GUIDE TO THE UNIVERSITIES OF EUROPE

Storm Boswick

Facts On File
New York • Oxford

*to the memory of Irene and Fridtjof Baadsvik
and John Grant*

GUIDE TO THE UNIVERSITIES OF EUROPE

For information contact:

Facts On File, Inc.
460 Park Avenue South
New York NY 10016
USA

Facts On File Limited
Collins Street
Oxford OX4 1XJ
United Kingdom

Library of Congress Cataloging-in-Publication Data

Boswick, Storm
Guide to the universities of Europe / Storm
Boswick.
p. cm.
Includes bibliographical references and index.
ISBN 0-8160-2359-X (alk. paper)
1. Universities and colleges—Europe—Directories.
I. Title.
L914.5.B67 1991
378.4—dc20   90-19169

A British CIP catalogue record for this book is available
from the British Library.

Facts On File books are available at special discounts
when purchased in bulk quantities for businesses,
associations, institutions or sales promotions. Please
call our Special Sales Department in New York at
212/683-2244 (dial 800/322-8755 except in NY, AK
or HI) or in Oxford at 865/728399.

Text Design by Ron Monteleone
Jacket design by Catherine Hyman
Composition by the Maple-Vail Book Manufacturing Group
Manufactured by the Maple-Vail Book Manufacturing Group
Printed in the United States of America

10 9 8 7 6 5 4 3 2 1

This book is printed on acid-free paper.

CONTENTS

ACKNOWLEDGMENTS

First of all, I wish to thank Michael J. Flynn Jr. for embarking upon this project with me three years ago. The book has changed a lot since then, Mike. I hope you approve.

I would like to take this opportunity to acknowledge Mark McWilliams, Paul Snyder and Gin Cambre for their help during the compilation of this book. Without their efforts, I am uncertain as to how successful this work would have been. Also, I would like to thank the following people for their support, suggestions and good humor over the past year: Chris Schmitz, Joshua Bruzzi, Angus Robb, Timothy Belk, Scott Winslow, Oliver Ortiz, John Hulsman, Jennifer Beales, Jane MacDonald, Katherine MacKinness, Dr. Myles Robertson and Dr. Mark Imber, Penny and Ron Hume, Kathy Lindsay, Crispin Jameson, Sarita Choudhury, and Glenn Unger.

I should thank the staffs of the University of St. Andrews Library and Hammersmith Public Library, London, for their cooperation during the collection of reference materials.

I am indebted to Hugh and George Riches for suggesting my publisher and am grateful to the people at Facts On File for their support, professionalism and understanding. In particular, I should thank Ed Knappman, Gerry Helferich and especially Deb Brody and Kathy Ishizuka.

While I understand that the correspondence between the administrations of the universities in this book and myself was fueled by mutual symbiosis, I remain thankful for their efforts and sincerely hope that their inclusion here will serve their best interests.

Finally, I should express my inestimable gratitude to my family for giving me the opportunity to study in Europe and for its encouragement over the past year. Most of all, I wish to thank my father, Tor Boswick, for financial support of this endeavor, for showing me through my own experience the value of studying and living in Europe, and for being my mentor. I aspire to you, Dad—there is no greater style than integrity.

INTRODUCTION

The *Guide to the Universities of Europe* is an attempt to provide North American students with important basic information on specific universities in Europe.

To study in Europe, as a North American, is a very valuable experience. It may serve to reinforce the faith one has in the bounties of the New World. On the other hand, one may succumb to the charms, civility and politics of the Old World. Certainly, the time spent in Europe will change one's perspective on wherever it is one calls home.

A university education has become very expensive in the United States. Tuition fees are exorbitant in many of the better universities of the land, and studying away from home—out of state or out of province—is also too pricey for most students. As the cost of studying away from home continues to rise in North America, the competition between the growing number of applicants for financial assistance and scholarships will increase accordingly. This heightened competition will result in a greater percentage of financial aid and scholarship applicants being denied the chance to study away from home, and more and more students will be forced to remain in state or in province. Consequently, those people who can not afford to study away from home or at one of the more expensive universities are often forced to select a prospective university based on financial considerations as well as its proximity to home.

Europe provides the ideal alternative. Most European countries have state-run, nonprofit university systems. In other words, a foreign student who can afford to attend a university in any given European country does not have to fear wild escalation of tuition fees when applying to different universities in that particular system. In fact, for many European countries, tuition fees are uniform at all universities. Some countries, such as Germany and Denmark, charge foreign students no tuition fees, while France, Portugal, Sweden, Finland, Spain, Italy, and the Eastern European countries, among others, charge foreign students very low tuition as compared to U.S. and Canadian standards. The faculties of the respective state institutions are usually made up of the finest doctors and professors in the country. Foreign students are considered essential to the reputations of European universities and are admitted to them more freely than foreign students are admitted to the better universities of the United States and Canada.

The value attached to foreign students studying in Europe can be traced to the European self-concept as treated in its own history—a concept of Europe as the seat of learning, not just for the individual nations but for the entire civilized world.

The rise of internationalism puts a premium on the ability to move between differing cultures and languages. Studying in Europe provides students with a first-rate education in internationalism. The opportunity to learn and use a foreign language while immersed in the culture of that language's people is, in itself, an education of tremendous value. North Americans who study in Europe have a chance to move freely and inexpensively throughout one of the most culturally diverse areas in the world. Student travel agencies, such as USIT and STA, are experts on how to see the most of Europe with the least money. In addition, most of the large national airlines in Europe offer reduced fares for students.

North American students who gain the experience of internationalism through studying in Europe enhance their employability in the job markets of the world. The advent of a single European Market in 1992 and the phenomena of glasnost and perestroika make the ability to understand and work within the new Europe an essential asset to any endeavor in the international arena. Whether a student's qualifications include a European university degree or proof of attendance at a European institution of higher learning for a term or a year, the benefits of an international education will stand out.

The purpose of *Guide to the Universities of Europe* is to help future internationalists select prospective institutions of higher learning. The systems of higher education vary greatly from one European country to another, and readers should not expect all of the universities reviewed in this guide to have similar information. The chapters are divided by countries, and there are two sections: one on the universities of Western Europe and one on the universities of Eastern Europe. Where the information was appropriate (the countries of Austria, Belgium, Denmark, Germany, France, the Republic of Ireland, Italy, the Netherlands, Portugal, Spain and the United Kingdom of Great Britain and Northern Ireland), the chapters include general university information. This section of the chapter gives information for foreign students on admission requirements, application procedures and deadlines, academic and degree requirements, accreditation, registration requirements, visa requirements and residence regulations, tuition fees, living expenses, scholarships and university calendar. This section also includes a short description of foreign student enrollment. Readers who are interested in finding out more about the higher education system in a particular country should contact that country's diplomatic mission in the reader's home country. For more information about a specific university reviewed within this guide, readers should contact the institution in question directly. In addition, the references mentioned in this guide's bibliography are excellent sources of information.

Finally, and on a personal note, I was applying to universities in Europe three years ago, and the lack of information about European universities was, at first, daunting. However, my decision to attend university in Europe is one I shall always consider fortuitous. I sincerely hope that this guide will encourage more North Americans to explore the exceptional and varied educational opportunities of this extraordinary continent. Europe awaits . . .

THE UNIVERSITIES OF WESTERN EUROPE

THE UNIVERSITIES OF AUSTRIA

GENERAL UNIVERSITY INFORMATION

Austrian universities are state-run, nonprofit institutions and, as such, follow similar rules regarding admission requirements, expenses and degree requirements. The following general information is relevant to all the institutions mentioned in this chapter.

ADMISSION REQUIREMENTS FOR FOREIGN STUDENTS

Foreign students must fulfill certain requirements in order to be admitted:

- Foreign students must have an adequate secondary school certificate (high school diploma, international baccalaureate, etc.) that is recognized by the Austrian academic authorities.
- Foreign students must be proficient in German.
- Foreign students must be in good health.
- Foreign students applying for transfer out of another university must submit a statement of honorable dismissal.
- If required by the intended program of studies, foreign students must produce evidence of special aptitude.

In addition, admission of foreign students as regular degree candidates to Austrian universities and art schools is subject to the following legal regulations:

Priority is given on the basis of academic qualifications as shown in the documents supporting the application. Foreign students may be admitted as regular degree students if their secondary school certificates prove the students have adequately prepared for university studies as required in the countries of the certificates' origin or as required by Austrian regulations. If an applicant's foreign qualifications are not equivalent to the requirements for the elected field of study at an Austrian university, then the applicant may not be admitted. However,

an applicant may alternatively gain admission by passing supplementary examinations. A two-semester preparatory course may be taken prior to these examinations.

Austria is a member of the Council of Europe and has agreed with 21 other countries upon standard university admission requirements. The other countries are Belgium, Cyprus, Denmark, France, Germany, Great Britain and Northern Ireland, Greece, Iceland, Ireland, Israel, Italy, Yugolavia, Luxembourg, Malta, Netherlands, New Zealand, Norway, Portugal, Spain, Sweden and Turkey.

Austria also has bilateral agreements on secondary school certificate equivalence with Bulgaria, Finland, Germany, Hungary, Liechtenstein and Romania. A secondary school certificate obtained in any of these countries entitles the holder to pursue any studies the certificate would allow within the country of its issue.

The language of instruction in all Austrian universities is German. However, some universities have courses conducted in English. If a student is not proficient in German or if the university's admissions department questions the proficiency of an applicant, the student must take an examination in German before beginning regular degree studies.

Submission of an official Austrian health certificate, no more than four months old, is also required for admission to Austrian universities. The foreign applicant is informed of the time and place of the medical examination, after which the health certificate will be issued.

A foreign applicant transferring from an institution of higher learning in another country must submit proof (a "Certificate") of honorable dismissal from the previous institution. The certificate must include the number of semesters attended and the names and grades of courses completed.

Certain academic programs require special qualifications. In such cases, the applicants must pass the specific entrance examinations required by the university.

APPLICATION PROCEDURE FOR FOREIGN STUDENTS

The applicant must send a letter to the desired *Studienabteilung* (admissions office for a department) at the applicant's chosen university. This letter serves as an application for admission to the studies selected by the applicant. Each university has special forms for this application procedure. The application must be accompanied by

1. a curriculum vita stating date of birth, nationality, educational background and the chosen academic program and subject area
2. a copy of the secondary school certificate, high school diploma or international baccalaureate containing the grades achieved in the various courses
3. for transfer applicants, all documents relating to previous academic history
4. evidence of proficiency in German language
5. evidence of the applicant's qualifications to pursue equivalent studies both in the applicant's home country and in the country of the secondary school certificate's origin

Applicants should submit notarized copies of these documents with certified German translations. A return address should be included as the applicant will be informed of the admission decision by mail.

APPLICATION DEADLINES

Any applications arriving later than the deadlines of September 1 for the winter semester and February 1 for the summer semester will not be considered until the subsequent semester's admissions review.

ACADEMIC PROGRAM AND DEGREE REQUIREMENTS

The academic program in Austrian universities and music and dramatic art schools is governed by the General Universities Studies Act. There are two degree programs: diploma studies (*Diplomstudien*) and doctoral studies (*Doktoratsstudien*).

Diploma studies offer professional training that is both practical and systematic and constitute the prerequisite for a diploma degree. The duration of diploma studies averages four to six years, though the number of semesters varies from degree program to degree program. Diploma degrees are awarded on the basis of the University Studies Act to candidates who have completed their regular degree studies and satisfactorily passed the prescribed diploma examinations. In order for students to achieve a master's degree, a thesis must be submitted prior to the final diploma examination.

Doctoral studies are available to students with master's degrees in the same or affiliated disciplines.

Doctorates are awarded on the basis of the University Studies Act to candidates who complete their regular degree studies, write a dissertation and pass the prescribed oral and written examinations.

ACCREDITATION

All universities are accredited by the State of Austria's Department of Science and Research in Vienna.

REGISTRATION REQUIREMENTS

Upon arriving in Austria, a foreign student must register with the police department (*Polizeikommissariat*) of the district in which the university is located. Registration forms can be obtained from any tobacconist (*Trafik*).

VISA REQUIREMENTS AND RESIDENCE REGULATIONS

The foreign student needs a valid passport in order to enter Austria. In addition, an Austrian visa is required for all students, excluding those from Liechtenstein, Luxembourg and Switzerland. Visas are issued by Austrian consulates and embassies abroad. The visa specifies how long the student may remain in Austria. The residence permit is extended in one year licenses by the Austrian police department.

TUITION FEES FOR FOREIGN STUDENTS

- AS 4,000 per semester for universities and art schools (roughly $320 US)
- AS 4,800 for *Wirtschaftsuniversität* (universities of economics and business administration)

Tuition fees must be paid in full by all students at the start of each semester. Exemption from the foreign student tuition fee is granted to the following:

1. students who during the past six years have been subject to unlimited income tax liability in Austria or who are supported by persons who have been subject to the unlimited top liability in Austria
2. students who have received scholarships to study at an Austrian university awarded by national, provincial or local authorities or another body incorporated under the public law. This scholarship must amount to no less than the minimum scholarship granted by the Study Promotion Act (Studienforderungsgesetz)
3. students whose home countries grant exemption from foreign student tuition fees to Austrian nationals
4. students from developing countries

5. stateless students with ordinary domicile in Austria for at least five years
6. students considered "refugees" according to the Refugee Convention

Application for exemption from foreign student tuition fees must be made to the prospective university (Fakultätskollegian) prior to registration/matriculation.

EXPENSES

Living expenses vary from city to city, particularly if the university is in a rural location. The following data was prepared by the Austrian Foreign Student Service (OÄD) and represents 1990 estimates. The housing cost corresponds to student hostel rates.

Housing (rent and utilities)	AS 2,100
Food (without tobacco and alcohol)	AS 2,200
Clothing, laundry	AS 600
Health care, hygiene	AS 450
Books, supplies	AS 450
Miscellaneous, entertainment	AS 700
Transportation	AS 500
Total per month in 1990	AS 7,000

The total cost of living corresponds to the amount a grantee of the Austrian federal government would receive in Austria.

FOREIGN STUDENT SCHOLARSHIPS

Scholarships provided by Austrian institutions are available to foreign students. Applications for scholarships offered by the Federal Ministry of Science and Research and the Federal Ministry of Foreign Affairs are to be submitted to the competent authority prescribed by the Austrian consulates and embassies in the applicant's home country.

UNIVERSITY CALENDAR

The academic year begins on October 1 and ends the following September 30. The year is divided into semesters:

• winter semester: October 1 until the completion of examinations in January
• summer semester: early February until the completion of examinations in June

FOREIGN STUDENTS IN AUSTRIA

Foreign students have a long and established tradition at Austrian universities. In the 1950s, as much as one-third of the total student enrollment was made up of foreigners. The number of foreign students has continued to increase over the past 30 years, though the percentage of the total enrollment has declined due to the rising numbers of Austrian students.

Austria ranks higher than the average European country in terms of foreign student enrollment.

In the 1980s, roughly 72% of foreign students enrolled in Austrian universities were from other European nations. However, in 1988, 107 different countries were represented. Certain universities attract more foreigners than others, but each of the Austrian universities has a large international student body.

Many foreign students study general subjects—humanities and natural sciences make up roughly 37% of the course programs selected; technical engineering accounts for about 20% and medicine, social sciences and economics account for about 14% each. There is also a large international contingent in the music and dramatic arts schools, especially in Vienna and Salzburg, where foreign students account for about 40% of the total enrollment.

It is estimated that the number of foreign students attending Austrian universities in the 1990s will be 12,500 to 13,000 per year.

BRANCH OFFICES OF THE AUSTRIAN FOREIGN STUDENT SERVICE (OÄD)

Most of the above information was provided by the OÄD. The OÄD provides any assistance foreign students and applicants need concerning studies and student life in Austria. The addresses of OÄD branches in Austria are

Headquarters in Vienna
Universität Wien, Stiege IX
Dr. Karl Lueger-Ring 1
A-1010 Vienna, Austria
Tel.# (0222) 42 67 42; 42 31 50
Office Hours: Mon.–Fri. 9 a.m.–12 a.m.
Tue. & Thur. 2 p.m.–4 p.m.

In Vienna
Universität Wien, Dr. Karl Lueger-Ring 1, Stiege I
A-1010 Vienna, Austria
Tel.# (0222) 43 00 / 26 29, 28 76
Office Hours: Mon.–Fri. 9 a.m.–12 a.m.
Tue. & Thur. 2 p.m.–4 p.m.

In Graz
Mandellstrasse 11
A-8010 Graz, Austria
Tel.# (0316, from Vienna 993) 70 77 93
Office Hours: Mon.–Fri. 9 a.m.–12 a.m.
Tue. & Thur. 2 p.m.–4 p.m.

In Innsbruck
Universität Innrain 52
A-6020 Innsbruck, Austria
Tel.# (05222, from Vienna 995) 724 / 20 55
Office Hours: Mon.–Fri. 9 a.m.–1 p.m.

In Salzburg
Akademiestrasse 20/2/229, 230

A-5020 Salzburg, Austria
Tel.# (0662, from Vienna 996) 84 36 51
Office Hours: Mon.–Fri. 9 a.m.–12 a.m.

In Leoben
Montanuniversität Leoben
Franz-Jozef Strasse 18
A-8700 Leoben, Austria
Tel.# (03842) 42 5 55
Office Hours: Mon.–Fri. 9.30 a.m.–2 p.m.

In Linz
Schloss Auhof
A-4040 Linz, Austria
Tel.# (0732, from Vienna 997) 24 68 0
Office Hours: Mon.–Thur. 9 a.m.–4.30 p.m.
                          Fri. 9 a.m.–2 p.m.

In Klagenfurt
Universität
Universitätsstrasse 67
A-9020 Klagenfurt, Austria
Tel.# (0463, from Vienna 994) 53 17
Office Hours: Mon., Wed., Fri. 9 a.m.–12 a.m.

KARL-FRANZENS-UNIVERSITÄT GRAZ
(Graz University)
8010 Graz, Universitätsplatz 3, Austria

CHARACTERISTICS OF INSTITUTION:
State-run, nonprofit university

DATE FOUNDED: 1585

TOTAL ENROLLMENT: 26,700 students

DEGREES AWARDED:
Magister in various fields
    five–six years required
Doctorate in various fields
    four–eight years required

ACADEMIC PROGRAMS:
Faculty of Business Administration and Economics
Faculty of Catholic Theology
Faculty of Law
Faculty of Liberal Arts
Faculty of Medicine
Faculty of Science

SPECIAL PROGRAMS:
Cooperative arrangements with universities in several countries

LANGUAGE OF INSTRUCTION: German

ADMISSION REQUIREMENTS FOR FOREIGN STUDENTS:
Secondary school certificate (*Reifezeugnis*) or recognized foreign equivalent

TUITION FOR FOREIGN STUDENTS:
AS 4,000 per semester. *See* GENERAL UNIVERSITY INFORMATION.

TOTAL INSTRUCTIONAL FACULTY:
1,975 fulltime faculty

LIBRARY COLLECTIONS:
University library—950,000 volumes

MUSEUMS AND GALLERIES:
Krimiologischer Museum

RECTOR: Dr. Thomas Kenner

LEOPOLD-FRANZENS-UNIVERSITÄT INNSBRUCK
(Leopold Franzens University of Innsbruck)
6020 Innsbruck, Innrain 52, Austria

CHARACTERISTICS OF INSTITUTION:
State-run, nonprofit university

DATE FOUNDED: 1669

TOTAL ENROLLMENT: 24,850 students

DEGREES AWARDED:
Diplom in various fields
    seven–ten semesters required
Magister in various fields
    six semesters required
Doctorate in various fields
    eight–twelve semesters required

ACADEMIC PROGRAMS:
Faculty of Arts
Faculty of Construction Engineering and Architecture
Faculty of Law
Faculty of Medicine
Faculty of Science
Faculty of Social and Economic Science
Faculty of Theology

SPECIAL PROGRAMS:
Cooperative arrangements with universities in several countries

LANGUAGE OF INSTRUCTION: German

ADMISSION REQUIREMENTS FOR FOREIGN STUDENTS:
Secondary school certificate (*Reifezeugnis*) or recognized foreign equivalent

TUITION FOR FOREIGN STUDENTS:
AS 4,000 per semester. *See* GENERAL UNIVERSITY INFORMATION.

TOTAL INSTRUCTIONAL FACULTY:
1,280 fulltime faculty

LIBRARY COLLECTIONS:
University library—500,000 volumes
Libraries of the institute—1,000,000 volumes

UNIVERSITY PUBLICATIONS:
Mitteilunsblatt, Veröffentlichungen, Vorlesungsverzeichnis

RECTOR: Prof. Dr. Rainer Sprung

UNIVERSITÄT SALZBURG
(Salzburg University)
5020 Salzburg, Residenzplatz 1, Austria

CHARACTERISTICS OF INSTITUTION:
State-run, nonprofit university

DATE FOUNDED: 1622

TOTAL ENROLLMENT: 12,100 students (including 1,400 foreign students)

DEGREES AWARDED:
Magister in various fields
    four years required
Doctorate in various fields
    five–seven years required

ACADEMIC PROGRAMS
Faculty of Arts
Faculty of Catholic Theology
Faculty of Law
Faculty of Natural Science

SPECIAL PROGRAMS:
Cooperative arrangements with universities in several countries

LANGUAGE OF INSTRUCTION: German

ADMISSION REQUIREMENTS FOR FOREIGN STUDENTS:
Secondary school certificate (*Reifezeugnis*) or recognized foreign equivalent

TUITION FOR FOREIGN STUDENTS:
AS 4,000 per semester. *See* GENERAL UNIVERSITY INFORMATION.

TOTAL INSTRUCTIONAL FACULTY:
750 fulltime faculty

MUSEUMS AND GALLERIES:
Museums of Fine Arts and Natural History
Several Galleries

LIBRARY COLLECTIONS:
University library—500,000 volumes
Libraries of the institute—1,000,000 volumes

UNIVERSITY PUBLICATIONS:
Jahrbuch, Universitätsreden

RECTOR: Prof. Dr. Theodor Köhler

UNIVERSITÄT WEIN
(Vienna University)
1010 Vienna, Austria

CHARACTERISTICS OF INSTITUTION:
State-run, nonprofit university

DATE FOUNDED: 1365

TOTAL ENROLLMENT: 85,400 (including 7,700 foreign students)

DEGREES AWARDED:
Diplom in various fields
    four years required
Magister in various fields
    four–five years required
Doctorate in various fields
    five–seven years required
Lehramtsprüfung (teaching qualification)
    five–six years required

ACADEMIC PROGRAMS:
Faculty of Catholic Theology
Faculty of Humanities
Faculty of Law and Political Science
Faculty of Medicine
Faculty of Natural Science
Faculty of Philosophy
Faculty of Protestant Theology
Faculty of Social and Economic Science

SPECIAL PROGRAMS:
Cooperative arrangements with universities in several countries

LANGUAGE OF INSTRUCTION: German

ADMISSION REQUIREMENTS FOR FOREIGN STUDENTS:
Secondary school certificate (*Reifezeugnis*) or recognized foreign equivalent

TUITION FOR FOREIGN STUDENTS:
AS 4,000 per semester. *See* GENERAL UNIVERSITY INFORMATION.

TOTAL INSTRUCTIONAL FACULTY:
2,500 fulltime faculty

LIBRARY COLLECTIONS:
University library—4,066,000 volumes

MUSEUMS AND GALLERIES:
Institute of Medical History Museum

RECTOR: Prof. Dr. Karl Wernhart

WIRTSCHAFTSUNIVERSITÄT WIEN
(Vienna University of Commerce)
A-10900 Vienna, Augasse 2-6, Austria

CHARACTERISTICS OF INSTITUTION:
State-run, nonprofit university

DATE FOUNDED: 1898

TOTAL ENROLLMENT: 18,000 fulltime students (including 1,850 foreign students from 85 countries)

DEGREES AWARDED:
Magister in various fields
    four–five years required
Doctorate in various fields
    four–six years required

ACADEMIC PROGRAMS:
Department of Business Administration
Department of Economics
Department of Human Science
Department of Law

SPECIAL PROGRAMS:
Cooperative arrangements with universities in several countries

LANGUAGES OF INSTRUCTION: German and English

ADMISSION REQUIREMENTS FOR FOREIGN STUDENTS:
Secondary school certificate (*Reifezeugnis*) or recognized foreign equivalent

TUITION FOR FOREIGN STUDENTS:
AS 4,800 per semester. *See* GENERAL UNIVERSITY INFORMATION.

TOTAL INSTRUCTIONAL FACULTY:
350 fulltime faculty

LIBRARY COLLECTIONS:
Central library—256,850 volumes
Departmental libraries—206,000 volumes

UNIVERSITY PUBLICATIONS:
Bankarchiv, Der Österriechische Betriebswirt, Zeitschrift für Ganzherisforschung

RECTOR: Prof. Dr. Hans Robert Hansen

TECHNISCHE UNIVERSITÄT GRAZ
(Graz Technical University)
8010 Graz, Rechbauerstrasse 12, Austria

CHARACTERISTICS OF INSTITUTION:
State-run, nonprofit university

DATE FOUNDED: 1811

TOTAL ENROLLMENT: 11,500 students

DEGREES AWARDED:
Diplom in various fields
    five years required
Magister in various fields
    seven years required

Doctorate in various fields
    seven years required

ACADEMIC PROGRAMS
Faculty of Architecture
Faculty of Constructional Engineering
Faculty of Electrical Engineering
Faculty of Mechanical Engineering
Faculty of Natural Science

SPECIAL PROGRAMS:
Cooperative arrangements with universities in several countries

LANGUAGE OF INSTRUCTION: German

ADMISSION REQUIREMENTS FOR FOREIGN STUDENTS:
Secondary school certificate (*Reifezeugnis*) or recognized foreign equivalent

TUITION FOR FOREIGN STUDENTS:
AS 4,000 per semester. *See* GENERAL UNIVERSITY INFORMATION.

TOTAL INSTRUCTIONAL FACULTY:
546 fulltime faculty
75 parttime faculty

LIBRARY COLLECTIONS:
University library—90,000 volumes

RECTOR: Prof. Dipl.-Ing. Dr. techn. Günther Schelling

TECHNISCHE UNIVERSITÄT WEIN
(Vienna Technical University)
1040 Vienna, Karlsplatz 13, Austria

CHARACTERISTICS OF INSTITUTION:
State-run, nonprofit university

DATE FOUNDED: 1815

TOTAL ENROLLMENT: 18,500 students (including 2,500 foreign students)

DEGREES AWARDED:
Diplom in various fields
    five years required
Magister in various fields
    five years required
Doctorate in various fields
    seven years and thesis required

ACADEMIC PROGRAMS:
Faculty of Civil Engineering
Faculty of Electrical Engineering
Faculty of Mechanical Engineering
Faculty of Natural Sciences
Faculty of Regional Planning and Architecture

SPECIAL PROGRAMS:
Cooperative arrangements with universities in several countries

LANGUAGE OF INSTRUCTION: German

ADMISSION REQUIREMENTS FOR FOREIGN STUDENTS:
Secondary school certificate (Reifezeugnis) or recognized foreign equivalent

TUITION FOR FOREIGN STUDENTS:
AS 4,000 per semester. See GENERAL UNIVERSITY INFORMATION.

TOTAL INSTRUCTIONAL FACULTY:
2,000 fulltime faculty

LIBRARY COLLECTIONS:
University library—800,000 volumes

UNIVERSITY PUBLICATIONS:
Mitteilunsblatt, Schriftenreihe, TU Aktuell

RECTOR: Prof. Dipl.-Ing. Dr. techn. Friedrich Moser

HOCHSCHULE FÜR MUSIK UND DARSTELLENDE KUNST IN WEIN
(University of Music and Dramatic Art in Vienna)
A-1037 Vienna III, Lothringerstrasse 18, Austria

CHARACTERISTICS OF INSTITUTION:
State-run, nonprofit university

DATE FOUNDED: 1812

TOTAL ENROLLMENT: 3,000 students

DEGREES AWARDED:
Diplom in various fields
    four--eight years required
Magister in various fields
    four–five years required
Doctorates in various fields
    four–six years required

ACADEMIC PROGRAMS:
Department of Church Music
Department of Drama and Production
Department of Film and Television
Department of Keyboard Instruments
Department of Music Education
Department of String Instruments
Department of Theory, Composition and Orchestral
    Conducting
Department of Voice and Operatic Art

LANGUAGE OF INSTRUCTION: German

ADMISSION REQUIREMENTS FOR FOREIGN STUDENTS:
Secondary school certificate (Reifezeugnis), or recognized foreign equivalent, and entrance examination in chosen artistic field

TUITION FOR FOREIGN STUDENTS:
See GENERAL UNIVERSITY INFORMATION.

TOTAL INSTRUCTIONAL FACULTY:
600 fulltime faculty

LIBRARY COLLECTIONS:
Central library and departmental library—90,000 volumes; 1,700 phonographic records; 700 audio tapes

RECTOR: Prof. Dr. Helmut Schwarz

HOCHSCHULE FÜR MUSIK UND DARSTELLENDE KUNST IN GRAZ
(University of Music and Dramatic Art in Graz)
A-8010 Graz Leonhardstrasse, 15, Austria

CHARACTERISTICS OF INSTITUTION:
State-run, nonprofit university

DATE FOUNDED: 1963

TOTAL ENROLLMENT: 1,500 students (including 275 foreign students)

DEGREES AWARDED:
Diplom
    three–six years required
Magister Artium
    five years required

ACADEMIC PROGRAMS:
Department of Church Music
Department of Jazz
Department of Keyboard Instruments
Department of Pedagogy
Department of Singing
Department of String Instruments
Department of Theory and Composition
Department of Wind and Percussion Instruments

ATTACHED INSTITUTES:
Jazz Research
Music Aesthetics
Music Ethnology
Performance Practice

LANGUAGE OF INSTRUCTION: German

ADMISSION REQUIREMENTS FOR FOREIGN STUDENTS:
Secondary school certificate (Reifezeugnis), or recognized foreign equivalent, and entrance examination in the chosen artistic field

TUITION FOR FOREIGN STUDENTS:
AS 1,500 per semester. See GENERAL UNIVERSITY INFORMATION.

TOTAL INSTRUCTIONAL FACULTY:
110 fulltime faculty

LIBRARY COLLECTIONS:
University library—90,000 volumes

UNIVERSITY PUBLICATIONS:
Mitteilunsblatt, Veroffentlichungen, Vorlesungsver-zeichnis

RECTOR: Prof. Dr. Sebastian Benda

HOCHSCHULE FÜR MUSIK UND DARSTELLENDE KUNST 'MOZARTIUM' IN SALZBURG
(Mozartium University of Music and Dramatic Art in Salzburg)
5020 Salzburg, Mirabellplatz 1, Austria

CHARACTERISTICS OF INSTITUTION:
State-run, nonprofit university

DATE FOUNDED: 1841

TOTAL ENROLLMENT: 1,550 students (including 600 foreign students)

DEGREES AWARDED:
Magister Artium

ACADEMIC PROGRAMS:
Department of Composition, Theory and Conducting
Department of Keyboard Instruments
Department of Instruction in Art
Department of Instruction in Music
Department of Music Education
Department of Performing Art
Department of Sacred Music
Department of Solo Singing and Dramatic Performance
Department of String Instruments
Department of Wind and Percussion Instruments
Orff Institute for Elemental Music and Movement Education

LANGUAGE OF INSTRUCTION: German

ADMISSION REQUIREMENTS FOR FOREIGN STUDENTS:
Entrance examination in chosen artistic field

TUITION FOR FOREIGN STUDENTS:
AS 4,000 per semester. *See* GENERAL UNIVERSITY INFORMATION.

TOTAL INSTRUCTIONAL FACULTY:
300 fulltime faculty
100 parttime faculty

LIBRARY COLLECTIONS:
Library—110,000 volumes

RECTOR: Prof. Dr. Günther Bauer

THE UNIVERSITIES OF BELGIUM

GENERAL UNIVERSITY INFORMATION

Belgian universities are state-run, nonprofit institutions and, as such, follow similar rules and regulations concerning admission requirements, expenses and degree requirements. The following general information is relevant to all institutions mentioned in this chapter.

ADMISSION REQUIREMENTS FOR FOREIGN STUDENTS

Foreign students applying to a Belgian university must hold either a Belgian secondary school certificate or one of the following recognized foreign equivalents:

- Baccalauréat Européen, issued by a secondary school in Belgium or abroad
- international baccalaureate, issued by the Office du Baccalaurat International in Geneva, Switzerland
- a secondary school certificate or high school diploma that has been approved as equivalent to Belgian standards by the Service des Équivalences de L'Administration de L'Enseignement Secondaire (for French institutions) or Dienst Gelijkwaardigheden van het Bestuur van het Hoger Onderwijs (for Dutch institutions)

Transfer applicants should contact either the French or Dutch agency or the school's admissions department for information on the educational qualifications required for transfer.

Recognition of foreign secondary school certificates, high school diplomas and university degrees is based upon Belgian equivalence. The law in Belgium ignores the level, the subject and the country in which the certificate, diploma or degree was achieved. The parameters for deciding equivalence are

- period of study
- examinations taken and passed
- certificates, diplomas and degrees acquired

In some cases only partial equivalence may be granted, and the student must take Belgian examinations to qualify for full equivalence. This proviso insures that equivalence is not granted to studies not comparable with the level of corresponding studies in Belgium and that a foreign applicant is not accepted at a Belgian university if the applicant would not be allowed to commence or continue corresponding studies in the country in which the certificate, diploma or degree was acquired.

If the foreign applicant has a secondary school certificate, high school diploma or university degree recognized as a Belgian equivalent, then the applicant is not required to take entry examinations. However, if the applicant wishes to study civil engineering, he or she will have to take the entrance examination required of all applicants, including Belgian students.

The language of instruction in Belgian universities is either French or Dutch, depending upon the region. Foreign applicants who cannot provide proof of proficiency in the language of instruction must take a language test prior to admission. All universities offer intensive language courses for those students who are accepted but do not have the adequate language proficiency level required.

APPLICATION PROCEDURE FOR FOREIGN STUDENTS

Foreign students applying to Belgian universities should contact the prospective institutions at least a year prior to planned enrollment.

First, foreign applicants should contact the Belgian embassy or consulate cultural office in their home countries for specific information regarding foreign student status in Belgium. Second, foreign applicants should contact the universities for specific information on application procedures and forms as well as on the academic programs.

Foreign student applications should be sent to the registrar's office (Service des Inscriptions or Inschrijvingsdienst) of the prospective university.

If an applicant is rejected by a state university in Belgium, the applicant has the right to appeal within 30 days of the decision. The appeal must be made to the minister for national education, who then has 30 days to appeal the rejection on behalf of the applicant.

APPLICATION DEADLINES

Foreign students must send the completed applications and all other required qualifications to the registrar's office before May 1 of the academic year.

ACADEMIC PROGRAM AND DEGREE REQUIREMENTS

The academic program at a Belgian university is organized in stages of studies (Cycles or Cycli) and academic years. After successfully completing a stage, or cycle, the student is admitted to the next stage of studies.

The first stage is completed after two or three years of course work. The student then obtains the qualification of Candidat or Kandidaat. The first stage is generally regarded as the basic academic training needed for the continuation of studies.

The second stage is usually completed after another two or three years of more rigorous and advanced course work, including specialized studies and the submission of a final thesis (*Mémoire* or *Verhandeling*). The resulting degree, the Licencié or Licentiaat, qualifies one to work as a doctor, a pharmacist or an engineer in the respective disciplines (all are four years of course work). In general, the second stage confers upon the graduate the right to undertake a profession.

The third stage in the academic program results in a Docteur or Doctor degree (the Belgian equivalent of a PhD). This stage is completed after at least one or two years of academic work following the Licencié or Licentiaat. The third stage often takes much longer than the stipulated one or two years and involves an original *Dissertation* or *Proefschrift* and a *Thèse Annexe* or *Bijkomende Stelling,* both of which must be publicly defended. Only students who are considered capable of independent research and scholarly endeavor are admitted to the third stage.

The fourth stage results in the highest qualification granted by Belgian universities, the Agrégé de L'Enseignement Supérieur or Geaggregeerde voor het Hoger Enderwijs. This qualification requires at least two years of independent scholarly research after being awarded the title of Docteur or Doctor. An original *Dissertation* or *Proefschrift* must be submitted and publicly defended, and three *Thèse Annexe* or *Bijkomende Stellingen* must be submitted and may require public defense as well. The degree obtained upon completion of the fourth stage is only awarded to extraordinary students.

In Belgium, there are three main types of university degrees:

1. The national degree (*Grades Légaux* or *Wetterlijke Graden*): National degrees are granted to graduates of university programs that have admission requirements, course work and duration of study defined by Belgian law. National degrees confer upon the graduate the right to practice a profession and follow the stages of studies described above.
2. The scientific degree (*Grades Scientifiques* or *Wetenschappelijike Graden*): Scientific degrees are granted to graduates of university programs with admission requirements, course work and length defined by the individual universities. Scientific degrees encompass subjects such as social sci-

ences and natural sciences and follow the stages of studies described above.
3. The specialized or supplementary degree (*Grades Complémentaire* or *Aanvullende Graden*): Specialized or supplementary degrees are granted to graduates of specialized programs of study. This course work usually follows either the Licencié/Licentiaat qualification or the Doctorat/Doctoraat qualification. The requirements for obtaining this degree are defined by the individual universities.

ACCREDITATION

All Belgian university degrees are accredited by the Coordinated Laws on Academic Degrees or the Law on the Protection of Titles of Higher Education.

REGISTRATION REQUIREMENTS

Foreign students must arrive in Belgium in September prior to the beginning of the term. A student must present his or her passport, the qualifications necessary for admission to the planned course of study, the notice of admission and certification of a recent medical examination. Foreign students must also pay tuition fees at this time.

VISA REQUIREMENTS AND RESIDENCE REGULATIONS

Belgium does not require a visa for foreign students. However, upon arrival at the university, foreign students must register with the local authorities. The requirements for this registration are:

- a passport
- a certificate of enrollment from the University
- proof of financial solvency—either a scholarship certificate or a certified document from the student's home embassy in Belgium stating that financial responsibility has been assumed personally by the student, by the student's family or by a Belgian citizen
- up to five passport-size photographs

After completing registration, the foreign student will receive a residence permit and be entered into the Alien's Register. The permit allows the foreign student legal residence in Belgium for one year. It must be renewed for each year of the student's course of studies.

TUITION FEES FOR FOREIGN STUDENTS

Tuition fees vary between Dutch- and French-speaking institutions. If a student falls into one of the following categories, he will be charged the same tuition fees as a Belgian student in the same academic program:

- foreign students who are citizens of Luxembourg
- foreign students whose parents or legal guardians have permanent or temporary residence in Belgium. The parents or legal guardians must also work or have worked in Belgium.
- foreign students who are citizens of a European Community member state and whose parents or legal guardians work or have worked in Belgium
- foreign students who are nationals of a European Community member state and are living and working, or have worked, in Belgium or foreign students whose spouses meet this criterion
- foreign students from European Community member states who plan to study in Belgium for only one year and can prove that they have been admitted to equivalent academic programs, for which they have paid the tuition fees, in their home countries
- foreign students who have permanent or temporary residence in Belgium and have refugee status accorded by the Belgian delegation of the United Nations High Commission for Refugees
- foreign students whose home countries are recognized by Belgium as "developing countries" and who have been admitted to a Belgian university by the minister responsible for cooperation with developing countries
- foreign students whose home countries have concluded cultural agreements with Belgium and who have received a scholarship within the framework of the cultural agreement from the ministries responsible for international cultural relations
- foreign students who do not fall into any of these categories and whose desired faculty limits the number of applicants accepted to 2% of the number of Belgian students enrolled in the respective academic program during the past academic year

Foreign students who are not covered by any of the above categories must pay the full foreign student fees. In 1989, tuition fees for a Belgian student were

- Dutch-speaking institution: BF 11,000–15,000
- French-speaking institution: BF 17,000–19,000

The 1989 tuition fees for foreign students who do not fulfill Belgian student tuition fee equivalence were

- From BF 95,000 to BF 300,000, depending upon the university and the academic program.

Tuition fees cover the costs of matriculation, the courses, examinations and student accident insurance. Foreign students shuld contact the university registrar office for specific tuition information.

EXPENSES

Expenses for foreign students will vary according to the location of the chosen university. The following data represents 1989 estimates:

Housing	BF	66,000
Books, supplies	BF	20,000
Food	BF	96,000
Transportation	BF	12,000
Health care, hygiene	BF	10,000
Clothing, laundry	BF	20,000
Miscellaneous, entertainment	BF	25,000
Total per year	BF	249,000

FOREIGN STUDENT SCHOLARSHIPS

Foreign students may be eligible for a variety of scholarships. The Belgian government grants scholarships under the auspices of Belgian cultural agreements with other countries and also to some foreign students holding temporary residence in Belgium. A foreign student's home government may offer scholarships for study at a Belgian university or at a university in the European community. There are also many scholarships offered by international organizations, foundations and universities.

Foreign students interested in researching a scholarship at a Belgian university should contact the cultural office at the Belgian embassy or consulate in their own countries. All scholarship applications should be made well in advance of the student's arrival in Belgium.

UNIVERSITY CALENDAR

The academic year begins in September or early October, depending upon the institution, and lasts 30 weeks. Examinations are given in June or early July. There are two holidays—one at Christmas and one near Easter. The academic year is split into three terms:

- 1st Term: September/October to December
- 2nd Term: January to March
- 3rd Term: April to June/July

FOREIGN STUDENTS IN BELGIUM

Foreign students are considered an essential asset to the universities of Belgium by both the government and the universities themselves. In 1986, approximately 13,000 foreign students were enrolled in Belgian universities—almost 13% of the total student population. Many of these students, nearly 40% of the 1980 foreign student contingent in Belgium, came from other European Community member states, but the majority of foreigners are non-European nationals. Certain institutions attract more foreign students than others, but each of the Belgian universities has a large international student body.

RIJKSUNIVERSITEIT TE GHENT
(State University of Ghent)
St.-Pietersnieuwstraat 25, 9000 Ghent, Belgium

CHARACTERISTICS OF INSTITUTION:
State-run, nonprofit university

DATE FOUNDED: 1817

TOTAL ENROLLMENT: 14,200 fulltime students (including 740 foreign students)

DEGREES AWARDED:
Kandidaat in various fields
   two–three years required
Licentiaat in various fields
   two years after Kandidaat required
Doctorate
   five–seven years required
Professional title of *Ingenieur* in various fields
   five years required
Geaggregeerde Middelbaar Onderwijs (secondary-level teaching qualification)
   after Licentiaat
Geaggregeerde Hoger Onderwijs (university-level teaching qualification)
   two years after doctorate required

ACADEMIC PROGRAMS:
Faculty of Agricultural Sciences
Faculty of Applied Sciences (including engineering)
Faculty of Economic Sciences
Faculty of Law
Faculty of Medicine
Faculty of Pharmacy
Faculty of Philosophy and Letters
Faculty of Psychological and Pedagogical Sciences
Faculty of Science
Faculty of Veterinary Sciences

SPECIAL PROGRAMS:
Center of Biochemistry
Computer Center
Institute of History of Art and Archaeology
Institute of Physical Education
Inter-Faculty Center for Environmental Sanitation
Inter-Faculty Center for Town Planning and Regional Development
Inter-Faculty Center for Development
School of Criminology
School of Management

LANGUAGE OF INSTRUCTION: Dutch

ADMISSION REQUIREMENTS FOR FOREIGN STUDENTS:
Secondary school certificate, or recognized foreign equivalent, and entrance examination

TUITION FOR FOREIGN STUDENTS:
BF 14,850 in 1989/90 (about $350 US) for students with Belgian student tuition fee equivalence. *See* GENERAL UNIVERSITY INFORMATION.

TOTAL INSTRUCTIONAL FACULTY:
1,200 fulltime faculty

LIBRARY COLLECTIONS:
University library—3,000,000 volumes
Faculty libraries

MUSEUMS AND GALLERIES:
Museum of the History of Science
University Museum of Science and Technology

UNIVERSITY PUBLICATIONS:
Gentse bijdragen tot de Kunstgeschiedenis en Oudheidkunde, Gids voor de student, Studiegids, various faculty publications

RECTOR: Dr. L. De Meyer

UNIVERSITÉ LIBRE DE BRUXELLES
(Free University of Brussels)
Avenue Franklin D. Roosevelt 50, 1050 Brussels, Belgium

CHARACTERISTICS OF INSTITUTION:
Private university

DATE FOUNDED: 1834

TOTAL ENROLLMENT: 15,000 fulltime students (including 4,300 foreign students)

DEGREES AWARDED:
Candidat
   two–three years required
Licencié in various fields
   two years after Candidat required
Doctorate
   one–four years required; thesis required in some fields
Professional titles in various fields
   one–five years required
Agrégation de l'enseignement secondaire et supérieur (secondary- and university-level teaching qualifications) in various fields

ACADEMIC PROGRAMS:
Faculty of Applied Sciences
Faculty of Law
Faculty of Medicine
Faculty of Philosophy and Letters
Faculty of Psychology and Education
Faculty of Science
Faculty of Social, Political and Economic Sciences

SPECIAL PROGRAMS:
Center for Current Affairs
Department of Applied Economy
Institute of European Studies
Institute of Labor
Institute of Pharmacy
Institute of Physical Education
Institute of Phonetics
Institute of Religious Studies
Institute of Statistics
School of Criminology
School of Nursing
School of Public Health

LANGUAGE OF INSTRUCTION: French

ADMISSION REQUIREMENTS FOR FOREIGN STUDENTS:
Secondary school certificate, or recognized foreign equivalent, and entrance examination

TUITION FOR FOREIGN STUDENTS:
See GENERAL UNIVERSITY INFORMATION.

TOTAL INSTRUCTIONAL FACULTY:
2,000 fulltime faculty (including 200 professors)

LIBRARY COLLECTIONS:
Total collection—1,210,000 volumes

UNIVERSITY PUBLICATIONS:
Bulletin d'Information, Revue de l'Université

PRESIDENT: Herve Hasquin

VRIJE UNIVERSITEIT BRUSSEL
(Free University of Brussels)
Pleinlaan 2, 1050 Brussels, Belgium

CHARACTERISTICS OF INSTITUTION:
State-run, nonprofit university

DATE FOUNDED: 1834 (separated from Université Libre de Bruxelles in 1970)

TOTAL ENROLLMENT: 7,500 fulltime students

DEGREES AWARDED:
Kandidaat in various fields
   two–three years required
Licentiaat in various fields
   five–seven years required
Doctorate
   two years after Licentiaat required
Professional titles in various fields
   five–seven years required
Geaggregeerde voor het Hogar Secundair Onderwijs (higher secondary-level teaching qualification)
   after Licentiaat
Geaggregeerde Hoger Onderwijs (University-level teaching qualification)
   two years after doctorate required

ACADEMIC PROGRAMS:
Faculty of Applied Sciences
Faculty of Law
Faculty of Medicine
Faculty of Philosophy and Letters
Faculty of Psychological and Educational Sciences
Faculty of Science
Faculty of Social, Political and Economic Sciences

SPECIAL PROGRAMS:
Institute of Physical Education

LANGUAGE OF INSTRUCTION: Dutch

ADMISSION REQUIREMENTS FOR FOREIGN STUDENTS:
Secondary school certificate, or recognized foreign equivalent, and entrance examination

TUITION FOR FOREIGN STUDENTS:
BF 11,000–15,000 per year in 1989. *See* GENERAL UNIVERSITY INFORMATION.

TOTAL INSTRUCTIONAL FACULTY:
500 fulltime faculty

LIBRARY COLLECTIONS:
Faculty libraries—147,000 volumes

UNIVERSITY PUBLICATIONS:
Aula, Universiteit Brussel

RECTOR: Sylvain Loccufier

UNIVERSITÉ DE L'ÉTAT À LIÈGE
(State University of Liège)
Place du 20-Août 7, 4000 Liège, Belgium

CHARACTERISTICS OF INSTITUTION:
State-run, nonprofit university

DATE FOUNDED: 1817

TOTAL ENROLLMENT: 11,000 fulltime students (including 1,500 foreign students)

DEGREES AWARDED:
Candidat
Licencié in various fields
   after Candidat
Doctorate
   at least one year after Licencié required
Professional titles in various fields
   five years required

ACADEMIC PROGRAMS:
Faculty of Applied Sciences
Faculty of Economics, Business Administration and
   Social Sciences
Faculty of Law
Faculty of Medicine
Faculty of Philosophy and Letters
Faculty of Psychology and Educational Science

Faculty of Science
Faculty of Veterinary Medicine

SPECIAL PROGRAMS:
Center for Studies of Developing Countries
Institute of Physical Education
Marine and Oceanographic Studies Station
Cooperative arrangements with 16 other universities, including Université de Montréal

LANGUAGE OF INSTRUCTION: French

ADMISSION REQUIREMENTS FOR FOREIGN STUDENTS:
Secondary school certificate, or recognized foreign equivalent, and entrance examination.

TUITION FOR FOREIGN STUDENTS:
BF 17,000–19,000 per year in 1989. *See* GENERAL UNIVERSITY INFORMATION.

TOTAL INSTRUCTIONAL FACULTY:
370 fulltime faculty (including 150 professors)

LIBRARY COLLECTIONS:
Central library—1,400,000 volumes
Law library—20,000 volumes

MUSEUMS AND GALLERIES:
Museum of Zoology
Aquarium

UNIVERSITY PUBLICATIONS:
Bulletin trimestriel de l'Association des Amis de l'Universite de Liege, Liege Universite

PRESIDENT: A. Bodson

KATHOLIEKE UNIVERSITEIT LEUVEN
(Catholic University of Louvain)
Naamsestraat 22, 3000 Louvain, Belgium

CHARACTERISTICS OF INSTITUTION:
Private, Catholic university

DATE FOUNDED: 1425

TOTAL ENROLLMENT: 24,000 fulltime students (including 1,600 foreign students)

DEGREES AWARDED:
Kandidaat in various fields
   two–three years required
Licentiaat in various fields
   two years after Kandidaat required
Doctorate
   two years after Licentiaat required
Magister
   two years after doctorate required
Professional titles in various fields
   three–four years required
Geaggregeerde voor het Hogar Secundair Onderwijs
(higher secondary-level teaching qualification)

ACADEMIC PROGRAMS:
Faculty of Agronomy
Faculty of Applied Sciences
Faculty of Arts
Faculty of Canon Law
Faculty of Economics and Applied Economics
Faculty of Law
Faculty of Medicine
Faculty of Psychology and Educational Science
Faculty of Sciences
Faculty of Social Sciences
Faculty of Theology
Higher Institute of Philosophy
Institute of Pharmacy
Institute of Physical Education

SPECIAL PROGRAMS:
China-Europe Institute
Higher Institute of Labor Relations
Institute of Actuaries
Institute of Engineering Preparatory Studies
Institute of Family and Sex Studies
Institute of Literary Studies
Institute of Modern Languages
Institute of Religious Sciences
Institute for the Study of Developing Countries
School of Public Health

LANGUAGES OF INSTRUCTION: Dutch and English

ADMISSION REQUIREMENTS FOR FOREIGN STUDENTS:
Secondary school certificate, or recognized foreign equivalent, and entrance examination

TUITION FOR FOREIGN STUDENTS:
BF 95,000 to BF 245,000. *See* GENERAL UNIVERSITY INFORMATION.

TOTAL INSTRUCTIONAL FACULTY:
1,900 fulltime faculty (including 790 professors)

LIBRARY COLLECTIONS:
Central library—1,370,000 volumes
Faculty libraries

MUSEUMS AND GALLERIES:
University museums

UNIVERSITY PUBLICATIONS:
Academische Agenda, Academische Tijdingen, Alumni Leuven, Jaarverslag, Veto

RECTOR: Prof. Dr. Roger Dillemans

UNIVERSITÉ CATHOLIQUE DE LOUVAIN
(Catholic University of Louvain)
Place de l'Université 1, 1348 Louvain La Neuve, Belgium

CHARACTERISTICS OF INSTITUTION:
Private, Catholic university

DATE FOUNDED: 1425 (separated from Katholieke Universiteit Leuven in 1970)

TOTAL ENROLLMENT: 18,000 fulltime students (including 3,500 foreign students)

DEGREES AWARDED:
Candidat
Licencié in various fields
    four–five years required
Maîtrise
    one year after Licencié required
Doctorate
    by thesis
Doctor of Medicine
    seven years required
Professional titles of *Ingenieur* in various fields
    five years required
Diplôme de Pharmacien (Pharmacy)
    five years required
Agrégé de l'enseignement secondaire supérieur (higher secondary-level teaching qualification)
    four years required
Agrégé de l'enseignement supérieur (university-level teaching qualification)
    at least two years after doctorate required

ACADEMIC PROGRAMS:
Faculty of Agriculture
Faculty of Applied Sciences
Faculty of Economic, Political and Social Sciences
Faculty of Law
Faculty of Medicine
Faculty of Philosophy and Letters
Faculty of Psychology and Education
Faculty of Sciences
Faculty of Theology
Higher Institute of Philosophy

SPECIAL PROGRAMS:
Center for Theater Studies
Center for Operations Research and Econometrics
Higher Institute of Religious Studies
Institute of Labor Studies
Institute of Logography
Institute for the Study of Developing Countries
Open Faculty of Economic and Social Politics

LANGUAGE OF INSTRUCTION: French

ADMISSION REQUIREMENTS FOR FOREIGN STUDENTS:
Secondary school certificate, or recognized foreign equivalent, and entrance examination

TUITION FOR FOREIGN STUDENTS:
BF 95,000 to 245,000 per year. *See* GENERAL UNIVERSITY INFORMATION.

TOTAL INSTRUCTIONAL FACULTY:
950 fulltime faculty (including 150 professors)

LIBRARY COLLECTIONS:
Total collection—1,000,000 volumes

MUSEUMS AND GALLERIES:
Museums of Art, Archaeology, History of Medicine

UNIVERSITY PUBLICATIONS:
Bulletin des Amis de Louvain, Le Porte-parole, Nouvelles Breves

RECTOR: Pierre Macq

UNIVERSITÉ DE L'ETAT A MONS
(State University of Mons)
20 Place du Parc, 7000 Mons, Belgium

CHARACTERISTICS OF INSTITUTION:
State-run, nonprofit university

DATE FOUNDED: 1965

TOTAL ENROLLMENT: 3,000 fulltime students (including 450 foreign students)

DEGREES AWARDED:
Candidat
    two–three years required
Licencié in various fields
    four years required
Doctorate
Professional titles in various fields
    three–five years required
Agrégé de l'enseignement secondaire supérieur (higher secondary-level teaching qualification) in various fields
    one year after Licencié required
Postgraduate certificates and diplomas

ACADEMIC PROGRAMS:
Faculty of Applied Economics
Faculty of Medicine
Faculty of Psychological and Educational Sciences
Faculty of Sciences

SPECIAL PROGRAM:
School of Translation and Interpretation

LANGUAGE OF INSTRUCTION: French

ADMISSION REQUIREMENTS FOR FOREIGN STUDENTS:
Secondary school certificate or recognized foreign equivalent

TUITION FOR FOREIGN STUDENTS:
BF 19,000. *See* GENERAL UNIVERSITY INFORMATION.

TOTAL INSTRUCTIONAL FACULTY:
170 fulltime faculty (including 45 professors)

LIBRARY COLLECTIONS:
Central library—500,000 volumes
Faculty libraries

UNIVERSITY PUBLICATIONS:
Cahiers Internationaux du Sybolisme, Reseaux, Revue de Phonetique Appliquee

RECTOR: Yves van Haverbeke

FACULTÉ POLYTECHNIQUE DE MONS
(Polytechnical Faculty of Mons)
Rue de Houdain, 7000 Mons, Belgium

CHARACTERISTICS OF INSTITUTION:
Independent, state-funded university

DATE FOUNDED: 1896

TOTAL ENROLLMENT: 1,000 fulltime students (including 150 foreign students)

DEGREES AWARDED:
Candidat Ingénieur civil
    two years required
Ingénieur civil in various fields
    three years after Candidat Ingénieur civil required
Maîtrise
    one year after Ingénieur civil required
Docteur en Sciences appliquées
Agrégé de l'enseignement supérieur (university-level teaching qualification) in various fields

ACADEMIC PROGRAM:
Faculty of Applied Sciences

SPECIAL PROGRAMS:
Interuniversity Institute of Nuclear Science
Computer Center
Cooperative arrangements with Brown University in Rhode Island

LANGUAGE OF INSTRUCTION: French

ADMISSION REQUIREMENTS FOR FOREIGN STUDENTS:
Entrance examination

TUITION FOR FOREIGN STUDENTS:
BF 17,000–19,000 per year in 1989. *See* GENERAL UNIVERSITY INFORMATION.

TOTAL INSTRUCTIONAL FACULTY:
80 fulltime faculty (including 60 professors)

LIBRARY COLLECTIONS:
Central library—50,000 volumes
Faculty libraries

MUSEUMS AND GALLERIES:
Museums of Architecture and Town Planning
Museum of Mineralogy and Geology

UNIVERSITY PUBLICATION:
Bulletin de l'Information de l'Association des Ingénieurs

RECTOR: Prof. C. Bouqueneau

FACULTÉS UNIVERSITAIRES NOTRE-DAME DE LA PAIX
(Polytechnical Faculty of Mons)
61 Rue de Bruxelles, 5000 Namur, Belgium

CHARACTERISTICS OF INSTITUTION:
Independent, state-funded university

DATE FOUNDED: 1831

TOTAL ENROLLMENT: 4,100 fulltime students (including 225 foreign students)

DEGREES AWARDED:
Candidat in various fields
    two–three years required
Licencié in various fields
    two–three years required
Doctorate
Agrégé de l'enseignement secondaire supérieur (higher secondary-level teaching qualification)

ACADEMIC PROGRAMS:
Faculty of Economics and Social Sciences
Faculty of Law
Faculty of Medicine
Faculty of Science
Faculty of Philosophy and Letters

SPECIAL PROGRAM:
Institute of Computer Science

LANGUAGE OF INSTRUCTION: French

ADMISSION REQUIREMENTS FOR FOREIGN STUDENTS:
Secondary school certificate or recognized foreign equivalent

TUITION FOR FOREIGN STUDENTS:
See GENERAL UNIVERSITY INFORMATION.

TOTAL INSTRUCTIONAL FACULTY:
180 fulltime faculty (including 80 professors)

LIBRARY COLLECTIONS:
Total collection—1,300,000 volumes

UNIVERSITY PUBLICATIONS:
Annales de la Société Scientifique de Bruxelles, Bibliothèque de la Faculté de Philosophie et Lettres de Namur, Les Etudes Classiques, Travaux de la Faculté de Droit, Travaux de la Faculté des Sciences économiques et sociales, Travaux de l'Institut d'Informatique

RECTOR: J. Berleur

COLLEGE OF EUROPE
Dijver 11, 8000 Bruges, Belgium

CHARACTERISTICS OF INSTITUTION:
State-run, nonprofit university

DATE FOUNDED: 1949

TOTAL ENROLLMENT: 200 fulltime students

DEGREES AWARDED:
Diploma of Advanced European Studies
Master's Degree of Advanced European Studies

ACADEMIC PROGRAMS:
European Studies—Administration
European Studies—Economics
European Studies—Law

SPECIAL PROGRAMS:
Annual symposia on aspects of the European Community

LANGUAGES OF INSTRUCTION: English and French

ADMISSION REQUIREMENTS FOR FOREIGN STUDENTS:
A recognized university degree in economics, law, political science or international relations

TUITION FOR FOREIGN STUDENTS:
BF 460,000 ($12,000 US) for foreign students from outside the European Community
BF 290,000 for European Community member state nationals

TOTAL INSTRUCTIONAL FACULTY:
60 fulltime professors

LIBRARY COLLECTIONS:
Total Collection—100,000 volumes (includes over 50 works published by the College of Europe on aspects of European unification)

UNIVERSITY PUBLICATIONS:
"Prospects for Agriculture in the EEC"; *Les Chemins de fer et l'Europe*; "In Search of a New Balance—The Community Institutions at the beginning of the '80's"; "European Monetary System and International Monetary Reform"; *Integrations regionales entre pays en voie de developpement*; "Community Bureaucracy at the Crossroads"; "The European Parliament on the Eve of the Second Direct Election: Balance Sheet and Prospects"; "Europe, America and the World Economy"; "The European Community's Development Policy: The strategies ahead"; "The European Community and the E.F.T.A. countries"; "The New Trends in EC and US Trade Laws"

RECTOR: J. Lukaszewski

FACULTEIT VOOR VERGELIJKENDE GODSDIENSTWETENSCHAPPEN
(Faculty for the Comparative Study of Religion)
Bist 164, 2610 Wilrijk-Antwerp, Belgium

CHARACTERISTICS OF INSTITUTION:
Independent faculty

DATE FOUNDED: 1980

TOTAL ENROLLMENT: 75 fulltime students (including 25 foreign students)

DEGREES AWARDED:
Bachelor of Arts (BA)
Master of Arts (MA)
Doctor of Philosophy (PhD)

ACADEMIC PROGRAMS:
Faculty of Comparative Religion (Judaism, general Christianity, Roman Catholicism, Protestantism, Eastern churches, Anglicanism, Islam, Vedism and Brahmanism, Hinduism, Buddhism, Shintoism, religious currents in China, nonecclesiastical Christian mysticism)

SPECIAL PROGRAMS:
Bilateral accords with the Eccumenical Research Society, Inc., Los Angeles, California; the Union of Arab Historians; Interfilm, Parijs/Hilversum

LANGUAGES OF INSTRUCTION: Dutch, English, French and German

ADMISSION REQUIREMENTS FOR FOREIGN STUDENTS:
Belgian secondary school certificate or recognized foreign equivalent. *See* GENERAL UNIVERSITY INFORMATION.

TUITION FOR FOREIGN STUDENTS:
BF equivalent of $400 US

TOTAL INSTRUCTIONAL FACULTY:
20 faculty (including 11 professors)

LIBRARY COLLECTIONS:
Total collection—7,000 volumes

UNIVERSITY PUBLICATIONS:
Faculty Prospectus, Acta Comparanda

RECTOR: Christiaan J. G. Vonck

THE UNIVERSITIES OF DENMARK

GENERAL UNIVERSITY INFORMATION

Danish universities are state-run, nonprofit institutions and, as such, follow similar rules and regulations concerning language requirements, expenses and degree requirements. The following general information is relevant to all the institutions mentioned in this chapter.

ADMISSION REQUIREMENTS FOR FOREIGN STUDENTS

Foreign students are not subject to uniform admission requirements when applying to Danish universities. There are many acceptable Danish and foreign qualifications for university admission in Denmark, and requirements are subject to the discretion of the individual institutions. Standard Danish requirements include

- the secondary school certificate, high school diploma or international baccalaureate (*studentereksamen*)
- the higher preparatory examination (*Højere Forberedelseseksamen*)
- the higher commercial examination (*Højere Handelseksamen*)

Equivalent foreign qualifications include the university admission qualification of a foreign student whose home country has a bilateral agreement with Denmark regarding university admission requirements. Also, university entrance examinations by a foreign student in a country with which Denmark has a bilateral agreement may be accepted. These agreements exist with the member states of the European Community, the Nordic countries, states in the Council of Europe which acceded to the European Convention on diploma equivalence and several UNESCO (United Nations Educational, Scientific, and Cultural Organization) countries.

Danish universities do not automatically recognize university degrees from foreign institutions due to variations in structure and content of the academic programs abroad. However, a foreign applicant can appeal for recognition of his qualifications by making an individual request to the university in question. The university will only grant equivalence to a foreign degree after reviewing the duration of study, the academic program and the examinations taken by the foreign applicant.

Before submitting qualifications for approval, the applicant should contact the Danish institution for any necessary forms. In general, however, the foreign applicant must provide the Danish university with the following documents:

- degree certificates
- grades
- a description of the academic program and degree requirements of the previous institution
- major papers written as required course work
- reading lists of the courses completed

Applications for Danish degree equivalence are answered in about two or three months by the university's admissions department.

In some instances, foreign students may be required to take entrance examinations in order to gain admission. All universities in Denmark require that students be proficient in the Danish language, and therefore, foreign students must either prove their proficiency or take a Danish language examination. No Danish language courses are available to foreign students at Danish universities, but such courses are conducted at the Studieskole in Copenhagen and at the Folkeuniversitet in Arhus and Odense. In addition, supplementary examinations may be required for admission to certain academic programs. Foreign students should request information regarding entrance examinations from the prospective Danish universities.

Since 1976, Denmark has regulated the number of its foreign students. Danish law restricts the admission of foreign students to less than 10% of the total student population. In practice, foreign student enrollment at Danish universities is usually between 2% and 4% of the total student population. This low number of foreign admissions is because of the "special tie" requirement of certain academic programs. To be admitted to a program such as medicine, dentistry, pharmacy, agriculture or civil engineering, it is necessary for a foreign student's home country to have "special ties" (agreements for reciprocal privileges, such as trade privileges and academic privileges) with Denmark.

Foreign students who meet the "special tie" requirements must also fulfill one of the following criteria:

- be a member of the specific group of European Community nationals covered by Article 12 of EEC Regulation No. 1612/68 concerning the freedom of movement of employees within the European Community
- have spent at least two years in Denmark since the age of seven before July 1st of the year in which

the application to the prospective Danish University was made
- have at least one Danish parent and be proficient in the Danish language
- be under the age of 22 years old and have foreign parents who are residents of Denmark and can prove they have reason for extended residence in Denmark

APPLICATION PROCEDURE FOR FOREIGN STUDENTS

Because foreign students are not subject to uniform admission requirements at Danish universities, application procedures vary from institution to institution. Foreign applicants should contact the prospective institutions directly for application information. They can also consult the Central Advisory Service (Studievejledning) at the University of Copenhagen (Københavns Universitet), which can provide application procedures of the other Danish universities. Foreign students are advised to contact the prospective institutions well in advance of the academic year in which they hope to be admitted.

Foreign applicants are expected to provide the following information and certified documents when applying to a Danish university:

- university admission qualification (secondary school certificates or high school diploma)
- proof of Danish language proficiency
- prospective academic program at the institution in question
- academic year in which the applicant hopes to enroll
- if a transfer applicant, validated results of present university studies
- specification of whether application is for a degree program or for temporary or course student status
- "special ties" with Denmark

Any photocopies of documents must be authenticated by the competent authorities.

Foreign students who apply to Danish institutions for temporary student status are not subject to regulatory quotas or application deadlines. However, they are advised to contact prospective Danish universities as early as possible.

APPLICATION DEADLINES

Foreign students must send complete applications for admission and all other requirements to the universities' admissions departments before March 15 of the year in which the applicant intends to commence studies. The applicant will receive notification concerning acceptance by June 1.

ACADEMIC PROGRAM AND DEGREE REQUIREMENTS

The individual Danish universities are responsible for specific regulations regarding examinations, grading and degree programs.

Undergraduate Degrees

There are two types of undergraduate degrees in Denmark. The kandidateksamen is a general degree awarded after the final examinations in the core curriculum (social sciences, theology, medicine, humanities and natural sciences). It is usually acquired in five to six years; however, this type of degree may take longer before the student is capable of passing the final examinations. The magisterkonferensen is a more advanced degree and takes at least six to eight years to complete. It involves intensive study in a particular discipline within the humanities, social sciences, or natural sciences.

Postgraduate Degrees

Two types of postgraduate degrees are generally offered at Danish universities: the Licentiatgrad degree and the Doktorgrad degree. Many specialized professional degrees may be attained at the postgraduate level, also.

The Licentiatgrad is the first postgraduate degree. The admission requirement to a Licentiatgrad program is a kandidateksamen degree in the same subject. The normal procedure for this degree is the submission of a study project, which must be approved by the faculty overseeing the degree. A proctor is appointed for the duration of the project (usually two to three years). The Licentiatgrad is roughly equivalent to a PhD but is less demanding than the doctoral thesis required to attain a Doktorgrad.

The Doktorgrad has no course requirements. Instead, the student must present a doctoral thesis, which usually involves several years of independent research at a scholarly level. The Doktorgrad is the highest degree available to students in Denmark.

Temporary Students

Foreign students can apply for temporary student status at Danish universities. Foreign applicants must have completed at least two years of the academic program to which they are applying at their current institutions. Temporary student status provides foreign students with the opportunity to engage in studies at a Danish university for a brief period of time. Temporary students (Gaestestuderende) are not allowed to attend introductory courses and are usually admitted for a maximum of two years; the usual duration of temporary studies is one year. Temporary students may attend lectures and take regular course examinations. They may also receive certificates validating completed course work at the Danish institution. Temporary students are not permitted to study for a full degree, though, as the admission requirements for temporary student status differ from those for degree students. Proficiency in the Danish language is still a requirement for admission as a temporary student.

Foreign applicants should contact the Danish institution in question to acquire the necessary information, since temporary student status may vary from one university to the next.

Course Students

Course students may only engage in individual courses and not as part of a degree program. The applicant must satisfy all equivalency requirements for each course, as well as provide evidence of proficiency in the Danish language in order to be accepted as a course student (Kursusstuderende). Only a few courses are available to such applicants, and the institution must have room in order to open admission to course student applicants. Course students may take the examinations offered in the program; however, they are not permitted to study for the kandidateksamen due to the different admission requirements for regular degree students.

ACCREDITATION

All Danish university degrees are accredited by the Danish government.

REGISTRATION REQUIREMENTS

Foreign applicants accepted at a Danish university must follow the instructions for registration at the relevant institution, since the requirements vary. The registration deadline (Tilmeldingsfristen) is July 1 for all Danish universities.

VISA REQUIREMENTS AND RESIDENCE REGULATIONS

Foreign students do not need a visa to enter Denmark but must apply for a residence permit upon arrival—or before arrival from Danish authorities, such as the Danish embassy or consulate, in their home countries.

When applying for a foreign student residence permit, the student must provide certified evidence of admission to a Danish university as well as the ability to finance the stay in Denmark.

Foreign students who are nationals of a European Community member state have more flexible residence regulations. They can register within five days of arrival in Denmark for an extended residence permit. Foreign students from the European Commu-

nity must register at the local Resident's Registration Office (Folkeregistret). After registration, the student will be issued a personal number certificate (Centrale Personregister—CPR).

TUITION FEES FOR FOREIGN STUDENTS

Foreign students pay no tuition fees at Danish universities. However, some universities may have an admission charge (such as the University of Odense, where foreign students pay DKr 500—roughly $70 US).

EXPENSES

Living expenses vary from location to location. The following is an estimate provided by the University of Copenhagen:

Housing, institutional food	DKr 36,000
Books, supplies	DKr 1,200
Clothing, laundry	DKr 1,200
Miscellaneous	DKr 12,000
Total per year	DKr 52,000

FOREIGN STUDENT SCHOLARSHIPS

Foreign students are entitled to Danish government assistance (Statens Uddannelsesstøtte—SU) if they are European Community member state nationals and are permanent residents of Denmark. Also, they must not be more than 20 years old when starting their Danish education. "Special ties" are required for the Danish government to offer any financial assistance to foreigners.

Foreign students who are from countries that do not have "special ties" with Denmark should inquire about scholarships at the Danish embassy or consulate in their home countries.

In general, the individual institutions do not offer financial assistance to foreign students.

UNIVERSITY CALENDAR

The academic year is divided into two semesters:

- fall semester: early September to mid/end of January
- spring semester: mid-February to mid/end of June

FOREIGN STUDENTS IN DENMARK

Foreign students can attend the universities of Denmark as regular degree students or as temporary and course students. In 1987, 3% of the total student enrollment was made up of foreign students; of that contingent, 25% were European Community nationals. Many foreign students in Denmark are from other nordic countries. Students from North America are also present in relatively large numbers. Certain institutions attract more foreigners than others, but each of the universities of Denmark has an international student body.

AALBORG UNIVERSITETS CENTER
(Aalborg University Center)
POB 159, Langagervej 2, 9100 Aalborg, Denmark

CHARACTERISTICS OF INSTITUTION:
State-run, nonprofit university

DATE FOUNDED: 1974

TOTAL ENROLLMENT: 6,500 students (including 250 foreign students)

DEGREES AWARDED:
Professional Titles in various fields
   three years required
Candidatus in various fields
   four and one-half to five and one-half years required
Postgraduate licentiate
   an additional two to three years required
Doctorate
   by thesis

ACADEMIC PROGRAMS:
Department of Building Technology and Structural Engineering
Department of Civil Engineering
Department of Communication
Department of Development and Planning
Department of Economics, Politics and Public Administration
Department of Electrical Systems
Department of Energy Technology
Department of Languages and Intercultural Studies
Department of Mechanical Engineering
Department of Music and Music Therapy
Department of Physics
Department of Production
Department of Social Studies and Organization

LANGUAGE OF INSTRUCTION: Danish

ADMISSION REQUIREMENTS FOR FOREIGN STUDENTS:
Secondary school certificate (studentereksamen) or recognized foreign equivalent

TUITION FOR FOREIGN STUDENTS:
None

TOTAL INSTRUCTIONAL FACULTY:
540

LIBRARY COLLECTIONS:
Central library—363,500 volumes

UNIVERSITY PUBLICATIONS:
Center nyt, Forskningsnyt, Årberetning

RECTOR: Sven Caspersen

AARHUS UNIVERSITET
(University Of Aarhus)
Ndr. Ringgade, 8000 Aarhus C, Denmark

CHARACTERISTICS OF INSTITUTION:
State-run, nonprofit university

DATE FOUNDED: 1928

TOTAL ENROLLMENT: 13,000 students

DEGREES AWARDED:
Candidatus in various fields, Magister Artium, Magister Scientiarum
   five to six years required
Candidatus Medicinae
   eight years required
Licentiate
   by thesis
Doctorate
   by thesis

ACADEMIC PROGRAM:
Faculty of Arts (humanities, including archaeology)
Faculty of Divinity
Faculty of Law and Economics (including political science and psychology)
Faculty of Medicine
Faculty of Natural Sciences (including biology)
School of Postbasic Nursing
Institute of Occupational Therapy and Physiotherapy
Institute of Home Economics

LANGUAGE OF INSTRUCTION: Danish

ADMISSION REQUIREMENTS FOR FOREIGN STUDENTS:
Secondary school certificate (studentereksamen) or recognized foreign equivalent

TUITION FOR FOREIGN STUDENTS:
None

TOTAL INSTRUCTIONAL FACULTY:
170

LIBRARY COLLECTIONS:
State and university library—1,740,000 volumes

MUSEUMS AND GALLERIES:
Museums of Classical Archaeology, History of Science, Medical History, Natural History

UNIVERSITY PUBLICATIONS:
Acta Jutlandica Årsberetning

RECTOR: H. Lehmann

KØBENHAVNS UNIVERSITET
(University of Copenhagen)
POB 2177, 1017 Copenhagen K, Denmark

CHARACTERISTICS OF INSTITUTION:
State-run, nonprofit university

DATE FOUNDED: 1479

TOTAL ENROLLMENT: 26,350 full-time students (including 720 foreign students)

DEGREES AWARDED:
Examinus Artium
    two years required
Candidatus in various fields
    four to seven years required
Magister in various fields
    seven to eight years required
Licentiate
    an additional three years required
Doctorate
    by thesis

ACADEMIC PROGRAMS:
Faculty of Arts
Faculty of Mathematics and Natural Science
Faculty of Medicine
Faculty of Social Sciences (including law and economics)
Faculty of Theology

SPECIAL PROGRAMS:
Cooperative arrangements with universities in several countries

LANGUAGE OF INSTRUCTION: Danish

ADMISSION REQUIREMENTS FOR FOREIGN STUDENTS:
Secondary school certificate (studentereksamen), or recognized foreign equivalent, and Danish language entrance examination

TUITION FOR FOREIGN STUDENTS:
None

TOTAL INSTRUCTIONAL FACULTY:
2,000

LIBRARY COLLECTIONS:
University and departmental libraries—1,000,000 volumes

MUSEUMS AND GALLERIES:
Museums of Botany, Medical History, Mineralogy, Zoology
Botanical Gardens

UNIVERSITY PUBLICATIONS:
Arbog for Københavns Universitet, Fetskrift i anledning af universitets arsfest, Lektionskatalogen

RECTOR: Prof. Dr. Phil. O. Nathan

ODENSE UNIVERSITET
(University of Odense)
Campusvej 55, DK-5230 Odense M, Denmark

CHARACTERISTICS OF INSTITUTION:
State-administered, academically autonomous, nonprofit university

DATE FOUNDED: 1966

TOTAL ENROLLMENT: 7,300 fulltime students (including 65 foreign students)

DEGREES AWARDED:
Examinus Artium
    two years required
Candidatus in various fields
    four to seven years required
Magister in various fields
    seven to eight years required
Licentiate
    an additional three years required
Doctorate
    by thesis

ACADEMIC PROGRAMS:
Faculty of Arts
Faculty of Medicine
Faculty of Natural Sciences
Faculty of Social Sciences and Management

SPECIAL PROGRAMS:
Cooperative arrangements with 10 other universities, including the University of Minnesota and the University of California at Berkeley
Scandinavian Area Studies

LANGUAGE OF INSTRUCTION: Danish

ADMISSION REQUIREMENTS FOR FOREIGN STUDENTS:
Secondary school certificate (studentereksamen) or Højere Forberedelseseksamen or Højere Handelseksamen or recognized foreign equivalent

TUITION FOR FOREIGN STUDENTS:
None (DKr 500 [$70 US] registration fee)

TOTAL INSTRUCTIONAL FACULTY:
575 (including 300 professors)

LIBRARY COLLECTIONS:
Central library—800,000 volumes

UNIVERSITY PUBLICATIONS:
Nyt fra Odense Universitet

RECTOR: Carl Th. Pedersen

HANDELSHOJSKOLEN I AARHUS
(The Aarhus School of Business)
Fuglesangs Alle 4, 8210 Aarhus V, Denmark

CHARACTERISTICS OF INSTITUTION:
State-run, nonprofit university

DATE FOUNDED: 1939

TOTAL ENROLLMENT: 6,500 students (including 60 foreign students)

DEGREES AWARDED:
Almen erhvervsokonomisk uddannelse (business economics and administration)
   three years required
Erhvervsretlig uddannelse (business law)
   three years required
Erhvervsokonomisk-sproglig uddannelse (business economics and modern languages)
   three years required
Erhvervsokonomisk uddannelse me datalogi (business economics and data processing)
   three years required
Candidatus Mercaturae
   an additional one to one and one-third years required
Erhvervsproglige afgangseksamen (modern languages)
   four years required
Candidatus Linguae Mercaturae
   a further two and one-half to three years after Erhvervsproglige afgangseksamen required
Diplomas for evening studies

ACADEMIC PROGRAMS:
Department of Accountancy
Department of Applied Statistics
Department of Auditing
Department of Business Law
Department of Business Organization and Management
Department of Economic Psychology
Department of English Language
Department of Finance
Department of Foreign Trade
Department of French Language
Department of German Language
Department of Macroeconomics
Department of Managerial Data Processing
Department of Marketing
Department of Operational Research

LANGUAGE OF INSTRUCTION: Danish

ADMISSION REQUIREMENTS FOR FOREIGN STUDENTS:
Secondary school certificate (studentereksamen) or Højere Forberedelseseksamen or Højere Handelseksamen or recognized foreign equivalent

TUITION FOR FOREIGN STUDENTS:
None

TOTAL INSTRUCTIONAL FACULTY:
150 fulltime faculty (including 16 professors)
300 parttime faculty

LIBRARY COLLECTIONS:
Total collection—110,000 volumes

RECTOR: Bent Provstgaard

HANDELSHØJSKOLEN I KØBENHAVN (Copenhagen Business School) Struenseegade 7–9, 2200 Copenhagen N, Denmark

CHARACTERISTICS OF INSTITUTION:
State-run, nonprofit university

DATE FOUNDED: 1917

TOTAL ENROLLMENT: 14,600 students (including 360 foreign students)

DEGREES AWARDED:
Almene erhvervsokonomisk eksamen (business economics and administration)
   three years required
Candidatus Mercaturae
   five years required
Erhvervesproglige afgangseksamen (modern languages)
   four years required
Candidatus Linguae Mercaturae
   an additional two years following completion of the Erhvervesproglige afgangseksamen required
Licentiate
Doctorate
Diplomas for evening studies

ACADEMIC PROGRAMS:
Faculty of Business Administration (including marketing, business administration, commercial law, sociology, transport and tourism and foreign trade)
Faculty of Modern Languages

SPECIAL PROGRAMS:
Cooperative arrangements with five other universities, including the University of Oregon, the University of Texas at Austin and Northwestern University in Illinois

LANGUAGE OF INSTRUCTION: Danish

ADMISSION REQUIREMENTS FOR FOREIGN STUDENTS:
Secondary school certificate (studentereksamen) or Højere Forberedelseseksamen or Højere Handelseksamen or recognized foreign equivalent

TUITION FOR FOREIGN STUDENTS:
None

TOTAL INSTRUCTIONAL FACULTY:
310 fulltime faculty (including 25 professors)
860 parttime faculty

LIBRARY COLLECTIONS:
Total collection—215,000 volumes

UNIVERSITY PUBLICATIONS:
Forskningsovisen, Ark, Cebal, Sprint

RECTOR: Finn Junge-Jensen

HANDELSHØJSKOLEN SYD
(Southern Denmark School of Business
Administration and Modern Languages)
Grundtvigsalle 150, 6400 Sonderborg, Denmark

CHARACTERISTICS OF INSTITUTION:
State-run, nonprofit, university-level school

DATE FOUNDED: 1984

TOTAL ENROLLMENT: 3,000 fulltime students

DEGREES AWARDED:
Almene erhvervsokonomisk eksamen (business economics and administration)
   three years required
Candidatus Mercaturae
   five years required
Erhvervsproglige afgangseksamen (modern languages)
   four years required
Candidatus Linguae Mercaturae
   an additional two years following completion of the Erhvervsproglige afgangseksamen

Licentiate
Doctorate
   by practical work and thesis

ACADEMIC PROGRAMS:
Faculty of Business Administration
Faculty of Modern Languages

SPECIAL PROGRAMS:
Cooperative arrangements with universities in several countries

LANGUAGE OF INSTRUCTION: Danish

ADMISSION REQUIREMENTS FOR FOREIGN STUDENTS:
Secondary school certificate *(studentereksamen)* or *Højere Forberedelseseksamen* or *Højere Handelseksamen* or recognized foreign equivalent

TUITION FOR FOREIGN STUDENTS:
None

TOTAL INSTRUCTIONAL FACULTY:
70 fulltime faculty
200 parttime faculty

LIBRARY COLLECTIONS:
Total collection—50,000 volumes

PUBLICATIONS:
School prospectus, research reports

PRESIDENT: Gert Engel

THE UNIVERSITIES OF FINLAND

ÅBO AKADEMI
(Swedish University of Åbo)
Domkyrkotorget 3, 20500 Åbo, Finland

CHARACTERISTICS OF INSTITUTION:
State-run, nonprofit university

DATE FOUNDED: 1917

TOTAL ENROLLMENT: 4,500 students

DEGREES AWARDED:
Kandidatexamen in various fields
  five to six years required
Licentiatexamen
  four to eight years (two to three years of course
  work after Kandidatexamen) required

ACADEMIC PROGRAMS:
Faculty of Arts
Faculty of Economics and Political Science
Faculty of Chemical Engineering
Faculty of Education
Faculty of Mathematics and Science
Faculty of Theology

SPECIAL PROGRAMS:
Archipelago Institute
Accelerator Laboratory
Computer Center
Institute of Parasitology
Institute of Religious and Cultural History
Institute of Social Research

LANGUAGE OF INSTRUCTION: Swedish

ADMISSION REQUIREMENTS FOR FOREIGN STUDENTS:
Documents required for admission to an equivalent
course of study at a university in their home countries

TUITION FOR FOREIGN STUDENTS:
None

TOTAL INSTRUCTIONAL FACULTY:
260 fulltime faculty
120 parttime faculty

LIBRARY COLLECTIONS:
Central library—6,000,000 volumes
Department libraries—400,000 volumes
Steiner Memorial Library—37,000 volumes

MUSEUMS AND GALLERIES:
Museum of Naval History, Sibelius Museum and the
"Ett hem"

UNIVERSITY PUBLICATIONS:
Acta Academiae Aboensis

CHANCELLOR: J. M. Jansson

HELSINGIN YLIOPISTO/HELSINGFORS UNIVERSITET
(University of Helsinki)
Hallituskatu 8, 00100 Helsinki, Finland

CHARACTERISTICS OF INSTITUTION:
Autonomous state institution

DATE FOUNDED: 1640

TOTAL ENROLLMENT: 27,000 students (including 500
foreign students)

DEGREES AWARDED:
Kandidaatti in various fields
  five to six years required
Licentiaatti in various fields
  four to six years (at least two to three years after
  Kandidaatti) required
Doctoral degrees in all fields

ACADEMIC PROGRAMS:
Department of Electron Microscopy
Department of Historical Research and Documenta-
  tion
Department of Seismology
Faculty of Agriculture and Forestry
Faculty of Arts
Faculty of Education
Faculty of Law
Faculty of Medicine
Faculty of Philosophy
Faculty of Social Sciences
Faculty of Science
Faculty of Theology

SPECIAL PROGRAMS:
Computer Center
Further Education Center
Institute of Development Studies
Language Center
Radiocarbon Dating Laboratory
Research and Educational Center
Research Institute for Theoretical Physics

LANGUAGES OF INSTRUCTION: Finnish and Swedish

ADMISSION REQUIREMENTS FOR FOREIGN STUDENTS:
Secondary school certificate or foreign equivalent

TUITION FOR FOREIGN STUDENTS:
None (Registration—$100 US [in Finnish markkas])

TOTAL INSTRUCTIONAL FACULTY:
1,700 fulltime faculty
1,300 parttime faculty

LIBRARY COLLECTIONS:
Central library—2,500,000 volumes
Departmental libraries—8,000,000

MUSEUMS AND GALLERIES
Museums of Agriculture, Medical History, Zoology

UNIVERSITY PUBLICATIONS:
Yliopisto, Helsingen Yliopiston Tiedotuslehti

CHANCELLOR: Acad. O. E. Lehto

JYVÄSKYLÄN YLIOPISTO
(University of Jyväskylä)
Seminaarinkatu 15, SF 40100 Jyvaskyla, Finland

CHARACTERISTICS OF INSTITUTION:
State-run, nonprofit university

DATE FOUNDED: 1863

TOTAL ENROLLMENT: 8,050 students (including 105 foreign students)

DEGREES AWARDED:
Kandidaatti in various fields
   five to six years required
Licentiaatti in various fields
   seven to eight (at least two to three years after Kandidaatti) required
Doctoral degrees in various fields
   by thesis

ACADEMIC PROGRAMS:
Faculty of Education
Faculty of Humanities
Faculty of Mathematics and Natural Sciences
Faculty of Physical and Health Education
Faculty of Social Sciences

SPECIAL PROGRAMS:
Center for Economic Research
Computer Center
Educational Research Institute
Further Education Center
Language Center
Nordplus Exchange
Cooperative arrangements with universities in several countries

LANGUAGES OF INSTRUCTION: Finnish and English

ADMISSION REQUIREMENTS FOR FOREIGN STUDENTS:
Entrance examinations and secondary school certificate or foreign equivalent

TUITION FOR FOREIGN STUDENTS:
None

TOTAL INSTRUCTIONAL FACULTY:
600 fulltime faculty

LIBRARY COLLECTIONS:
Central library—1,000,000 volumes
Departmental libraries—200,000 volumes

MUSEUMS AND GALLERIES:
University Museum

UNIVERSITY PUBLICATIONS:
Kasvatu; Acta Academia; Paedogogicae Jyväskyläensis; Jyväskylä Studies in Education, Psychology and Social Research; Studia Historica Jyväskyläensis; Studia Philologica Jyväskyläensis; Studies in Sport, Physical Education and Health; Jyväskylä Studies in the Arts, etc.

RECTOR: Prof. Antti Tanskanen

KUOPION YLIOPISTO
(University of Kuopio)
Box 6, SF 70211 Kuopio, Finland

CHARACTERISTICS OF INSTITUTION:
State-run, nonprofit university

DATE FOUNDED: 1966

TOTAL ENROLLMENT: 2,600 students (including 10 foreign students)

DEGREES AWARDED:
Kandidaatti in various fields
   three to five years required
Licentiaatti in various fields
   seven to eight years (at least three to four years after Kandidaatti) required
Doctoral degrees in various fields
   by thesis

ACADEMIC PROGRAMS:
Department of Environmental Hygiene
Faculty of Dentistry
Faculty of Medicine
Faculty of Natural and Environmental Sciences
Faculty of Pharmacy

SPECIAL PROGRAMS:
Center for Supplementary Education
Computer Center
Language Center
Public Health Research Institute

LANGUAGES OF INSTRUCTION: Finnish

ADMISSION REQUIREMENTS FOR FOREIGN STUDENTS:
Secondary school certificate with placement determined by examination results

TUITION FOR FOREIGN STUDENTS:
None

TOTAL INSTRUCTIONAL FACULTY:
300 fulltime faculty
200 parttime faculty

LIBRARY COLLECTIONS:
Central library—110,000 volumes

UNIVERSITY PUBLICATIONS:
Various university publications

RECTOR: O. V. Lindqvist

TAMPEREEN YLIOPISTO
(University of Tampere)
PI 607, Kalevantiea, 33101 Tampere, Finland

CHARACTERISTICS OF INSTITUTION:
State-run, nonprofit university

DATE FOUNDED: 1925

TOTAL ENROLLMENT: 14,000 (including 80 foreign students)

DEGREES AWARDED:
Kandidaatti in various fields
   five to seven years required
Licentiaatti in various fields
   three to four years after Kandidaatti required
Doctoral degrees in various fields
Professional titles

ACADEMIC PROGRAMS:
Faculty of Economics and Administration
Faculty of Education
Faculty of Humanities
Faculty of Medicine
Faculty of Social Sciences
Vocational Section for Public Administration
Vocational Section for Social Security
Vocational Section for Social Studies

SPECIAL PROGRAMS:
Computer Center
General Language Teaching Center
Institute for Extension Studies
Institute for Speech Studies
Research Institute for Social Sciences

LANGUAGE OF INSTRUCTION:
Finnish

ADMISSION REQUIREMENTS FOR FOREIGN STUDENTS:
Entrance examination and secondary school certificate or foreign equivalent

TUITION FOR FOREIGN STUDENTS:
None

TOTAL INSTRUCTIONAL FACULTY:
600 fulltime faculty
275 parttime faculty

LIBRARY COLLECTIONS:
Central library—1,314,000 volumes

MUSEUMS AND GALLERIES:
Museum of Folk Music Instruments

UNIVERSITY PUBLICATIONS:
Acta Universitatis Tamperensis

CHANCELLOR: Prof. K. Sipponen

TURUN YLIOPISTO
(University of Turku)
20500 Turku 50, Finland

CHARACTERISTICS OF INSTITUTION:
State-run, nonprofit university

DATE FOUNDED: 1920

TOTAL ENROLLMENT: 10,500 students (including 25 foreign students)

DEGREES AWARDED:
Kandidaatti in various fields
   five to six years required
Licentiaatti in various fields
   four to six years (at least two to three years after Kandidaatti) required
Doctoral degrees in all fields

ACADEMIC PROGRAMS:
Faculty of Education
Faculty of Humanities
Faculty of Mathematics and Natural Sciences
Faculty of Medicine
Faculty of Law
Faculty of Social Sciences

SPECIAL PROGRAMS:
Adult Education Center
Archipelago Research Institute
Cardiorespiratory Research Unit
Center for Maritime Studies
Computer Center
Institute for Extension Studies
Language Center

LANGUAGE OF INSTRUCTION: Finnish

ADMISSION REQUIREMENTS FOR FOREIGN STUDENTS:
Entrance examination and secondary school certificate or foreign equivalent

TUITION FOR FOREIGN STUDENTS:
None

TOTAL INSTRUCTIONAL FACULTY:
700 fulltime faculty
300 parttime faculty

LIBRARY COLLECTIONS:
Central library—1,500,000 volumes

MUSEUMS AND GALLERIES:
Museums of Botany and Zoology; Ethnological and Archaeological Museum

UNIVERSITY PUBLICATIONS:
Various university publications

CHANCELLOR: O. J. Granö

TEKNILLINEN KORKEAKOULU
(Helsinki University of Technology)
02150 Espoo 15, Finland

CHARACTERISTICS OF INSTITUTION:
State-run, nonprofit university

DATE FOUNDED: 1908

TOTAL ENROLLMENT: 10,500 students (including 200 foreign students)

DEGREES AWARDED:
Professional titles
   six years required
Licentiaatti in various fields
   a minimum of two more years required
Doctoral degrees in technology
   by thesis (a minimum of four years after degree)

ACADEMIC PROGRAMS:
Faculty of Architecture
Faculty of Electrical Engineering
Faculty of Mechanical Engineering
Faculty of Process Engineering and Materials
Faculty of Surveying and Civil Engineering

SPECIAL PROGRAMS:
Arctic Offshore Research Center
Center for Urban and Regional Studies
Computer Center
Continuing Education Center
Language Center
Metashov Radio Research Station

LANGUAGES OF INSTRUCTION: Finnish, with some lectures in English or Swedish

ADMISSION REQUIREMENTS FOR FOREIGN STUDENTS:
Entrance examination and secondary school certificate or foreign equivalent

TUITION FOR FOREIGN STUDENTS:
None

TOTAL INSTRUCTIONAL FACULTY:
400 fulltime faculty
1,000 parttime faculty

LIBRARY COLLECTIONS:
Central library and departmental libraries—700,000

RECTOR: Prof. Jussi Hyyppä

HELSINGIN KAUPPAKORKEAKOULU
(Helsinki School of Economics and Business Administration)
Runeberginkatu, 14–16, 00100 Helsinki, Finland

CHARACTERISTICS OF INSTITUTION:
State-run, nonprofit university

DATE FOUNDED: 1917

TOTAL ENROLLMENT: 3,600 students

DEGREES AWARDED:
Degree of Kauppatieteiden Maisteri (KTM)
   four to five years required
Kauppatieteiden Lisensiaatti (KTL)
   an additional two to three years required
Kauppatieteiden Tohtori (KTT) (a doctorate)
   an additional four years after Kauppatieteiden Lisensiaatti required

ACADEMIC PROGRAM:
Department of Accountancy and Finance
Department of Administration and Decision Systems
Department of Economics
Department of Law and Social Sciences
Department of Marketing and Production
Department of Methodological Sciences
Department of Modern Languages

SPECIAL PROGRAMS:
Center for Continuing Education
Computer Center
International Center
Program for Developmental Cooperation

LANGUAGE OF INSTRUCTION: Finnish

ADMISSION REQUIREMENTS FOR FOREIGN STUDENTS:
Entrance examination and a secondary school certificate or a foreign equivalent

TUITION FOR FOREIGN STUDENTS:
None

TOTAL INSTRUCTIONAL FACULTY:
260 fulltime faculty
100 parttime faculty

LIBRARY COLLECTIONS:
Library—210,000

UNIVERSITY PUBLICATIONS:
Journal of Business Economics, Acta Academiae Oeconemicae Hesingiensis

CHANCELLOR: J. Lassila

VAASAN KORKEAKOULU
(University of Vaasa)
POB 297, 65101 Vaasa, Finland

CHARACTERISTICS OF INSTITUTION:
State-run, nonprofit university

DATE FOUNDED: 1966

TOTAL ENROLLMENT: 2,000 students

DEGREES AWARDED:
Ekonomi and Kirjeenvaihtaja
    four years required
Kauppatieteiden Kandidaatti
    five years required
Kauppatieteiden Lisensiaatti (KTL)
    an additional two to three years required
Kauppatieteiden Tohtori (KTT) (a doctorate)
    an additional four years after Kauppatieteiden
    Lisensiaatti required

ACADEMIC PROGRAMS:
Department of Accountancy, Business Finance and
    Methodological Sciences
Department of Administration and Marketing

Department of Administrative Sciences
Department of Economics and Law
Department of Modern Languages

SPECIAL PROGRAMS:
Computer Center
Center for Continuing Education
Western-Finland Center for Economic Research

LANGUAGES OF INSTRUCTION: Finnish and Swedish

ADMISSION REQUIREMENTS FOR FOREIGN STUDENTS:
Secondary school certificate

TUITION FOR FOREIGN STUDENTS:
None

TOTAL INSTRUCTIONAL FACULTY:
260 fulltime faculty
120 parttime faculty

LIBRARY COLLECTIONS:
Central library—70,000

UNIVERSITY PUBLICATIONS:
Acta Wasaensia, Proceedings of the University of Vaasa

RECTOR: I. Virtanen

THE UNIVERSITIES OF FRANCE

GENERAL UNIVERSITY INFORMATION

Two types of French universities are reviewed in this chapter: *universitaires* and *grandes écoles*.

French universities *(universitaires)* are state-run, nonprofit institutions and, as such, follow similar rules and regulations concerning admission and degree requirements. The general information given is relevant to all universities mentioned in this chapter.

French *grandes écoles* can be either state-run or private institutions. All *grandes écoles* are autonomous and requirements vary from institution to institution. The general information in this chapter will not cover the *grandes écoles*. However, these institutions are represented in the listing of individual universities.

ADMISSION REQUIREMENTS FOR FOREIGN STUDENTS

Foreign students applying for admission to *universitaires* or *grandes écoles* must hold either a French secondary school certificate *(baccalauréat)* or a recognized foreign equivalent.

With the exception of the secondary school certificate of Germany, French universities do not automatically recognize any foreign qualification as equivalent to the *baccalauréat*.

Foreign students must submit their foreign qualifications in formal applications to the universities, which, after reviewing the candidate's documents and transcripts, make proposals to the president or director of the university for a final decision.

A foreign applicant must also have maintained an acceptable academic standard in an equivalent academic program at a university in his or her home country. Foreign student admission is granted based on the following axioms:

- the equality of rights between French and foreign students
- the equality of foreign applicants in admission procedures
- the adherence to the autonomy of the respective French universities in admission decisions

French universities operate according to a strict three-stage system.

Stage I *(premier cycle)* is the first two years of undergraduate studies and corresponds to the level at which foreign students apply after obtaining a recognized secondary school certificate.

Stage II *(deuxième cycle)* is the continuation of an undergraduate academic program. Transfer students may apply directly to this stage of an academic program. However, the French university in question may not recognize the foreign student's previous educational experience as equivalent to its *premier cycle*. In such cases, foreign transfer applicants may be advised to enroll in the *premier cycle*.

Stage III *(troisième cycle)* is postgraduate level studies. Foreign students wishing to undertake postgraduate work at a French university must have obtained a recognized undergraduate degree and have contacted the chairman of the prospective postgraduate program before the admission procedure can begin.

French universities have individual admissions requirements, and these can vary from one academic program to another. Also, foreign student qualifications may be recognized as equivalent at one French university but not at another. Therefore, foreign students wishing to attend a university in France are advised to apply to a variety of institutions.

Limitations on the admission of foreign students to French universities exists only for the first year of the *premier cycle* in medical and dental departments in the universities of the Paris region. The quota on foreign students in this sector is 5% of the total French student enrollment for that academic year.

The language of instruction at French universities is French. All foreign students are required to be proficient in the French language before enrollment. Admission to the *premier cycle* requires a French language proficiency test. The proficiency level necessitated by a Stage I program is the Diplôme Approfondi de Langue Français (DALF). Admission to the *deuxième* and *troisième cycles* may also require a proficiency test, depending on the regulations of the respective universities. Applicants who obtain a *Baccalauréat* or a secondary school certificate from a recognized French secondary school abroad may be exempt from the proficiency test, depending on the individual universities' regulations. Foreign students are advised to contact the cultural office of the French embassy or consulate in their home countries for information on French language courses available there or in France during the academic year and the summer.

APPLICATION PROCEDURE FOR FOREIGN STUDENTS

All foreign applications to Stage I must complete and submit an initial registration form *(dossier de demande de Première admission en premier cycle)*. This registration form can be obtained from the cultural office of

French embassies and consulates abroad, as well as from the individual universities. The registration form must be completed and returned to the university admissions departments by February 1 of the academic year in which the foreign applicant hopes to enroll.

The foreign applicant must select three institutions, at least two of which must be from the provinces (not Parisian). The following foreign applicants are not required to submit the registration form:

1. any student who holds the

   - French *baccalauréat*
   - French *baccalauréat* with an international option
   - Franco-German *baccalauréat*
   - European *baccalauréat*
   - any French certificate equivalent to the French *Baccalauréat*

2. any applicant who is under the auspices of a transnational governmental agreement between France and the student's home country or a transnational agreement between the student's previous university and a French institution

3. any student who holds a scholarship provided by the French government, international organizations or foreign governments—if the scholarship is administered by CNOUS or CIES (French governmental organizations)

4. any student who is a refugee or stateless person or is waiting for the French government's reply to a request for political asylum

The specific application requirements for foreign students may vary among universities, but each applicant must provide the following information as part of the formal application: proof of previous studies—secondary school certificate, university transcript or university degree (all information must be accompanied by certified French translations authorized by the French embassy or consulate in the foreign student's home country)—and a certificate of proficiency in the French language—even though all foreign students entering the *premier cycle* must take the French language test. It is often possible to submit this formal application well in advance of the anticipated enrollment date.

Application Deadlines

Foreign students are encouraged to submit the initial registration form as soon as possible after December 1 of the year prior to the anticipated academic year. The deadline for receipt of the initial registration form is February 1.

The deadline for formal application may vary from university to university. Since formal applications entail translations of documents and certificates, foreign students are encouraged to start this process as early as possible.

ACADEMIC PROGRAMS AND DEGREE REQUIREMENTS

University academic programs in France are called *études longues* and are in successive stages (*cycles*).The first stage, the *premier cycle*, is two years long and consists of orientation to university studies following the achievement of a *Baccalauréat* or a recognized foreign equivalent. It comprises general courses offered within the framework of multidisciplinary education. Upon completion of the Stage I, the student obtains the Diplôme d'études universitaires générales (DEUG). The DEUG specifies the courses taken during the first stage and the grades achieved by the student. The first stage prepares the student to continue the *études longues,* and the DEUG signifies successful preparation for the second stage.

In certain subject areas, students can complete their university education by graduating from the *premier cycle* with a DEUST degree (Diplôme d'études universitaires scientifiques et techniques). The student must fulfill national or regional requirements before receiving this degree.

The second stage, the *deuxième cycle*, is two or three years in duration. Students must have completed the first stage and obtained a satisfactory DEUG in order to be admitted to the second stage. The academic programs offered in the second stage represent more intensive and specialized academic training. The completion of a second stage program results in professional status for the graduate.

Several degrees are offered within the academic framework of the *deuxième cycle:*

1. Licence and Maîtrise degrees:

   - Licence degrees require one year of basic course work following the DEUG.
   - Maîtrise degrees require one year of professional and specialized course work following the Licence.

2. Maîtrise des sciences et techniques (MST), Maîtrise de sciences de gestion (MSG) and Maîtrise de méthodes informatiques appliquées a la gestion (MIAGE) degrees
   These degrees require two successive years of course work following the DEUG, which result in the single qualification.

3. Engineering degrees
   All engineering degrees involve three years of successive course work after the DEUG, which result in the professional qualification.

4. Magistère degree
   This degree encompasses all university degrees

that consist of three successive years of course work following the DEUG and do not lead to a professional qualification. This includes law, economics and business administration, social sciences, human sciences, regional planning, chemistry, mathematics, computer science, geoscience, natural sciences, physics, physical chemistry and industrial science. Students undergo a competitive application/admissions procedure in order to gain entrance to this second stage degree program.

The third stage, the *troisième cycle*, consists of highly specialized studies and individual research. Certain programs also include one or two years of course work. Admission to this stage is competitive, and applicants must obtain a Maîtrise degree, an engineering degree or a recognized equivalent in order to be fully considered. Two types of degrees are offered in the third stage:

1. Diplôme d'études supérieures specialisées (DESS) degree
   The DESS degree requires one year of professional training plus a period of practical work within a business or firm.
2. Diplôme d'études approfondis (DEA) and Doctorat degrees
   The first year of the third stage in certain programs consists of one year of professional training and results in the DEA degree. The DEA allows students to continue independent research for two more years before obtaining the Doctorat degree.

Études longues in the study of medicine, dentistry, pharmacy and human biology is completed following three stages of studies and results in the national degree of doctor. The duration of study required for the various disciplines is as follows:

- Doctor of Medicine—eight to 10 years
- Doctor of Dentistry—a minimum of five years
- Doctor of Pharmacy—a minimum of six years
- Doctor of Human Biology—a minimum of six years

All candidates for the national degree of Doctor of Medicine must satisfactorily pass an examination after the first year of study before being admitted to the second year. Even foreign students who have completed medical studies abroad are still required to take the first year examination. This test is designed to reduce the number of medical students by 80%, and only those students who pass are admitted to the second year of study. No students, French or foreign, are allowed to observe advanced studies in the faculties of medicine.

The quota for the amount of students admitted to the second year is regulated by the French Ministry of Education. At the end of the second year, students must take another competitive examination for admission to the third year of study (*Internat en Médicine*).

ACCREDITATION

All university degrees, at every stage, are accredited by the French government.

REGISTRATION REQUIREMENTS

After receiving notification of admission, foreign students must register with the universities' *Service de Scolarité* by July 15 of the year in which they intend commencing academic studies. Foreign students must then register in person by October 15; some universities may hold definitive registration prior to October 15.

While registration requirements may vary, each foreign student must present, in person, the following information to the *Service de Scolarité*:

- authenticated proof of previous studies (secondary school certificate or university transcripts or degrees) accompanied by certified French translations authorized by the French embassy or consulate in the foreign student's home country
- certificate of proficiency in the French language
- proof of family status

The foreign student must also at this time pay tuition fees and contributions for medical insurance, medical care, social insurance and any membership dues to athletic facilities. Upon payment of these fees and the presentation of the stated requirements, the foreign student is given a student identity card (*Carte d'Étudiant*). The *Carte d'Étudiant* allows the student to proceed to course registration.

Registration (*Inscription Pédagogique*) takes place at the beginning of the academic year. There, the foreign student must register for optional courses as well as seminars and/or practical course work.

VISA REQUIREMENTS AND RESIDENCE REGULATIONS

Foreign students who are not European Community nationals need a French visa in order to attend a university in France. Visas are obtained from French embassies and consulates abroad. Foreign students also must apply for temporary residence permits (*Cartes de Séjour Temporaire*) once at the university. The temporary residence permit is obtained from the Ministry of the Interior in Paris (*Préfecture de Police*). Proof of financial solvency equivalent to the amount of scholarship provided by the French government to French students is required for foreign students applying for this permit. The amount of government scholarships to individual French students in 1989–1990 was Fr 3,000 per month. Foreign students should expect the amount to increase after 1990 and should inquire as to the amount of finances necessary to gain the temporary residence permit.

Foreign students who are European Community member state nationals do not need a French visa in order to enter France. However, the regulations regarding temporary residence permits remain the same for all foreign students, except that European Community member state nationals are allowed to reside in France for three months before registering with the Ministry of the Interior in Paris.

TUITION FEES FOR FOREIGN STUDENTS

Foreign student tuition fees for the 1989–1990 academic year ranged from Fr 500 to Fr 600. Tuition at the grandes ecoles varies widely. Specific academic programs at the individual institutions must be contacted for accurate information.

EXPENSES

Living expenses vary from city to city with Parisian universities having the highest cost of living. Costs for housing, food, transportation, clothing, entertainment and miscellaneous expenses in 1990 were

- Parisian universities: Rented accommodations + expenses—Fr 5,000 per month
  University residences + expenses—Fr 3,500–4,500 per month
- Provincial universities: Rented accommodations + expenses—Fr 4,500 per month
  University residences + expenses—Fr 3,000–4,000 per month

FOREIGN STUDENT SCHOLARSHIPS

Foreign students are eligible for scholarships from the French embassies and consulates in their home countries. No foreign student scholarships are granted to foreign students by the French government in France. Foreign students should inquire about scholarship opportunities at least 18 months prior to the academic year in which they plan to enroll. Information on foreign student scholarships is available from the cultural office of French embassies and consulates.

These scholarships generally exempt the foreign student from paying tuition fees. However, foreign student scholarships offered by international orga-

nizations may also include transportation costs and living expenses while the foreign student attends university in France. Information on scholarships offered by international organizations is available from the cultural office of French embassies and consulates.

Any foreign student whose parents have held residence in France for at least two years prior to that student's commencement of study at a French university is eligible for a university scholarship from the French government's Ministry of Education. Inquiries about such scholarships can be made to the Ministry of Education in Paris.

UNIVERSITY CALENDAR

The academic year runs from October until June and is divided into three terms:

- fall term: October to December
- winter term: January to March
- spring term: April to June

Students should contact their respective universities for the exact dates of registration and the beginning of classes.

FOREIGN STUDENTS IN FRANCE

Foreign student enrollment at French universities is by far the highest in all of Europe. Approximately 150,000 foreign students were registered at French universities in 1990. In 1986 foreign student enrollment was broken down as follows:

- Stage I (premier cycle): 41.2%
- Stage II (deuxième cycle): 32.9%
- Stage III (troisième cycle): 25.9%

The majority of foreign students study the arts, while the remainder are divided among economics and law (about 17%), medicine (about 12%) and the sciences (about 13%).

Recent figures show that only 14.4% of foreign students came from European Community member states. The vast majority came from other European countries, Asia, Africa, and North America and came to France on Junior Year Abroad programs or as full-time students.

Further information about French universities is available from the following institutions:

The Information Bureau and the Orientation Bureau of the Ministry of Education and Sport
61–65 rue Dutot
75015 Paris, France
Tel.#   (1) 45 39 25 75
        ext. (32 70) & (37 47)

Office National d'Information sur les Enseignements et les Professions (O.N.I.S.E.P.)
168 boulevard du Montparnasse
75014 Paris, France

Office National d'Information sur les Enseignments
et les Professions (O.N.I.S.E.P.) Diffusion
75635 Paris Cedex 13
France

UNIVERSITÉ D'AIX-MARSEILLE I
(UNIVERSITÉ DE PROVENCE)
(University of Provence [Aix-Marseille I])
3 place Victor Hugo, 13331 Marseille Cedex 3, France

CHARACTERISTICS OF INSTITUTION:
State-run, nonprofit university

DATE FOUNDED: 1970

TOTAL ENROLLMENT: 18,700 fulltime students

DEGREES AWARDED:
State qualifications
Sciences:
   Diplôme d'études universitaires générales (DEUG)
      two years required
   Diplôme d'études universitaires scientifiques et
   techniques (DEUST)
      two years required
   Licence ès Sciences
      one year after DEUG required
   Maîtrise
      one year after Licence, or equivalent, required
   Diplôme d'études supérieures spécialisées (DESS)
      one year after Maîtrise required
   Diplôme d'études appropfondies (DEA)
      one year after Maîtrise required
   Doctorat
      two to four years after DEA required
Letters and Human Sciences:
   Diplôme d'études universitaires générales (DEUG)
      two years required
   Licence ès Lettres
      one year after DEUG required
   Magistère
      three years after DEUG required
   Maîtrise
      one year after Licence, or equivalent, required
   Diplôme d'études approfondies (DEA)
      one year after Maîtrise required
   Doctorat
      two to four years after DEA required

ACADEMIC PROGRAMS:
Aix-en-Provence:
   Unit of Anglo-Saxon and Germanic Languages

   Unit of Civilization and Humanities
   Unit of Oriental, Slavonic and Romance Languages
      and Latin American Studies
   Unit of Literature, Art, Communication and Lin-
      guistics
   Unit of Psychology and Education Sciences
   Institute for the Training of Musicians at Nursery
      and Primary Schools
Marseille:
   Unit of Life Sciences, Earth Sciences and Environ-
      ment
   Unit of Mathematics, Computer Science and Me-
      chanics
   Unit of Physical Sciences
   Astronomy

LANGUAGE OF INSTRUCTION: French

ADMISSION REQUIREMENTS FOR FOREIGN STUDENTS:
Secondary school certificate *(baccalauréat)*, or recognized foreign equivalent, or special entrance examination

TUITION FOR FOREIGN STUDENTS:
Fr 500–600 per year in 1990

TOTAL INSTRUCTIONAL FACULTY:
760

LIBRARY COLLECTIONS:
Interuniversity library

PRESIDENT: Jean-Claude Bouvier

UNIVERSITÉ D'AIX-MARSEILLE II
(University of Aix-Marseille II)
Jardin du Pharo, 58 blvd Charles Livon, 13007 Marseille, France

CHARACTERISTICS OF INSTITUTION:
State-run, nonprofit university

DATE FOUNDED: 1973

TOTAL ENROLLMENT: 19,150 fulltime students (including 1,600 foreign students)

DEGREES AWARDED:
State qualifications
Economics:
   Diplôme d'études universitaires générales (DEUG)
      two years required
   Licence ès Sciences économiques
      one year after DEUG required
   Maîtrise
      one year after Licence required
   Diplôme d'études supérieures spécialisées (DESS)
      a minimum of two semesters following Maîtrise
      required
   Dîplôme d'études approfondies (DEA)

a minimum of one year following Maîtrise required
Doctorat en Sciences économiques
two to four years following DEA required
Medicine:
Doctorat en Médecine
six years plus one year hospital practice and thesis required
Certificats de spécialité
a minimum of two years following doctorate required
Chirurgien-Dentiste
five years required
Pharmacy:
Diplôme de Pharmacien
four years plus one year practical work required
Doctorat en Pharmacie
two certificats (études supérieures ou spéciales ou sciences) and thesis after Diplôme required
Science:
Diplôme d'études universitaires générales (DEUG)
two years required
Licence ès Sciences
one year after DEUG required
Maîtrise
one year after Licence, or equivalent, required
Diplôme d'études supérieures spécialisées (DESS)
one year after Maîtrise required
Diplôme d'études approfondies (DEA)
one year after Maîtrise required
Doctorat en Sciences
two to four years after DEA required
Diplôme universitaire de technologie (DUT)
two years required

ACADEMIC PROGRAMS:
Faculty of Dental Surgery
Faculty of Economic Science
Faculty of Medicine
Faculty of Pharmacy
Unit of Science
Institute of Fluid Mechanics
Institute of Geography
Institute of Labor, Economic and Social Research
Institute of Physical Education
Institute of Technology
Institute of Turbulence Statistics Mechanics
Center for Communication
Center for Tropical Health and Medicine

SPECIAL PROGRAMS:
Cooperative arrangements with 24 other universities, including the University of California (Berkeley and San Francisco) and Université du Québec

LANGUAGE OF INSTRUCTION: French

ADMISSION REQUIREMENTS FOR FOREIGN STUDENTS:
Secondary school certificate (baccalauréat) or recognized foreign equivalent, or special entrance examinations.

TUITION FOR FOREIGN STUDENTS:
Fr 500–600 per year in 1990

TOTAL INSTRUCTIONAL FACULTY:
1,166

LIBRARY COLLECTIONS:
Interuniversity library
Units libraries

PRESIDENT: Claude Mercier

UNIVERSITÉ D'AIX-MARSEILLE III (UNIVERSITÉ DE DROIT, D'ÉCONOMIE ET DE SCIENCES) (University of Law, Economics and Science [Aix-Marseille III]) 3 ave Robert Schuman, 13628 Aix-en-Provence Cedex, France

CHARACTERISTICS OF INSTITUTION:
State-run, nonprofit university

DATE FOUNDED: 1973

TOTAL ENROLLMENT: 18,000 fulltime students (including 2,500 foreign students)

DEGREES AWARDED:
State qualifications
Law and Economics:
Diplôme d'études universitaires générales (DEUG)
two years required
Licence
one year after DEUG required
Magistère
three years after DEUG required
Maîtrise
one year after Licence required
Diplôme d'études supérieures spécialisées (DESS)
at least one year following Maîtrise required
Diplôme d'études approfondies (DEA)
one year after Maîtrise required
Doctorat en Sciences économiques
two–four years after DEA required
Certificat de Capacité en Droit (law)
two years after Maîtrise required
Science:
Diplôme d'études universitaires générales (DEUG)
two years required
Licence ès Sciences
one year after DEUG required
Maîtrise

one year after Licence, or equivalent, required
Maîtrise de Sciences et Techniques
  one year after DEUG
Diplôme d'études supérieures spécialisées (DESS)
  one year after Maîtrise required
Diplôme d'études approfondies (DEA)
  one year after Maîtrise required
Doctorat en Sciences
  two–four years after DEA required
Diplôme universitaire de technologie (DUT)
  two years required

ACADEMIC PROGRAMS:
Aix-en-Provence—Social Sciences:
  Institute of Business Law
  Institute of Business Management
  Institute of French Studies for Foreign Students
  Institute of Penal Sciences and Criminology
  Institute of Political Studies
  Institute of Regional Development
  Legal Research Unit
Marseille—Sciences and Technology:
  Professional Training Unit
  Propaedeutical Sciences Unit
  Science Teacher Training Unit
  Scientific and Technical Research Unit
  Higher National School of Physics
  Institute of Petrochemistry and Organic Industrial
    Synthesis
  University Institute of Engineering Sciences
  University Institute of Technology

SPECIAL PROGRAMS:
Cooperative arrangements with universities in 34
countries

LANGUAGE OF INSTRUCTION: French

ADMISSION REQUIREMENTS FOR FOREIGN STUDENTS:
Secondary school certificate *(baccalauréat)*, or recognized foreign equivalent, or special entrance examination

TUITION FOR FOREIGN STUDENTS:
Fr 500–600 per year in 1990

TOTAL INSTRUCTIONAL FACULTY:
664

LIBRARY COLLECTIONS:
Total collection—220,000 volumes
Interuniversity library
Law and Economics section (Aix-en-Provence)
Science section (Marseille)
Specialized libraries

UNIVERSITY PUBLICATIONS:
U3 Infos, Lettre Flash, Livret de l'Étudiant, annual research reports

PRESIDENT: L. Capella

UNIVERSITÉ DE BORDEAUX I
(University of Bordeaux I)
351 cours de la Libération, 33405 Talence Cedex, France

CHARACTERISTICS OF INSTITUTION:
State-run, nonprofit university

DATE FOUNDED: 1970

TOTAL ENROLLMENT: 18,650 fulltime students (including 2,000 foreign students)

DEGREES AWARDED:
State qualifications
Law and Economics:
  Certificat de Capacité en Droit (law)
    two years required
  Diplôme d'études universitaires générales (DEUG)
    two years required
  Licence
    one year after DEUG required
  Maîtrise
    one year after Licence required
  Diplôme d'études supérieures spécialisées (DESS)
    a minimum of two semesters after following
    Maîtrise required
  Diplôme d'études approfondies (DEA)
    one year after Maîtrise required
  Doctorat en Sciences économiques
    two–four years after DEA required
Science:
  Diplôme d'études universitaires générales (DEUG)
    two years required
  Licence ès Sciences
    one year after DEUG required
  Maîtrise
    one year after Licence or equivalent, required
  Diplôme d'études supérieures spécialisées (DESS)
    one year after Maîtrise required
  Diplôme d'études approfondies (DEA)
    two years after Maîtrise required
  Doctorat en Sciences
    two–four years after DEA required
  Diplôme universitaire de technologie (DUT)
    two years required

ACADEMIC PROGRAMS:
Unit of Astronomy
Unit of Basic Economic Studies
Unit of Biology
Unit of Chemistry
Unit of Geological Studies and Research on Aquitaine
Unit of Higher Economic Studies
Unit of Juridical Sciences (first cycle)
Unit of Land and Regional Development
Unit of Mathematics

Unit of Physics
Unit of Private Law
Unit of Public Law and Political Science
Unit of Scientific Studies (first cycle)
Higher National School of Chemistry
Higher School of Electronics and Radioelectricity
Institute of Criminal Studies
Institute of Labor
Institute of Legal Studies
Institute of Political Sciences
Institute of Quaternary and Prehistoric Geology
Pine Research Institute
Perigueux Municipal Institute of Legal and Economic
    Studies
Research Institute on Mathematics Teaching
Regional Institute of Business Studies
Regional Institute of Management
University Institute of Marine Biology
University Institute of Technology
Electronic Microscopy Center
Metal Assaying

SPECIAL PROGRAMS:
Cooperative arrangements with 33 other universities, including the University of California

LANGUAGE OF INSTRUCTION: French

ADMISSION REQUIREMENTS FOR FOREIGN STUDENTS:
Secondary school certificate (baccalauréat), or recognized foreign equivalent, or special entrance examination

TUITION FOR FOREIGN STUDENTS:
Fr 500–600 per year in 1990

TOTAL INSTRUCTIONAL FACULTY:
819

LIBRARY COLLECTIONS:
Interuniversity library
Specialized libraries

UNIVERSITY PUBLICATIONS:
Revue Économique de Sud-Ouest, Flash, Bulletin

PRESIDENT: Jean Lascombe

UNIVERSITÉ DE BORDEAUX II
(University of Bordeaux II)
146 rue Léo-Saignat, 33076 Bordeaux Cedex,
France

CHARACTERISTICS OF INSTITUTION:
State-run, nonprofit university

DATE FOUNDED: 1970

TOTAL ENROLLMENT: 14,000 fulltime students

DEGREES AWARDED:
State qualifications
Medicine:
    Doctorat en Médecine
        six years plus one year hospital practice and thesis
        required
    Certificats de spécialité
        a minimum of two years following doctorate required
    Chirurgien-Dentiste
        five years required
Pharmacy:
    Diplôme de Pharmacien
        four years and one year practical work required
    Doctorat en Pharmacie
        two certificats (études supérieures ou speciales ou
        sciences) and thesis after Diplôme required
Social and Psychological Sciences:
    Diplôme d'études universitaires générales (DEUG)
        two years required
    Licence
        one year after DEUG required
    Maîtrise
        one year after Licence required
    Diplôme d'études supérieures spécialisées (DESS)
        one year after Maîtrise required
    Diplôme d'études approfondies (DEA)
        one year after Maîtrise required
    Doctorat
        two–four years after DEA required
Science:
    Diplôme d'études universitaires générales (DEUG)
        two years required
    Licence ès Sciences
        one year after DEUG required
    Maîtrise
        one year after Licence, or equivalent, required
    Diplôme d'études approfondies (DEA)
        one year after Maîtrise required
    Doctorat en Sciences
        two–four years after DEA required

ACADEMIC PROGRAMS:
Unit of Biochemistry and Cellular Biology
Unit of Biology and Physiopathology
Unit of Medical Sciences I
Unit of Medical Sciences II
Unit of Medical Sciences III
Unit of Odontology
Unit of Pharmacy
Unit of Social and Psychological Sciences
Unit of Tropical Medicine
Institute of Applied Human Sciences
Research Institute of Physical Education

LANGUAGE OF INSTRUCTION: French

ADMISSION REQUIREMENTS FOR FOREIGN STUDENTS:
Secondary school certificate *(baccalauréat)*, or recognized foreign equivalent, or special entrance examination

TUITION FOR FOREIGN STUDENTS:
Fr 500–600 per year in 1990

TOTAL INSTRUCTIONAL FACULTY:
750

LIBRARY COLLECTIONS:
Interuniversity library

UNIVERSITY PUBLICATIONS:
Comte rendu de l'activité scientifique, Bulletin d'information de l'Université, Flashes d'information

PRESIDENT: D. Ducassou

UNIVERSITÉ DE BORDEAUX III
(University of Bordeaux III)
espl Michel-Montaigne, Domaine Universitaire, 33405 Talence Cedex, France

CHARACTERISTICS OF INSTITUTION:
State-run, nonprofit university

DATE FOUNDED: 1970

TOTAL ENROLLMENT: 14,800 fulltime students (including 1,000 foreign students)

DEGREES AWARDED:
State qualifications
Science:
　Diplôme d'études universitaires générales (DEUG)
　　Two years required
　Licence ès Sciences
　　one year after DEUG required
　Maîtrise
　　one year after Licence, or equivalent, required
　Maîtrise de Sciences et Techniques
　　two years after DEGU required
　Diplôme d'études approfondies (DEA)
　　one year after Maîtrise required
　Doctorat en Sciences
　　two–four years after DEA required
Letters and Human Sciences:
　Diplôme d'études universitaires générales (DEUG)
　　two years required
　Licence ès Lettres
　　one year after DEUG required
　Maîtrise
　　one year after Licence, or equivalent, required
　Diplôme d'etudes supérieures spécialisées (DESS)
　　one year after Maîtrise required
　Diplôme d'études approfondies (DEA)
　　one year after Maîtrise required
　Doctorat

　　two–four years after DEA required
　Diplôme universitaire de technologie (DUT)
　　two years required

ACADEMIC PROGRAMS:
Unit of Development and Natural Resources
Unit of Foreign Languages and Literature
Unit of Geography
Unit of Germanic Studies
Unit of History
Unit of Iberian and Latin American Studies
Unit of Language, Literature and Civilization of Anglophone Countries
Unit of Letters and Arts
Unit of Philosophy
Department of French (for foreign students)
Institute of Information and Communication Sciences
University Institute of Technology

SPECIAL PROGRAMS:
Cooperative arrangements with universities in 14 countries

LANGUAGE OF INSTRUCTION: French

ADMISSION REQUIREMENTS FOR FOREIGN STUDENTS:
Secondary school certificate *(baccalauréat)*, or recognized foreign equivalent, or special entrance examination/linguistic test

TUITION FOR FOREIGN STUDENTS:
Fr. 530–600 per year in 1990

TOTAL INSTRUCTIONAL FACULTY:
360

LIBRARY COLLECTIONS:
Interuniversity library—250,000 volumes
Unit libraries—194,500 volumes

UNIVERSITY PUBLICATIONS:
10, including *Revue des études anciennes, Cahiers d'outre-mer, Bulletin hispanique*

PRESIDENT: Prof. Régis Ritz

UNIVERSITÉ DE CAEN
(University of Caen)
espl de la Paix, 14032 Caen Cedex, France

CHARACTERISTICS OF INSTITUTION:
State-run, nonprofit university

DATE FOUNDED: 1432

TOTAL ENROLLMENT: 21,000 fulltime students (including 2,100 foreign students)

DEGREES AWARDED:
State qualifications
Law and Economics:

Diplôme d'études universitaires générales (DEUG)
   two years required
Licence
   one year after DEUG required
Maîtrise
   one year after Licence required
Diplôme d'études supérieures spécialisées (DESS)
   a minimum of two semesters following Maîtrise required
Diplôme d'études approfondies (DEA)
   one year after Maîtrise required
Doctorat
   two–four years after DEA required
Certificat de Capacité en Droit (law)
   two years required
Medicine:
Doctorat en Médecine
   six years plus one year hospital practice and thesis required
Certificats de spécialité
   a minimum of two years following doctorate required
Pharmacy:
Diplôme de Pharmacien
   four years and one year practical work required
Doctorat en Pharmacie
   two certificats (études supérieures ou spéciales ou sciences) and thesis after Diplôme required
Science:
Diplôme d'études universitaires générales (DEUG)
   two years required
Licence ès Sciences
   one year after DEUG required
Maîtrise
   one year after Licence, or equivalent, required
Diplôme d'études approfondies (DEA)
   one year after Maîtrise required
Doctorat en Sciences
   two–four years after DEA required
Letters and Human Sciences:
Diplôme d'études universitaires générales (DEUG)
   two years required
Licence ès Lettres
   one year after DEUG required
Maîtrise
   one year after Licence, or equivalent, required
Diplôme d'études approfondies (DEA)
   one year after Maîtrise required
Doctorat
   two–four years after DEA required
Diplôme universitaire de technologie (DUT)
   two years required

ACADEMIC PROGRAMS:
Unit of Business Studies
Unit of Earth Sciences and Regional Planning
Unit of Economics and Management Science
Unit of General Administration Studies
Unit of History
Unit of Law and Political Science
Unit of Life Sciences and Behavioral Sciences
Unit of Medicine
Unit of Modern Languages
Unit of Pharmacy
Unit of Science of Man
Unit of Sciences
Center for French (for foreign students)
Material Sciences and Radiation Institute
Regional Institute for Physical Education and Sport
Institute of Biochemistry and Applied Biology
University Institute of Technology

SPECIAL PROGRAMS:
Cooperative arrangements with 21 other universities, including Georgetown University in Washington, DC, and Vanderbilt University in Tennessee

LANGUAGE OF INSTRUCTION: French

ADMISSION REQUIREMENTS FOR FOREIGN STUDENTS:
Secondary school certificate (baccalauréat), or recognized foreign equivalent, or special entrance examination

TUITION FOR FOREIGN STUDENTS:
Fr 500–600 per year in 1990

TOTAL INSTRUCTIONAL FACULTY:
858

LIBRARY COLLECTIONS:
Total collection—600,000 volumes

UNIVERSITY PUBLICATIONS:
Bulletin, Journal

PRESIDENT: Max Robba

UNIVERSITÉ DE GRENOBLE I
(UNIVERSITÉ JOSEPH FOURIER)
(University of Grenoble I)
BP 53 X, 38041 Grenoble Cedex, France

CHARACTERISTICS OF INSTITUTION:
State-run, nonprofit university.

DATE FOUNDED: 1970

TOTAL ENROLLMENT: 11,650 fulltime students (including 1,600 foreign students)

DEGREES AWARDED:
State qualifications
Medicine:
   Doctorat en Médecine
      six years plus one year hospital practice and thesis required

Certificats de spécialité
    a minimum of at least two years following doctorate required
Pharmacy:
    Diplôme de Pharmacien
        four years plus one year practical work required
    Doctorat en Pharmacie
        two *certificats* (études supérieures ou spéciales ou sciences) and thesis after Diplôme required
Science:
    Diplôme d'études universitaires générales (DEUG)
        two years required
    Licence ès Sciences
        two years after DEUG required
    Magistère in Physics
        three years after DEUG required
    Maîtrise
        one year after Licence, or equivalent, required
    Diplôme d'études approfondies (DEA)
        one year after Maîtrise required
    Diplôme d'études supérieures spécialisées (DESS)
        one year after Maîtrise required
    Doctorate en Sciences
        two–four years after DEA required
    Diplôme universitaire de technologie (DUT)
        two years required

ACADEMIC PROGRAMS:
Unit of Applied Mathematics and Computer Sciences
Unit of Biology
Unit of Chemistry
Unit of Geography
Unit of Geology
Unit of Mathematics
Unit of Mechanical Engineering
Unit of Medicine
Unit of Pharmacy
Unit of Physical Education and Sport
Unit of Physics
Unit of Science and Technology

LANGUAGE OF INSTRUCTION: French

ADMISSION REQUIREMENTS FOR FOREIGN STUDENTS:
Secondary school certificate *(baccalauréat)*, or recognized foreign equivalent, or special entrance examination

TUITION FOR FOREIGN STUDENTS:
Fr. 450 per year for European Community students
Fr 1,126 per year for non-European Community students

TOTAL INSTRUCTIONAL FACULTY:
930

LIBRARY COLLECTIONS:
Total collection—80,000 volumes

UNIVERSITY PUBLICATIONS:
Bulletin d'Information, various research publications

PRESIDENT: Alain Nemoz

UNIVERSITÉ DE GRENOBLE II (UNIVERSITÉ DES SCIENCES SOCIALES) (University of Grenoble II) BP 47 X, 38040 Grenoble Cedex, France

CHARACTERISTICS OF INSTITUTION:
State-run, nonprofit university

DATE FOUNDED: 1970

TOTAL ENROLLMENT: 14,000 fulltime students (including 1,300 foreign students)

DEGREES AWARDED:
State qualifications
Law and Economics:
    Diplôme d'études universitaires générales (DEUG)
        two years required
    Licence
        one year after DEUG required
    Magistère
        three years after DEUG required
    Maîtrise
        one year after Licence required
    Diplôme d'études supérieures spécialisées (DESS)
        a minimum of one year following Maîtrise required
    Diplôme d'études approfondies (DEA)
        one year after Maîtrise required
    Doctorat
        two–four years after DEA required
    Certificat de Capacité en Droit (law)
        two years required
Science:
    Diplôme d'études universitaires générales (DEUG)
        two years required
    Licence ès Sciences
        one year after DEUG required
    Maîtrise
        one year after Licence, or equivalent, required
    Maîtrise of Sciences et Techniques
        two years after DEUG required
    Diplôme d'études approfondies (DEA)
        one year after Maîtrise required
    Doctorat en Sciences
        two–four years after DEA required
    Diplôme universitaire de technologie (DUT)
        two years required

ACADEMIC PROGRAMS:
Unit of Development, Society and Economic Management
Unit of Economic Sciences

Unit of Human and Social Sciences
Unit of Humanities
Unit of Law
Center for Research with Data Processing (in the field
  of social sciences)
Higher Institute of Business
Institute of Energy Policy and Economics
Institute for Political Studies
University Institute of Technology

SPECIAL PROGRAMS:
Cooperative arrangements with universities in six
countries

LANGUAGE OF INSTRUCTION: French

ADMISSION REQUIREMENTS FOR FOREIGN STUDENTS:
Secondary school certificate (baccalauréat), or recognized foreign equivalent, or special entrance examination

TUITION FOR FOREIGN STUDENTS:
Fr 520–600 per year in 1990

TOTAL INSTRUCTIONAL FACULTY:
500

LIBRARY COLLECTIONS:
Central library—7,000 volumes
Interuniversity Libraries of Grenoble—120,000 vol-
umes

UNIVERSITY PUBLICATIONS:
Guide de l'Etudiant, Intercours, various scientific publications

RECTOR: Michel Treuil

UNIVERSITÉ DE GRENOBLE III
(UNIVERSITÉ STENDHAL)
(University of Grenoble III)
BP 25X, 38040 Grenoble Cedex, France

CHARACTERISTICS OF INSTITUTION:
State-run, nonprofit university

DATE FOUNDED: 1810

TOTAL ENROLLMENT: 5,100 fulltime students

DEGREES AWARDED:
State qualifications
Letters and Human Sciences:
  Diplôme d'études universitaires générales (DEUG)
    two years required
  Licence ès Lettres
    one year after DEUG required
  Maîtrise
    one year after Licence, or equivalent, required
  Diplôme d'études supérieures spécialisées (DESS)
    one year after Maîtrise required

Diplôme d'études approfondies (DEA)
  one year after Maîtrise required
Doctorat
  two–four years after DEA required

ADADEMIC PROGRAMS:
Unit of Classical Studies
Unit of Languages
Unit of Letters
Center for French Studies (for foreign students)

SPECIAL PROGRAMS:
Cooperative arrangements with eight other universities, including Georgetown University in Washington, DC, Purdue University in Indiana and the University of Alberta in Canada

LANGUAGE OF INSTRUCTION: French

ADMISSION REQUIREMENTS FOR FOREIGN STUDENTS:
Secondary school certificate (baccalauréat), or recognized foreign equivalent, or special entrance examination

TUITION FOR FOREIGN STUDENTS:
Fr. 520–600 per year in 1990

TOTAL INSTRUCTIONAL FACULTY:
200

LIBRARY COLLECTIONS:
Interuniversity library

UNIVERSITY PUBLICATIONS:
Livret de l'étudiant, Bulletin d'Information du Centre de
documentation et de Recherches Bibliographiques, Recherches et Travaux, Bulletin de l'Institut de Phonetique,
Bulletin d'Informations administratives

PRESIDENT: B. Miège

UNIVERSITÉ DE LILLE I
(UNIVERSITÉ DES SCIENCES ET TECHNIQUES
DE LILLE FLANDERS ARTOIS)
(University of Science and Technology [Lille])
59655 Villeneuve d'Ascq Cedex, France

CHARACTERISTICS OF INSTITUTION:
State-run, nonprofit university

DATE FOUNDED: 1855

TOTAL ENROLLMENT: 17,000 fulltime students (including 2,300 foreign students)

DEGREES AWARDED:
State qualifications
Science:
  Diplôme d'études universitaires générales (DEUG)
    two years required
  Diplôme d'études universitaires de scientifiques et
  techniques (DEUST)

two years required
Diplôme universitaires de sciences et techniques (DUST)
    two years required
Licence ès Sciences
    one year after DEUG required
Maîtrise
    one–two years after Licence or equivalent, required
Maîtrise de sciences et techniques
    two years after DEUG required
Magistère
    three years after DEUG required
Diplôme d'études approfondies (DEA)
    one year after Maîtrise required
Diplôme d'études supérieures spécialisées
    one year after Maîtrise required
Doctorat en Sciences
    two–four years after DEA required
Diplôme d'Ingénieur
    five years required
Diplôme universitaire de technologie (DUT)
    two years required
Certificats and Diplômes in various fields

ACADEMIC PROGRAMS:
Unit of Biology
Unit of Chemistry
Unit of Computer Science, Electronics, Electrical Engineering and Automation
Unit of Earth Sciences
Unit of Economics and Social Sciences
Unit of Exact and Natural Sciences (Calais)
Unit of Geology and Spatial Development
Unit of Physics
Unit of Pure and Applied Mathematics
Higher National School of Chemistry in Lille
Agricultural Institute
Institute of Business Studies
University Center for the Economics of Permanent Education
University Institute of Technology
University Institute of Technology (Bethune)
University Institute of Technology of the Littoral
University School of Engineers in Lille

LANGUAGE OF INSTRUCTION: French

ADMISSION REQUIREMENTS FOR FOREIGN STUDENTS:
Secondary school certificate *(baccalauréat)*, or recognized foreign equivalent, or special entrance examination

TUITION FOR FOREIGN STUDENTS:
Fr 450 per year for European Community students
Fr 1,725 for non-European Community students

TOTAL INSTRUCTIONAL FACULTY:
858

LIBRARY COLLECTIONS:
Interuniversity library (section sciences)—120,000 volumes

UNIVERSITY PUBLICATIONS:
Hommes et Terres du Nord; Espace, populations, sociétés; Les Cahiers lillois d'Économie et de Sociologie; Le Bulletin de l'Institute de Recherche dans l'enseignement des Mathématiques; Les Cahiers du Laboratoire d'Économie publique et regionale; Les Cahiers du Laboratoire de Sociologie du Travail, de l'Education et l'Emploi; Les Cahiers du Centre d'Étude et de Recherche en Epistémologie de Lille; Les Cahiers du Centre de recherches européenes et internationales; Les Cahiers de l'Institut d'administration des entreprises; Les Cahiers de l'Institute de Recherches sur les mathématiques avancées; Les Cahiers de Géographie physique

PRESIDENT: Alain Dubrulle

UNIVERSITÉ DE LILLE II
(UNIVERSITÉ DU DROIT ET DE LA SANTÉ)
(University of Law and Health Sciences [Lille II])
42 rue Paul Duez, 59800 Lille, France

CHARACTERISTICS OF INSTITUTION:
State-run, nonprofit university

DATE FOUNDED: 1969

TOTAL ENROLLMENT: 17,500 fulltime students (including 1,700 foreign students)

DEGREES AWARDED:
State qualifications
Law and Economics:
    Diplôme d'études universitaires générales (DEUG)
        two years required
    Licence
        one year after DEUG required
    Maîtrise
        one year after Licence required
    Diplôme d'études supérieures spécialisées (DESS)
        one year after Maîtrise required
    Diplôme d'études approfondies (DEA)
        one year after Maîtrise required
    Doctorat
        two–four years after DEA required
    Certificat de Capacité en Droit (law)
        two years required
Medicine:
    Doctorat en Médecine
        six years plus one year hospital practice and thesis required
    Certificats de spécialité
        a minimum of two years following doctorate required
    Chirurgien-Dentiste

five years required
Pharmacy:
Diplôme de Pharmacien
four years plus one year practical work required
Doctorat en Pharmacie
two *certificats* (études supérieures ou spéciales ou sciences) and thesis after Diplôme required
Diplôme universitaire de technologie (DUT)
two years required

ACADEMIC PROGRAMS:
Unit of Dentistry
Unit of Law
Unit of Medicine
Unit of Pharmacy
Unit of Physical Education and Sport
Institute of Forensic and Social Medicine
Institute of Pharmaceutical Chemistry
Institute of Speech Therapy
Labor Studies Institute
University Institute of Technology

SPECIAL PROGRAMS:
Cooperative arrangements with eight other universities, including the University of Salt Lake City

LANGUAGE OF INSTRUCTION: French

ADMISSION REQUIREMENTS FOR FOREIGN STUDENTS:
Secondary school certificate *(baccalauréat)*, or recognized foreign equivalent, or special entrance examination

TUITION FOR FOREIGN STUDENTS:
Fr. 540–640 per year, depending on field of study

TOTAL INSTRUCTIONAL FACULTY:
710

LIBRARY COLLECTIONS:
Interuniversity Library of Lille—725,000 volumes

PRESIDENT: José Savoye

UNIVERSITÉ DE LILLE III
(UNIVERSITÉ DES SCIENCES HUMAINES, LETTRES ET ARTS)
(University of Human Sciences, Literature and Arts [Lille III])
BP 149, 59653 Villenueve d'Ascq Cedex, France

CHARACTERISTICS OF INSTITUTION:
State-run, nonprofit university

DATE FOUNDED: 1560

TOTAL ENROLLMENT: 18,375 fulltime students

DEGREES AWARDED:
State qualifications
Letters and Human Sciences:

Diplôme d'études universitaires générales (DEUG)
two years required
Licence ès Lettres
one year after DEUG required
Maîtrise
one year after Licence, or equivalent, required
Diplôme d'études approfondies (DEA)
one year after Maîtrise
Diplôme d'études supérieures spécialisées (DESS)
one year after Maîtrise required
Doctorat
two–four years after DEA required
Diplôme universitaire de technologie (DUT)
two years required

ACADEMIC PROGRAMS:
Unit of Applied Foreign Languages
Unit of Classical Languages
Unit of Education
Unit of English
Unit of French Linguistics and Literature
Unit of German Studies
Unit of History, History of Art and Archaeology
Unit of Mathematics, Economics and Social Sciences
Unit of Philosophy
Unit of Psychology and Social Sciences
Unit of Romance, Semitic, Slav and Hungarian Studies
University Institute of Technology

SPECIAL PROGRAMS:
Cooperative arrangements with 10 other universities

LANGUAGE OF INSTRUCTION: French

ADMISSION REQUIREMENTS FOR FOREIGN STUDENTS:
Secondary school certificate *(baccalauréat)*, or recognized foreign equivalent, or special entrance examination

TUITION FOR FOREIGN STUDENTS:
Fr. 520–600 per year in 1990

TOTAL INSTRUCTIONAL FACULTY:
434

LIBRARY COLLECTIONS:
Interuniversity library

MUSEUMS AND GALLERIES:
Museum of Egyptology

UNIVERSITY PUBLICATIONS:
Revue du Nord, Revue des Sciences Humaines, Études Irlandaises

PRESIDENT: Alain Lottin

UNIVERSITÉ DE LYON I
(UNIVERSITÉ CLAUDE-BERNARD)

(University Claude Bernard [Lyons I])
43 blvd du 11 Novembre 1918, 69622 Villeurbanne
Cedex, France

CHARACTERISTICS OF INSTITUTION:
State-run, nonprofit university

DATE FOUNDED: 1970

TOTAL ENROLLMENT: 23,000 fulltime students (including 2,600 foreign students)

DEGREES AWARDED:
State qualifications
Medicine:
  Doctorat en Médecine
    six years plus one year hospital practice and thesis required
  Certificats de spécialité
    a minimum of two years following doctorate required
  Diplôme d'études et de recherche en Biologie humaine
    two years required
  Doctorat en Biologie humain
    five years required
  Chirurgien-Dentiste
    five years required
Pharmacy:
  Diplôme de Pharmacien
    four years plus one year practical work required
  Doctorat en Pharmacie
    two years required
Science:
  Diplôme d'études universitaires générales (DEUG)
    two years required
  Licence ès Sciences
    one year after DEUG required
  Maîtrise
    one year after Licence, or equivalent, required
  Diplôme d'études approfondies (DEA)
    one year after Maîtrise required
  Doctorat en Sciences
    two–four years after DEA required
  Diplôme universitaire de technologie (DUT)
    two years required
  Diplôme d'études universitaires générales (DEUG) in physical education
    two years required
  Licence in physical education
    one year required

ACADEMIC PROGRAMS:
Medicine:
  Unit of Dentistry
  Unit of Medicine (Grange-Blanche)
  Unit of Medicine (Alexis-Carrel)
  Unit of Medicine (Lyon-Nord)
  Unit of Medicine (Suc)
  Unit of Pharmacy
  Unit of Rehabilitation
Sciences:
  Unit of Chemistry and Molecular and Cellular Biology
  Unit of Earth, Ocean, Atmospheric Space and Environmental Sciences
  Unit of Engineering and Technological Development
  Unit of Material Sciences
  Unit of Physical Education and Sport
  Unit of Systems Analysis (biology and socioeconomics)
  University Institute of Technology

SPECIAL PROGRAMS:
Cooperative arrangements with 26 other universities, including the University of Calgary, New York University and The Rensselaer Polytechnic Institute in New York

LANGUAGE OF INSTRUCTION: French

ADMISSION REQUIREMENTS FOR FOREIGN STUDENTS:
Secondary school certificate (baccalauréat), or recognized foreign equivalent, or special entrance examination

TUITION FOR FOREIGN STUDENTS:
Fr. 520–600 per year in 1990

TOTAL INSTRUCTIONAL FACULTY:
1,500

LIBRARY COLLECTIONS:
Interuniversity library Bibliothèque Santé—350,000 volumes; sciences library—331,500 volumes

MUSEUMS AND GALLERIES:
Museum of the History of Medicine

UNIVERSITY PUBLICATIONS:
Lettre UCB/INFO, Livret de l'Étudiant, Annuaire sur la Recherche

PRESIDENT: Paul Zech

UNIVERSITÉ DE LYON II
(UNIVERSITÉ LUMIÈRE)
(University of Lyons II)
86 rue Pasteur, 69365 Lyon Cedex, France

CHARACTERISTICS OF INSTITUTION:
State-run, nonprofit university

DATE FOUNDED: 1970

TOTAL ENROLLMENT: 21,000 fulltime students (including 2,500 foreign students)

DEGREES AWARDED:
State qualifications
Law and Economics:
    Diplôme d'études universitaires générales (DEUG)
        two years required
    Licence
        one year after DEUG required
    Maîtrise
        one year after Licence required
    Diplôme d'études supérieures spécialisées (DESS)
        a minimum of two semesters following Maîtrise
        required
    Diplôme d'études approfondies (DEA)
        one year after Maîtrise required
    Doctorat
        two–four years after DEA required
    Certificat de Capacité en Droit (law)
        two years
Letters and Human Sciences:
    Diplôme d'études universitaires générales (DEUG)
        two years required
    Licence ès Lettres
        one year after DEUG required
    Maîtrise
        one year after Licence, or equivalent, required
    Diplôme d'études supérieures spécialisées (DESS)
        one year after Maîtrise required
    Diplome d'études approfondies (DEA)
        one year after Maîtrise required
    Doctorat
        two–four years after DEA required

ACADEMIC PROGRAMS:
Faculty of Economics and Business Sciences
Faculty of Geography, History, History of Art and
    Tourism
Faculty of Law
Faculty of Literature, Science of Language and Arts
Faculty of Modern Languages
Faculty of Psychology and Social Sciences
Center of French (for foreign students)
Institute of Labor Studies
Institute of Political Studies
Institute of Teacher Training

SPECIAL PROGRAMS:
Cooperative arrangements with 30 other universities, including the University of Montreal, Wright State University, Brown University, the University of Rhode Island, Dartmouth College and the University of New Hampshire

LANGUAGE OF INSTRUCTION: French

ADMISSION REQUIREMENTS FOR FOREIGN STUDENTS:
Secondary school certificate (baccalauréat), or recognized foreign equivalent, or special entrance examination

TUITION FOR FOREIGN STUDENTS:
Fr 600 per year in 1990

TOTAL INSTRUCTIONAL FACULTY:
380 full-time faculty
220 parttime faculty

LIBRARY COLLECTIONS:
Interuniversity library

MUSEUMS AND GALLERIES:
Museum of Sculpture

UNIVERSITY PUBLICATIONS:
Bulletin Express d'Information, Bulletin des Rélations Internationales, Bulletin de la Recherche

PRESIDENT: Michel Cusin

UNIVERSITÉ DE LYON III
(UNIVERSITÉ JEAN MOULIN)
(University Jean Moulin [Lyons III])
BP 0638, 69299 Lyon Cedex 02, France

CHARACTERISTICS OF INSTITUTION:
State-run, nonprofit university

DATE FOUNDED: 1973

TOTAL ENROLLMENT: 13,300 fulltime students (including 2,000 foreign students)

DEGREES AWARDED:
State qualifications
Law:
    Diplôme d'études universitaires générales (DEUG)
        two years required
    Licence en Droit
        one year after DEUG required
    Maitrise
        one year after Licence required
    Diplôme d'études supérieures spécialisées (DESS)
        a minimum of two semesters following Maîtrise
        required
    Diplôme d'études approfondies (DEA)
        a minimum of two semesters following Maîtrise
        required
    Doctorat
        two–four years after DEA required
    Certificat de Capacité en Droit (law)
        two years required
Letters and Human Sciences:
    Diplôme d'études universitaires générales (DEUG)
        two years required
    Licence ès Lettres
        one year after DEUG required
    Maîtrise
        one year after Licence, or equivalent, required
    Diplôme d'études approfondies (DEA)
        one year after Maîtrise required

Doctorat
   two–four years after DEA required
Diplôme d'études supérieures spécialisées (DESS)
de gestion des entreprises
   one year after Maîtrise required
Certificat d'études supérieures de Droit social
(CESDS)

ACADEMIC PROGRAMS:
Faculty of Languages
Faculty of Law
Faculty of Letters and Civilizations
Faculty of Philosophy
Department of Communications Technology
Computer Science
Institute of Business Administration and Management
Institute of History of Christianity
Institute of Indo-European Studies
Institute of Population Studies
Institute of Rhone Studies
Institute of Work and Social Security Studies

SPECIAL PROGRAMS:
Cooperative arrangements with 13 other universities, including the University of Montreal, Georgetown University in Washington, DC, and the University of Minnesota

LANGUAGE OF INSTRUCTION: French

ADMISSION REQUIREMENTS FOR FOREIGN STUDENTS:
Secondary school certificate (baccalauréat), or recognized foreign equivalent, or special entrance examination

TUITION FOR FOREIGN STUDENTS:
Fr. 520–1,000, depending of field of study in 1990

TOTAL INSTRUCTIONAL FACULTY:
270

LIBRARY COLLECTIONS:
Interuniversity library—610,000 volumes
Languages—20,000 volumes
Law—15,000 volumes
Letters—10,000 volumes
Philosophy—6,000 volumes
Institute of Business Administration—5,950 volumes
Institute of Labor Studies—4,300 volumes

UNIVERSITY PUBLICATIONS:
Annales de la Faculté de Droit, Annuaire ARES Défense et securité, Bulletin de l'Institut de Droit de l'Environnement, Annales de l'Institut d'Études du Travail et de la Securité Sociale, Revue d'Études indo-européennes

PRESIDENT: Pierre Vialle

UNIVERSITÉ DE MONTPELLIER I
(University Montpellier I)
BP 1017, 34006 Montpellier Cedex, France

CHARACTERISTICS OF INSTITUTION:
State-run, nonprofit university

DATE FOUNDED: 1970

TOTAL ENROLLMENT: 17,900 fulltime students

DEGREES AWARDED:
State qualifications
Law and Economics:
   Diplôme d'études universitaires générales (DEUG)
      two years required
   Licence
      one year after DEUG required
   Maîtrise
      one year after Licence required
   Diplôme d'études approfondies (DEA)
      a minimum of one year following Maîtrise required
   Doctorat
      two–four years after DEA required
   Certificat de Capacité en Droit (law)
      two years required
Medicine:
   Maîtrise de Biologie humain and Doctorat de Biologie humain
      six years required for combination of the two
   Doctorat en Médecine
      six years plus one year hospital practice and thesis required
   Certificats de spécialité
      a minimum of two years following doctorate required
   Chirurgien-Dentiste
      five years required
Pharmacy:
   Diplôme de Pharmacien
      four years plus one year practical work required
   Doctorat en Pharmacie
      two *certificats* (études supérieures ou spéciales ou sciences) and thesis after Diplôme required

ACADEMIC PROGRAMS:
Unit of Alimentary, Enological and Environmental Studies
Unit of Economic and Social Administration
Unit of Economics
Unit of Industrial Pharmacy
Unit of Law and Social Sciences
Unit of Medicine
Unit of Odontology
Unit of Pharmaceutical and Biological Science
Unit of Physical Education and Sport
Higher Institute for Montpellier Enterprise

Research Institute for the Study of Juridical Information
Regional Institute for Economic Study
Institute for Preparation for General Administration

LANGUAGE OF INSTRUCTION: French

ADMISSION REQUIREMENTS FOR FOREIGN STUDENTS:
Secondary school certificate *(baccalauréat)*, or recognized foreign equivalent, or special entrance examination

TUITION FOR FOREIGN STUDENTS:
Fr. 520–600 per year in 1990

TOTAL INSTRUCTIONAL FACULTY:
309

LIBRARY COLLECTIONS:
Specialized libraries

UNIVERSITY PUBLICATIONS:
L'Economie Méridionale, Revue de la Société d'Histoire du Droit, Journal de Médecine, du Ligament

PRESIDENT: Jacques Demaille

UNIVERSITÉ DE MONTPELLIER II
(UNIVERSITÉ DES SCIENCES ET TECHNIQUES DU LANGUEDOC)
(Languedoc University of Science and Technology [Montpellier II])
place Eugene Bataillon, 34060 Montpellier Cedex, France

CHARACTERISTICS OF INSTITUTION:
State-run, nonprofit university

DATE FOUNDED: 1970

TOTAL ENROLLMENT: 7,500 fulltime students

DEGREES AWARDED:
State qualifications
Science:
   Diplôme d'études universitaires générales (DEUG)
      two years required
   Licence ès Sciences
      one year after DEUG required
   Maîtrise
      one year after Licence, or equivalent, required
   Diplôme d'études approfondies (DEA)
      one year after Maîtrise required
   Doctorat en Sciences
      two–four years after DEA required
   Diplôme universitaire de technologie (DUT)
      two years required

ACADEMIC PROGRAMS:
Unit of Chemistry

Unit of Earth Sciences (including Botanical Institute)
Unit of Life Sciences
Unit of Mathematics
Unit of Physics
Unit of General and Scientific Training (first cycle)
Unit of Basic Science and Introduction to Research (second cycle)
Unit of Pedagogic and Scientific Teacher Training (second cycle)
Higher National School of Chemical Engineers
Institute of Engineering Sciences
University Institute of Technology of Montpellier-Nimes

LANGUAGE OF INSTRUCTION: French

ADMISSION REQUIREMENTS FOR FOREIGN STUDENTS:
Secondary school certificate *(baccalauréat)*, or recognized foreign equivalent, or special entrance examination

TUITION FOR FOREIGN STUDENTS:
Fr 520–600 per year in 1990

TOTAL INSTRUCTIONAL FACULTY:
750

LIBRARY COLLECTIONS:
Interuniversity library (section sciences)

MUSEUMS AND GALLERIES:
Museum of Natural History

UNIVERSITY PUBLICATIONS:
Naturalia Monspelianesia, Paléobilogie Contientale—Paléovertebrata, Cahiers de Mathématics

PRESIDENT: Jean Lagarrigue

UNIVERSITÉ DE MONTPELLIER III
(UNIVERSITÉ PAUL VALÉRY)
(University Paul Valéry [Montpellier III])
place de la Voie Domitienne, BP 5043, 34032 Montpellier Cedex, France

CHARACTERISTICS OF INSTITUTION:
State-run, nonprofit university

DATE FOUNDED:
1970

TOTAL ENROLLMENT: 13,000 fulltime students (including 2,000 foreign students)

DEGREES AWARDED:
State qualifications
Letters and Human Sciences:
   Diplôme d'études universitaires générales (DEUG)
      two years required
   Licence ès Lettres
      one year after DEUG required

Maîtrise
    one year after Licence, or equivalent, required
Diplôme d'études supérieures spécialisées (DESS)
    one year after Maîtrise required
Diplôme d'études approfondies (DEA)
    one year after Maîtrise required
Doctorat
    two–four years after DEA required

ACADEMIC PROGRAMS:
Unit of Economic, Mathematic and Social Sciences
Unit of Human and Environmental Sciences
Unit of Languages, Literature and Foreign Civilizations
Unit of Letters, Arts, Philosophy and Linguistics
Unit of Science of Society
Center of Teacher Training

LANGUAGE OF INSTRUCTION: French

ADMISSION REQUIREMENTS FOR FOREIGN STUDENTS:
Secondary school certificate (baccalauréat), or recognized foreign equivalent, or special entrance examination

TUITION FOR FOREIGN STUDENTS:
Fr 520–600 per year in 1990

TOTAL INSTRUCTIONAL FACULTY:
344

LIBRARY COLLECTIONS:
Interuniversity library

MUSEUMS AND GALLERIES:
Museum of Sculpture

UNIVERSITY PUBLICATIONS:
Études valeryennes, Revue des Langues romanes, Lengas, Imprévue, Revue archéologique "La Narbonnaise," Centre d'histoire contemporaine du Languedoc-Roussillon, Annales du Midi, Cahiers Elisabethains, Études Victoriennes et Edouardiennes, Delta, Sigma, Bulletin de la Société languedocienne de Geographie, Mentalités et Croyances contemporaines, Revue Languedocienne de Sociologie-Ethnologie

PRESIDENT: Michel Gayraud

UNIVERSITÉ DE NANCY I
(University of Nancy I)
24 rue Lionnois, BP 3137, 54013 Nancy Cedex,
France

CHARACTERISTICS OF INSTITUTION:
State-run, nonprofit university

DATE FOUNDED: 1970

TOTAL ENROLLMENT: 14,600 fulltime students

DEGREES AWARDED:
State qualifications
Medicine:
    Doctorat en Médecine
        six years plus one year hospital practice and thesis required
    Certificats de spécialité
        a minimum of two years following doctorate required
    Chirurgien-Dentiste
        five years required
    Magistère in microbiology
        five years required
Pharmacy:
    Diplôme de Pharmacien
        four years plus one year practical work required
    Doctorat en Pharmacie
        two certificats (études supérieures ou spéciales ou sciences) and thesis after Diplôme required
Science:
    Diplôme d'études universitaires générales (DEUG)
        two years required
    Licence ès Sciences
        one year after DEUG required
    Maîtrise
        one year after Licence, or equivalent, required
    Maîtrise en sciences et techniques
        two years after DEUG required
    Diplôme d'études approfondies (DEA)
        one year after Maîtrise
    Diplôme d'études supérieures spécialisées (DESS)
        one year after Maîtrise required
    Doctorat en Sciences
        two–four years after DEA required
    Diplôme universitaire de technologies (DUT)
        two years required

ACADEMIC PROGRAMS:
Unit of Biological Sciences
Unit of Dental Surgery
Unit of Earth Sciences and Materials
Unit of Material Sciences
Unit of Mathematical Sciences
Unit of Medical Sciences A
Unit of Medical Sciences B
Unit of Nutrition and Alimentation
Unit of Pharmaceutical and Biological Sciences
Unit of Physics, Chemistry and Biology
Unit of Sport and Physical Education
Higher School of the Science and Technology of Engineering
Higher School of the Science and Technology of the Wood Industry
Institute of Computer Sciences
University Institute of Technology
Interuniversity Center for Preventive Medicine

Center for the Effects of Medicines on Biological Systems

SPECIAL PROGRAMS:
Cooperative arrangements with 10 other universities.

LANGUAGE OF INSTRUCTION: French

ADMISSION REQUIREMENTS FOR FOREIGN STUDENTS:
Secondary school certificate *(baccalauréat)*, or recognized foreign equivalent, or special entrance examination

TUITION FOR FOREIGN STUDENTS:
Fr. 520–600 per year in 1990

TOTAL INSTRUCTIONAL FACULTY:
961

LIBRARY COLLECTIONS:
Interuniversity library—164,000 volumes

UNIVERSITY PUBLICATIONS:
Revue française d'aquariologie; Revue de réadaptation fonctionnelle, professionnelle et sociale; Annales Médicales de Nancy; Publications de l'Institute Elie Cartan; Rapports du Centre d'Informatique de Nancy

PRESIDENT: Michel Boulangé

UNIVERSITÉ DE NANCY II
(University of Nancy II)
25 rue Baron Louis, BP 454, 54001 Nancy Cedex, France

CHARACTERISTICS OF INSTITUTION:
State-run, nonprofit university

DATE FOUNDED: 1970

TOTAL ENROLLMENT: 12,500 fulltime students (including 1,300 foreign students)

DEGREES AWARDED:
State qualifications
Law and Economics:
  Diplôme d'études universitaires générales (DEUG)
    two years required
  Licence
    one year after DEUG required
  Maîtrise
    one year after Licence required
  Diplôme d'études supérieures spécialisées (DESS)
    a minimum of one year following Maîtrise required
  Diplôme d'études approfondies (DEA)
    one year after Maîtrise required
  Doctorat
    two–four years after DEA required
  Certificat de Capacite en Droit (law)

two years required
Letters and Human Sciences:
  Diplôme d'études universitaires générales (DEUG)
    two years required
  Licence ès Lettres
    one year after DEUG required
  Maîtrise
    one year after Licence, or equivalent, required
  Diplôme d'études approfondies (DEA)
    one year after Maîtrise required
  Doctorat
    two–four years after DEA required
  Diplôme universitaire de technologie (DUT)
    two years required

ACADEMIC PROGRAMS:
Unit of Foreign Languages and Literature
Unit of Historical and Geographical Sciences
Unit of Languages
Unit of Literature
Unit of Mathematics and Informatics
Unit of Philosophy, Psychology, Sociology and Educational Sciences
Faculty of Law, Economic Sciences and Management
European University Center
Institute of Administrative and Political Studies
Institute of Commerce
Institute for Preparation for General Administration
Regional Institute of Labor
University Institute of Technology

SPECIAL PROGRAMS:
Cooperative arrangements with 13 other universities, including the University of Indiana and Austin College in Texas

LANGUAGE OF INSTRUCTION: French

ADMISSION REQUIREMENTS FOR FOREIGN STUDENTS:
Secondary school certificate *(baccalauréat)*, or recognized foreign equivalent, or special entrance examination

TUITION FOR FOREIGN STUDENTS:
Fr. 520–600 per year in 1990

TOTAL INSTRUCTIONAL FACULTY:
370

LIBRARY COLLECTIONS:
Interuniversity library—700,000 volumes

UNIVERSITY PUBLICATIONS:
Les Annales de l'Est, Verbum, Revue Géographique de l'Est, Autrement Dire, Études d'archéologie classique, La Revue française d'études americaines, Cahier d' Économistes

PRESIDENT: Gérard Druesne

UNIVERSITÉ DE NICE
(University of Nice)
28 parc Valrose, 06034 Nice Cedex, France

CHARACTERISTICS OF INSTITUTION:
State-ran, nonprofit university

DATE FOUNDED: 1971

TOTAL ENROLLMENT: 19,200 fulltime students

DEGREES AWARDED:
State qualifications
Law, Economics and Management:
Diplôme d'études universitaires générales (DEUG)
two years required
Licence
one year after DEUG required
Maîtrise
one year after Licence required
Diplôme d'études supérieures spécialisées (DESS)
one year after Maîtrise required
Diplôme d'études approfondies (DEA)
one year after Maîtrise required
Doctorat
two–four years after DEA required
Certificat de Capacité en Droit (law)
two years required
Medicine:
Doctorat en Médecine
six years plus one year hospital practice and thesis
required
Certificats de spécialité
a minimum of two years following doctorate required
Chirurgien-Dentiste
five years required
Science:
Diplôme d'études universitaires générales (DEUG)
two years required
Licence ès Sciences
one year after DEUG required
Magistère in computer science
three years after DEUG or DUT required
Maîtrise
one year after Licence, or equivalent, required
Diplôme d'études approfondies (DEA)
one year after Maîtrise required
Diplôme d'études supérieures spécialisées (DESS)
one year after Maîtrise required
Doctorat en Sciences
two–four years after DEA required
Letters and Human Sciences:
Diplôme d'études universitaires générales (DEUG)
two years required
Licence ès Lettres
one year after DEUG required
Maîtrise
one year after Licence, or equivalent, required
Diplôme d'études approfondies (DEA)
one year after Maîtrise required
Doctorat
two–four years after DEA required
Diplôme universitaire de technologie (DUT)
two years required

ACADEMIC PROGRAMS:
Unit of Civilizations
Unit of Dentistry
Unit of Law and Economics
Unit of Law of Peace of Development
Unit of Literature and Human Sciences
Unit of Medicine
Unit of Physical Education and Sport
Faculty of Sciences
Higher School of Computer Sciences
Institute of Business Administration
Interethnic and Intercultural Research Studies Institute
Mathematics Teaching Research Institute
University Institute of Technology
Center for Geodynamic and Astronomical Studies (research)
Center for Preventive Medicine
Mediterranean Studies Center

SPECIAL PROGRAMS:
Cooperative arrangements with 48 other universities, including: Georgetown University, University of Vermont, State University of New York (Albany), University of San Diego, University of Pennsylvania, University of California (Santa Barbara), University of Colorado (Boulder), Louisiana State University, Université du Québec, University of Texas (Austin), California Institute of Technology and Randolph-Macon College

LANGUAGE OF INSTRUCTION: French

ADMISSION REQUIREMENTS FOR FOREIGN STUDENTS:
Secondary school certificate (baccalauréat), or recognized foreign equivalent, or special entrance examination

TUITION FOR FOREIGN STUDENTS:
Fr. 520–600 per year in 1990

TOTAL INSTRUCTIONAL FACULTY:
960

LIBRARY COLLECTIONS:
Central library—172,000 volumes

UNIVERSITY PUBLICATIONS:
Annuaire, Guide des formations de Recherche, Revue d'Odontostomatologie tropicale

RECTOR: R. Blanchet

**UNIVERSITÉ DE PARIS I
(PANTHÉON-SORBONNE)
(University of Paris I [Pantheon-Sorbonne])
12 place du Panthéon, 75231 Paris Cedex 05,
France**

CHARACTERISTICS OF INSTITUTION:
State-run, non-profit university

DATE FOUNDED: 1971

TOTAL ENROLLMENT: 35,250 fulltime students (including 6,000 foreign students)

DEGREES AWARDED:
State qualifications
Law and Economics:
   Diplôme d'études universitaires générales (DEUG)
      two years required
   Licence
      one year after DEUG required
   Maîtrise
      one year after Licence required
   Diplôme d'études supérieures spécialisées (DESS)
      one year after Maîtrise
   Diplôme d'études approfondies (DEA)
      one year after Maîtrise
   Doctorat in various fields
      two–four years after DEA required
   Certificat de Capacité en Droit (law)
      two years required
Letters and Human Sciences:
   Diplôme d'études universitaires générales (DEUG)
      two years required
   Licence ès Lettres
      one year after DEUG required
   Maîtrise
      one year after Licence, or equivalent, required
   Diplôme d'études approfondies (DEA)
      one year after Maîtrise required
   Diplôme d'études supérieures spécialisées (DESS)
      one year after Maîtrise required
   Doctorat
      two–four years after DEA required
   Diplôme in various fields

ACADEMIC PROGRAMS:
Unit of Business Law
Unit of Development, International, European and Comparative Studies
Unit of Economic Analysis and Politics, Econometrics, Labor and Human Resources
Unit of Economic and Social Administration, Labor and Social Studies
Unit of General Economics and Business Administration
Unit of Geography
Unit of History

Unit of History of Art and Archaeology
Unit of Mathematics, Statistics and Informatics
Unit of Philosophy
Unit of Plastic Arts and Science of Art
Unit of Political Science
Unit of Public Administration and Public Law
Department of Applied Modern Languages, Economics and Law
Department of Applied Modern Languages, Humanities
Department of Coordination of Juridic and Political Sciences
Department of Social Sciences
Institute of Business Administration
Institute of Demography
Institute of Economic and Social Development Studies
Institute of Mathematics and Applied Economics
Institute of Social Sciences of Labor
Institute of Tourism
Regional Center for Municipal Studies

SPECIAL PROGRAMS:
Cooperative arrangements with 22 other universities, including the University of California at Berkeley, New York University and the University of Maryland.

LANGUAGE OF INSTRUCTION: French

ADMISSION REQUIREMENTS FOR FOREIGN STUDENTS:
Secondary school certificate (baccalauréat), or recognized foreign equivalent, or special entrance examination

TUITION FOR FOREIGN STUDENTS:
Fr. 520–600 per year in 1990

TOTAL INSTRUCTIONAL FACULTY:
687

LIBRARY COLLECTIONS:
Interuniversity library
Specialized libraries

UNIVERSITY PUBLICATIONS:
Bulletin

PRESIDENT: Georges Haddad

**UNIVERSITÉ DE PARIS II
(UNIVERSITÉ DE DROIT, D'ÉCONOMIE ET DES
SCIENCES SOCIALES)
(University of Paris II [University of Law, Economics
and Social Sciences])
12 place du Panthéon, 75231 Paris Cedex 05,
France**

CHARACTERISTICS OF INSTITUTION:
State-run, nonprofit university

DATE FOUNDED:
1970

TOTAL ENROLLMENT: 17,850 fulltime students

DEGREES AWARDED:
State qualifications
Diplôme d'études universitaires générales (DEUG)
  two years required
Licence in various fields
  one year after DEUG required
Magistère
  three years after DEUG required
Maîtrise
  one year after Licence required
Diplôme d'études supérieures spécialisées (DESS)
  one year after Maîtrise
Diplôme d'études approfondies (DEA)
  one year after Maîtrise required
Doctorat
  two–four years after DEA required
Certificat de Capacité en Droit (law)
  two years required

ACADEMIC PROGRAMS:
Unit of Advanced International Studies
Unit of Business Law
Unit of Comparative Law
Unit of Economic Science
Unit of General Private Law and Juridicial Law
Unit of Information Sciences
Unit of Institutional and Economic History and Sociology
Unit of Juridicial Studies
Unit of Legal and Economic Studies in International, European and Comparative Law
Unit of Penal, Criminological and Social Adjustment Studies
Unit of Political Science
Unit of Public Law and Public Administration
Department of Computer Sciences
Department of Labor Studies
Department of Modern Languages and Civilizations
Department of Social Psychology and Juridicial Sociology
French Press Institute
Institute of Business Law
Institute of Criminology
Institute of Judicial Studies
Institute of Roman Law
Center of Philosophy of Law
Center for Studies and Research in International Law

LANGUAGE OF INSTRUCTION: French

ADMISSION REQUIREMENTS FOR FOREIGN STUDENTS:
Secondary school certificate (baccalauréat), or recognized foreign equivalent, or special entrance examination

TUITION FOR FOREIGN STUDENTS:
Fr. 520–600 per year in 1990

TOTAL INSTRUCTIONAL FACULTY:
256

LIBRARY COLLECTIONS:
Interuniversity library

UNIVERSITY PUBLICATIONS:
Travaux et recherches

PRESIDENT: Georges Durry

UNIVERSITÉ DE PARIS III (SORBONNE-NOUVELLE) (University of Paris III [Sorbonne-Nouvelle]) 17 rue de la Sorbonne, 75230 Paris Cedex 05, France

CHARACTERISTICS OF INSTITUTION:
State-run, nonprofit university

DATE FOUNDED: 1970

TOTAL ENROLLMENT: 17,100 fulltime students

DEGREES AWARDED:
State qualifications
Diplôme d'études universitaires générales (DEUG)
  two years required
Licence
  one year after DEUG required
Maîtrise
  one year after Licence required
Diplôme d'études supérieures spécialisées (DESS)
  a minimum of two semesters following Maîtrise required
Diplôme d'études approfondies (DEA)
  one year after Maîtrise required
Doctorat
  two–four years after DEA required
Diplômes and Certificats in various fields

ACADEMIC PROGRAMS:
Unit of Cinematographic Studies
Unit of French as a Foreign Language
Unit of French Language and Literature
Unit of Finnish and Hungarian Studies
Unit of General and Comparative Literature
Unit of Iberian Studies
Unit of Indian, Oriental and North African Languages and Civilizations
Unit of Italian and Romanian Studies
Unit of Languages, Literatures and Civilizations of English-speaking Countries
Unit of Phonetics and Speech
Unit of Theater Studies
Higher School of Interpreters and Translators

Department of Historical, Economic and Political Sciences

Department of Physical Education, Sport and Open-air Activities

Department of Techniques of Expression and Communication

German Institute

Institute of Latin American Studies

National Institute of Oriental Languages and Civilizations

SPECIAL PROGRAMS:
Cooperative arrangements with 51 other universities, including: University of New Mexico, University of California (Berkeley), City University of New York, University of Iowa, Tufts University in Massachusetts, New York University, University of Ottawa, Université du Québec and Sweet Briar College in Virginia

TUITION FOR FOREIGN STUDENTS:
Fr. 520–600 per year in 1990

TOTAL INSTRUCTIONAL FACULTY:
374

LIBRARY COLLECTIONS:
Three interuniversity libraries
Unit libraries—255,000 volumes

UNIVERSITY PUBLICATIONS:
Trema, Cahiers de l'Unit des Études Iberiques, Lalies, Italique, Aggiornamento, Publication du Centre de la Renaissance, Publication du Centre Interuniversitaire de Recherche des Études Roumaines, Cahiers de la Bibliotéque Gaston Baty

PRESIDENT: Robert Ellrodt

UNIVERSITÉ DE PARIS IV (PARIS-SORBONNE)
(University of Paris IV [Paris-Sorbonne])
1 rue Victor Cousin, 75230 Paris Cedex 05, France

CHARACTERISTICS OF INSTITUTION:
State-run, nonprofit university

DATE FOUNDED: 1970

TOTAL ENROLLMENT: 21,625 fulltime students (including 3,000 foreign students)

DEGREES AWARDED:
State qualifications
Diplôme d'études universitaires générales (DEUG) in various fields
  two years required
Licence
  one year after DEUG required
Maîtrise
  one year after Licence required
Maîtrise spécialisées
  two years after Licence required
Diplôme d'études supérieures spécialisées (DESS)
  a minimum of two semesters following Maîtrise required
Diplôme d'études approfondies (DEA)
  one year after Maîtrise required
Doctorat
  two–four years after DEA required
Diplômes in various fields

ACADEMIC PROGRAMS:
Unit of English
Unit of French Language
Unit of French Literature
Unit of Geography
Unit of Germanic Studies
Unit of Greek Studies
Unit of History
Unit of History of Art
Unit of Iberian Studies
Unit of Italian and Romanian Studies
Unit of Latin Language and Literature
Unit of Modern Western Civilization
Unit of Musicology
Unit of Philosophy
Unit of Slavonic Studies
Department of Applied Modern Languages
Department of Classical Civilizations
Department of Dance
Department of Information Science Applied to Humanities
Department of Islamic Studies
Department of Linguistics
Department of Medieval Studies
Department of Science of Religions
Experimental Department of French Civilization
Center for Applied Iberian and Latin American Studies
Center of Applied Literary and Scientific Studies
Center for Neo-Hellenic Studies
Center for Polish Studies
International Center for Francophone Studies
University Center for Catalan Studies
Institute of Applied Humanities
Institute for Languedoc Studies
Institute of Urban Studies

SPECIAL PROGRAMS:
Cooperative arrangements with 18 other universities, including the State University of New York, the University of Pennsylvania and Tulane University in Louisiana

LANGUAGE OF INSTRUCTION: French

ADMISSION REQUIREMENTS FOR FOREIGN STUDENTS:
Secondary school certificate *(baccalauréat)*, or recognized foreign equivalent, or special entrance examination

TUITION FOR FOREIGN STUDENTS:
Fr. 700 per year in 1990

TOTAL INSTRUCTIONAL FACULTY:
527

LIBRARY COLLECTIONS:
Main collection—125,000 volumes
Specialized libraries

UNIVERSITY PUBLICATIONS:
Bulletin, Actes de Colloques

PRESIDENT: M. Meslin

UNIVERSITÉ DE PARIS V
(RÉNÉ DESCARTES)
(University of Paris V [René Descartes])
12 rue de L'Ecole de Médecine, 75270 Paris Cedex 06, France

CHARACTERISTICS OF INSTITUTION:
State-run, nonprofit university

DATE FOUNDED: 1970

TOTAL ENROLLMENT: 30,000 fulltime students (including 5,000 foreign students)

DEGREES AWARDED:
State qualifications
Human Sciences:
    Diplôme d'études universitaires générales (DEUG)
        two years required
    Licence
        one year after DEUG required
    Magistère in social sciences
        three years after DEUG required
    Maîtrise
        one year after Licence required
    Maîtrise spécialisées in various fields
        four years required
    Diplôme d'études approfondies (DEA)
        one year after Maîtrise
    Doctorat
        two–four years after DEA Maîtrise and thesis required
Biomedical and Pharmaceutical Sciences:
    Doctorat en Médecine
        six years plus one year hospital practice and thesis required
    Certificats de spécialité
        a minimum of two years following doctorate required
    Chirurgien-Dentiste

five years required
Diplôme de Pharmacien
    four years plus one year practical work required
Doctorat en Pharmacie
    two *certificats* (études supérieures ou spéciales ou sciences) and thesis after Diplôme required
Maîtrise en Biologie humain
    four years required
Doctorat en Biologie humain
    an additional two–four years following Maîtrise en Biologie humain required
Diplôme universitaire de technologie (DUT)
    two years required

ACADEMIC PROGRAMS:
Unit of Biomedicine
Unit of Dentistry
Unit of Educational Sciences
Unit of Forensic Medicine, Medical Law and Deontology
Unit of General and Applied Linguistics
Unit of Mathematics, Statistics and Data Processing
Unit of Medical and Biological Studies
Unit of Medicine (Cochin-Port Royal)
Unit of Medicine (Necker-Enfants Malades)
Unit of Medicine (Paris-Ouest)
Unit of Pharmaceutical and Biological Sciences
Unit of Physical Education and Sport
Unit of Psychology
Unit of Social Sciences
Faculty of Law
Institute of Psychology
University Institute of Technology

SPECIAL PROGRAMS:
Cooperative arrangements with 34 other universities, including Université du Quebec, University of Minnesota, University of California (Berkeley), City University of New York, University of Boston and Harvard Medical School

LANGUAGE OF INSTRUCTION: French

ADMISSION REQUIREMENTS FOR FOREIGN STUDENTS:
Secondary school certificate *(baccalauréat)*, or recognized foreign equivalent, or special entrance examination

TUITION FOR FOREIGN STUDENTS:
Fr. 700 per year in 1990

TOTAL INSTRUCTIONAL FACULTY:
1,665

LIBRARY COLLECTIONS:
Interuniversity libraries
Library of the University of Paris V
Unit libraries

MUSEUMS AND GALLERIES:
Museum of the History of Medicine

PRESIDENT: G. Cremer

UNIVERSITÉ DE PARIS VI
(PIERRE ET MARIE CURIE)
(University of Paris VI [Pierre and Marie Curie])
4 place Jussieu, 75252 Paris Cedex 05, France

CHARACTERISTICS OF INSTITUTION:
State-run, nonprofit university

DATE FOUNDED: 1970

TOTAL ENROLLMENT: 33,900 fulltime students

DEGREES AWARDED:
State qualifications
Science:
  Diplôme d'études universitaires générales (DEUG)
    two years required
  Licence ès Sciences
    one year after DEUG required
  Magistère in various fields
    three years after DEUG or DUT required
  Maîtrise
    one year after Licence required
  Diplôme d'études supérieures spécialisées (DESS)
    one year after Maîtrise required
  Diplôme d'études approfondies (DEA)
    one year after Maîtrise required
  Doctorat en Sciences
    two–four years after DEA required
  Certificats and Diplômes in statistics and computer programming
Medicine:
  Doctorat en Médecine
    six years plus one year hospital practice and thesis required
  Certificats de spécialité
    a minimum of two years following doctorate required
  Maîtrise en Biologie humain
    four years required
  Doctorat en Biologie humain
    an additional two–four years following Maîtrise en Biologie humain required

ACADEMIC PROGRAMS:
Unit of Analysis, Probability and Application
Unit of Animal Physiology
Unit of Applied Physics
Unit of Biochemistry
Unit of Computer Science, Statistics and Application
Unit of Condensed State Physics
Unit of Earth Sciences
Unit of Genetics
Unit of Inorganic Chemistry
Unit of Medicine (Saint-Antoine)
Unit of Medicine (Pitie-Salpetriere)
Unit of Medicine (Broussais Hotel-Dieu)
Unit of Optic, Atomic, Molecular and Crystalline Physics
Unit of Organic Chemistry
Unit of Physical Chemistry
Unit of Theoretical Physics
Unit of Zoology
Department of Modern Languages
Department of Physical, Sporting and Outdoor Activities
Department of Public Health
Department of Sciences and Technology
National Higher School of Chemistry of Paris
Geophysics Institute
Institute of Plant Biology
Institute of Pure and Applied Mathematics
Institute of Stomatology
Institute of Theoretical and Applied Mechanics
Statistics Institute of Paris

LANGUAGE OF INSTRUCTION: French

ADMISSION REQUIREMENTS FOR FOREIGN STUDENTS:
Secondary school certificate (baccalauréat), or recognized foreign equivalent, or special entrance examination

TUITION FOR FOREIGN STUDENTS:
Fr. 520–700 per year in 1990

TOTAL INSTRUCTIONAL FACULTY:
6,100

LIBRARY COLLECTIONS:
Interuniversity libraries
Medical libraries
Scientific libraries

MUSEUMS AND GALLERIES:
Mineral Collection

UNIVERSITY PUBLICATIONS:
Bulletin d'information, Livret de l'Étudiant

PRESIDENT: M. Garnier

UNIVERSITÉ DE PARIS VII
(University of Paris VII)
2 place Jussieu, 75221 Paris Cedex 05, France

CHARACTERISTICS OF INSTITUTION:
State-run, nonprofit university

DATE FOUNDED: 1970

TOTAL ENROLLMENT: 35,000 fulltime students (including 6,000 foreign students)

DEGREES AWARDED:
State qualifications
Human Sciences:
Diplôme d'études universitaires générales (DEUG)
two years required
Licence ès Lettres
one year after DEUG required
Maîtrise
one year after Licence required
Maîtrise spécialisées
two years after DEUG required
Diplôme d'études supérieures spécialisées (DESS)
one year after Maîtrise required
Diplôme d'études approfondies (DEA)
one year after Maîtrise required
Doctorat
one year after DEA required
Diplômes in various fields
Exact Sciences:
Diplôme d'études universitaires générales (DEUG)
two years required
Licence ès Sciences
one year after DEUG required
Magistère in various fields
three years after DEUG or DUT required
Maîtrise
one year after Licence required
Maîtrise de Sciences et Techniques
one year after Licence required
Diplôme d'études supérieures spécialisées (DESS)
one year after Maîtrise
Diplôme d'études approfondies (DEA)
one year after Maîtrise required
Doctorat
one year after DEA required
Medicine:
Doctorat en Médecine
six years plus one year hospital practice and thesis
required
Certificats de spécialité
a minimum of two years following doctorate required
Chirurgien-Dentiste
five years required
Maîtrise en Biologie humain
four years required
Doctorat en Biologie humain
an additional two–four years after Maîtrise en
Biologie humain required

ACADEMIC PROGRAMS:
Unit of Anthropology, Ethnology and Religious
Studies
Unit of Biochemistry
Unit of Biology and Natural Sciences
Unit of Chemistry

Unit of Clinical Human Sciences
Unit of Computer Studies
Unit of Dental Surgery
Unit of Didactics of Disciplines
Unit of Earth and Physical Sciences
Unit of East Asian Languages and Literature
Unit of Film, Communication and Information Stud-
ies
Unit of Geography and Social Sciences
Unit of Human Biology
Unit of Intercultural Studies in Applied Languages
Unit of Linguistic Research
Unit of Management and Environmental Protection
Unit of Mathematics
Unit of Medicine (Lariboisiere-Saint-Louis)
Unit of Medicine (Xavier-Bichat)
Unit of Physics
Unit of Sciences of Texts and Documents
Unit of Social Sciences
Institute of English
Institute of Hematology

LANGUAGE OF INSTRUCTION: French

ADMISSION REQUIREMENTS FOR FOREIGN STUDENTS:
Secondary school certificate (baccalauréat), or recognized foreign equivalent, or special entrance examination

TUITION FOR FOREIGN STUDENTS:
Fr. 520–700 per annum in 1990

TOTAL INSTRUCTIONAL FACULTY:
1,645

LIBRARY COLLECTIONS:
Interuniversity library
Specialized libraries—67,000 volumes

UNIVERSITY PUBLICATIONS:
Cahiers Jussieu

PRESIDENT:
Mme. Nadine Forest

UNIVERSITÉ DE PARIS VIII
(VINCENNES À SAINT-DENIS)
(University of Paris VIII [Vincennes at Saint-Denis])
2 rue de la Liberté, 93526 Saint-Denis Cedex 02,
France

CHARACTERISTICS OF INSTITUTION:
State-run, nonprofit university

DATE FOUNDED: 1969

TOTAL ENROLLMENT: 18,800 fulltime students (including 6,000 foreign students)

DEGREES AWARDED:
State qualifications

Diplôme d'études universitaires générales (DEUG)
   two years required
Licence ès Lettres
   one year after DEUG required
Magistère
   three years after DEUG required
Maîtrise
   one year after Licence required
Diplôme d'études supérieures spécialisées (DESS)
   one year after Maîtrise required
Diplôme d'études approfondies (DEA)
   one year after Maîtrise required
Doctorat
   two–four years after DEA required
Licence libre in various fields

ACADEMIC PROGRAMS:
Unit of Arts, Philosophy and Aesthetics
Unit of Communication, Animation and Teaching
Unit of History, Literature and Society
Unit of Languages, Societies and Foreign Cultures
Unit of Linguistics, Computer Studies and Technology
Unit of Power, Administration and Trade
Unit of Psychology, Clinical and Social Practices
Unit of Territory, Economics and Society
Institute of Urban Studies

SPECIAL PROGRAMS:
Cooperative arrangements with 20 universities, including Université du Québec, the University of Chicago and Northwestern University in Illinois

LANGUAGE OF INSTRUCTION: French

ADMISSION REQUIREMENTS FOR FOREIGN STUDENTS:
Secondary school certificate (baccalauréat), or recognized foreign equivalent, or special entrance examination

TUITION FOR FOREIGN STUDENTS:
Fr. 520–700 per year in 1990

TOTAL INSTRUCTIONAL FACULTY:
550

LIBRARY COLLECTIONS:
Total collection—100,000 volumes

UNIVERSITY PUBLICATIONS:
Revue Litterature, Bulletin de linguistique allemande, Bulletin de la RDA, Bulletin de la France au XXe siècle, Travaux sur le capitalisme et l'économie politique, Art et Info

PRESIDENT: Francine Demichel

UNIVERSITÉ DE PARIS IX
(PARIS-DAUPHINE)
(University of Paris IX [Paris-Dauphine])

2 rue de la Liberté, 93526 Saint-Denis Cedex 02, France

CHARACTERISTICS OF INSTITUTION:
State-run, nonprofit university

DATE FOUNDED: 1968

TOTAL ENROLLMENT: 5,600 fulltime students

DEGREES AWARDED:
State qualifications
Diplôme d'études universitaires générales (DEUG)
   two years required
Licence in various fields
   one year after DEUG required
Maîtrise in various fields
   three years after DEUG required
Magistère in mathematics and management
   three years after DEUG required
Diplôme d'études approfondies (DEA) in decision mathematics
   one year after Maîtrise requirements
Diplôme d'études supérieures spécialisées (DESS)
   one year after Maîtrise required
Doctorat
   two–four years after DEA required

ACADEMIC PROGRAMS:
Unit of Applied Economics
Unit of Applied Mathematics
Unit of Business Computer Science
Unit of Business Studies
Unit of Business Studies and Applied Economics
Unit of Organization Sciences

LANGUAGE OF INSTRUCTION: French

ADMISSION REQUIREMENTS FOR FOREIGN STUDENTS:
Secondary school certificate (baccalauréat), or recognized foreign equivalent, or special entrance examination

TUITION FOR FOREIGN STUDENTS:
Fr 520–700 per year in 1990

TOTAL INSTRUCTIONAL FACULTY:
880

LIBRARY COLLECTIONS:
Center for the Acquisition and Diffusion of Scientific and Technological Information—60,000 volumes

UNIVERSITY PUBLICATIONS:
Brochures des enseignements pour châque diplôme

PRESIDENT: I. Ekelano

UNIVERSITÉ DE PARIS X
(PARIS-NANTERRE)
(University of Paris X [Paris-Nanterre])

200 ave de la République, 92001 Nanterre Cedex, France

CHARACTERISTICS OF INSTITUTION:
State-run, nonprofit university

DATE FOUNDED: 1970

TOTAL ENROLLMENT: 26,500 fulltime students (including 3,300 foreign students)

DEGREES AWARDED:
State qualifications
Law and Economics:
  Diplôme d'études universitaires générales (DEUG)
    two years required
  Licence
    one year after DEUG required
  Maîtrise
    one year after license required
  Diplôme d'études supérieures spécialisées (DESS)
    one year after Maîtrise required
  Diplôme d'études approfondies (DEA)
    one year after Maîtrise required
  Doctorat
    two–four years after DEA required
Letters and Human Sciences:
  Diplôme d'études universitaires générales (DEUG)
    two years required
  Licence ès Lettres
    one year after DEUG required
  Maîtrise
    one year after Licence, or equivalent, required
  Diplôme d'études supérieures spécialisées (DESS)
    one year after Maîtrise required
  Diplôme d'études approfondies (DEA)
    one year after Maîtrise required
  Doctorat
    two–four years after DEA required
  Diplôme universitaire de technologie (DUT)
    two years required

ACADEMIC PROGRAMS:
Unit of Anglo-American Studies
Unit of Economic Sciences
Unit of German, Romance Languages, Slav and Applied Foreign Languages
Unit of History, Geography and Sociology
Unit of Juridicial Studies
Unit of Letters, Linguistics and Philosophy
Unit of Psychology and Education Sciences
Unit of Science and Techniques of Physical and Sporting Activities
Institute of Technology (Ville d'Avray)

SPECIAL PROGRAMS:
Cooperative arrangements with 18 other universities, including Columbia University, City University of New York, University of Massachusetts and Université du Quebec

LANGUAGE OF INSTRUCTION: French

ADMISSION REQUIREMENTS FOR FOREIGN STUDENTS:
Secondary school certificate *(baccalauréat)*, or recognized foreign equivalent or special entrance examination

TUITION FOR FOREIGN STUDENTS:
Fr 520–700 per year in 1990

TOTAL INSTRUCTIONAL FACULTY:
750

LIBRARY COLLECTIONS:
Interuniversity library—350,000 volumes

UNIVERSITY PUBLICATIONS:
Droit et Cultures, Collection (Cinéma et Sciences humaines)

PRESIDENT: Paul Larivaille

UNIVERSITÉ DE PARIS XI
(PARIS-SUD)
(University of Paris XI [Paris-Sud])
15 rue de G. Clemenceau, 91405 Orsay Cedex, France

CHARACTERISTICS OF INSTITUTION:
State-run, nonprofit university

DATE FOUNDED: 1970

TOTAL ENROLLMENT: 25,000 fulltime students

DEGREES AWARDED:
State qualifications
Exact Sciences:
  Diplôme d'études universitaires scientifiques et techniques (DEUST)
    two years required
  Diplôme d'études universitaires générales (DEUG)
    two years required
  Licence ès Sciences
    one year after DEUG required
  Magistère in various fields
    three years after DEUG or DUT required
  Maîtrise
    one year after Licence, or equivalent, required
  Diplôme d'études approfondies (DEA)
    one year after Maîtrise required
  Doctorat
    two–four years after DEA required
Biomedical Sciences:
  Doctorat en Médecine
    six years plus one year hospital practice and thesis required
  Certificats de specialité

a minimum of two years following doctorate required

Diplôme de Pharmacien
  four years plus one year practical work required

Doctorat en Pharmacie
  two *certificats* (études supérieures ou spéciales ou sciences) and thesis after Diplôme required

Maîtrise en Biologie humain
  four years required

Doctorat en Biologie humain
  an additional two to four years following Maîtrise en Biologie humain required

Law:

Diplôme d'études universitaires générales (DEUG)
  two years required

Licence en Droit
  three years required

Maîtrise
  one year after Licence required

Diplôme d'études approfondies (DEA)
  one year after Maîtrise required

Doctorat
  two–four years after DEA required

Certificat de Capacité en Droit (law)
  two years required

Diplôme universitaire de technologie (DUT)
  two years required

ACADEMIC PROGRAMS:
Unit of Law and Economic Science (Sceaux)
Unit of Medicine (Kremlin-Bicetre)
Unit of Pharmacy (Chatenay-Malabry)
Unit of Sciences (Orsay)
University Institute of Technology at Cachan
University Institute of Technology at Orsay
University Institute of Technology at Sceaux

SPECIAL PROGRAMS:
Cooperative arrangements with seven universities

LANGUAGE OF INSTRUCTION: French

ADMISSION REQUIREMENTS FOR FOREIGN STUDENTS:
Secondary school certificate *(baccalauréat)*, or recognized foreign equivalent, or special entrance examination

TUITION FOR FOREIGN STUDENTS:
Fr 520–700 per year in 1990

TOTAL INSTRUCTIONAL FACULTY:
2,900

LIBRARY COLLECTIONS:
Central library
Specialized libraries—250,000 volumes

UNIVERSITY PUBLICATIONS:
Aspects de la recherche, Paris-Sud Université

PRESIDENT: Jack Robert

UNIVERSITÉ DE PARIS XII (PARIS-VAL-DE-MARNE) (University of Paris XII [Paris-Val-de-Marne]) ave du Général de Gaulle, 94010 Cretail Cedex, France

CHARACTERISTICS OF INSTITUTION:
State-run, nonprofit university

DATE FOUNDED: 1970

TOTAL ENROLLMENT: 15,000 fulltime students (including 2,000 foreign students)

DEGREES AWARDED:
State qualifications
Law:

Diplôme d'études universitaires générales (DEUG)
  two years required

Licence en Droit
  one year after DEUG required

Maîtrise
  one year after Licence required

Diplôme d'études supérieures spécialisées (DESS)
  one year after Maîtrise required

Diplôme d'études approfondies (DEA)
  one year after Maîtrise required

Economics:

Diplôme d'études universitaires scientifiques et techniques (DEUST)
  two years required

Diplôme d'études universitaires générales (DEUG)
  two years required

Licence en Sciences économiques
  one year after DEUG required

Maîtrise
  one year after Licence required

Diplôme d'études approfondies (DEA)
  one to two years following Maîtrise required

Biomedical Sciences

Doctorat en Médecine
  six years plus one year hospital practice and thesis required

Diplôme d'études approfondies (DEA)
  one to two years following Maîtrise required

Certificats d'études spéciales de Psychiatrie
  a minimum of two years following Doctorat

Diplômes in various fields

Science:

Diplôme d'études universitaires générales (DEUG)
  two years required

Maîtrise de sciences et techniques
  one year after Licence, or equivalent, required

Diplôme d'études approfondies (DEA)
  one year after Maîtrise required

Diplôme d'études supérieures spécialisées (DESS)
  one year after Maîtrise required

Letters and Human Sciences:
   Diplôme d'études universitaires générales (DEUG)
      two years required
   Licence ès Lettres
      one year after DEUG required
   Maîtrise
      one year after Licence, or equivalent, required
   Diplôme d'études approfondies (DEA)
      one year after Maîtrise required
   Doctorat
      two–four years after DEA required
Town Planning:
   Diplôme d'études approfondies (DEA) (postgraduate)
      one to two years following Maîtrise required
   Diplôme d'Etat d'Ergotherapeute
      one to two years following Maîtrise required
   Maîtrise de Sciences sociales appliquees au travail
      one to two years following Licence required
   Diplôme universitaire de technologie (DUT)
      two years following Maîtrise required

ACADEMIC PROGRAMS:
Unit of Communication and Social Interface
Unit of Economic Sciences
Unit of Law and Politics
Unit of Letters and Humanities
Unit of Medicine
Unit of Public and Social Administration
Unit of Science
Institute of General Administration
Institute of Technology (Creteil-Evry)
Institute of Town Planning

SPECIAL PROGRAMS:
Cooperative arrangements with universities in 25 other countries, including Canada and the U.S.A.

LANGUAGE OF INSTRUCTION: French

ADMISSION REQUIREMENTS FOR FOREIGN STUDENTS:
Secondary school certificate (baccalauréat), or recognized foreign equivalent, or special entrance examination

TUITION FOR FOREIGN STUDENTS:
Fr 520–700 per year in 1990

TOTAL INSTRUCTIONAL FACULTY:
776

LIBRARY COLLECTIONS:
Central library—45,000 volumes
Law and economics—22,000 volumes
Medicine—15,000 volumes

PRESIDENT: Daniel Laurent

UNIVERSITÉ DE PARIS XIII (PARIS-NORD) (University of Paris XIII [Paris-Nord]) ave J. B. Clement, 93430 Villetaneuse, France

CHARACTERISTICS OF INSTITUTION:
State-run, nonprofit university

DATE FOUNDED: 1970

TOTAL ENROLLMENT: 13,450 fulltime students

DEGREES AWARDED:
State qualifications
Law and Economics:
   Diplôme d'études universitaires générales (DEUG)
      two years required
   Licence
      one year after DEUG required
   Maîtrise
      one year after Licence required
   Diplôme d'études approfondies (DEA)
      one year after Maîtrise required
   Doctorat
      two–four years after DEA required
   Capacité en Droit (law)
      two–four years following DEA required
Medical and Biomedical Sciences:
   Doctorat en Médecine
      six years plus one year hospital practice and thesis required
   Diplômes and Certificats in various fields
Exact Sciences:
   Diplôme d'études universitaires générales (DEUG)
      two years required
   Licence ès Sciences
      one year after DEUG required
   Magistère in various fields
      three years after DEUG or DUT required
   Maîtrise
      one year after Licence, or equivalent, required
   Diplôme d'études approfondies (DEA)
      one year after Maîtrise required
   Doctorat
      two–four years after DEA required
Letters and Human Sciences:
   Diplôme d'études universitaires générales (DEUG)
      two years required
   Licence ès Lettres
      one year after DEUG
   Maîtrise
      one year after Licence, or equivalent, required
   Diplôme d'études supérieures spécialisées (DESS)
      one year after Maîtrise required
   Diplôme d'études approfondies (DEA)
      one year after Maîtrise required
   Doctorat

two–four years after DEA required
Diplôme universitaire de technologie (DUT)
    two years required

ACADEMIC PROGRAMS:
Unit of Economic Sciences and Business Administration
Unit of Expression and Communications Sciences
Unit of Law and Political Science
Unit of Letters and Humanities
University Institute of Technology
Medicine and Human Biology Experimental Center
Scientific and Polytechnic Center

LANGUAGE OF INSTRUCTION: French

ADMISSION REQUIREMENTS FOR FOREIGN STUDENTS:
Secondary school certificate *(baccalauréat)*, or recognized foreign equivalent, or special entrance examination

TUITION FOR FOREIGN STUDENTS:
Fr 520–700 per year in 1990

TOTAL INSTRUCTIONAL FACULTY:
669

LIBRARY COLLECTIONS:
Central library
Scientific library (Saint-Denis)

PRESIDENT: Pierre Cornillot

UNIVERSITÉ DE PICARDIE
(University of Picardie)
rue Solomon Mahlangu, 80025 Amiens Cedex, France

CHARACTERISTICS OF INSTITUTION:
State-run, nonprofit university

DATE FOUNDED: 1965

TOTAL ENROLLMENT: 10,000 fulltime students

DEGREES AWARDED:
State qualifications
Law and Economics:
    Diplôme d'études universitaires générales (DEUG)
        two years required
    Licence
        one year after DEUG required
    Maîtrise
        one year after Licence required
    Diplôme d'études supérieures spécialisées (DESS)
        a minimum of two semesters following Maîtrise required
    Diplôme d'études approfondies (DEA)
        one year after Maîtrise required
    Doctorat
        two–four years after DEA required

Certificat de Capacité en Droit (law)
    two years required
Medicine:
    Doctorat en Médecine
        six years plus one year hospital practice and thesis required
    Certificats de spécialité
        a minimum of two years following doctorate required
    Chirurgien-Dentiste
        five years
Pharmacy:
    Diplôme de Pharmacien
        four years plus one year practical work required
    Doctorat en Pharmacie
        two *certificats* (études supérieures ou spéciales ou sciences) and thesis after Diplôme required
Science:
    Diplôme d'études universitaires générales (DEUG)
        two years required
    Licence ès Sciences
        one year after DEUG required
    Maîtrise
        one year after Licence, or equivalent, required
    Diplôme d'études approfondies (DEA)
        one year after Maîtrise required
    Diplôme d'études supérieures spécialisées (DESS)
        a minimum of two semesters following Maîtrise required
    Doctorat en Sciences
        two–four years after DEA required
Letters and Human Sciences:
    Diplôme d'études universitaires générales (DEUG)
        two years required
    Licence ès Lettres
        one year after DEUG required
    Maîtrise
        one year after Licence, or equivalent, required
    Diplôme d'études approfondies (DEA)
        one year after Maîtrise required
    Doctorat
        two–four years after DEA required
    Diplôme universitaire de technologie (DUT)
        two years required

ACADEMIC PROGRAMS:
Unit of Art
Unit of Economics
Unit of History and Geography
Unit of Law
Unit of Literature
Unit of Mathematics
Unit of Medicine
Unit of Modern Languages
Unit of Philosophy and Human Sciences
Unit of Pharmacy

Unit of Sciences
School of Commerce
Institute of Juridicial Sciences
University Institute of Technology

SPECIAL PROGRAMS:
Cooperative arrangements with two universities

LANGUAGE OF INSTRUCTION: French

ADMISSION REQUIREMENTS FOR FOREIGN STUDENTS:
Secondary school certificate *(baccalauréat), brevet supérieur* or recognized foreign equivalent or special entrance examination

TUITION FOR FOREIGN STUDENTS:
Fr 520–600 per year in 1990

TOTAL INSTRUCTIONAL FACULTY:
540

LIBRARY COLLECTIONS:
Central library

PRESIDENT: Bernard Nemitz

UNIVERSITÉ DE REIMS CHAMPAGNE-ARDENNE
(University of Reims, Champagne-Ardenne)
23 rue Boulard, 51097 Reims Cedex, France

CHARACTERISTICS OF INSTITUTION:
State-run, nonprofit university

DATE FOUNDED: 1548

TOTAL ENROLLMENT: 17,000 fulltime students (including 1,500 foreign students)

DEGREES AWARDED:
State qualifications
Law and Economics:
  Diplôme d'études universitaires générales (DEUG)
    two years required
  Licence
    one year after DEUG required
  Maîtrise
    one year after Licence required
  Diplôme d'études approfondies (DEA)
    one year after Maîtrise required
  Doctorat
    two–four years after DEA required
Medicine:
  Doctorat en Médecine
    six years plus one year hospital practice and thesis required
  Certificats de specialité
    a minimum of two years following doctorate required
  Chirurgien-Dentiste
    five years required
Pharmacy:

Diplôme de Pharmacien
  four years plus one year practical work required
Doctorat en Pharmacie
  two *certificats* (études supérieures ou spéciales ou sciences) and thesis after Diplôme required
Science:
  Diplôme d'études universitaires générales (DEUG)
    two years required
  Licence ès Sciences
    one year after DEUG required
  Maîtrise
    one year after Licence, or equivalent, required
  Diplôme d'études approfondies (DEA)
    one year after Maîtrise required
  Doctorat en Sciences
    two–four years after DEA required
Viticulture:
  Diplôme national d'oenologie
    two years required
Letters and Human Sciences:
  Diplôme d'études universitaires générales (DEUG)
    two years required
  Licence ès Lettres
    one year after DEUG required
  Maîtrise
    one year after Licence, or equivalent, required
  Diplôme d'études approfondies (DEA)
    one year after Maîtrise required
  Doctorat
    two–four years after DEA required
  Diplôme universitaire de technologie (DUT)
    two years required

ACADEMIC PROGRAMS:
Unit of Economic Sciences and Management
Unit of Exact and Natural Sciences
Unit of Law and Political Sciences
Unit of Letters and Human Sciences
Unit of Medicine
Unit of Odontology
Unit of Pharmacy
University Institute of Technology in Reims
University Institute of Technology in Troyes
University Institute of Technical Training in Charleville

SPECIAL PROGRAMS:
Cooperative arrangements with 10 other universities

LANGUAGE OF INSTRUCTION: French

ADMISSION REQUIREMENTS FOR FOREIGN STUDENTS:
Secondary school certificate *(baccalauréat),* or recognized foreign equivalent, or special entrance examination

TUITION FOR FOREIGN STUDENTS:
Fr 550–600 per year in 1990

TOTAL INSTRUCTIONAL FACULTY:
540

LIBRARY COLLECTIONS:
Total collection—235,000 volumes

UNIVERSITY PUBLICATIONS:
Bulletin de Liaison de l'Université de Reims champagne-Ardenne, Realités du Droit International contemporain, Livret de l'Université, Publications du département d'anglais, Etudes Champenoises, Revue de l'Institut de Géographie, Jurisprudence Cour d'appel, Cahiers de l'Institut du Territoire et de l'Environnement de l'Université de Reims, Cahiers du Centre de Recherches sur la Décentralisation Territoriale

PRESIDENT: Jean Raimond

UNIVERSITÉ DE ROUEN
(University of Rouen)
1 rue Thomas Becket, BP 138, 76134 Mont-Saint-Aignan Cedex, France

CHARACTERISTICS OF INSTITUTION:
State-run, nonprofit university

DATE FOUNDED: 1966

TOTAL ENROLLMENT: 16,000 fulltime students

DEGREES AWARDED:
State qualifications
Law and Economics:
   Diplôme d'études universitaires générales (DEUG)
      two years required
   Licence
      one year after DEUG required
   Maîtrise
      one year after Licence required
   Diplôme d'études supérieures spécialisées (DESS)
      one year after Maîtrise required
   Diplôme d'études approfondies (DEA)
      one year after Maîtrise required
   Doctorat
      two–four years after DEA required
   Certificat de Capacité en Droit (law)
      two years required
Medicine:
   Doctorat en Médecine
      six years plus one year hospital practice and thesis required
   Certificats de spécialité
      a minimum two years following doctorate required
   Chirurgien-Dentiste
      five years required
Pharmacy:
   Diplôme de Pharmacien
      four years plus one year practical work required

Doctorat en Pharmacie
   two *certificats* (études supérieures ou spéciales ou sciences) and thesis after Diplôme required
Science:
   Diplôme d'études universitaires générales (DEUG)
      two years required
   Licence ès Sciences
      one year after DEUG required
   Maîtrise
      one year after Licence, or equivalent, required
   Diplôme d'études supérieures spécialisées (DESS)
      one year after Maîtrise required
   Diplôme d'études approfondies (DEA)
      one year after Maîtrise required
   Doctorat en Sciences
      two–four years after DEA required
Letters and Human Sciences:
   Diplôme d'études universitaires générales (DEUG)
      two years required
   Licence ès Lettres
      one year after DEUG required
   Maîtrise
      one year after Licence, or equivalent, required
   Diplôme d'études approfondies (DEA)
      one year after Maîtrise required
   Doctorat
      two–four years after DEA required
   Diplôme universitaire de technologie (DUT)
      two years required

ACADEMIC PROGRAMS:
Unit of Behavioral and Educational Sciences
Unit of Law and Economic Sciences
Unit of Letters and Humanities
Unit of Medicine and Pharmacy
Unit of Sciences and Technology
University Institute of Technology

SPECIAL PROGRAMS:
Cooperative arrangements with 10 other universities, including St. Lawrence University of Connecticut

LANGUAGE OF INSTRUCTION: French

ADMISSION REQUIREMENTS FOR FOREIGN STUDENTS:
Secondary school certificate (*baccalauréat*), or recognized foreign equivalent or special entrance examination

TUITION FOR FOREIGN STUDENTS:
Fr 520–600 per year in 1990

TOTAL INSTRUCTIONAL FACULTY:
700

LIBRARY COLLECTIONS:
University library—127,000 volumes

UNIVERSITY PUBLICATIONS:
Cahiers de CRIAR, France-Autriche, AUSTRIACA, Cahiers de geographie

PRESIDENT: Patrick Boucly

UNIVERSITÉ DE SAINT-ÉTIENNE
(University of Saint-Étienne)
34 rue Francis Baulier, 42023 Saint-Étienne Cedex, France

CHARACTERISTICS OF INSTITUTION:
State-run nonprofit university

DATE FOUNDED: 1969

TOTAL ENROLLMENT: 10,000 fulltime students (including 1,000 foreign students)

DEGREES AWARDED:
State qualifications
Law and Economics:
  Diplôme d'études universitaires générales (DEUG)
    two years required
  Licence
    one year after DEUG
  Maîtrise
    one year after Licence
  Diplôme d'études supérieures spécialisées (DESS)
    one year after Maîtrise required
  Diplôme d'études approfondies (DEA)
    one year after Maîtrise required
  Doctorat
    two–four years after DEA required
  Certificat de Capacité en Droit (law)
    two years required
Medicine:
  Doctorat en Médecine
    six years plus one year hospital practice and thesis required
  Certificats de spécialité
    a minimum of two years following doctorate required
  Chirurgien-Dentiste
    five years required
Science:
  Diplôme d'études universitaires générales (DEUG)
    two years required
  Licence ès Sciences
    one year after DEUG required
  Maîtrise
    one year after Licence, or equivalent, required
  Diplôme d'études approfondies (DEA)
    one year after Maîtrise required
  Doctorat en Sciences
    two–four years after DEA required
Letters and Human Sciences:
  Diplôme d'études universitaires générales (DEUG)
    two years required
  Licence ès Lettres
    one year after DEUG required
  Maîtrise
    one year after Licence, or equivalent, required
  Diplôme d'études approfondies (DEA)
    one year after Maîtrise required
  Doctorat
    two–four years after DEA required
  Diplôme universitaire de technologie (DUT)
    two years required

ACADEMIC PROGRAMS:
Unit of Arts, Communication and Pedagogy
Unit of Law and Economics
Unit of Letters and Human Sciences
Unit of Management, Administration and Applied Foreign Languages
Unit of Medicine
Unit of Sciences
Institute of French Language (for foreign students)
University Institute of Technology

SPECIAL PROGRAMS:
Cooperative arrangements with six other universities

LANGUAGE OF INSTRUCTION: French

ADMISSION REQUIREMENTS FOR FOREIGN STUDENTS:
Secondary school certificate *(baccalauréat)*, or recognized foreign equivalent, or special entrance examination

TUITION FOR FOREIGN STUDENTS:
Fr 520–600 per year in 1990

TOTAL INSTRUCTIONAL FACULTY:
450

LIBRARY COLLECTIONS:
Humanities, law, economics—45,000 volumes
Science, medicine—10,000 volumes

UNIVERSITY PUBLICATIONS:
L'Université, Publications des Centres de Recherche

PRESIDENT: B. Lauras

UNIVERSITÉ DE STRASBOURG I
(UNIVERSITÉ LOUIS PASTEUR)
(University of Strasbourg I [University Louis Pasteur])
Institut Le Bel, 4 rue Blaise Pascal, 67070 Strasbourg Cedex, France

CHARACTERISTICS OF INSTITUTION:
State-run, nonprofit university

DATE FOUNDED: 1971

TOTAL ENROLLMENT: 14,300 fulltime students (including 2,400 foreign students)

DEGREES AWARDED:
State qualifications
Medicine:
  Doctorat en Médecine
    six years plus one year hospital practice and thesis
    required
  Certificats de spécialité
    a minimum of two years following doctorate re-
    quired
  Chirurgien-Dentiste
    five years required
  Doctorat de 3e cycle en Sciences ondontolgiques
    two certificats d'études supérieures and thesis
    required
Pharmacy:
  Diplôme de Pharmacien
    four years plus one year practical work required
  Doctorat en Pharmacie
    two *certificats* (études supérieures ou spéciales ou
    sciences) and thesis after Diplôme required
Psychology and Geography:
  Diplôme d'études universitaires générales (DEUG)
    two years required
  Licence ès Lettres
    one year after DEUG required
  Maîtrise
    one year after Licence required
  Diplôme d'études approfondies (DEA)
    one year after Maîtrise required
  Diplôme d'études supérieures spécialisées (DESS)
    one year after Maîtrise required
  Doctorat
    two–four years after DEA required
Science:
  Diplôme d'études universitaires générales (DEUG)
    two years required
  Licence ès Sciences
    one year after DEUG required
  Maîtrise
    one year after Licence, or equivalent, required
  Diplôme d'études approfondies (DEA)
    one year after Maîtrise required
  Doctorat en Sciences
    two–four years after DEA required
Economics:
  Diplôme d'études universitaires générales (DEUG)
    two years required
  Licence
    one year after DEUG required
  Maîtrise
    one year after Licence required
  Diplôme d'études supérieures spécialisées (DESS)
    one year after Maîtrise required
  Diplôme d'études approfondies (DEA)
    one year after Maîtrise required
  Doctorat

    two–four years after DEA required
  Diplôme universitaire de technologie (DUT)
    two years required

ACADEMIC PROGRAMS:
Unit of Behavioral and Environmental Sciences
Unit of Dentistry
Unit of Earth and Life Sciences
Unit of Economic Sciences
Unit of Geography
Unit of Materials Sciences
Unit of Mathematics and Computer Science
Unit of Medical Sciences
Unit of Pharmacy
Higher National School of Biotechnology
Higher National School of Physical Engineering
School of Polymer Science
Astronomy
Institute of Geophysics
University Institute of Technology (applied biology)

SPECIAL PROGRAMS:
Cooperative arrangements with 41 other universities, including Clark University, University of Virginia, University of California (Los Angeles), Pennsylvania State University, Duke University, University
of Arizona and Harvard Medical School

LANGUAGE OF INSTRUCTION: French

ADMISSION REQUIREMENTS FOR FOREIGN STUDENTS:
Secondary school certificate *(baccalauréat)*, or recognized foreign equivalent, or special entrance examination

TUITION FOR FOREIGN STUDENTS:
Fr. 520–600 per year in 1990

TOTAL INSTRUCTIONAL FACULTY:
920

LIBRARY COLLECTIONS:
National university library

MUSEUMS AND GALLERIES:
Museums of Zoology, Strasbourg and the Louis Pasteur University of Strasbourg

UNIVERSITY PUBLICATIONS:
*Journal de Médecine, Sciences géologiques, Marcellia (Re-
vue internationale de cécidologie), Annales de l'Institute
de Physique du Globe, Revue de Géomorphologie Dyna-
mique, Revue géographique de l'Est, Atlas Regional de la
France de l'Est*

PRESIDENT: Gilbert Laustriat

**UNIVERSITÉ DE STRASBOURG II
(UNIVERSITÉ DES SCIENCES HUMAINES)**

(University of Strasbourg II [University of Human Sciences])
22 rue Descartes, 67084 Strasbourg Cedex, France

CHARACTERISTICS OF INSTITUTION:
State-run, nonprofit university

DATE FOUNDED: 1538

TOTAL ENROLLMENT: 10,500 fulltime students (including 2,000 foreign students)

DEGREES AWARDED:
State qualifications
Letters and Human Sciences:
Diplôme d'études universitaires générales (DEUG)
two years required
Licence ès Lettres
one year after DEUG required
Maîtrise
one year after Licence, or equivalent, required
Diplôme d'études supérieures spécialisées (DESS)
one year after Maîtrise required
Diplôme d'études approfondies (DEA)
one year after Maîtrise required
Doctorat
two–four years after DEA required
Certificat and Diplôme d'études françaises (for foreign students)

ACADEMIC PROGRAMS:
Unit of Art
Unit of Catholic Theology
Unit of Classics
Unit of French and Comparative Linguistics and Literature
Unit of History
Unit of Languages and Applied Human Sciences
Unit of Modern Languages, Literature and Civilization
Unit of Philosophy and Communication
Unit of Protestant Theology
Unit of Social Sciences
Unit of Sport Science
Institute of French Studies (for foreign students)

SPECIAL PROGRAMS:
Cooperative arrangements with 23 other universities, including Purdue University, University of Houston, University of Seattle, University of Indiana, Pennsylvania State University and Syracuse University

LANGUAGE OF INSTRUCTION: French

ADMISSION REQUIREMENTS FOR FOREIGN STUDENTS:
Secondary school certificate (baccalauréat), or recognized foreign equivalent, or special entrance examination

TUITION FOR FOREIGN STUDENTS:
Fr 520–600 per year in 1990

TOTAL INSTRUCTIONAL FACULTY:
400

LIBRARY COLLECTIONS:
National and university library
Specialized libraries

MUSEUMS AND GALLERIES:
Museum of Mediterranean and Oriental Antiquities

UNIVERSITY PUBLICATIONS:
Recherches anglaises et nord-americaines, Recherches iberiques et ibero-americaines, Recherches germaniques, Bulletin analytique d'histoire romaine, Revue des sciences sociales de la France de l'Est, Travaux de l'Institut de Phonétique, KTEMA (Civilisations de l'Orient de la Grèce et de Rome antique), Revue de Droit Canonique, Revue des Sciences Religieuses

PRESIDENT: Claude Regnier

UNIVERSITÉ DE STRASBOURG III
(UNIVERSITÉ ROBERT SCHUMAN)
(University of Strasbourg III [University Robert Schuman])
22 rue Descartes, 67084 Strasbourg Cedex, France

CHARACTERISTICS OF INSTITUTION:
State-run, nonprofit university

DATE FOUNDED: 1970

TOTAL ENROLLMENT: 7,600 fulltime students (including 800 foreign students)

DEGREES AWARDED:
State qualifications
Law:
Diplôme d'études universitaires générales (DEUG)
two years required
Licence en Droit (law)
three years required
Maîtrise de Droit (law)
four years required
Maîtrise de sciences et techniques (journalism)
four years required
Diplôme d'études supérieures spécialisées (DESS)
one year after Maîtrise required
Diplôme d'études approfondies (DEA)
one year after Maîtrise required
Doctorat
two–four years after DEA required
Certificat de Capacité en Droit (law)
two years required
Diplôme universitaire de technologie (DUT)
two years required

ACADEMIC PROGRAMS:
Unit of Law, Political Sciences and Management
Unit of Law, Political and Social Research
Unit of Technological Research
European Institute for Advanced Commercial Studies
Institute of Advanced European Studies
Institute of Business Economics
Institute of Labor
Institute of Political Studies
Institute of Preparation for General Administration
University Institute of Technology
Adult Education Service
Center for International Patent Rights
University Center for Journalistic Studies
Language Center

SPECIAL PROGRAMS:
Cooperative arrangements with 18 other universities, including Purdue University in Indiana, University of Indiana and Tulane University in Louisiana

LANGUAGE OF INSTRUCTION: French

ADMISSION REQUIREMENTS FOR FOREIGN STUDENTS:
Secondary school certificate (baccalauréat), or recognized foreign equivalent, or special entrance examination

TUITION FOR FOREIGN STUDENTS:
Fr 520–600 per year in 1990

TOTAL INSTRUCTIONAL FACULTY:
1,089 (200 fulltime)

LIBRARY COLLECTIONS:
Strasbourg national university library
Specialized libraries—70,000 volumes

UNIVERSITY PUBLICATIONS:
Annales de la Facultié de Droit, Revue Allemagne du Centre d'Études germaniques

PRESIDENT: Jean-Paul Jacqué

UNIVERSITÉ DE TOULOUSE I
(SCIENCES SOCIALES)
(University of Toulouse I [Social Sciences])
place Anatole France, 31042 Toulouse Cedex, France

CHARACTERISTICS OF INSTITUTION:
State-run, nonprofit university

DATE FOUNDED: 1229

TOTAL ENROLLMENT: 14,700 fulltime students (including 1,000 foreign students)

DEGREES AWARDED:
State qualifications
Law and Economics:
   Diplôme d'études universitaires générales (DEUG)
      two years required
   Licence
      one year after DEUG required
   Magistère in economics and statistics
      three years after DEUG required
   Maîtrise en Administration économique et sociale
      one year after Licence required
   Diplôme d'études supérieures spécialisées (DESS)
      a minimum of one year following Maîtrise required
   Diplôme d'études approfondies (DEA)
      one year after Maîtrise required
   Doctorat
      two–four years after DEA required
   Certificat de Capacite en Droit (law)
      two years required

ACADEMIC PROGRAMS:
Unit of Economics
Unit of Economic and Social Administration
Unit of Information Science
Unit of Law (first cycle)
Unit of Law (second and third cycles)
Unit of Politics
Unit of Special Studies

SPECIAL PROGRAMS:
Cooperative arrangements with 11 other universities, including Nicholls State University in Louisiana, Longwood College in Virginia and Dickinson College in Pennsylvania

LANGUAGE OF INSTRUCTION: French

ADMISSION REQUIREMENTS FOR FOREIGN STUDENTS:
Secondary school certificate (baccalauréat), or recognized foreign equivalent, or special entrance examination

TUITION FOR FOREIGN STUDENTS:
Fr 520–600 per year in 1990

TOTAL INSTRUCTIONAL FACULTY:
232

LIBRARY COLLECTIONS:
Central library—30,000 volumes
Interuniversity library—1,000,000 volumes

UNIVERSITY PUBLICATIONS:
Livret de l'Étudiant, Annales, Livre de la Recherche, UT1 Magazine

PRESIDENT: Claude Gour

UNIVERSITÉ DE TOULOUSE II
(LE MIRAIL)

(University of Toulouse II [Le-Mirail])
5 alle Antonio Machado, 31058 Toulouse Cedex,
France

CHARACTERISTICS OF INSTITUTION:
State-run, nonprofit university

DATE FOUNDED: 1970

TOTAL ENROLLMENT: 18,400 fulltime students (including 2,000 foreign students)

DEGREES AWARDED:
State qualifications
Letters and Human Sciences:
  Diplôme d'études universitaires générales (DEUG)
    two years required
  Licence ès Lettres
    one year after DEUG required
  Magistère in economics and statistics
    three years after DEUG required
  Maîtrise
    one year after Licence, or equivalent, required
  Diplôme d'études supérieures spécialisées (DESS)
    a minimum of one year following Maîtrise required
  Diplôme d'études approfondies (DEA)
    one year after Maîtrise required
  Doctorat
    two–four years after DEA required
  Diplôme universitaire de technologie (DUT)
    two years required

ACADEMIC PROGRAMS:
Unit of Ancient Literature and Languages
Unit of Behavioral Sciences
Unit of Continuing Education
Unit of Economics and Business Studies
Unit of French Literature and Comparative Literature
Unit of Geography
Unit of Hispanic and Hispano-American Studies
Unit of History, Archaeology and History of Art
Unit of Mathematics, Computer Science and Statistics
Unit of Modern Languages, Literatures and Civilizations and General Linguistics
Unit of Philosophy and Politics
Unit of Social Sciences
School of Interpretation and Translation
University Institute of Technology
Center of French (for foreign students)

LANGUAGE OF INSTRUCTION: French

ADMISSION REQUIREMENTS FOR FOREIGN STUDENTS:
Secondary school certificate (baccalauréat), or recognized foreign equivalent, or special entrance examination

TUITION FOR FOREIGN STUDENTS:
Fr 520–600 per year in 1990

TOTAL INSTRUCTIONAL FACULTY:
460

LIBRARY COLLECTIONS:
Interuniversity library—100,000 volumes

UNIVERSITY PUBLICATIONS:
Annales de l'Université, Revue d'Art préhistorique, Caravelle, Revue Géographique des Pyrénées et du Sud-Ouest, Psychologie et Éducation, Litteratures, Pallas (Revue d'Etudes antiques)

PRESIDENT: G. Bertrand

UNIVERSITÉ DE TOULOUSE III
(UNIVERSITÉ PAUL SABATIER)
(University of Toulouse III [University Paul Sabatier])
118 route de Narbonne, 31062 Toulouse Cedex,
France

CHARACTERISTICS OF INSTITUTION:
State-run, nonprofit university

DATE FOUNDED: 1970

TOTAL ENROLLMENT: 22,750 fulltime students (including 2,500 foreign students)

DEGREES AWARDED:
State qualifications
Medicine:
  Doctorat en Médecine
    six years plus one year hospital practice and thesis required
  Certificats de spécialité
    a minimum of two years following doctorate required
  Chirurgien-Dentiste
    five years required
Pharmacy:
  Diplôme de Pharmacien
    four years plus one year practical work required
  Doctorat en Pharmacie
    two *certificats* (études supérieures ou spéciales ou sciences) and thesis after Diplôme required
  Maîtrise de Sciences et Techniques en Genie biologique et médicale
Science:
  Diplôme d'études universitaires générales (DEUG)
    two years required
  Licence ès Sciences
    one year after DEUG required
  Maîtrise
    one year after Licence, or equivalent, required
  Diplôme d'études approfondies (DEA)
    one year after Maîtrise required

Diplôme d'études supérieures spécialisées (DESS)
   one year after Maîtrise required
Doctorat
   two–four years after DEA required
Diplôme universitaire de technologie (DUT)
   two years required

ACADEMIC PROGRAMS:
Unit of Dental Surgery
Unit of Earth and Life Sciences
Unit of Mathematics, Information Science and Man-
   agement
Unit of Medical Sciences (Purpan)
Unit of Medical Sciences (Rangueil)
Unit of Modern Languages
Unit of Pharmaceutical Sciences
Unit of Physics, Chemistry and Automation
Unit of Readaptation Technology
Unit of Scientific Study of Physical and Sporting Ac-
   tivities
University Institute of Technology
Observatory and Space Sciences Institute

SPECIAL PROGRAMS:
Cooperative arrangements with universities in 27
countries, including Canada and the U.S.A.

LANGUAGE OF INSTRUCTION: French

ADMISSION REQUIREMENTS FOR FOREIGN STUDENTS:
Secondary school certificate (baccalauréat), or recognized foreign equivalent, or special entrance examination

TUITION FOR FOREIGN STUDENTS:
Fr 520–600 per year in 1990

TOTAL INSTRUCTIONAL FACULTY:
1,500

LIBRARY COLLECTIONS:
Medical library
Science library

UNIVERSITY PUBLICATIONS:
*Annales de la Faculté des Sciences, Bulletin, Annales de
Limnologie, Publication du Laboratoire de Statistiques*

PRESIDENT: Prof. Jean J. Conte

UNIVERSITÉ D'ANGERS
(University of Angers)
30 rue de Arènes, BP 3532, 49035 Angers Cedex,
France

CHARACTERISTICS OF INSTITUTION:
State-run, nonprofit university

DATE FOUNDED: 1971

TOTAL ENROLLMENT: 9,500 fulltime students (including 500 foreign students)

DEGREES AWARDED:
State qualifications
Law and Economics:
   Diplôme d'études universitaires générales (DEUG)
      two years required
   Licence
      one year after DEUG required
   Maîtrise
      one year after Licence required
   Maîtrise de sciences et techniques
      two years after DEUG required
   Diplôme d'études supérieures spécialisées (DESS)
      a minimum of one year following Maîtrise re-
      quired
   Diplôme d'études approfondies (DEA)
      one year after Maîtrise required
   Doctorat
      two–four years after DEA required
   Certificat de Capacité en Droit (law)
      two years required
Medicine:
   Doctorat en Médecine
      six years plus one year hospital practice and thesis
      required
   Certificats de spécialité
      a minimum of two years following doctorate re-
      quired
   Chirurgien-Dentiste
      five years required
Pharmacy:
   Diplôme de Pharmacien
      four years plus one year practical work required
   Doctorat en Pharmacie
      two *certificats* (études supérieures ou spéciales ou
      sciences) and thesis after Diplôme required
Science:
   Diplôme d'études universitaires générales (DEUG)
      two years required
   Licence ès Sciences
      one year after DEUG required
   Magistère de Tourisme
      one year after Licence required
   Maîtrise
      one year after Licence, or equivalent, required
   Maîtrise de sciences et techniques
      two years after DEUG required
   Diplôme d'études approfondies (DEA)
      one year after Maîtrise required
   Diplôme d'études supérieures spécialisées (DESS)
      one year after Maîtrise required
   Doctorat
      two–four years after DEA required
Letters and Human Sciences:

Diplôme d'études universitaires générales (DEUG)
  two years required
Licence ès Lettres
  one year after DEUG required
Maîtrise
  one year after Licence, or equivalent, required
Diplôme d'études approfondies (DEA)
  one year after Maîtrise required
Doctorat
  two–four years after DEA required
Diplôme universitaire de technologie (DUT)
  two years required

ACADEMIC PROGRAMS:
Faculty of Environment
Faculty of Law, Economic Sciences and Social Sciences
Faculty of Letters and Human Sciences
Faculty of Medicine and Pharmacy
Faculty of Structures and Materials
University Institute of Technology

SPECIAL PROGRAMS:
Cooperative arrangements with universities in 13 countries, including Canada and the United States

LANGUAGE OF INSTRUCTION: French

ADMISSION REQUIREMENTS FOR FOREIGN STUDENTS:
Secondary school certificate (baccalauréat), or recognized foreign equivalent, or special entrance examination

TUITION FOR FOREIGN STUDENTS:
Fr 520–600 per year in 1990

TOTAL INSTRUCTIONAL FACULTY:
412

LIBRARY COLLECTIONS:
Central library—50,000 volumes

UNIVERSITY PUBLICATIONS:
Plantes médicinales et phytothérapie

PRESIDENT: M. Bonneau

UNIVERSITÉ DE FRANCHE-COMTÉ
(University of Franche-Comté)
30 ave de l'Observatoire, 25030 Besançon Cedex, France

CHARACTERISTICS OF INSTITUTION:
State-run, nonprofit university

DATE FOUNDED: 1422

TOTAL ENROLLMENT: 16,000 fulltime students (including 2,000 foreign students)

DEGREES AWARDED:
State qualifications

Law and Economics:
  Diplôme d'études universitaires générales (DEUG)
    two years required
  Licence
    one year after DEUG required
  Maîtrise
    one year after Licence required
  Maîtrise de sciences et techniques
    two years after DEUG required
  Diplôme d'études supérieures spécialisées (DESS)
    a minimum of one year following Maîtrise required
  Diplôme d'études approfondies (DEA)
    one year after Maîtrise required
  Doctorat
    two–four years after DEA required
  Certificat de Capacité en Droit (law)
    two years required
Medicine:
  Doctorat en Médecine
    six years plus one year hospital practice and thesis required
  Certificats de spécialité
    a minimum of two years following doctorate required
  Chirurgien-Dentiste
    five years required
Pharmacy:
  Diplôme de Pharmacien
    four years plus one year practical work required
  Doctorat en Pharmacie
    two certificats (études supérieures ou spéciales ou sciences) and thesis after Diplôme required
Science:
  Diplôme d'études universitaires générales (DEUG)
    two years required
  Diplôme d'études universitaires scientifiques et techniques (DEUST)
    two years required
  Diplôme d'études universitaires de formation générale scientifique (DUFGS)
    two years required
  Licence ès Sciences
    one year after DEUG required
  Maîtrise
    one year after Licence, or equivalent, required
  Diplôme d'études approfondies (DEA)
    one year after Maîtrise required
  Diplôme d'études supérieures spécialisées (DESS)
    one year after Maîtrise required
  Doctorat
    two–four years after DEA required
Letters and Human Sciences:
  Diplôme d'études universitaires générales (DEUG)
    two years required
  Licence ès Lettres

one year after DEUG required
Maîtrise
  one year after Licence, or equivalent, required
Diplôme d'études supérieures spécialisées (DESS)
  one year after Maîtrise required
Diplôme d'études approfondies (DEA)
  one year after Maîtrise required
Doctorat
  two–four years after DEA required
Diplôme universitaire de technologie (DUT)
  two years required
Diplôme d'études universitaires générales (DEUG)
in physical education
Certificats and Diplômes d'études françaises (for foreign students)

ACADEMIC PROGRAMS:
Unit of Law, Economics and Politics
Unit of Literature and Human Sciences
Unit of Medicine and Pharmacy
Unit of Physical Education and Sport
Unit of Science and Technology
University Institute of Technology (Besançon)
University Institute of Technology (Belfort)

SPECIAL PROGRAMS:
Cooperative arrangements with 30 other universities, including Université du Québec, State University of New York, the University of Baltimore and the University of Washington

LANGUAGE OF INSTRUCTION: French

ADMISSION REQUIREMENTS FOR FOREIGN STUDENTS:
Secondary school certificate *(baccalauréat)*, or recognized foreign equivalent, or special entrance examination

TUITION FOR FOREIGN STUDENTS:
Fr 520–600 per year in 1990

TOTAL INSTRUCTIONAL FACULTY:
840

LIBRARY COLLECTIONS:
Central library—300,000 volumes
Scientific library

UNIVERSITY PUBLICATIONS:
Annales Litteratures de l'Université, Journal de Médecine de Besançon, Annales Scientifiques de l'Université, Revue Géographique de l'Est, Annales de l'Observatoire de Besançon, Annales économiques de l'Université, Annales médicales de l'Université

PRESIDENT: Jean-François Robert

UNIVERSITÉ DE CLERMONT-FERRAND I
(University of Clermont-Ferrand I)

49 blvd Gergovia, BP 32, 63001 Clermont-Ferrand Cedex, France

CHARACTERISTICS OF INSTITUTION:
State-run, nonprofit university

DATE FOUNDED: 1976

TOTAL ENROLLMENT: 8,300 fulltime students

DEGREES AWARDED:
State qualifications
Law and Economics:
  Diplôme d'études universitaires générales (DEUG)
    two years required
  Licence
    one year after DEUG required
  Maîtrise
    one year after Licence required
  Diplôme d'études supérieures spécialisées (DESS)
    a minimum of two semesters following Maîtrise required
  Diplôme d'études approfondies (DEA)
    one year after Maîtrise required
  Doctorat
    two–four years after DEA required
  Certificat de Capacité en Droit (law)
    two years required
Medicine:
  Doctorat en Médecine
    six years plus one year hospital practice and thesis required
  Certificats de spécialité
    a minimum of two years following doctorate required
  Chirurgien-Dentiste
    five years required
Pharmacy:
  Diplôme de Pharmacien
    four years plus one year practical work required
  Doctorat en Pharmacie
    two *certificats* (études supérieures ou spéciales ou sciences) and thesis after Diplôme required
  Diplôme universitaire de technologie (DUT)
    two years required

ACADEMIC PROGRAMS:
Unit of Dentistry
Unit of Economic and Social Sciences
Unit of Law and Politics
Unit of Medicine
Unit of Pharmacy
University Institute of Technology
Institute of Hydrology and Bioclimatology

SPECIAL PROGRAMS:
Cooperative arrangements with seven other universities, including the University of Michigan

LANGUAGE OF INSTRUCTION: French

ADMISSION REQUIREMENTS FOR FOREIGN STUDENTS:
Secondary school certificate (baccalauréat), brevet supérieur or recognized foreign equivalent, or special entrance examination

TUITION FOR FOREIGN STUDENTS:
Fr 520–600 per year in 1990

TOTAL INSTRUCTIONAL FACULTY:
500

LIBRARY COLLECTIONS:
Central library—327,000 volumes
Medicine and pharmacy library—31,000 volumes
Law library—65,000 volumes

PRESIDENT: Annie Rouhette

UNIVERSITÉ DE CLERMONT-FERRAND II
(UNIVERSITÉ BLAISE PASCAL)
(University of Clermont-Ferrand II [University Blaise Pascal])
34 ave Carnot, BP 185, 63006 Clermont-Ferrand Cedex, France

CHARACTERISTICS OF INSTITUTION:
State-run, nonprofit university

DATE FOUNDED: 1810

TOTAL ENROLLMENT: 11,150 fulltime students (including 1,000 foreign students)

DEGREES AWARDED:
State qualifications
Science:
    Diplôme d'études universitaires générales (DEUG)
        two years required
    Diplôme d'études universitaires scientifiques et techniques (DEUST)
        two years required
    Licence ès Sciences
        one year after DEUG required
    Maîtrise
        one year after Licence, or equivalent, required
    Diplôme d'Ingenieur
        one year after Maîtrise de sciences et techniques required
    Diplôme d'études approfondies (DEA)
        one year after Maîtrise required
    Doctorat
        two–four years after DEA required
Letters and Human Sciences:
    Diplôme d'études universitaires générales (DEUG)
        two years required
    Licence ès Lettres
        one year after DEUG required
    Maîtrise
        one year after Licence, or equivalent, required

Diplôme d'études approfondies (DEA)
    one year after Maîtrise required
Doctorat
    two–four years after DEA required
Diplôme universitaire de technologie (DUT)
    two years required

ACADEMIC PROGRAMS:
Unit of Applied Language and Communication
Unit of Engineering Sciences
Unit of Exact and Natural Sciences
Unit of Literature and Human Sciences
Unit of Physical Education and Sport
Unit of Psychology, Social Sciences and Educational Science
Unit of Scientific and Technical Research
National Higher School of Chemistry
Geophysics Institute and Observatory
Mathematics Research Institute
University Institute of Technology
Computer Center

SPECIAL PROGRAMS:
Cooperative arrangements with 20 other universities, including the University of California (Los Angeles), the University of Delaware and the University of Oklahoma

LANGUAGE OF INSTRUCTION: French

ADMISSION REQUIREMENTS FOR FOREIGN STUDENTS:
Secondary school certificate (baccalauréat), brevet supérieur or recognized foreign equivalent, or special entrance examination

TUITION FOR FOREIGN STUDENTS:
Fr 520–600 per year in 1990

TOTAL INSTRUCTIONAL FACULTY:
652

LIBRARY COLLECTIONS:
Central library—350,000 volumes
Letters library—14 volumes
Sciences library—50,000 volumes

PRESIDENT: C. Boutin

UNIVERSITÉ DE BOURGOGNE
(University of Bourgogne)
Campus de Montmuzard, BP 138, 21004 Dijon Cedex, France

CHARACTERISTICS OF INSTITUTION:
State-run, nonprofit university

DATE FOUNDED: 1970

TOTAL ENROLLMENT: 20,600 fulltime students (including 1,450 foreign students)

DEGREES AWARDED:
State qualifications
Law and Economics:
  Diplôme d'études universitaires générales (DEUG)
    two years required
  Licence
    three years required
  Maîtrise
    one year after Licence required
  Diplôme d'études supérieures spécialisées (DESS)
    one year after Maîtrise required
  Doctorat
    two–four years after DEA required
  Certificat de Capacité en Droit (law)
    two years required
Science:
  Diplôme d'études universitaires générales (DEUG)
    two years required
  Licence ès Sciences
    one year after DEUG required
  Maîtrise
    one year after Licence, or equivalent, required
  Diplôme d'études approfondies (DEA)
    one year after Maîtrise required
  Diplôme d'études supérieures spécialisées (DESS)
    one year after Maîtrise required
  Doctorat de spécialité
    two–four years after DEA required
Medicine:
  Doctorat en Médecine
    six years plus one year hospital practice and thesis
    required
  Certificats de spécialité
    a minimum of two years following doctorate re-
    quired
Pharmacy:
  Diplôme de Pharmacien
    four years plus one year practical work required
  Doctorat en Pharmacie
    two *certificats* (études supérieures ou spéciales ou
    sciences) and thesis after Diplôme required
  Diplôme d'études supérieures spécialisées (DESS)
    one year required
Viticulture:
  Diplôme de technicien d'oenology
    one year required
  Diplôme national d'oenology
    two years required
Letters and Human Sciences:
  Diplôme d'études universitaires générales (DEUG)
    two years required
  Licence ès Lettres
    one year after DEUG required
  Maîtrise
    one year after Licence, or equivalent, required
  Diplôme d'études supérieures spécialisées (DESS)

    one year after Maîtrise required
  Diplôme d'études approfondies (DEA)
    one year after Maîtrise required
  Doctorat
    two–four years after DEA required
  Diplôme universitaire de technologie (DUT)
    two years required
  Licence en sciences et techniques des Activities
  physiques et sportives
    one–two years following DEUG required
  Certificat and Diplômes d'études françaises (for
  foreign students)

ACADEMIC PROGRAMS:
Faculty of Earth Sciences
Faculty of Economics and Business Administration
Faculty of Foreign Languages and Civilizations
Faculty of Human Sciences
Faculty of Law and Political Sciences
Faculty of Letters and Philosophy
Faculty of Medicine
Faculty of Pharmaceutical and Biological Sciences
Faculty of Science and Technology (including math-
    ematics, data processing, physics and chemistry)
Unit of Physical Education and Sport
Unit of Science (Life and Environmental Sciences)
Institute of Nutritional Biology
University Institute of Technology (Dijon)
University Institute of Technology (Le Creusot)

SPECIAL PROGRAMS:
Cooperative arrangements with 11 other universities, including Université du Québec, University of
New Hampshire, University of Illinois and Worcester State University in Massachusetts

LANGUAGE OF INSTRUCTION: French

ADMISSION REQUIREMENTS FOR FOREIGN STUDENTS:
Secondary school certificate (*baccalauréat*), or recognized foreign equivalent, or special entrance examination

TUITION FOR FOREIGN STUDENTS:
Fr 520–600 per year in 1990

TOTAL INSTRUCTIONAL FACULTY:
880

LIBRARY COLLECTIONS:
Central library—505,000 volumes

UNIVERSITY PUBLICATIONS:
Bulletin, Livret de la Recherche

PRESIDENT: Gilles Bertrand

UNIVERSITÉ DE LIMOGES
(University of Limoges)

Hôtel Burgy, 13 rue de Genève, 87065 Limoges Cedex, France

CHARACTERISTICS OF INSTITUTION:
State-run, nonprofit university

DATE FOUNDED: 1970

TOTAL ENROLLMENT: 10,000 fulltime students (including 750 foreign students)

DEGREES AWARDED:
State qualifications
Law and Economics:
Diplôme d'études universitaires scientifiques et techniques (DEUST)
two years required
Diplôme d'études universitaires générales (DEUG)
two years required
Licence
three years required
Maîtrise
one year after Licence required
Diplôme d'études supérieures spécialisées (DESS)
a minimum of two semesters following Maîtrise required
Diplôme d'études approfondies (DEA)
one year after Maîtrise required
Doctorat
two–four years after DEA required
Certificat de Capacité en Droit (law)
two years required
Medicine:
Doctorat en Médecine
six years plus one year hospital practice and thesis required
Certificats de spécialité
a minimum of two years following doctorate required
Pharmacy:
Diplôme de Pharmacien
four years plus one year practical work required
Doctorat en Pharmacie
two *certificats* (études supérieures ou spéciales ou sciences) and thesis after Diplôme required
Diplôme d'études supérieures spécialisées (DESS) en Pharmacotechnie-vétérinaire
four–five years required
Science:
Diplôme d'études universitaires générales (DEUG)
two years required
Licence ès Sciences
one year after DEUG required
Maîtrise
one year after Licence, or equivalent, required
Diplôme d'études approfondies (DEA)
one year after Maîtrise required
Diplôme d'études supérieures spécialisées (DESS)

one year after Maîtrise required
Doctorat de spécialité
two–four years after DEA required
Letters and Human Sciences:
Diplôme d'études universitaires générales (DEUG)
two years required
Licence ès Lettres
one year after DEUG required
Maîtrise
one year after Licence, or equivalent, required
Diplôme d'études approfondies (DEA)
one year after Maîtrise required
Doctorat
two–four years after DEA required
Diplôme universitaire de technologie (DUT)
two years required
Certificat and Diplôme d'études françaises (for foreign students)

ACADEMIC PROGRAMS:
Unit of Law and Economic Sciences
Unit of Letters and Social Sciences
Unit of Medicine
Unit of Pharmacy
Unit of Sciences
University Institute of Technology

SPECIAL PROGRAMS: Cooperative arrangements with 16 other universities, including McGill University in Canada

LANGUAGE OF INSTRUCTION: French

ADMISSION REQUIREMENTS FOR FOREIGN STUDENTS:
Secondary school certificate *(baccalauréat)*, or recognized foreign equivalent, or special entrance examination

TUITION FOR FOREIGN STUDENTS:
Fr 520–600 per year in 1990

TOTAL INSTRUCTIONAL FACULTY:
559

LIBRARY COLLECTIONS:
Total collection—181,800 volumes

PRESIDENT: Pierre Pouthier

UNIVERSITÉ DE METZ
(University of Metz)
Île de Saulcy, BP 794, 57012 Metz Cedex 1, France

CHARACTERISTICS OF INSTITUTION:
State-run nonprofit university

DATE FOUNDED: 1971

TOTAL ENROLLMENT: 9,100 fulltime students

DEGREES AWARDED:
State qualifications
Law:
  Diplôme d'études universitaires générales (DEUG)
    two years required
  Licence en Droit
    one year after DEUG required
  Maîtrise de sciences de gestion
    one–two years after Licence required
  Certificat de Capacité en Droit (law)
    two years required
Science:
  Diplôme d'études universitaires générales (DEUG)
    two years required
  Licence ès Sciences
    one year after DEUG required
  Maîtrise
    one year after Licence, or equivalent, required
  Diplôme d'études approfondies (DEA)
    one year after Maîtrise required
  Doctorat
    two–four years after DEA required
Letters and Human Sciences:
  Diplôme d'études universitaires générales (DEUG)
    two years required
  Licence ès Lettres
    one year after DEUG required
  Maîtrise
    one year after Licence, or equivalent, required
  Diplôme d'études approfondies (DEA)
    one year after Maîtrise required
  Doctorat
    two–four years after DEA required
  Diplôme universitaire de technologie (DUT)
    two years required
  Diplôme universitaire d'Écologie générale et des
  Sciences de l'Environment
    two years required

ACADEMIC PROGRAMS:
Unit of Economic, Social and Legal Sciences
Unit of Exact and Natural Sciences
Unit of Letters and Human Sciences
University Institute of Technology

LANGUAGE OF INSTRUCTION: French

ADMISSION REQUIREMENTS FOR FOREIGN STUDENTS:
Secondary school certificate (baccalauréat), or recognized foreign equivalent, or special entrance examination

TUITION FOR FOREIGN STUDENTS:
Fr 520–600 per year in 1990

TOTAL INSTRUCTIONAL FACULTY:
309

LIBRARY COLLECTIONS:
Total collection—70,000 volumes

PRESIDENT: D. Durand

UNIVERSITÉ DU MAINE
(University of Maine)
route de Laval, BP 535, 72017 Le Mans Cedex, France

CHARACTERISTICS OF INSTITUTION:
State-run, nonprofit university

DATE FOUNDED: 1969

TOTAL ENROLLMENT: 7,050 fulltime students (including 500 foreign students)

DEGREES AWARDED:
State qualifications
Law and Economics:
  Diplôme d'études universitaires générales (DEUG)
    two years required
  Licence
    one year after DEUG required
  Maîtrise
    one year after Licence required
  Diplôme d'études supérieures spécialisées (DESS)
    a minimum of two semesters following Maîtrise
    required
  Diplôme d'études approfondies (DEA)
    one year after Maîtrise required
  Doctorat
    two–four years after DEA required
  Certificat de Capacité en Droit (law)
    two years required
Science:
  Diplôme d'études universitaires générales (DEUG)
    two years required
  Licence ès Sciences
    one year after DEUG required
  Maîtrise
    one year after Licence, or equivalent, required
  Diplôme d'études approfondies (DEA)
    one year after Maîtrise required
  Doctorat
    two–four years after DEA required
Letters and Human Sciences:
  Diplôme d'études universitaires générales (DEUG)
    two years required
  Licence ès Lettres
    one year after DEUG required
  Maîtrise
    one year after Licence, or equivalent, required
  Diplôme d'études approfondies (DEA)
    one year after Maîtrise required
  Doctorat
    two–four years after DEA required

Diplôme universitaire de technologie (DUT)
two years required
Certificat and Diplôme d'études françaises (for foreign students)

ACADEMIC PROGRAMS:
Faculty of Economic, Legal and Social Sciences
Faculty of Letters and Human Sciences
Faculty of Sciences
University Institute of Technology

SPECIAL PROGRAMS:
Cooperative arrangements with nine other universities, including Stanford University in California and the University of Maine at Farmington

LANGUAGE OF INSTRUCTION: French

ADMISSION REQUIREMENTS FOR FOREIGN STUDENTS:
Secondary school certificate (baccalauréat), or recognized foreign equivalent, or special entrance examination

TUITION FOR FOREIGN STUDENTS:
Fr 520–600 per year in 1990

TOTAL INSTRUCTIONAL FACULTY:
280

LIBRARY COLLECTIONS:
Interuniversity library
Science—8,500 volumes
Letters and Law—28,300 volumes
Technology—7,500 volumes

UNIVERSITY PUBLICATIONS:
Livret de l'Etudiant

PRESIDENT: J. L. Jolivet

UNIVERSITÉ DE NANTES
(University of Nantes)
1 quai de Tourville, BP 1026, 44035 Nantes Cedex 01, France

CHARACTERISTICS OF INSTITUTION:
State-run, nonprofit university

DATE FOUNDED: 1970

TOTAL ENROLLMENT: 20,000 fulltime students (including 1,750 foreign students)

DEGREES AWARDED:
State qualifications
Law and Economics:
Diplôme d'études universitaires générales (DEUG)
two years required
Licence
one year after DEUG required
Maîtrise
one year after Licence required

Diplôme d'études supérieures spécialisées (DESS)
a minimum two semesters following Maîtrise required
Diplôme d'études approfondies (DEA)
one year after Maîtrise required
Doctorat
two–four years after DEA required
Certificat de Capacité en Droit (law)
two years required
Medicine:
Doctorat en Médecine
six years plus one year hospital practice and thesis required
Certificats de spécialité
a minimum two years following doctorate required
Chirurgien-Dentiste
five years required
Pharmacy:
Diplôme de Pharmacien
four years plus one year practical work required
Doctorat en Pharmacie
two certificats (études supérieures ou spéciales ou sciences)
and thesis after Diplôme required
Science:
Diplôme d'études universitaires générales (DEUG)
two years required
Diplôme d'études universitaires scientifiques et techniques (DEUST)
two years required
Licence ès Sciences
one year after DEUG required
Maîtrise
one year after Licence, or equivalent, required
Diplôme d'études approfondies (DEA)
one year after Maîtrise required
Diplôme d'études supérieures spécialisées (DESS)
one year after Maîtrise required
Doctorat
two–four years after DEA required
Letters and Human Sciences:
Diplôme d'études universitaires générales (DEUG)
two years required
Licence ès Lettres
one year after DEUG required
Maîtrise
one year after Licence, or equivalent, required
Diplôme d'études approfondies (DEA)
one year after Maîtrise required
Doctorat
two–four years after DEA required
Diplôme Universitaire de technologie (DUT)
two years required

ACADEMIC PROGRAMS:
Unit of Arts and Human Sciences
Unit of Business Studies
Unit of Dentistry
Unit of Economics
Unit of Geography
Unit of History and Sociology
Unit of Languages
Unit of Law
Unit of Medicine
Unit of Pharmacology
Unit of Sciences
National Higher School of Mechanical Engineering
Higher Institute of Electronics
Institute of Technology (Nantes)
Institute of Technology (St.-Nazaire)
Institute of Preparatory Administrative Studies
Institute of Thermodynamics and Materials

SPECIAL PROGRAMS:
Cooperative arrangements with nine other universities, including Université du Québec and Seattle University

LANGUAGE OF INSTRUCTION: French

ADMISSION REQUIREMENTS FOR FOREIGN STUDENTS:
Secondary school certificate (baccalauréat), or recognized foreign equivalent, or special entrance examination

TUITION FOR FOREIGN STUDENTS:
Fr 520–600 per year in 1990

TOTAL INSTRUCTIONAL FACULTY:
911

LIBRARY COLLECTIONS:
University library—166,000 volumes
Specialized libraries

PRESIDENT: S. Renaudin

UNIVERSITÉ DE PERPIGNAN
(University of Perpignan)
ave de Villeneuve, 66025 Perpignan Cedex, France

CHARACTERISTICS OF INSTITUTION:
State-run, nonprofit university

DATE FOUNDED: 1971

TOTAL ENROLLMENT: 4,500 fulltime students (including 550 foreign students)

DEGREES AWARDED:
State qualifications
Science:
  Diplôme d'études universitaires générales (DEUG)
    two years required

Licence ès Sciences
  one year after DEUG required
Maîtrise
  one year after Licence, or equivalent, required
Diplôme d'études approfondies (DEA)
  one year after Maîtrise required
Doctorat
  two–four years after DEA required
Letters and Human Sciences:
  Diplôme d'études universitaires générales (DEUG)
    two years required
  Licence ès Lettres
    one year after DEUG required
  Maîtrise
    one year after Licence, or equivalent, required
  Diplôme d'études approfondies (DEA)
    one year after Maîtrise required
  Doctorat
    two–four years after DEA required
  Diplôme universitaire de technologie (DUT)
    two years required
  Certificat and Diplôme d'études françaises (for foreign students)

ACADEMIC PROGRAMS:
Unit of Exact and Natural Sciences
Unit of Humanities and Social Sciences (including law and economics)
University Institute of Technology

SPECIAL PROGRAMS:
Cooperative arrangements with universities in 38 other countries

LANGUAGE OF INSTRUCTION: French

ADMISSION REQUIREMENTS FOR FOREIGN STUDENTS:
Secondary school certificate (baccalauréat), or recognized foreign equivalent, or special entrance examination

TUITION FOR FOREIGN STUDENTS:
Fr 520–600 per year in 1990

TOTAL INSTRUCTIONAL FACULTY:
230

LIBRARY COLLECTIONS:
Central library
Law library
Science library

PRESIDENT: Henri Got

UNIVERSITÉ D'ORLÉANS
(University of Orléans)
Château de la Source, BP 6749,
45067 Orléans Cedex 2, France

CHARACTERISTICS OF INSTITUTION:
State-run, nonprofit university

DATE FOUNDED: 1971

TOTAL ENROLLMENT: 9,200 fulltime students

DEGREES AWARDED:
State qualifications
Law and Economics:
  Diplôme d'études universitaires générales (DEUG)
    two years required
  Licence
    one year after DEUG required
  Maîtrise
    one year after Licence required
  Diplôme d'études supérieures spécialisées (DESS)
    a minimum of one semester following Maîtrise
    required
  Diplôme d'études approfondies (DEA)
    one year after Maîtrise required
  Doctorat
    two–four years after DEA required
  Certificat de Capacité en Droit (law)
    two years required
Science:
  Diplôme d'études universitaires générales (DEUG)
    two years required
  Maîtrise
    two years after DEUG required
  Diplôme d'études supérieures spécialisées (DESS)
    one year after Maîtrise required
  Diplôme d'études approfondies (DEA)
    one year after Maîtrise required
  Doctorat en Sciences
    two–four years after DEA required
Letters and Human Sciences:
  Diplôme d'études universitaires générales (DEUG)
    two years required
  Licence ès Lettres
    one year after DEUG required
  Maîtrise
    one year after Licence, or equivalent, required
  Diplôme d'études approfondies (DEA)
    one year after Maîtrise required
  Doctorat
    two–four years after DEA required
  Diplôme universitaire de technologie (DUT)
    two years required

ACADEMIC PROGRAMS:
Unit of Law, Economics and Management
Unit of Letters, Languages and Human Sciences
Unit of Sciences
Higher School of Energy and Material Resources
Mathematics Teaching Research Institute
University Institute of Technology (Orleans)
University Institute of Technology (Bourges)

Institute of Biological Sciences
Institute of Economic Law
Institute of Financial and Monetary Research
Institute of Juridicial Studies

LANGUAGE OF INSTRUCTION: French

ADMISSION REQUIREMENTS FOR FOREIGN STUDENTS:
Secondary school certificate (baccalauréat), or recognized foreign equivalent, or special entrance examination

TUITION FOR FOREIGN STUDENTS:
Fr 520–600 per year in 1990

TOTAL INSTRUCTIONAL FACULTY:
398

LIBRARY COLLECTIONS:
Central library—60,000 volumes
Specialized libraries

UNIVERSITY PUBLICATIONS:
Bulletin d'informations de l'Université, Plaquette en direction des entreprises, Revue "Symbioses" Biologie

PRESIDENT: William Marois

UNIVERSITÉ DE POITIERS
(University of Poitiers)
15 rue de Blossac, 86034 Poitiers Cedex, France

CHARACTERISTICS OF INSTITUTION:
State-run, nonprofit university

DATE FOUNDED: 1432

TOTAL ENROLLMENT: 22,000 fulltime students (including 1,700 foreign students)

DEGREES AWARDED:
State qualifications
Law and Economics:
  Diplôme d'études universitaires générales (DEUG)
    two years required
  Licence
    one year after DEUG required
  Maîtrise
    one year after Licence required
  Diplôme d'études supérieures spécialisées (DESS)
    a minimum of two semesters following Maîtrise
    required
  Diplôme d'études approfondies (DEA)
    one year after Maîtrise required
  Doctorat
    two–four years after DEA required
  Certificat de Capacité en Droit (law)
    two years required

Medicine:
  Doctorat en Médecine
    six years plus 1 year hospital practice and thesis
    required
  Certificats de spécialité
    a minimum of two years following doctorate re-
    quired
Pharmacy:
  Diplôme de Pharmacien
    four years plus one year practical work required
  Doctorat en Pharmacie
    two *certificats* (études supérieures ou spéciales ou
    sciences) and thesis after Diplôme required
Science:
  Diplôme d'études universitaires générales (DEUG)
    two years required
  Licence ès Sciences
    one year after DEUG required
  Maîtrise
    one year after Licence, or equivalent, required
  Diplôme d'études approfondies (DEA)
    one year after Maîtrise required
  Doctorat en Sciences
    two–four years after DEA required
Letters and Human Sciences:
  Diplôme d'études universitaires générales (DEUG)
    two years required
  Licence ès Lettres
    one year after DEUG required
  Maîtrise
    one year after Licence, or equivalent, required
  Diplôme d'études approfondies (DEA)
    one year after Maîtrise required
  Doctorat
    two–four years after DEA required
  Diplôme universitaire de technologie (DUT)
    two years required

ACADEMIC PROGRAMS:
Unit of Economics
Unit of Exact and Natural Sciences
Unit of Fundamental and Applied Sciences
Unit of Human Sciences
Unit of Languages and Literatures
Unit of Law and Social Sciences
Unit of Medicine and Pharmacy
Unit of Science and Technology
National Higher School of Mechanical and Aeronau-
  tical Engineering
Regional Institute for Physical Education and Sport
University Institute of Business Administration
University Institute of Technology (Poitiers)
University Institute of Technology (La Rochelle)
Center for Aerodynamic and Thermal Studies
Center for Higher Studies of Medieval Civilization

SPECIAL PROGRAMS:
Cooperative arrangements with 23 universities, including the University of California and Université
du Québec

LANGUAGE OF INSTRUCTION: French

ADMISSION REQUIREMENTS FOR FOREIGN STUDENTS:
Secondary school certificate (*baccalauréat*), or recognized foreign equivalent, or special entrance examination

TUITION FOR FOREIGN STUDENTS:
Fr 520–600 per year in 1990
French studies for foreign students—Fr 2,600 per year
in 1990

TOTAL INSTRUCTIONAL FACULTY:
595

LIBRARY COLLECTIONS:
Total collection—322,500 volumes

UNIVERSITY PUBLICATIONS:
Cahiers de civilisation médievale, La Licorne

PRESIDENT: Réné Giraud

UNIVERSITÉ DE RENNES I
(University of Rennes I)
2 rue du Thàbor, 35000 Rennes, France

CHARACTERISTICS OF INSTITUTION:
State-run, nonprofit university

DATE FOUNDED: 1970

TOTAL ENROLLMENT: 21,150 fulltime students (including 1,300 foreign students)

DEGREES AWARDED:
State qualifications
Law and Economics:
  Diplôme d'études universitaires générales (DEUG)
    two years required
  Licence
    one year after DEUG required
  Maîtrise
    one year after Licence required
  Diplôme d'études supérieures spécialisées (DESS)
    a minimum of one year following Maîtrise re-
    quired
  Diplôme d'études approfondies (DEA)
    one year after Maîtrise required
  Doctorat
    two–four years after DEA required
  Certificat de Capacité en Droit (law)
    two years required
Medicine:
  Doctorat en Médecine

six years plus one year hospital practice and thesis required

Certificats de spécialité
a minimum of two years following doctorate required

Chirurgien-Dentiste
five years required

Pharmacy:
Diplôme de Pharmacien
four years plus one year practical work required

Doctorat en Pharmacie
two *certificats* (études supérieures ou spéciales ou sciences) and thesis after Diplôme required

Science:
Diplôme d'études universitaires générales (DEUG)
two years required

Licence ès Sciences
one year after DEUG required

Magistère in mathematics
three years after DEUG or DUT required

Maîtrise
one year after Licence, or equivalent, required

Diplôme d'études approfondies (DEA)
one year after Maîtrise required

Doctorat
two–four years after DEA required

Letters and Human Sciences:
Diplôme d'études universitaires générales (DEUG)
two years required

Licence ès Lettres
one year after DEUG required

Maîtrise
one year after Licence, or equivalent, required

Diplôme d'études approfondies (DEA)
one year after Maîtrise required

Doctorat
two–four years after DEA required

Diplôme universitaire de technologie (DUT)
two years required

ACADEMIC PROGRAMS:
Unit of Behavioral and Environmental Sciences
Unit of Clinical and Therapeutic Medicine
Unit of Dentistry
Unit of Economics and Management Economics
Unit of Juridicial Sciences
Unit of Mathematics and Computer Sciences
Unit of Medicaments
Unit of Philosophy
Unit of Physio-Chemistry and Biology
Unit of Public Health
Unit of Structure and Properties of Matter
School of Applied Sciences and Technology
Mathematics Teaching Research Institute
Institute of Technology (Rennes)
Institute of Technology (Lannion)

SPECIAL PROGRAMS:
Cooperative arrangements with 21 universities, including the University of California at Davis

LANGUAGE OF INSTRUCTION: French

ADMISSION REQUIREMENTS FOR FOREIGN STUDENTS:
Secondary school certificate *(baccalauréat)*, or recognized foreign equivalent, or special entrance examination

TUITION FOR FOREIGN STUDENTS:
Fr 520–600 year in 1990

TOTAL INSTRUCTIONAL FACULTY:
1,060

LIBRARY COLLECTIONS:
Interuniversity library
Specialized libraries

MUSEUMS AND GALLERIES:
Musée préhistorique Armoricain de Penmarc'h (Finistère)

UNIVERSITY PUBLICATIONS:
Bulletin "Université-Informations," Bulletin de la Société Scientifique de Bretagne

PRESIDENT: J.-C. Hardouin

UNIVERSITÉ DE RENNES II
(UNIVERSITÉ DE HAUTE BRETAGNE)
(University of Rennes II [University of Haute-Bretagne])
6 ave Gaston Berger, 35043 Rennes Cedex, France

CHARACTERISTICS OF INSTITUTION:
State-run, nonprofit university

DATE FOUNDED: 1970

TOTAL ENROLLMENT: 13,000 fulltime students

DEGREES AWARDED:
State qualifications
Letters and Human Sciences:
Diplôme d'études universitaires générales (DEUG)
two years required

Licence ès Lettres
one year after DEUG required

Maîtrise
one year after Licence, or equivalent, required

Diplôme d'études supérieures spécialisées (DESS)
one year after Maîtrise required

Diplôme d'études approfondies (DEA)
one year after Maîtrise required

Doctorat
two–four years after DEA required

Diplôme universitaire de technologie (DUT)
two years required

Certificat and Diplômes d'études françaises (for foreign students)

ACADEMIC PROGRAMS:
Unit of Arts
Unit of Economic and Social Administration
Unit of English
Unit of Geography and Environment
Unit of History and Political Sciences
Unit of Language and Culture
Unit of Literature
Unit of Modern Languages
Unit of Physical Education and Sport
Unit of Psychology, Sociology and Education
Armoricain Institute of Economic and Human Research
Institute of the Social Sciences of Employment
University Institute of Technology (Vannes)

SPECIAL PROGRAMS:
Cooperative arrangements with 30 universities, including the University of Rochester in New York, Beloit College in Wisconsin, Occidental College in Los Angeles, Nazareth College of Rochester in New York and Rice University in Texas

TUITION FOR FOREIGN STUDENTS:
Fr 520–600 per year in 1990

TOTAL INSTRUCTIONAL FACULTY:
360

LIBRARY COLLECTIONS:
Interuniversity library—397,550 volumes

UNIVERSITY PUBLICATIONS:
Rennes 2 Actualites, R2 Recherche, Tetrologiques, Interférences, Mondes hispanophones, Annales de Bretagne et des Pays de l'Ouest, Norois (Revue de Géographes), Arts de l'Ouest, Annales du Lévant, Dossiers de Télédetection

PRESIDENT: Jean Mounier

UNIVERSITÉ DE TOURS
(UNIVERSITÉ FRANÇOIS RABELAIS)
(University of Tours [University François Rabelais])
3 rue des Tanneurs, 37041 Tours Cedex, France

CHARACTERISTICS OF INSTITUTION:
State-run, nonprofit university

DATE FOUNDED: 1970

TOTAL ENROLLMENT: 20,000 fulltime students (including 2,000 foreign students)

DEGREES AWARDED:
State qualifications
Law and Economics:
Diplôme d'études universitaires générales (DEUG)
two years required

Licence
one year after DEUG required
Maîtrise
one year after Licence required
Diplôme d'études supérieures spécialisées (DESS)
a minimum of one year following Maîtrise required
Diplôme d'études approfondies (DEA)
one year after Maîtrise required
Doctorat
two–four years after DEA required
Certificat de Capacité en Droit (law)
two years required
Medicine:
Doctorat en Médecine
six years plus one year hospital practice and thesis required
Certificats de spécialité
a minimum of two years following doctorate required
Chirurgien-Dentiste
five years required
Diplôme de Sage-Femme (midwifery)
three years required
Pharmacy:
Diplôme de Pharmacien
four years plus one year practical work required
Doctorat en Pharmacie
two *certificats* (études supérieures ou spéciales ou sciences) and thesis after Diplôme required
Science:
Diplôme d'études universitaires scientifiques et techniques (DEUST)
two years required
Diplôme d'études universitaires générales (DEUG)
two years required
Licence ès Sciences
one year after DEUG required
Maîtrise
one year after Licence, or equivalent, required
Maîtrise des sciences et techniques
one–two years following Licence required
Diplôme d'études supérieures spécialisées (DESS)
one year after Maîtrise required
Diplôme d'études approfondies (DEA)
one year after Maîtrise required
Doctorat en Sciences
two–four years after DEA required
Letters and Human Sciences:
Diplôme d'études universitaires générales (DEUG)
two years required
Licence ès Lettres
one year after DEUG required
Maîtrise
one year after Licence, or equivalent, required
Diplôme d'études approfondies (DEA)

one year after Maîtrise required
Doctorat
two–four years after DEA required
Diplôme universitaire de technologie (DUT)
two years required
Certificat and Diplôme d'études françaises (for foreign students)

ACADEMIC PROGRAMS:
Unit of Art and Science of Man
Unit of Classical and Modern Languages, Literatures and Civilizations
Unit of Exact and Natural Sciences
Unit of Language, Literature and Civilization of English-speaking Countries
Unit of Law, Economics and Social Sciences
Unit of Medicine
Unit of Pharmacy
Unit of Town Planning and Geography
University Institute of Technology
Center for Renaissance Studies

SPECIAL PROGRAMS:
Cooperative arrangements with 24 universities, including Rutgers—The State University in New Jersey, Stanford University in California and Sweet Briar College in Virginia

LANGUAGE OF INSTRUCTION: French

ADMISSION REQUIREMENTS FOR FOREIGN STUDENTS:
Secondary school certificate (baccalauréat), or recognized foreign equivalent, or special entrance examination

TUITION FOR FOREIGN STUDENTS:
Fr 520–600 per year in 1990

TOTAL INSTRUCTIONAL FACULTY:
700

LIBRARY COLLECTIONS:
Letters and Law—91,500 volumes
Medicine—17,500 volumes
Science—12,400 volumes

UNIVERSITY PUBLICATIONS:
François Rabelais Informations, Études du XVIIe, Cahiers de l'Institut d'Histoire de la Presse et de l'Opinion, Bulletin de la Société ligèrienne de Philosophie, Cahiers de l'Analyse sociologique, L'Emploi des Femmes, Bulletin de Psychologie, Textes et documents du XVIe, Cahiers de la Loire moyenne, Bulletin de Recherche sur l'Enseignement du Français, Études Latines "Caesarodunum"

PRESIDENT: Jean Germain

COLLÈGE DE FRANCE
(College of France)

11 place Marcelin-Berthélot, 75231 Paris Cedex 05, France

CHARACTERISTICS OF INSTITUTION:
State-run, nonprofit university

DATE FOUNDED: 1530

DEGREES AWARDED:
None

ACADEMIC PROGRAMS:
Faculty of Letters
Faculty of Science

LANGUAGE OF INSTRUCTION: French

ADMISSION REQUIREMENTS FOR FOREIGN STUDENTS:
None. Courses are open to the public.

TUITION FOR FOREIGN STUDENTS:
None

TOTAL INSTRUCTIONAL FACULTY:
130 (52 professors)

LIBRARY COLLECTIONS:
Library of the College—85,000 volumes (for professors only)

UNIVERSITY PUBLICATIONS:
Annuaire, Leçons inaugurales des professeurs, Documents Inédits

PRESIDENT: Y. Laporte

THE AMERICAN UNIVERSITY OF PARIS
31 ave Bosquet, 75007 Paris, France

CHARACTERISTICS OF INSTITUTION:
Independent, private university

DATE FOUNDED: 1962

TOTAL ENROLLMENT: 1,000 fulltime students

ACADEMIC PROGRAMS:
Faculty of Arts
Faculty of Science

SPECIAL PROGRAMS:
Adult education program
Computer Science Laboratory
Summer session

LANGUAGE OF INSTRUCTION: English

ADMISSION REQUIREMENTS FOR FOREIGN STUDENTS:
Secondary school certificate recognized as equivalent to a U.S. high school diploma

TUITION FOR FOREIGN STUDENTS:
Not available and subject to change in the coming year

TOTAL INSTRUCTIONAL FACULTY:
Not available

LIBRARY COLLECTIONS:
Total collection—over 100,000 volumes

PRESIDENT: Dr. Catherine W. Ingold

INSTITUTE EUROPÉEN DE L'ADMINISTRATION DES AFFAIRES
(EUROPEAN INSTITUTE OF BUSINESS ADMINISTRATION)
blvd. de Constance, 77305 Fontainebleau, France

CHARACTERISTICS OF INSTITUTION:
Independent *Grande École*

DATE FOUNDED: 1958

TOTAL ENROLLMENT: 2,400 (including 80%–90% foreign students [5%–10% are North American])

DEGREES AWARDED:
Diplôme
   one year

ACADEMIC PROGRAMS:
Post-graduate MBA Program (80% English Language/20% French Language)
Executive Development Program

SPECIAL PROGRAMS:
Cooperative arrangements with Harvard Business School in Massachusetts and Stanford Business School in California

LANGUAGES OF INSTRUCTION: French, English and German

ADMISSION REQUIREMENTS FOR FOREIGN STUDENTS:
University degree or equivalent

TUITION FOR FOREIGN STUDENTS:
MBA—Fr 108,000 per year

TOTAL INSTRUCTIONAL FACULTY:
75 fulltime professors
50 part time professors

LIBRARY COLLECTIONS:
Total collection—35,000 volumes

CHAIR, BOARD OF GOVERNORS: Claude Janssen

GROUPE ÉCOLE SUPÉRIEUR DE COMMERCE DE REIMS
(Grande École of Commerce of Reims)
59 rue Pierre-Taittinger, BP 302, 51061 Reims Cedex, France

CHARACTERISTICS OF INSTITUTION:
Independent *Grande École*

DATE FOUNDED: 1928

TOTAL ENROLLMENT: 1,000 fulltime students (including 200 foreign students)

DEGREES AWARDED:
Diplôme d'études supérieures commerciales, administratives et financières (state diploma)
   three years required
Magistère
   one year required

ACADEMIC PROGRAMS:
Unit of Commerce
Unit of Business Administration

SPECIAL PROGRAMS:
Cooperative arrangements with seven universities, including Northeastern University in Massachusetts

LANGUAGE OF INSTRUCTION: French

ADMISSION REQUIREMENTS FOR FOREIGN STUDENTS:
Entrance by competition following 1–2 years study after secondary school certificate *(baccalauréat),* or following first university qualification (DUT, BTS or DEUG). Direct entrance to second year by competition following appropriate university degree (Licence).

TUITION FOR FOREIGN STUDENTS:
Fr 15,000–34,000 per year

TOTAL INSTRUCTIONAL FACULTY:
160

LIBRARY COLLECTIONS:
Total collection—7,500 volumes

DIRECTOR: Pierre Lamborelle

ÉCOLE SUPÉRIEUR DE COMMERCE DE PARIS
(Grande École of Commerce of Paris)
79 ave de la République, 75543 Paris Cedex 11, France

CHARACTERISTICS OF INSTITUTION:
Independent *Grande École*

DATE FOUNDED: 1819

TOTAL ENROLLMENT: 950 fulltime students (including 100 foreign students)

DEGREES AWARDED:
Three-year diploma courses
Continuing education programs
Master's degree programs

ACADEMIC PROGRAMS:
Commerce
Research Center

SPECIAL PROGRAMS:
Cooperative arrangements with 23 universities from around the world. A minimum of three compulsory internships as part of regular degree curriculum.

TUITION FEES FOR FOREIGN STUDENTS:
Fr 20,000 per year

TOTAL INSTRUCTIONAL FACULTY:
76 fulltime professors
600 parttime faculty

LIBRARY COLLECTIONS:
Total collection—20,000 volumes

UNIVERSITY PUBLICATIONS:
Numerous research papers and books published each year

DEAN: Veronique de Chantérac

ÉCOLE DU LOUVRE
(School of the Louvre)
34 quai du Louvre, 75001 Paris, France

CHARACTERISTICS OF INSTITUTION:
Independent *Grande École*

DATE FOUNDED: 1882

TOTAL ENROLLMENT: 3,000 fulltime students

DEGREES AWARDED:
Titre d'Ancien Elève de l'École du Louvre
   three years required
Diplôme de l'École du Louvre
   five–eight years required

ACADEMIC PROGRAMS:
Fine Arts (archaeology, musicology)

LANGUAGE OF INSTRUCTION: French

ADMISSION REQUIREMENTS FOR FOREIGN STUDENTS:
Secondary school certificate *(baccalauréat),* or recognized foreign equivalent

TUITION FOR FOREIGN STUDENTS:
Not available

TOTAL INSTRUCTIONAL FACULTY:
50

LIBRARY COLLECTIONS:
Total collection—20,000 volumes

UNIVERSITY PUBLICATIONS:
École du Louvre, Notices d'Histoire de l'Art, Actes des Colloques et Recontres de l'École du Louvre

PRINCIPAL: D. Ponnau

SCHILLER INTERNATIONAL UNIVERSITY
103 rue de Lille, 75007 Paris, France
Château Portales, rue Melanie, 67000 Strasburg, France

CHARACTERISTICS OF INSTITUTION:
Private, independent university chartered by the State of Delaware, U.S.A.

DATE FOUNDED: 1964

TOTAL ENROLLMENT: 1,500 foreign students from 98 different countries enrolled at various study centers

DEGREES AWARDED:
Associate of Arts (AA and AAS)
Bachelor of Arts (BA)
Associate of Business Administration (ABA)
Bachelor of Business Administration (BBA)
Bachelor of Public Administration (BPA)
Master of Arts (MA)
Master of Business Administration (MBA)
Master of International Management (MIM)

ACADEMIC PROGRAMS:
Department of Business Administration
Department of Law/Public Administration
Department of Applied Sciences (including premedicine, preengineering and preveterinary Sciences)
Department of General Studies (including economics, languages and arts courses)
Department of International Relations and Diplomacy
Department of Hotel Management

SPECIAL PROGRAMS:
Study centers located in:
England—London and West Wickham
France—Paris and Strasbourg
Germany—Heidelberg
Spain—Madrid
Switzerland—Engelberg
Hotel management internships

LANGUAGE OF INSTRUCTION: English

ADMISSION REQUIREMENTS FOR FOREIGN STUDENTS:
Any foreign secondary school diploma recognized as equivalent to the high school diploma issued in the State of Delaware, U.S.A.

TUITION FOR FOREIGN STUDENTS:
Undergraduate—$8,700 US in 1990
Postgraduate—$9,050 US in 1990

TOTAL INSTRUCTIONAL FACULTY:
190 teachers and lecturers

LIBRARY COLLECTION:
Total collection—36,000 volumes

UNIVERSITY PUBLICATIONS:
Schiller Newsletter, Hotel Management Newsletter

DIRECTORS: J. Nagourney (Paris), C. Parisel (Strasbourg)

ÉCOLE SUPÉRIEURE DE JOURNALISME
(Grande École of Journalisme)
4 place Saint-Germain des Pres, 75006 Paris, France

CHARACTERISTICS OF INSTITUTION:
Independent *Grande École*

DATE FOUNDED: 1899

TOTAL ENROLLMENT: 400 fulltime students (including 90 foreign students)

DEGREES AWARDED:
Certificat
   one year required
Diplôme de l'École
   two years required
Diplôme de Formation supérieure
   three years and thesis required

ACADEMIC PROGRAM:
Journalism

SPECIAL PROGRAMS:
Cooperative arrangements with the University of Wisconsin and Columbia University in New York

LANGUAGE OF INSTRUCTION: French

ADMISSION REQUIREMENTS FOR FOREIGN STUDENTS:
Secondary school certificate *(baccalauréat)*

TUITION FOR FOREIGN STUDENTS:
Fr 6,500 per year in 1990

TOTAL INSTRUCTIONAL FACULTY:
20

PRESIDENT: M. Schumann

ÉCOLE DES HAUTES ÉTUDES EN SCIENCES SOCIALES
(Grande École of Social Sciences)
54 blvd Raspail, 75006 Paris, France

CHARACTERISTICS OF INSTITUTION:
State-administrated, academically autonomous *Grande École*

DATE FOUNDED: 1947

TOTAL ENROLLMENT: 4,000 fulltime students (including 2,000 foreign students)

DEGREES AWARDED:
Diplôme
   three years required

Diplôme d'études approfondies (DEA)
   one year required
Doctorat
   two–four years after DEA required

ACADEMIC PROGRAMS:
Department of History
Department of Sociology, Social Anthropology and
   Psychology
Department of Economics
Department of Cultural Affairs
Department of Artic and Asian Studies

LANGUAGE OF INSTRUCTION: French

ADMISSION REQUIREMENTS FOR FOREIGN STUDENTS:
None. Courses are open to the public

TUITION FOR FOREIGN STUDENTS:
None

TOTAL INSTRUCTIONAL FACULTY:
300

LIBRARY COLLECTIONS:
Foundation of the House of Sciences of Mankind—
50,000 volumes
Libraries of the research centers—65,000 volumes

UNIVERSITY PUBLICATIONS:
Revues, Bullletin des centres de recherches

PRESIDENT: Marc Augé

INSTITUT D'ÉTUDES POLITIQUES DE PARIS
(Political Institute of Paris)
27 rue Saint-Guillaume, 75341 Paris Cedex 07, France

CHARACTERISTICS OF INSTITUTION:
State-run nonprofit institution

DATE FOUNDED: 1945

TOTAL ENROLLMENT: 5,000 fulltime students

DEGREES AWARDED:
Diplôme
   three years required
Diplôme d'études approfondies (DEA)
   one further year required
Doctorat
   two–four years after DEA required
Certificate for foreign students
   one year required

ACADEMIC PROGRAMS:
Unit of Political, Social and Economic Sciences
Unit of Lifelong Education

LANGUAGE OF INSTRUCTION: French

ADMISSION REQUIREMENTS FOR FOREIGN STUDENTS:
Entrance by competition following one year of study after secondary school certificate *(baccalauréat)*. Direct entrance to second year by competition following appropriate university degree.

TUITION FOR FOREIGN STUDENTS:
See GENERAL UNIVERSITY INFORMATION.

TOTAL INSTRUCTIONAL FACULTY:
900

LIBRARY COLLECTIONS:
Total Collection—700,000 volumes

UNIVERSITY PUBLICATIONS:
Revue française de Science politique; Bulletin analytique de documentation politique, économique et sociale contemporaine; Revue économique; "M.O.T.S." Lexicologie, Critiques et comptes rendus dans le domaine du vocabulaire socio-politique

DIRECTOR: A. Lancelot

ÉCOLE NATIONALE SUPÉRIEURE DES BEAUX-ARTS
17 quai Malaquais, 75006 Paris, France

CHARACTERISTICS OF INSTITUTION:
Independent *Grande École*

DATE FOUNDED: 1648

TOTAL ENROLLMENT: 500 fulltime students (including 400 foreign students)

DEGREES AWARDED:
Diplôme supérieur d'Arts plastique (DSAP)
   four–five years required

ACADEMIC PROGRAMS:
Painting and Sculpture

SPECIAL PROGRAMS:
Cooperative arrangements with the Academy of Fine Arts, in Taiwan, Parsons School in New York and the School of Fine Arts in Beijing.

LANGUAGE OF INSTRUCTION: French

ADMISSION REQUIREMENTS FOR FOREIGN STUDENTS:
Competitive entrance tests for painting and sculpture

TUITION FOR FOREIGN STUDENTS:
Not available

TOTAL INSTRUCTIONAL FACULTY:
75

LIBRARY COLLECTIONS:
Total collection—120,000 volumes

UNIVERSITY PUBLICATIONS:
Bulletin Signaletique, arts plastiques; Cahiers de psychologie de l'Art et de la Culture

DIRECTOR: Y. Michaud

ÉCOLE DES HAUTES ÉTUDES INTERNATIONALES
(School of International Studies)
4 place Saint-Germain des Pres, 77553 Paris Cedex II, France

CHARACTERISTICS OF INSTITUTION:
Independent *Grande École*

DATE FOUNDED: 1904

TOTAL ENROLLMENT: 210 fulltime students (including 146 foreign students)

DEGREES AWARDED:
Certificat
   one year required
Diplôme de l'École
   two years required
Diplôme de la Formation supérieure
   three years and thesis required

ACADEMIC PROGRAMS:
Diplomatic Studies

SPECIAL PROGRAMS:
Cooperative arrangements with the University of Wisconsin and Columbia University in New York

LANGUAGE OF INSTRUCTION: French

ADMISSION REQUIREMENTS FOR FOREIGN STUDENTS:
Secondary school certificate *(baccalauréat)*

TUITION FOR FOREIGN STUDENTS:
Fr 6,500 per year

TOTAL INSTRUCTIONAL FACULTY:
24

PRESIDENT: M. Schumann

THE UNIVERSITIES OF GERMANY

GENERAL UNIVERSITY INFORMATION

German universities are state-run, nonprofit institutions and, as such, follow similar rules and regulations concerning admission and language requirements, tuition and degree requirements. The general information given is relevant to all the universities mentioned in this chapter.

ADMISSION REQUIREMENTS FOR FOREIGN STUDENTS

Foreign students applying to a German university must hold either a German secondary school certificate (*Allgemeine Hochschulreife, Reifezeugnis* or *Abitur*) or one of the following recognized foreign equivalents:

- high school diploma from the United States
- Baccalaureat Européen, issued by a secondary school in Germany or abroad
- international baccalaureate, issued by the Office du Baccalaureat International in Geneva, Switzerland
- secondary school certificate issued by the competent authorities in a European Community member state, provided that the foreign students have documented proof that their prior education is sufficient for admission to a university in their home countries and that they are proficient in German
- secondary school certificate from a recognized German secondary school abroad
- secondary school certificate that has been approved as equivalent to German standards by the university to which the foreign student applies

If a foreign applicant's secondary school certificate or high school diploma is not considered equivalent to the West German qualification necessary to gain admission, the foreign applicant will not be admitted directly to an academic program. In such cases, the foreign applicant must take a standardized eligibility/admission examination (*Prüfung zur Feststellung der Hochschulreife—Feststellungsprüfung*). This examination is designed to test the applicant's knowledge in the subjects of his chosen academic program and is taken upon completion of a preparatory course for foreign students (*Studienkolleg*), which is usually two terms in duration. The test is not required of all foreign students; if an applicant wishes, he or she may take the *Feststellungsprüfung* without German preparation. Foreign students who prefer to take the en-trance examination without preparation should contact the university's foreign student office. This examination may be repeated only once.

The *Studienkollegs* are offered in the following areas:

- T course: engineering, mathematics and sciences
- M course: medicine, pharmacy, biology and similar subjects
- W course: economics and social sciences
- G course: German language and literature, history and philosophy
- S course: linguistic subjects, excluding German language and literature

The *Feststellungsprüfung* examine the following subjects and include a German language proficiency test:

- T examination: mathematics, physics, chemistry and/or technical drawing
- M examination: biology, chemistry, physics and mathematics
- W examination: mathematics, economics, history/geography and other social science subjects
- G examination: history, German literature and social science/geography
- S examination: second languages, third language/history/mathematics and history/social science/geography

Information regarding entrance examination requirements can be obtained from university foreign student offices (*Akademische Auslandsämter*) and the *Studienkollegs*.

Foreign transfer students must apply directly to the desired university for recognition and accreditation of their previous academic work. Germany has agreements on reciprocal recognition and accreditation of degrees and academic programs with France, the Netherlands, Italy, the United States and other countries that are not European Community member states. But foreign students must still apply for recognition of their foreign qualifications, even though their qualifications may be covered by transnational, bilateral agreements. When applying to transfer to a German university, foreign students should include complete transcripts and German translations of all relevant certificates and information. Additional forms may be required, and the transfer applicant should contact the university directly for the specific procedures of application.

The language of instruction at all German universities is German. All foreign applicants must prove they are proficient in German before being admitted to a university. All foreign students not from a German-speaking country must take the German language examination—the PNdS test (*Prüfung zum Nachweis deutscher Sprachkenntnisse*). This examination is administered by the respective universities. All foreign students who attended recognized German schools abroad or achieved their secondary school certificates in German are exempt from this examination. German courses are offered to foreign students in Germany by the Goethe Institutes, the Carl Duisberg Centers and the individual universities themselves. If a foreign applicant requires training in German, he should enroll in a language school in his home country or contact the prospective German university for advice about the degree of proficiency required by the PNdS test and information regarding available language schools.

APPLICATION PROCEDURE FOR FOREIGN STUDENTS

The general application procedure for foreign students is the submission of the Application for Admission to University/Matriculation (*Antrag auf Zulassung zum Studium und auf Immatrikulation*). This application and any forms and information regarding the application procedure for foreign students can be obtained from the *Akademische Auslandsämter* of the prospective universities, German embassies and consulates abroad and the branch offices of the German Academic Exchange Service (Deutscher Akademischer Austauschdienst [DAAD]).

There are limitations on the numbers of foreign students accepted to certain academic programs because of specific enrollment capacities (*Numerus Clausus*). For example, in 1987, the national regulation on foreign student enrollment to medicine, dentistry, veterinary medicine and pharmacy programs was 6% of total student enrollment; the quota for agricultural and forest sciences, architecture, biology, home economics and food science, food chemistry and psychology programs was 8% of total student enrollment. In addition some academic programs are only available for winter semester enrollment. Foreign students are advised to contact the prospective universities well in advance of application deadlines for the specific information regarding enrollment capacities and the academic calendar for their particular programs.

Universities will notify foreign applicants of admission or rejection in February/March of the year prior to the summer semester or August/September of the year prior to the winter semester. The notification of admission is only valid for a specific program and semester and becomes invalid if the foreign student fails to matriculate in the semester to which he was admitted.

APPLICATION DEADLINES

Foreign applicants are encouraged to send their admission applications as early as possible to the prospective universities' admissions departments. Closing dates for all foreign applications are

- July 15 for the winter semester
- January 15 for the summer semester

Late applications will be invalid for the following semester's admissions as well.

ACADEMIC PROGRAMS AND DEGREE REQUIREMENTS

The degrees issued by the universities of Germany are arranged around examination regulations stipulating the duration of the academic programs. The examination regulations indicate a period of time in which the student must complete the course work required to pass the set examinations in the respective programs. Most university programs comprise eight to ten semesters of course work. Some programs, such as medicine, take longer to complete and may include a semester or two of practical training.

Undergraduate programs are divided into two stages:

- stage I (*Grundstudium*): the first four or five semesters of course work, culminating in an intermediate examination (*Zwischenprüfung*)
- stage II (*Hauptstudium*): the final four or five semesters of course work culminating in a final examination. The final examination may be either a state examination (*Staatsprüfung*) or, depending upon the program, an examination arranged by the individual universities. The two types of university examinations are the *Diplomprüfung* and the *Magisterprüfung*.

Academic programs that culminate in a *Staatsprüfung* have course work and academic performance standards designated by state authorities. Degrees that are under the auspices of the state are medicine, veterinary medicine, dentistry, teaching, law, pharmacy and food chemistry. The degree confered following the passing of the *Staatsprüfung* is the *Doktor* (Dr.).

Programs that culminate in a *Diplomprüfung* have course work and academic standards regulated by the independent universities. After completing the course work and passing the *Diplomprüfung*, the graduate obtains the degree of Diplom. The academic programs for the Diplom are concentrated on one subject, and usually cover social sciences, economics, engineering or natural sciences. Programs culminating in a *Magisterprüfung* result in the degree of Magister and are also regulated by the independent universities. The Magister degree provides for the combination of several different subjects and usually covers modern languages, cultural studies, social sciences and economics.

Postgraduate degrees are offered at most West German universities. The student must have gained a Doktor, Diplom or Magister degree or a recognized foreign equivalent in order to be admitted to a postgraduate program. The first postgraduate degree offered by German universities is the Promotion (Ph.D.). The postgraduate programs are arranged by the *Promotionsordnung* of the corresponding faculty (*Fakultät*) or department (*Fachbereich*) of the university. The Promotion degree requires an independently researched doctoral thesis and an oral examination that includes a public defense of the thesis. The duration of the program is usually between two and four years. The state requires that the postgraduate student must have studied at least two semesters of the doctoral degree at the university in question.

Other specific postgraduate degrees are offered by particular institutions. Foreign students are advised to fully research the various postgraduate opportunities available.

ACCREDITATION

The accreditation of a state degree of a German university (Doktor) is the responsibility of the federal government of Germany.

Accreditation of the university degrees under the auspices of the individual universities (Diplom and Magister) are the responsibility of the federative states of Germany: Baden-Wurtemberg, Bavaria, Bremen, Hamburg, Hesse, Lower Saxony, North Rhine-Westphalia, Rhineland-Palatinate, Saarland, Schleswig-Holstein, West Berlin and all the recently reintegrated states of what was East Germany.

REGISTRATION REQUIREMENTS

Foreign students must register and matriculate in person prior to beginning studies. When matriculating (*Immatrikulation*), the foreign student must present the following documents:

1. the letter of acceptance
2. all originals of certified copies of documents (including translations) sent to the university as part of the formal application for admission
3. a statement of honorable dismissal if transferring from another German university or from a university abroad
4. examination results if the foreign applicant had to take the *Feststellungsprüfung*

5. proof of financial solvency, either by producing a certified bank guarantee or a statement from an individual who has agreed to support the foreign student during his education
6. a passport or identity card with a valid residence permit
7. a certificate of registration from the local resident registration office
8. a health certificate issued by a local public health authority
9. certificate of foreign student medical health insurance, either from a German authority or from an authority in the student's home country
10. receipt from the semester's contribution to the Student Welfare Organization (Studentenwerk)
11. if required by the academic program, a certificate indicating the foreign student's qualifications for specific course work
12. a minimum of four passport photographs

After registration, the foreign applicant becomes a matriculated foreign student and obtains a student identity card.

VISA REQUIREMENTS AND RESIDENCE REGULATIONS

Foreign students need a student visa and a residence permit for study in Germany. If the foreign student is from another European Community member state or from Austria, Switzerland or the United States of America, a visa is not needed. However, the residence permit regulations still apply.

Foreign students needing visas should apply as early as possible at the German embassy or consulate in their home countries. It usually takes several weeks to process a student visa and residence permit. In order to be issued a student visa and residence permit, the foreign student must present the following documents to the competent German authorities in the student's home country:

- a valid passport
- notification of admission or a place reservation for admission at a later date (including preparatory institutions—*Studienkollegs*) to a German university
- proof of financial solvency for tuition and expenses while in Germany

Foreign students can obtain a student applicant visa (*Bewerbervisum*) if the notification of admission has not arrived prior to departure to Germany. The applicants must provide the German authorities in their home countries with all application materials required by the prospective universities' admissions departments. Foreign students in Germany with student applicant visas must prove that they are admitted to a university within the expiry date of the visa (presently three months). The advantage of this visa is that the foreign applicant can research universities in person before making formal applications.

Upon arrival at a university, the foreign student must register with the alien authority (Ausländerbrhorde) of the local district. Within a week of arrival, the foreign student should also report to the resident registration office (Einwohnermeldeamt).

Foreign students are strongly advised against coming to Germany on a tourist visa because such a document cannot be converted to a student visa or residence permit upon acceptance to a university. On the other hand, a student applicant visa is easily transferable. Students must also apply for an extension of the residence permit before it expires.

TUITION FEES FOR FOREIGN STUDENTS

There are no tuition fees for German or foreign students at the state-run universities of Germany. Some private institutions, however, do charge tuition.

EXPENSES

Expenses for a foreign student at a German university include

- semester contribution (between DM 20 and DM 50 per six-month period in 1989) for the social welfare benefits provided by the Student Welfare Organization (Studentenwerk) to the student body at all West German universities
- medical insurance (roughly DM 350 per semester in 1989). All matriculated students must be insured in a statutory health insurance plan covering doctor's fees, prescriptions and hospital costs. If uninsured by an agent in the home country, medical insurance is paid to the insurance office at the university prior to matriculation. No foreign students are exempt.
- living expenses, such as food, clothing, entertainment, transportation and other miscellaneous expenses (about DM 1,000 per month). Books and supplies vary from DM 450 to DM 600 per semester, depending on the student's program of study.

FOREIGN STUDENT SCHOLARSHIPS

In general, universities of Germany do not offer foreign student scholarships. However, other organizations do offer scholarships to foreign students, awarded mainly on the basis of academic achievement and financial need. Information on foreign student scholarships can be obtained from the German embassy or consulate in the applicant's home country, the Goethe Institutes abroad or the German Academic Exchange Service (DAAD) branch offices.

Financial assistance for certain foreign students is also available through the Federal Educational Assistance Act (BAföG). According to the BAföG, foreign students can be awarded grants if they have the same legal status as German citizens. The foreign student must fulfill one of the following categories in order to be considered by the BAföG:

- the student is stateless;
- the student has residence in Germany and is recognized as a "refugee" under Section 1 of the law concerning measures for refugees received within the framework of humanitarian relief action or has been accorded political asylum under the corresponding law (Asylverfahrensgesetz);
- the student has permanent residence in Germany and has at least one German parent; or,
- the student has parents who are citizens of a European Community member state and are employed in Germany or have been employed there in the past.

The BAföG will give financial assistance to foreign students who do not fulfill one of these criteria only if

- the foreign student has lived in Germany for at least five years prior to the commencement of studies and has been a German taxpayer.
- the parent or parents of the foreign student has been living and working in Germany for at least three of the six years prior to the student's enrollment in a university academic program. If the foreign student fulfills this stipulation while still enrolled in the program, he or she will become eligible for financial assistance through BAföG.

UNIVERSITY CALENDAR

The academic year is divided into two semesters:

- winter semester: October to March
- summer semester: April to September

Students should contact the school for the exact date of registration and the start of classes.

FOREIGN STUDENTS IN GERMANY

Foreign students find German universities particularly attractive due to the absence of tuition fees. There are exceptional educational facilities available in Germany and, though some universities attract more foreign students than others, each university has an international student body.

In 1986, German universities contained 74,344 foreign students—5.6% of total student enrollment. Roughly 25% of foreign student enrollment was made up of European Community member state nationals. Many foreign students come from the United States and Canada as part of Junior Year Abroad programs.

BRANCH OFFICES OF THE GERMAN ACADEMIC EXCHANGE SERVICE (DAAD)

Most of the above information was provided by DAAD. It is the job of the DAAD to provide any help, advice and assistance foreign students and applicants need in matters related to studies and student life in Germany. The addresses of DAAD branch offices in Germany and abroad are:

Head Office in Bonn-Bad Godesberg
Deutscher Akademischer Austauschdienst
Kennedyallee 50
D-5300 Bonn 2
Germany
Tel. # 88 20/88 21
Telex # 885515

Berlin Office
Deutscher Akademischer Austauschdienst
Steinplatz 2
D-1000 Berlin 12
Germany
Tel. # 31 00 030
Telex # 184766

London Office
German Academic Exchange Service
17, Bloomsbury Square
London WC1A 2LP
England, U.K.
Tel. # (071) 404 4065

Paris Office
Office Allemand d'Echanges Universitaires
15, rue de Verneuil
F-75007 Paris, France
Tel. # 45 61 58 57

Paris Office
Maison Heinrich Heine
27 C, blvd. Jourdan
F-75014 Paris, France
Tel. # 45 89 32 26

New York Office
German Academic Exchange Service
950 Third Ave., 19th Floor
New York, NY, 10022
U.S.A.
Tel. # (212) 758 3223
Telex # WUI 667691 DAAD-NY

FREIE UNIVERSITÄT BERLIN
(Free University of Berlin)
1000 Berlin 33 (Dahlem), Altensteinstrasse 40, Germany

CHARACTERISTICS OF INSTITUTION:
State-run, nonprofit university

DATE FOUNDED: 1948

TOTAL ENROLLMENT: 60,000 fulltime students (including 4,500 foreign students)

DEGREES AWARDED:
State examination in various fields
Diplom in various fields
    four–six years required
Magister Artium (arts)
    four–six years required
Doktor in various fields
    one–six years required
Zahnarztliche Staatsprüfung and Dr.med.dent.
    ten semesters required
Medizinische Staatsprüfung and Dr.med.
    twelve semesters required
Habilitation (university teaching qualification)
    a minimum of three years following doctorate required

ACADEMIC PROGRAMS:
Department of Basic Medicine and Medical Ecology
Department of Biology
Department of Classics and Archaeology
Department of Chemistry
Department of Dentistry
Department of Economics and Business Administration
Department of Education
Department of History
Department of Law
Department of Mass Communications
Department of Geosciences
Department of German Language and Philology
Department of Mathematics
Department of Modern Languages and Literatures
Department of Pharmacy
Department of Philosophy and Social Sciences I
    (psychology, philosophy and sociology)
Department of Philosophy and Social Sciences II
    (theology, Islamic studies, Iranian studies, East Asian studies and ethnology)
Department of Physics
Department of Political Science
Department of Veterinary Medicine

SPECIAL PROGRAMS:
University Hospital (Steglitz)
University Hospital (Rudolf Virchow)
Central Institute of Didactics and Curricular Development
Central Institute of Latin American Studies
Central Institute of Social Science Research
East European Institute
John F. Kennedy Institute of North American Studies
Center for Foreign Students

Cooperative arrangements with 40 other universities, including Duke University, Wake Forest University, University of Minnesota, University of Indiana, Vanderbilt University, University of Washington, University of Texas, Cornell University, University of Maryland, Tulane University, University of Wisconsin, and Stanford University

LANGUAGE OF INSTRUCTION: German

ADMISSION REQUIREMENTS FOR FOREIGN STUDENTS:
Secondary school certificate *(Reifezeugnis)* or recognized foreign equivalent

TUITION FOR FOREIGN STUDENTS:
None

TOTAL INSTRUCTIONAL FACULTY:
4,000

LIBRARY COLLECTIONS:
Central library—1,550,000 volumes
Departmental libraries and Central Institute library

UNIVERSITY PUBLICATIONS:
FU-Info, FU-Dokumentation, Mitteilungen fur Dozenten und Studenten, Pressedienst Wissenschaft

PRESIDENT: Prof. Dr.iur. Dieter Heckelmann

RHEINISCHE FRIEDRICH-WILHEMS-UNIVERSITÄT BONN
(Rhenish Friedrich-Wilhelm University of Bonn)
5300 Bonn, Regina-Pacis-Weg 3, Germany

CHARACTERISTICS OF INSTITUTION:
State-run, nonprofit university

DATE FOUNDED: 1786

TOTAL ENROLLMENT: 40,150 fulltime students (including 1,500 foreign students)

DEGREES AWARDED:
State examinations in various fields
Diplom in various fields
Doktor in various fields
    approximately eight semesters required (except Dr.med.dent. and Zahnarztliche Staatsprüfung, 10 semesters required)
Medizinische Staatsprüfung and Dr.med.
    11 semesters required
Habilitation (university teaching qualification)
    a minimum of three years following doctorate required

ACADEMIC PROGRAMS:
Faculty of Agriculture
Faculty of Catholic Theology
Faculty of Education
Faculty of Evangelical Theology
Faculty of Law and Economics

Faculty of Mathematics and Natural Sciences (including pharmacy)
Faculty of Medicine (including dentistry)
Faculty of Philosophy (including liberal arts, psychology, political science and musicology)

SPECIAL PROGRAMS:
Institute of Bank and Credit Finance
Institute of French Culture
Institute of Mathematics
Institute of Orthodox Theology
Institute for Water Conservation Law
Max Plack Institute for Radioastronomy
Center for Foreign Students
Cooperative arrangements with the University of Toulouse in France, the University of Warsaw in Poland and Waseda University in Tokyo

LANGUAGE OF INSTRUCTION: German

ADMISSION REQUIREMENTS FOR FOREIGN STUDENTS:
Secondary school certificate *(Reifezeugnis)* or recognized foreign equivalent

TUITION FOR FOREIGN STUDENTS:
None

TOTAL INSTRUCTIONAL FACULTY:
2,062 (including 295 professors)

LIBRARY COLLECTIONS:
University library—1,500,000 volumes

MUSEUMS AND GALLERIES:
Classical Art Museum, Collection of Mineralogy

UNIVERSITY PUBLICATIONS:
Akademica Bonnensia, Alma Mater, Bonner Akaemische Reden, Bonner Universitäts-Nachrichten, Politeia

RECTOR: Prof. Dr. Kurt Fleischhauer

UNIVERSITÄT BREMEN
(University of Bremen)
2800 Bremen 33, Bibliothekstrasse, Germany

CHARACTERISTICS OF INSTITUTION:
State-run, nonprofit university

DATE FOUNDED: 1971

TOTAL ENROLLMENT: 13,100 fulltime students (including 600 foreign students)

DEGREES AWARDED:
State teaching qualifications, secondary level
    four years required
Juristische Staatsprüfung (law)
    five years required
Diplom in various fields
    four–five years

Doktor in various fields
five–six years required

ACADEMIC PROGRAMS:
Department 1 (physics and electrical engineering)
Department 2 (biology and chemistry)
Department 3 (mathematics and computer science)
Department 4 (engineering)
Department 5 (geology)
Department 6 (law)
Department 7 (economics)
Department 8 (sociology, geography and history)
Department 9 (politics and community studies, psychology, theology and social science)
Department 10 (communication, art and music)
Department of Educational Sciences
Department of Sport, Labor and Cultural Sciences

SPECIAL PROGRAMS:
Center for European Law Policy
German Press Research Institute
Research Institute for Independent Literature and Social Movement in Eastern Europe
Cooperative arrangements with the University of Toulouse in France, the University of Warsaw in Poland and Waseda University in Tokyo

LANGUAGE OF INSTRUCTION: German

ADMISSION REQUIREMENTS FOR FOREIGN STUDENTS:
Secondary school certificate (Reifezeugnis) or recognized foreign equivalent

TUITION FOR FOREIGN STUDENTS:
None

TOTAL INSTRUCTIONAL FACULTY:
359

LIBRARY COLLECTIONS:
University library—1,200,000 volumes

UNIVERSITY PUBLICATIONS:
Veranstaltungsverzeichnis, Rechenschaftsbericht, Impulse aus der Forschung, Research Report

RECTOR: Prof. Dr. Jürgen Timm

HEINRICH-HEINE-UNIVERSITÄT DUSSELDORF
(Heinrich-Heine University of Dusseldorf)
4000 Dusseldorf 1, Universitatsstrasse 1, Germany

CHARACTERISTICS OF INSTITUTION:
State-run, nonprofit university

DATE FOUNDED: 1965
(Formerly Medizinische Akademie, founded in 1907)

TOTAL ENROLLMENT: 16,000 fulltime students (including 1,000 foreign students)

DEGREES AWARDED:
State examinations in various fields
State teaching qualification, secondary level
Magisterprüfung (arts)
four years required
Diplom in various fields
four years required
Doktor in various fields
six years required

ACADEMIC PROGRAMS:
Faculty of Mathematics and Natural Sciences (including pharmacy and psychology)
Faculty of Medicine (including dentistry)
Faculty of Philosophy

SPECIAL PROGRAMS:
Air Pollution and Silicosis Research Institute
Diabetic Research Institute
Institute of Dietetics and Nutrition
Cooperative arrangements with the University of Nantes in France and the University of Naples in Italy

LANGUAGE OF INSTRUCTION: German

ADMISSION REQUIREMENTS FOR FOREIGN STUDENTS:
Secondary school certificate (Reifezeugnis) or recognized foreign equivalent

TUITION FOR FOREIGN STUDENTS:
None

TOTAL INSTRUCTIONAL FACULTY:
2,600

LIBRARY COLLECTIONS:
Central library—2,000,000 volumes
Medicine library—400,000 volumes
Specialized libraries—490,000 volumes

UNIVERSITY PUBLICATIONS:
Amtliche, BekanntmachungenStudienfuhrer, Jahrbuch der Universität, Personen- und Vorlesungsverzeichnis, Universitätszeitung

RECTOR: Prof. Dr. G. Kaiser

FRIEDRICH-ALEXANDER-UNIVERSITÄT ERLANGEN-NÜRNBERG
(Friedrich Alexander University of Erlangen-Nuremberg)
8520 Erlangen, Schlossplatz 4, Germany

CHARACTERISTICS OF INSTITUTION:
State-run, nonprofit university

DATE FOUNDED: 1743

TOTAL ENROLLMENT: 27,000 fulltime students (including 950 foreign students)

DEGREES AWARDED:
State examinations in various fields
State teaching qualification, secondary level
Magister Artium (arts)
    four years required
Diplom in various fields
    four years required
Doktor in various fields
    four years required
Habilitation (university teaching qualification)
    a minimum of three years following doctorate required

ACADEMIC PROGRAMS:
Faculty of Biology and Chemistry
Faculty of Economic and Social Sciences
Faculty of Education
Faculty of Geosciences
Faculty of Languages and Literatures
Faculty of Law
Faculty of Mathematics and Physics
Faculty of Medicine (including dentistry)
Faculty of Philosophy, History and Social Sciences
Faculty of Technology
Faculty of Theology

SPECIAL PROGRAMS:
Astrophysics Center
Institute of Biomedical Technology
Social Science Research Center
Computer Center
Physical Education Center
Cooperative arrangements with the University of Rennes I and the University of Rennes II, both in France, Ain-Shams University, the University of Cracow in Poland and the University of St. Andrews in Scotland

LANGUAGE OF INSTRUCTION: German

ADMISSION REQUIREMENTS FOR FOREIGN STUDENTS:
Secondary school certificate (Reifezeugnis) or recognized foreign equivalent

TUITION FOR FOREIGN STUDENTS:
None.

TOTAL INSTRUCTIONAL FACULTY:
1,775 (including 230 professors)

LIBRARY COLLECTIONS:
Central library—3,456,000 volumes
Faculty of economic and social sciences—164,000 volumes
Faculty of education—68,000 volumes
Faculty of engineering—70,000 volumes

UNIVERSITY PUBLICATIONS:
Unikurier, Jahresbibliographie und Forschungsbericht, Jahrsbericht, Personal- und Vorlesungsverzeichnis, Erlanger Bausteine zur frankischen Heimatforschung, Erlanger Forschungen, Geologische Blatter für Nordost-Bayern und angrenzende Gebiete, Jahrbuch für frankische Landesforschung, Sitzungsberichte der Physikalich-Medizinischen Societat zu Erlangen, Erlanger Universitätsreden

PRESIDENT: Prof. G. Jasper

JOHANN WOLFGANG GOETHE-UNIVERSITÄT FRANKFURT
(Johann Wolfgang Goethe University of Frankfurt)
6000 Frankfurt am Main, Senckenberganlage 31, Postfach 111932, Germany

CHARACTERISTICS OF INSTITUTION:
State-run, nonprofit university

DATE FOUNDED: 1914

TOTAL ENROLLMENT: 34,000 fulltime students (including 2,500 foreign students)

DEGREES AWARDED:
State examinations in various fields
State teaching qualification (elementary, primary or secondary level and for the teaching of the handicapped)
Magister Artium (arts)
    eight semesters required
Diplom in various fields
    four years required
Doktor in various fields
    approximately eight semesters required
Medizinische Staatsprüfung and Dr.med.
    eleven semesters required
Habilitation (university teaching qualification)
    a minimum of three years following doctorate required

ACADEMIC PROGRAMS:
Department of Biology
Department of Biochemistry, Pharmacy and Food Chemistry
Department of Catholic Theology
Department of Chemistry
Department of Classical Languages and Arts
Department of East European and Non-European Languages and Cultures
Department of Economics
Department of Education
Department of Geography
Department of Geosciences
Department of History
Department of Human Medicine
Department of Information Science
Department of Law
Department of Modern Languages
Department of Mathematics

Department of Philosophy
Department of Physics
Department of Psychology
Department of Social Science
Department of Sport

SPECIAL PROGRAMS:
Cooperative arrangements with 10 universities, including Trenton State College in New Jersey, Eastern Illinois University, and the University of Wisconsin—Milwaukee

LANGUAGE OF INSTRUCTION: German

ADMISSION REQUIREMENTS FOR FOREIGN STUDENTS:
Secondary school certificate (Reifezeugnis) or recognized foreign equivalent

TUITION FOR FOREIGN STUDENTS:
None

TOTAL INSTRUCTIONAL FACULTY:
2,000 (including 603 professors)

LIBRARY COLLECTIONS:
Municipal and university library—2,400,000 volumes
Senckenberg Library—930,000 volumes
Libraries of the departments and institutes—2,000,000 volumes

MUSEUMS AND GALLERIES:
Senckenberg Museum

UNIVERSITY PUBLICATIONS:
Forschung Frankfurt, Forschungsbericht, Studienfuhrer, Rechenschaftsbericht, Vorlesungs- und Personalverzeichnis, UniReport

PRESIDENT: Prof. Dr. K. Ring

ALBERT-LUDWIG-UNIVERSITÄT FREIBURG
(Albert Ludwig University of Freiburg)
7800 Freiburg i. Br., Werthmannplatz, Germany

CHARACTERISTICS OF INSTITUTION:
State-run, nonprofit university

DATE FOUNDED: 1457

TOTAL ENROLLMENT: 22,600 fulltime students (including 1,600 foreign students)

DEGREES AWARDED:
State examinations in various fields
State teaching qualification, secondary level
Magister Artium (arts)
    eight semesters required
Diplom in various fields
    four years required
Doktor in various fields
    approximately eight semesters required
Medizinische Staatsprüfung and Dr.med.

eleven semesters required
Habilitation (teaching qualification, university level)
    a minimum of three years following doctorate required

ACADEMIC PROGRAMS:
Faculty of Biology
Faculty of Chemistry and Pharmacology
Faculty of Economics
Faculty of Law
Faculty of Mathematics
Faculty of Medicine
Faculty of Philosophy I (fine arts)
Faculty of Philosophy II (foreign languages and literatures)
Faculty of Philosophy III (Germanic and English studies)
Faculty of Philosophy IV (history, political and social sciences)
Faculty of Physics
Faculty of Theology
Department of Forestry
Department of Geosciences

SPECIAL PROGRAMS:
Cooperative arrangements with 20 universities including: University of Massachusetts, University of Texas (Austin), Wayne State University, University of Michigan, Michigan State University and the Institute of European Studies (Chicago)

LANGUAGE OF INSTRUCTION: German

ADMISSION REQUIREMENTS FOR FOREIGN STUDENTS:
Secondary school certificate (Reifezeugnis) or recognized foreign equivalent

TUITION FOR FOREIGN STUDENTS:
None

TOTAL INSTRUCTIONAL FACULTY:
2,400

LIBRARY COLLECTIONS:
University library—2,000,000 volumes

UNIVERSITY PUBLICATIONS:
Freiburger Universitätsblatter, Uni-Aktuell

RECTOR: Prof. Dr. Christoph Rüchardt

JUSTUS-LIEBIG-UNIVERSITÄT GIESSIN
(Justus Liebig University of Giessin)
6300 Giessin, Ludwigstrasse 23, Germany

CHARACTERISTICS OF INSTITUTION:
State-run, nonprofit university

DATE FOUNDED: 1607

TOTAL ENROLLMENT: 19,000 fulltime students (including 1,000 foreign students)

DEGREES AWARDED:
State examinations in law and medicine
Magister Artium (arts)
  four years required
Diplom in various fields
  four–six years required
Doktor in various fields
  eight–fourteen semesters required
Habilitation (teaching qualification, university level)
  a minimum of three years following doctorate required

ACADEMIC PROGRAMS:
Department of Agriculture
Department of Arts, Music and Sport
Department of Biology
Department of Chemistry
Department of Economics
Department of Education
Department of English and Anglo-American Literature
Department of Geology and Geography
Department of German
Department of History
Department of Law
Department of Mathematics
Department of Medicine (including pharmacy and dentistry)
Department of Mediterranean and East European Studies
Department of Nutrition and Home Economics
Department of Physics
Department of Psychology
Department of Religion
Department of Social Sciences
Department of Veterinary Medicine

SPECIAL PROGRAMS:
Center for the Basic Philosophy of Science
Center for Data Processing
Center for Regional Development Research
Radiation Center (including Nuclear Physics and Radiation Protection)
Teacher Training Center
Institute of Tropical Studies
Cooperative arrangements with 15 universities, including Kansas State University and the University of Wisconsin (Milwaukee and Madison)

LANGUAGE OF INSTRUCTION: German

ADMISSION REQUIREMENTS FOR FOREIGN STUDENTS:
Secondary school certificate (*Reifezeugnis*) or recognized foreign equivalent

TUITION FOR FOREIGN STUDENTS:
None

TOTAL INSTRUCTIONAL FACULTY:
518

LIBRARY COLLECTIONS:
University library—450,000 volumes

UNIVERSITY PUBLICATIONS:
Personal- und Vorlesungsverzeichnis der Justus-Liebig-Universitat

PRESIDENT: Prof. Dr. Heinz Bauer

UNIVERSITÄT HAMBURG
(University of Hamburg)
2000 Hamburg 13, Edmund-Siemers-Allee 1, Germany

CHARACTERISTICS OF INSTITUTION:
State-run, nonprofit university

DATE FOUNDED: 1919

TOTAL ENROLLMENT: 43,100 fulltime students (including 2,060 foreign students)

DEGREES AWARDED:
State examinations in various fields
State teaching qualification, secondary level
Magister (Mag.theol. or Mag.phil.)
  four years required
Diplom in various fields
  three–five years required
Doktor in various fields
  four–five years required (except Dr.med.—ten–twelve semesters required)
Habilitation (teaching qualification, university level)
  a minimum of three years following doctorate required

ACADEMIC PROGRAMS:
Department of Biology
Department of Chemistry
Department of Computer Science
Department of Economic Sciences
Department of Education
Department of of Geographical Sciences
Department of History
Department of History of Culture
Department of Law I
Department of Law II
Department of Mathematics
Department of Medicine
Department of Oriental Studies
Department of Philology
Department of Philosophy and Social Sciences
Department of Physical Education
Department of Physics

Department of Protestant Theology
Department of Psychology

SPECIAL PROGRAMS:
Institute for Integration Research
Institute for Peace Research and Security
Institute for Radio and Television
Institute for Shipbuilding
Interdisciplinary Center for University Didatics
Computer Center
Cooperative arrangements with 28 universities, including Smith College, Indiana University, Purdue University, Tulane University, Johns Hopkins University, Cornell University and Temple University

LANGUAGE OF INSTRUCTION: German

ADMISSION REQUIREMENTS FOR FOREIGN STUDENTS:
Secondary school certificate (Reifezeugnis) or recognized foreign equivalent

TUITION FOR FOREIGN STUDENTS:
None

TOTAL INSTRUCTIONAL FACULTY:
2,498

LIBRARY COLLECTIONS:
State and university library—2,000,000 volumes
Hamburg Research Center and Archives of World Economies—850,000 volumes

MUSEUMS AND GALLERIES:
Museums of Applied Botany, Geology, Mineralogy, Zoology
Botanical Garden

UNIVERSITY PUBLICATIONS:
Wegweiser durch die Universitat, uni hh Berichte und Meinungen, uni hh Reform, uni hh Forchung, uni hh Planung, Informationen zum Stadium in Humburg, Informationen für auslandische Studenten, Jahrsbericht des Prasidenten

PRESIDENT: Prof. Dr. Peter Fischer-Appelt

UNIVERSITÄT HANNOVER
(University of Hanover)
3000 Hannover, Welfengarten 1, German

CHARACTERISTICS OF INSTITUTION:
State-run, nonprofit university

DATE FOUNDED: 1831

TOTAL ENROLLMENT: 28,000 fulltime students (including 1,000 foreign students)

DEGREES AWARDED:
State examinations in law
State teaching qualification, secondary level

Magister Artium (arts)
four years required
Diplom in various fields
four–five years required
Doktor in various fields
four–five years required
Habilitation (teaching qualification, university level)
a minimum of three years following doctorate required

ACADEMIC PROGRAMS:
Department of Architecture
Department of Biology
Department of Chemistry
Department of Civil Engineering
Department of Earth Sciences
Department of Economics
Department of Education I
Department of Education II
Department of Electrical Engineering
Department of History, Philosophy and Social Sciences
Department of Horticulture
Department of Landscape Development and Planning
Department of Law
Department of Literature and Linguistics
Department of Mathematics
Department of Mechanical Engineering
Department of Physics

SPECIAL PROGRAMS:
Cooperative arrangements with seven universities, including the University of Nebraska and San Diego State University in California

LANGUAGE OF INSTRUCTION: German

ADMISSION REQUIREMENTS FOR FOREIGN STUDENTS:
Secondary school certificate (Reifezeugnis) or recognized foreign equivalent

TUITION FOR FOREIGN STUDENTS:
None

TOTAL INSTRUCTIONAL FACULTY:
1,340

LIBRARY COLLECTIONS:
University library—1,000,000 volumes
Technical information library—835,000 volumes

PRESIDENT: Prof. Heinrich Seidel

RUPRECHT-KARLS-UNIVERSITÄT HEIDELBURG
(Rupert Charles University of Heidelburg)
6900 Heidelburg, Grabengasse 1, Postfach 105760, Germany

CHARACTERISTICS OF INSTITUTION:
State-run, nonprofit university

DATE FOUNDED: 1386

TOTAL ENROLLMENT: 26,850 fulltime students (including 2,400 foreign students)

DEGREES AWARDED:
State examinations in law, medicine and dentistry
State teaching qualification, secondary level
Magister der Theologie, Magister Artium
    four years required
Diplom in various fields
    four–five years required
Doktor in various fields
    approximately eight semesters required
Zahnarztliche Staatsprüfung and Dr.med.dent
    ten semesters required
Medizinische Staatsprüfung and Dr.med
    twelve semesters required
Habilitation (teaching qualification, university level)
    a minimum of three years following doctorate required

ACADEMIC PROGRAMS:
Faculty of Chemistry
Faculty of Biology
Faculty of Clinical Medicine I
Faculty of Clinical Medicine II
Faculty of Clinical Medicine (Mannheim)
Faculty of Economic Sciences
Faculty of Geosciences
Faculty of Law
Faculty of Mathematics
Faculty of Modern Philology
Faculty of Oriental and Classical Studies
Faculty of Pharmacy
Faculty of Philosophy and History
Faculty of Physics and Astronomy
Faculty of Scientific Medicine
Faculty of Social and Behavioral Sciences
Faculty of Theology
Faculty of Theoretical Medicine

SPECIAL PROGRAMS:
Astronomic Institute
South Asia Institute
Observatory
Cancer Research Center
Computer Center
Nuclear Research Center
Cooperative arrangements with 31 universities, including Cornell University, University of Kentucky, Bucknell University, California State University, Wesleyan University, University of Massachusetts, University of Oregon, Randolf-Macon Woman's College, Sweet Briar College, Arizona State University, University of Miami, University of New Mexico, University of Kansas and University of Utah.

LANGUAGE OF INSTRUCTION: German

ADMISSION REQUIREMENTS FOR FOREIGN STUDENTS:
Secondary school certificate (Reifezeugnis) or recognized foreign equivalent

TUITION FOR FOREIGN STUDENTS:
None

TOTAL INSTRUCTIONAL FACULTY:
1,300

LIBRARY COLLECTIONS:
University library—2,316,000 volumes
Institute and seminar libraries

MUSEUMS AND GALLERIES:
Museums of Antiquities, Egyptology, Zoology, Geology and Paleontology, Mineralogy
Botanical Garden
Archaeological Collection of Plaster Casts, Prehistory Collection, Collection of Historical Instruments

UNIVERSITY PUBLICATIONS:
Unispeigel, Mitteilungsblatt des Rektors, Ruperto Carola, Pressemitteilungen Personalia, Heidelberger Jahrbucher

PRESIDENT: Prof. Dr. Volker Sellin

UNIVERSITÄT FRIDERICIANA KARLSRUHE
(University of Karlsruhe)
7500 Karlsruhe, Kaiserstrasse 12, Germany

CHARACTERISTICS OF INSTITUTION:
State-run, nonprofit university

DATE FOUNDED: 1825

TOTAL ENROLLMENT: 20,100 fulltime students (including 1,330 foreign students)

DEGREES AWARDED:
State examination in food chemistry
State teaching qualification, secondary level
Magister Artium (arts)
    four years required
Diplom in various fields
    four–five years required
Licentiate (Lic.rer.)
    an additional two years required
Doktor in various fields
    two–four years required
Habilitation (teaching qualification, university level)
    a minimum of three years following doctorate required

ACADEMIC PROGRAMS:
Faculty of Architecture
Faculty of Art and Social Sciences

Faculty of Biological and Geosciences
Faculty of Chemical Engineering
Faculty of Chemistry
Faculty of Construction Engineering
Faculty of Economics
Faculty of Electrical Engineering
Faculty of Information Sciences
Faculty of Mathematics
Faculty of Physics
Faculty of Mechanical Engineering

SPECIAL PROGRAMS:
Institute for Applied Computer Sciences
Institute for Regional Planning
Computer Center
Cooperative arrangements with 11 universities, including the University of California at Berkeley

LANGUAGE OF INSTRUCTION: German

ADMISSION REQUIREMENTS FOR FOREIGN STUDENTS:
Secondary school certificate (Reifezeugnis) or recognized foreign equivalent

TUITION FOR FOREIGN STUDENTS:
None

TOTAL INSTRUCTIONAL FACULTY:
1,143

LIBRARY COLLECTIONS:
University library—650,000 volumes
Faculty and institute libraries

UNIVERSITY PUBLICATIONS:
Universitätsfuhrer, Vorlesungsverzeichnis, Fridericiana, Uni-Information, Veroffentlichungsverzeichnis, Mitteilungsblatt

PRESIDENT: Prof. Dr. H. Kunle

CHRISTIAN-ALBRECHTS UNIVERSITÄT ZU KIEL
(Christian Albrect University of Kiel)
2300 Kiel, Neue Universitat, Olshausenstrasse 40, Germany

CHARACTERISTICS OF INSTITUTION:
State-run, nonprofit university

DATE FOUNDED: 1665

TOTAL ENROLLMENT: 18,000 fulltime students (including 900 foreign students)

DEGREES AWARDED:
State examinations in various fields
State teaching qualification, secondary level
Magister Artium (arts)
    four years required
Diplom in various fields
    four–four and one-half years required

Doktor in various fields
    approximately eight semesters (seven semesters for Dr.iur.) required
Zahnarztliche Staatsprüfung, Dr.med.dent, Dr.rer.pol.
    ten semesters required
Arztliche Staatsprüfung and Dr.med.
    eleven semesters required
Habilitation (teaching qualification, university level)
    a minimum of three years following doctorate required

ACADEMIC PROGRAMS:
Faculty of Agriculture
Faculty of Economics and Social Sciences
Faculty of Law
Faculty of Mathematics and Natural Sciences
Faculty of Medicine
Faculty of Philosophy
Faculty of Theology

SPECIAL PROGRAMS:
Institute of World Economics
Institute of Oceanography
Institute for the Teaching of Sciences
Cooperative arrangements with 10 universities, including Pennsylvania State University and the University of Indiana

LANGUAGE OF INSTRUCTION: German

ADMISSION REQUIREMENTS FOR FOREIGN STUDENTS:
Secondary school certificate (Reifezeugnis) or recognized foreign equivalent

TUITION FOR FOREIGN STUDENTS:
None

TOTAL INSTRUCTIONAL FACULTY:
470 (including 350 professors)

LIBRARY COLLECTIONS:
University library—1,400,000 volumes
Institute of World Economics library—1,600,000 volumes

MUSEUMS AND GALLERIES:
Museums of Zoology, Minerals and Petrographics, Geology and Paleontology
Museum of Ancient and Early History
Theater History Collection and Hebbel Collection
Wanderndes Museum

UNIVERSITY PUBLICATIONS:
Personal-und Vorlesungsverzeichnis, Christiana-Albertina, Jahresbericht, Universitätsreden

RECTOR: Prof. Dr. Michael Mülle-Wille

JOHANNES GUTTENBERG-UNIVERSITÄT MAINZ
(Johannes Guttenberg University of Mainz)

6500 Mainz, Saarstrasse 21, Postfach 3980, Germany

CHARACTERISTICS OF INSTITUTION:
State-run, nonprofit university

DATE FOUNDED: 1477

TOTAL ENROLLMENT: 26,000 fulltime students (including 1,500 foreign students)

DEGREES AWARDED:
State examinations in various fields
State teaching qualification, secondary level
Magister Artium (arts)
   eight semesters required
Diplom in various fields
   four–five years required
Doktor in various fields
   approximately eight semesters required
Zahnarztliche Staatsprüfung and Dr.med.dent.
   ten semesters required
Medizinische Staatsprüfung and Dr.med.
   eleven semesters required
Habilitation (teaching qualification, university level)
   a minimum of three years following doctorate required

ACADEMIC PROGRAMS:
Faculty of Applied Linguistics
Faculty of Biology
Faculty of Catholic Theology
Faculty of Chemistry and Pharmacy
Faculty of Evangelical Theology
Faculty of Fine Arts
Faculty of Geosciences
Faculty of History
Faculty of Law and Economics
Faculty of Mathematics
Faculty of Medicine (including dentistry)
Faculty of Music
Faculty of Philology I (German)
Faculty of Philology II (English)
Faculty of Philology III (romance, Slav, classical, history of art, Indology, Egyptology, Oriental studies)
Faculty of Philosophy and Pedagogy
Faculty of Physical Training
Faculty of Physics
Faculty of Social Sciences

SPECIAL PROGRAMS:
Cooperative arrangements with nine universities

LANGUAGE OF INSTRUCTION: German

ADMISSION REQUIREMENTS FOR FOREIGN STUDENTS:
Secondary school certificate (*Reifezeugnis*) or recognized foreign equivalent

TUITION FOR FOREIGN STUDENTS:
None

TOTAL INSTRUCTIONAL FACULTY:
1,256

LIBRARY COLLECTIONS:
University library—1,018,000 volumes

UNIVERSITY PUBLICATIONS:
Bericht des Prasidenten, Personen- und Studienverzeichnis, Universitätszeitung "JOGU," Forschungsmagazin, Forschungsbericht, Antrittsoverlesungen

PRESIDENT: Prof. Dr. E. J. Zöllner

**PHILIPPS-UNIVERSITÄT MARBURG
(Philipps University of Marburg)
3550 Marburg, Biegenstrasse 10–12, Germany**

CHARACTERISTICS OF INSTITUTION:
State-run, nonprofit university

DATE FOUNDED: 1527

TOTAL ENROLLMENT: 15,200 fulltime students

DEGREES AWARDED:
State examinations in various fields
   seven–twelve semesters required
State teaching qualification, secondary level
Magister Artium (arts)
   eight semesters required
Diplom in various fields
   four–five years required
Doktor in various fields
   approximately eight semesters required
Zahnarztliche Staatsprüfung and Dr.med.dent.
   ten semesters required
Medizinische Staatsprüfung and Dr.med.
   twelve semesters required
Habilitation (teaching qualification, university level)
   a minimum of three years following doctorate required

ACADEMIC PROGRAMS:
Department of Antiquities
Department of Biology
Department of Chemistry
Department of Economics
Department of Education (including physical education)
Department of General Linguistics and German Philology
Department of Geography
Department of Geosciences
Department of History
Department of Human Medicine (including dentistry)

Department of Law
Department of Mathematics
Department of Modern German Literature and Arts
Department of Modern Languages and Literature
Department of Non-European Languages and Literature
Department of Pharmacy and Food Chemistry
Department of Physical Chemistry
Department of Physics
Department of Psychology
Department of Social Sciences and Philosophy
Department of Theology

SPECIAL PROGRAMS:
Cooperative arrangements with nine universities, including Syracuse University in New York

LANGUAGE OF INSTRUCTION: German

ADMISSION REQUIREMENTS FOR FOREIGN STUDENTS:
Secondary school certificate (Reifezeugnis) or recognized foreign equivalent

TUITION FOR FOREIGN STUDENTS:
None

TOTAL INSTRUCTIONAL FACULTY:
650

LIBRARY COLLECTIONS:
University library—1,000,000 volumes
Libraries of the departments and institutes

MUSEUMS AND GALLERIES:
Museum of Art and Cultural History
Collection of Religious Art and Ceremonial Utensils

UNIVERSITY PUBLICATIONS:
Marburger Universitätszeitung

PRESIDENT: Prof. Dr. Dietrich Simon

TECHNISCHE UNIVERSITÄT MUNCHEN
(Technical University Of Munich)
8000 Munich 2, Arcisstrasse 21, Germany

CHARACTERISTICS OF INSTITUTION:
State-run, nonprofit university

DATE FOUNDED: 1868

TOTAL ENROLLMENT: 23,250 fulltime students

DEGREES AWARDED:
State examinations in Food Chemistry and Medicine
    four–six years required
State teaching qualification, secondary level
Diplom in various fields
    two–five years required
Doktor in various fields
    a minimum of two years following the completion
    of studies required

Habilitation (teaching qualification, university level)
    a minimum of two years of scientific research following doctorate required

ACADEMIC PROGRAMS:
Faculty of Agriculture and Horticulture
Faculty of Architecture
Faculty of Brewing, Food Technology and Dairy Science
Faculty of Chemistry, Biology and Geosciences
Faculty of Civil Engineering and Surveying
Faculty of Economics and Social Sciences
Faculty of Electrical Engineering
Faculty of Mathematics and Informatics
Faculty of Mechanical Engineering
Faculty of Medicine
Faculty of Physics

SPECIAL PROGRAMS:
Institute of Environmental Planning and Research
    Center for Physical Education
Cooperative arrangements with four universities, including the University of Illinois

LANGUAGE OF INSTRUCTION: German

ADMISSION REQUIREMENTS FOR FOREIGN STUDENTS:
Secondary school certificate (Reifezeugnis) or recognized foreign equivalent

TUITION FOR FOREIGN STUDENTS:
None

TOTAL INSTRUCTIONAL FACULTY:
3,406

LIBRARY COLLECTIONS:
University library—1,250,000 volumes

UNIVERSITY PUBLICATIONS:
Personen- und Vorlesungsverzeichnis, Jahrbuch

PRESIDENT: Prof. Dr.Ing. Otto Meitinger

WESTFALISCHE WILHELMS-UNIVERSITÄT MÜNSTER
(Westfalische Wilhelms University of Münster)
4400 Munster, Schlossplatz 2, Germany

CHARACTERISTICS OF INSTITUTION:
State-run, nonprofit university

DATE FOUNDED: 1780

TOTAL ENROLLMENT: 45,600 fulltime students (including 1,800 foreign students)

DEGREES AWARDED:
State examinations in various fields
State teaching qualification, secondary level
Magister Artium (arts)
    eight semesters required
Diplom in various fields

eight–ten semesters required
Doktor in various fields
   six–ten semesters required
Habilitation (teaching qualification, university level)
   a minimum of three years following doctorate required

ACADEMIC PROGRAMS:
Department of Biology
Department of Catholic Theology
Department of Chemistry
Department of Classical and Non-European Studies
Department of Earth Sciences
Department of Economic Sciences
Department of Education
Department of English Studies
Department of Germanic Studies
Department of German Language, Literature and Arts (teacher training)
Department of History
Department of Law
Department of Mathematics
Department of Medicine
Department of Philosophy
Department of Physics
Department of Protestant Theology
Department of Psychology
Department of Romance and Slavonic Studies
Department of Social Sciences
Department of Sport Sciences

SPECIAL PROGRAMS:
Center for Mature Students
Cooperative arrangements with 17 universities, including California State University

LANGUAGE OF INSTRUCTION: German

ADMISSION REQUIREMENTS FOR FOREIGN STUDENTS:
Secondary school certificate (*Reifezeugnis*) or recognized foreign equivalent

TUITION FOR FOREIGN STUDENTS:
None

TOTAL INSTRUCTIONAL FACULTY:
2,176 fulltime faculty (including 675 professors)
700 parttime faculty

LIBRARY COLLECTIONS:
University library—1,655,000 volumes
Institute and seminar libraries

MUSEUMS AND GALLERIES:
Museums of Geology, Mineralogy, Archaeology

UNIVERSITY PUBLICATIONS:
Personal- und Vorlesungs- Verzeichnis der WWU, Jahresbericht des Rektors, Jahresschrift der Gesellschaft zur Forderung der WWU, Universitäts-Zeitung, Dissertationen der Mathematischen- Naturwissenschaftlichen Fakulttät in Referaten, Struktur der Studeierenden der WWU, Amtliche Bekanntmachungen der WWU

RECTOR: Prof. Dr. Maria Wasna

UNIVERSITÄT TRIER
(University of Trier)
5500 Trier, Postfach 3825, Germany

CHARACTERISTICS OF INSTITUTION:
State-run, nonprofit university

DATE FOUNDED: 1970

TOTAL ENROLLMENT: 8,750 fulltime students (including 510 foreign students)

DEGREES AWARDED:
State examination in law
   six years required
State teaching qualification, secondary level
   four–five years required
Magister Artium (arts)
   five years required
Diplom in various fields
   five years required
Doktor in various fields
   eight–ten semesters required
Habilitation (teaching qualification, university level)
   a minimum of three years following doctorate required

ACADEMIC PROGRAMS:
Faculty of Geography/Geosciences, History, Political Sciences, Classical Archaeology, Egyptology, Art History and Papyrology
Faculty of Language and Literature
Faculty of Law
Faculty of Management, Economics, Sociology, Political Economy, Applied Mathematics and Ethnology
Faculty of Pedagogy, Philosophy and Psychology

SPECIAL PROGRAMS:
Institute for Cusanus Studies
Institute for Labor Legislation and Labor Relations in the European Community
Cooperative arrangements with seven universities, including Clark University in Massachusetts

LANGUAGE OF INSTRUCTION: German

ADMISSION REQUIREMENTS FOR FOREIGN STUDENTS:
Secondary school certificate (*Reifezeugnis*) or recognized foreign equivalent

TUITION FOR FOREIGN STUDENTS:
None

TOTAL INSTRUCTIONAL FACULTY:
550

LIBRARY COLLECTIONS:
Central library—900,000 volumes

UNIVERSITY PUBLICATIONS:
UNI-Journal, Studienfuhrer, Vorlesungsverzeichnis, Trierer Beitrage, Trierer Universitätsreden, Forschungsbericht, Jahresbericht

PRESIDENT: Prof. Dr. Jörg Hasler

EBERHARD-KARLS-UNIVERSITÄT TÜBINGEN
(Eberhard Karl University of Tübingen)
7400 Tubingen 1, Wilhelmstrasse 5, Germany

CHARACTERISTICS OF INSTITUTION:
State-run, nonprofit university

DATE FOUNDED: 1477

TOTAL ENROLLMENT: 23,550 fulltime students (including 1,060 foreign students)

DEGREES AWARDED:
State examinations in various fields
    four–six years required
State teaching qualification, secondary level
    four years required
Magister Artium (arts)
    four years required
Diplom in various fields
    four–four and one-half years required
Doktor in various fields
    approximately eight semesters required
Zahnarztliche Staatsprüfung and Dr.med.dent.
    ten semesters required
Medizinische Staatsprüfung and Dr.med.
    eleven semesters required
Habilitation (teaching qualification, university level)
    a minimum of three years following doctorate required

ACADEMIC PROGRAMS:
Department of Biology
Department of Catholic Theology
Department of Chemistry and Pharmacy
Department of Clinical Medicine
Department of Cultural Sciences
Department of Economics
Department of Geosciences
Department of History
Department of Law
Department of Mathematics
Department of Modern Languages
Department of Philosophy
Department of Physics
Department of Protestant Theology
Department of Social and Behavioral Sciences
Department of Theoretical Medicine

SPECIAL PROGRAMS:
German Institute for Distance Studies
Institute for Special Pedagogies
Data Processing Center
Cooperative arrangements with 49 universities, including: University of Flordia, University of Iowa, University of Kansas, University of Michigan, State University of New York at Stony Brook, Tufts University, University of Washington (Seattle), Washington University (St. Louis), Antioch College, University of California at Berkeley, California State University, University of Denver, University of Maryland, University of Oregon, Oregon State University, Wittenberg University, Arizona State University, University of Colorado, Georgetown University, Louisiana State University, McMaster University in Canada, Temple University, Texas A&M University, University of Virginia, University of North Carolina, and Brown University

LANGUAGE OF INSTRUCTION: German

ADMISSION REQUIREMENTS FOR FOREIGN STUDENTS:
Secondary school certificate *(Reifezeugnis)* or recognized foreign equivalent

TUITION FOR FOREIGN STUDENTS:
None

TOTAL INSTRUCTIONAL FACULTY:
1,825

LIBRARY COLLECTIONS:
University library—2,200,000 volumes
100 institute libraries—2,500,000 volumes

MUSEUMS AND GALLERIES:
Museums of Archaeology, Egyptology, Geology and Paleontology, Zoology
Botanical Gardens

UNIVERSITY PUBLICATIONS:
Attempto, Amtliche Mitteilungen, Tubinger Universitätszeitung, Tubinger Universitätsnachrichten, Forschungsbericht

PRESIDENT: Adolf Theis

BÄYERISCHE-JULIUS-MAXIMILIANS-UNIVERSITÄT WÜRZBERG
(Bavarian Julius Maximilian University of Würzberg)
8700 Wurzberg, Sanderring 2, Germany

CHARACTERISTICS OF INSTITUTION:
State-run, nonprofit university

DATE FOUNDED: 1582

TOTAL ENROLLMENT: 17,450 fulltime students (including 630 foreign students)

DEGREES AWARDED:
State examinations in various fields
    four–six years required
State teaching qualification, secondary level
Magister Artium (arts)
    four years required
Diplom in various fields
    four–five years required
Doktor in various fields
    approximately four years required
Dr.med.dent and Dr.med
    five and one-half years required
Dr.theol
    six years required
Habilitation (teaching qualification, university level)
    a minimum of three years following doctorate required

ACADEMIC PROGRAMS:
Faculty of Biology
Faculty of Catholic Theology
Faculty of Chemistry and Pharmacy (including food technology)
Faculty of Geosciences
Faculty of Economics
Faculty of Law
Faculty of Mathematics
Faculty of Medicine (including dentistry)
Faculty of Philosophy I (antiquity and cultural studies)
Faculty of Philosophy II (philology, history and history of art)
Faculty of Philosophy III (philosophy, education and social sciences)
Faculty of Physics and Astronomy
Faculty of Social and Behavioral Sciences
School of Child Care
School of Dietetics
School of Medical Technology
School of Midwifery
School of Nursing
School of Physical Rehabilitation
School of Physiotherapy

SPECIAL PROGRAMS:
Cooperative arrangements with 17 universities, including the State University of New York (Oneonta, Buffalo and Albany) and Davidson College in North Carolina

LANGUAGE OF INSTRUCTION: German

ADMISSION REQUIREMENTS FOR FOREIGN STUDENTS:
Secondary school certificate (Reifezeugnis) or recognized foreign equivalent

TUITION FOR FOREIGN STUDENTS:
None

TOTAL INSTRUCTIONAL FACULTY:
661

LIBRARY COLLECTIONS:
University library—1,000,000 volumes
Institute libraries—1,400,000 volumes

MUSEUMS AND GALLERIES:
Martin von Wagner Museum, Mineralogy Museum

UNIVERSITY PUBLICATIONS:
Personal- und Volesungsverzeichnis, Jahresbericht, Informationsblatt, Wurzberg Heute

PRESIDENT: Prof. Dr.phil. Th. Berchem

RHEINISCHE-WESTFALISCHE TECHNISCHE HOCHSCULE AACHEN
(Rhenish Westphalian Technical University)
5100 Aachen, Templergraben 55, Germany

CHARACTERISTICS OF INSTITUTION:
State-run, nonprofit university

DATE FOUNDED: 1870

TOTAL ENROLLMENT: 36,500 fulltime students (including 3,800 foreign students)

DEGREES AWARDED:
State examination in medicine
    five and one-half years required
State teaching qualification, secondary level
    four years required
Magister Artium (arts)
    four years required
Diplom in various fields
    two–four years required
Doktor in various fields
    three–four years after diploma required
Habilitation (teaching qualification, university level)
    a minimum of three years following doctorate required

ACADEMIC PROGRAMS:
Faculty of Architecture
Faculty of Arts
Faculty of Civil Engineering and Surveying
Faculty of Economics
Faculty of Education
Faculty of Electrical Engineering
Faculty of Mathematics and Natural Sciences
Faculty of Mechanical Engineering
Faculty of Medicine
Faculty of Mining, Metallurgy and Geological Science

Institute of Plastic Technology
Preuniversity Course for Foreign Students.

SPECIAL PROGRAMS:
Interdisciplinary Center for Environmental Protection
Institute of Biomedical Technology
Rationalization Research Institute
Research Center for Technical and Economic Structures of the Steel Industry
Research Institute for Hydrotechnology
Research Institute for Laser Technoloogy
Research Institute for Production Technology
Wood Research Institute
Cooperative arrangements with 25 universities, including Florida Atlantic University, Columbia University and the Space Institute of the University of Tennessee

LANGUAGE OF INSTRUCTION: German

ADMISSION REQUIREMENTS FOR FOREIGN STUDENTS:
Secondary school certificate (Reifezeugnis) or recognized foreign equivalent

TUITION FOR FOREIGN STUDENTS:
None

TOTAL INSTRUCTIONAL FACULTY:
2,027 (including 510 professors)

LIBRARY COLLECTIONS:
Central library—570,000 volumes
Institute libraries

UNIVERSITY PUBLICATIONS:
Vorlesungsverzeichnis, Alma Mater Aquensis, RWTH-Themen

PRESIDENT: Prof. Dr.rer.nat. K. Habetha

UNIVERSITÄT AUGSBURG
(University of Augsburg)
8900 Augsburg, Universitätsstrasse 2, Germany

CHARACTERISTICS OF INSTITUTION:
State-run, nonprofit university

DATE FOUNDED: 1970

TOTAL ENROLLMENT: 11,200 fulltime students (including 400 foreign students)

DEGREES AWARDED:
State examination in law
State teaching qualification, primary and secondary levels
Diplom in various fields
    four years required
Magister Artium (arts)
    four years required

Doktor in various fields
    four–five years required
Habilitation (university teaching qualification)
    a minimum of three years following doctorate required

ACADEMIC PROGRAMS:
Faculty of Catholic Theology
Faculty of Economics and Social Science
Faculty of Jurisprudence
Faculty of Natural Sciences
Faculty of Philosophy I (human sciences)
Faculty of Philosophy II (modern languages)

SPECIAL PROGRAMS:
Cooperative arrangements with 12 other universities, including Emory University in Georgia and the University of Pittsburgh in Pennsylvania

LANGUAGE OF INSTRUCTION: German

ADMISSION REQUIREMENTS FOR FOREIGN STUDENTS:
Secondary school certificate (Reifezeugnis) or recognized foreign equivalent

TUITION FOR FOREIGN STUDENTS:
None

TOTAL INSTRUCTIONAL FACULTY:
430

LIBRARY COLLECTIONS:
Central library—1,400,000 volumes

PRESIDENT: Prof. Dr. Josef Becker

UNIVERSITÄT BAMBERG
(University of Bamberg)
8600 Bamberg, Kapuzinerstrasse 16, Germany

CHARACTERISTICS OF INSTITUTION:
State-run, nonprofit university

DATE FOUNDED: 1648

TOTAL ENROLLMENT: 5,500 fulltime students (including 150 foreign students)

DEGREES AWARDED:
State teaching qualification, primary level
    four–five years required
Diplom in various fields
    four–five years required
Lizentiat in Theology
    five years required
Magister Artium (arts)
    four–five years required
Doktor in various fields
    eight–ten semesters required
Habilitation (teaching qualification, university level)
    at least three years after doctorate required

ACADEMIC PROGRAMS:
Faculty of Catholic Theology
Faculty of Education, Philosophy and Psychology
Faculty of History and Earth Sciences
Faculty of Languages and Literature
Faculty of Social and Economic Sciences
School of Social Work

SPECIAL PROGRAMS:
Computer Center
Sociological Research Center
Institute of Physical Education
Cooperative arrangements with four universities, including Brown University in Rhode Island and the University of South Carolina

LANGUAGE OF INSTRUCTION: German

ADMISSION REQUIREMENTS FOR FOREIGN STUDENTS:
Secondary school certificate *(Reifezeugnis)* or recognized foreign equivalent

TUITION FOR FOREIGN STUDENTS:
None

TOTAL INSTRUCTIONAL FACULTY:
300

LIBRARY COLLECTIONS:
Central library—550,000 volumes

UNIVERSITY PUBLICATIONS:
Bamberger Universitätszeitung, Bamberger Geographische Schriften, Bamberger Beitrage zur Englischen Sprachwissenschaft, Gratia, Bamberger Schriften zur Renaissanceforschung, Bamberger Hochschulscriften, Pressemitteilungen, Informationen, Personal- und Vorlesungsverzeichnis Bericht des Prasidenten, Forschungsbericht

PRESIDENT: Prof. Dr. Siegfried Oppolzer

TECHNISCHE UNIVERSITÄT BERLIN
(Technical University of Berlin)
1000 Berlin 12, Strasse des 17 Juni 135, Germany

CHARACTERISTICS OF INSTITUTION:
State-run, nonprofit university

DATE FOUNDED: The *Bauakademie* (founded 1799) merged with the *Gewerbeakademie* (founded 1821) in 1879 to become the *Technische Hochschule Berlin.* Opened under present name in 1946.

TOTAL ENROLLMENT: 33,000 fulltime students (including 5,000 foreign students)

DEGREES AWARDED:
State teaching qualification, secondary level in technical sciences
Diplom in various fields
    four–five years required

Magister Artium (arts)
    four years required
Doktor in various fields
    five years required
Habilitation (teaching qualification, university level)
    a minimum of three years following doctorate required

ACADEMIC PROGRAMS:
Department of Architecture
Department of Building and Geodetic Sciences
Department of Chemistry
Department of Communications and Humanities
Department of Computer Science
Department of Construction and Manufacturing
Department of Economics
Department of Electrical Engineering
Department of Environmental Science
Department of Education
Department of International Agricultural Development
Department of Mathematics
Department of Materials Science
Department of Mining and Earth Sciences
Department of Nutrition and Biotechnology
Department of Physical and Applied Chemistry
Department of Physical Engineering
Department of Physics
Department of Process Engineering
Department of Regional Development
Department of Social Sciences and Planning
Department of Transport Engineering

SPECIAL PROGRAMS:
Institute of Turbulence Research
Cooperative arrangements with 39 universities, including the University of Michigan, the University of California at Berkeley, the University of Oklahoma, the University of North Carolina at Chapel Hill and the Massachusetts Institute of Technology

LANGUAGE OF INSTRUCTION: German

ADMISSION REQUIREMENTS FOR FOREIGN STUDENTS:
Secondary school certificate *(Reifezeugnis)* or recognized foreign equivalent

TUITION FOR FOREIGN STUDENTS:
None

TOTAL INSTRUCTIONAL FACULTY:
674

LIBRARY COLLECTIONS:
University library—1,000,000 volumes

UNIVERSITY PUBLICATIONS:
Humanismus und Technik, Mitteilungsblatt der TUB, Vorlesungsverzeichnis, Universitätsfuhrer, Forshung Ak-

tuel, Wissenschaftsmagazin der TU Berlin, TU International, TU intern

PRESIDENT: Prof. Dr.Ing. Manfred Fricke

RUHR-UNIVERSITÄT BOCHUM
(University of the Ruhr at Bochum)
4630 Bochum, Universitätsstrasse 150, Germany

CHARACTERISTICS OF INSTITUTION:
State-run, nonprofit university

DATE FOUNDED: 1961

TOTAL ENROLLMENT: 34,500 fulltime students (including 1,700 foreign students)

DEGREES AWARDED:
State examination in law
  seven semesters required
State teaching qualification, secondary level
  eight semesters required
Diplom in various fields
  eight semesters required
Magister Artium (arts)
  eight semesters required
Doktor in various fields
  approximately eight semesters required
Habilitation (teaching qualification, university level)
  a minimum of three years following doctorate required

ACADEMIC PROGRAMS:
Faculty of Biology
Faculty of Catholic Theology
Faculty of Chemistry
Faculty of Civil Engineering
Faculty of East Asian Studies
Faculty of Economics
Faculty of Electrical Engineering
Faculty of Geosciences
Faculty of History
Faculty of Law
Faculty of Mathematics
Faculty of Mechanical Engineering
Faculty of Medicine
Faculty of Philosophy, Pedagogy and Journalism
Faculty of Philology
Faculty of Physics and Astronomy
Faculty of Protestant Theology
Faculty of Psychology
Faculty of Social Sciences
Faculty of Sport Science

SPECIAL PROGRAMS:
Cooperative arrangements with 16 universities, including Texas A & M University

LANGUAGE OF INSTRUCTION: German

ADMISSION REQUIREMENTS FOR FOREIGN STUDENTS:
Secondary school certificate *(Reifezeugnis)* or recognized foreign equivalent

TUITION FOR FOREIGN STUDENTS:
None

TOTAL INSTRUCTIONAL FACULTY:
1,650 (including 510 professors)

LIBRARY COLLECTIONS:
University library—700,000 volumes
Faculty and institute libraries

UNIVERSITY PUBLICATIONS:
RUB-aktuell, Zeitung der Ruhr-Universität Bochum, Rechenschaftsbericht des Rektorates, Jarbuch, Amtliche Bekanntmachungen, RUB-international, News from Ruhr University, the City of Bochum and the Region, Bochumer Universitätsreden

RECTOR: Prof. Dr. Wolfgang Massberg

TECHNISCHE UNIVERSITÄT CAROLO-WILHELINA ZU BRAUNSCHWEIG
(Carolo-Wilhelmina Technical University of Braunschweig)
3300 Braunschweig, Pockelsstrasse 14, Germany

CHARACTERISTICS OF INSTITUTION:
State-run, nonprofit university

DATE FOUNDED: 1745

TOTAL ENROLLMENT: 17,000 fulltime students (including 620 foreign students)

DEGREES AWARDED:
State teaching qualification, secondary level in natural sciences
Diplom in various fields
  seven–ten semesters required
Magister Artium (arts)
  eight semesters required
Doktor in various fields
  approximately eight semesters required
Habilitation (teaching qualification, university level)
  a minimum of three years following doctorate required

ACADEMIC PROGRAMS:
Department 1 (mathematics, informatics and economic sciences)
Department 2 (physics and geosciences)
Department 3 (chemistry, pharmacy and biosciences)
Department 4 (architecture)
Department 5 (building engineering)
Department 6 (mechanical engineering)
Department 7 (electrical engineering)

Department 8 (philosophy and social science)
Department 9 (education)

SPECIAL PROGRAMS:
Cooperative arrangements with nine other universities, including the State University of Nebraska and the University of New York

LANGUAGE OF INSTRUCTION: German

ADMISSION REQUIREMENTS FOR FOREIGN STUDENTS:
Secondary school certificate (Reifezeugnis) or recognized foreign equivalent

TUITION FOR FOREIGN STUDENTS:
None

TOTAL INSTRUCTIONAL FACULTY:
270 fulltime professors

LIBRARY COLLECTIONS:
University library—770,000 volumes

MUSEUMS AND GALLERIES:
Botanical gardens

UNIVERSITY PUBLICATIONS:
Mitteilungen, Personal- und Vorlesungsverzeichnis, TU-aktuell Forschungsberichtsband, Veroffentlichung der Technischen Universität

PRESIDENT: Prof. Dr.Iur. Bernd Rebe

TECHNISCHE HOCHSCULE DARMSTADT
(Technical University of Darmstadt)
6100 Darmstadt, Karolinenplatz 5, Germany

CHARACTERISTICS OF INSTITUTION:
State-run, nonprofit university

DATE FOUNDED: 1836

TOTAL ENROLLMENT: 16,500 fulltime students (including 1,500 foreign students)

DEGREES AWARDED:
State teaching qualification, secondary and technical level
   four years required
Diplom in various fields
   eleven–fourteen semesters required
Doktor in various fields
   an additional two–three years required
Habilitation (teaching qualification, university level)
   a minimum of three years following doctorate required

ACADEMIC PROGRAMS:
Department 1 (law and economics)
Department 2 (history and social sciences)
Department 3 (education science, psychology and sports science)

Department 4 (mathematics)
Department 5 (physics)
Department 6 (mechanics)
Department 7 (physical chemistry and chemical technology)
Department 8 (inorganic chemistry and nuclear chemistry)
Department 9 (organic, bio- and macromolecular chemistry)
Department 10 (biology)
Department 11 (geosciences and geography)
Department 12 (surveying)
Department 13 (water and transport)
Department 14 (constructional engineering)
Department 15 (architecture)
Department 16 (mechanical engineering)
Department 17 (electrical energy technology)
Department 18 (electrical communications technology)
Department 19 (control and data technology)
Department 20 (computer science)
Department 21 (material science)

SPECIAL PROGRAMS:
Cooperative arrangements with 22 other universities, including the State University of New York at Buffalo and the University of Illinois

LANGUAGE OF INSTRUCTION: German

ADMISSION REQUIREMENTS FOR FOREIGN STUDENTS:
Secondary school certificate (Reifezeugnis) or recognized foreign equivalent

TUITION FOR FOREIGN STUDENTS:
None

TOTAL INSTRUCTIONAL FACULTY:
334 fulltime professors

LIBRARY COLLECTIONS:
Land (state) and university library—900,000 volumes

UNIVERSITY PUBLICATIONS:
Die Hochschule, Personal- und Studienplanverzeichnis, Jahrbuch, Rechenschaftsbericht des Prasidenten, Forschungsbericht

PRESIDENT: Prof. Dr.phil. Helmut Böhme

UNIVERSITÄT DORTMUND
(University of Dortmund)
4600 Dortmund-Eichlinghofen, August-Schmidt-Strasse, Germany

CHARACTERISTICS OF INSTITUTION:
State-run, nonprofit university

DATE FOUNDED: 1966

TOTAL ENROLLMENT: 20,300 fulltime students (including 800 foreign students)

DEGREES AWARDED:
State teaching qualification, secondary level and vocational schools
three–four years required
Diplom in various fields
four–five years required
Doktor in various fields
three–four years after diplom required
Habilitation (teaching qualification, university level)
a minimum of three years following doctorate required

ACADEMIC PROGRAMS:
Department of Building Construction and Architecture
Department of Chemical Engineering
Department of Chemistry
Department of Computer Sciences
Department of Economic and Social Sciences
Department of Education and Biology
Department of Electrical Engineering
Department of Language and Literature, Journalism and History
Department of Mathematics
Department of Mechanical Engineering
Department of Music, Arts, Sport and Geography
Department of Physics
Department of Sociology, Philosophy and Theology
Department of Special Education and Rehabilitation
Department of Statistics
Department of Urban and Regional Planning

SPECIAL PROGRAMS:
Institute of Environmental Studies
Institute of Occupational Health
Institute for Robotics Research
Institute of Spectrochemistry
Institute for Transport Technology
Computer Center
Center for Didactics
Center for Lifelong Education
Cooperative arrangements with 12 other universities, including the State University of New York at Buffalo

LANGUAGE OF INSTRUCTION: German

ADMISSION REQUIREMENTS FOR FOREIGN STUDENTS:
Secondary school certificate (Reifezeugnis) or recognized foreign equivalent

TUITION FOR FOREIGN STUDENTS:
None

TOTAL INSTRUCTIONAL FACULTY:
1,000

LIBRARY COLLECTIONS:
Total collection—1,318,000 volumes

UNIVERSITY PUBLICATIONS:
Forschungsbericht, Amtliche Mitteilungen, Vorlesungsverzeichnis, Uni-Report

RECTOR: Prof. Dr. D. Müller-Bölling

UNIVERSITÄT DUISBERG GESAMTHOCHSCHULE (Polytechnic University of Duisberg)
4100 Duisberg, Lotharstrasse 65, Germany

CHARACTERISTICS OF INSTITUTION:
State-run, nonprofit university

DATE FOUNDED: 1972

TOTAL ENROLLMENT: 12,400 fulltime students (including 700 foreign students)

DEGREES AWARDED:
State teaching qualification, secondary level
four years required
Diplom in various fields
three years required
Doktor in various fields
a minimum of three years following doctorate required
Habilitation (teaching qualification, university level)
at least three years after Doktor required

ACADEMIC PROGRAMS:
Department 1 (philosophy, evangelical and Catholic theology, social sciences)
Department 2 (educational science, psychology, physical education)
Department 3 (linguistics)
Department 4 (art and music)
Department 5 (economics)
Department 6 (biology, chemistry and geography)
Department 7 (construction engineering)
Department 8 (metallurgy and ceramics)
Department 9 (electrical and control engineering)
Department 10 (physics and technology)
Department 11 (mathematics)

SPECIAL PROGRAMS:
Cooperative arrangements with nine other universities, including the University of Minnesota and the University of Washington

LANGUAGE OF INSTRUCTION: German

ADMISSION REQUIREMENTS FOR FOREIGN STUDENTS:
Secondary school certificate (Reifezeugnis) or recognized foreign equivalent

TUITION FOR FOREIGN STUDENTS:
None

TOTAL INSTRUCTIONAL FACULTY:
750

LIBRARY COLLECTIONS:
University library—650,500 volumes
Departmental libraries

UNIVERSITY PUBLICATIONS:
Amtliche Mitteilungen, Universitäts-Report, Vorlesungs-verzeichnis

RECTOR: Prof. Dr.rer.nat. Gernot Born

GEORG-AUGUST-UNIVERSITÄT GOTTINGEN
(George August University of Gottingen)
3400 Gottingen, Postfach 3744, Germany

CHARACTERISTICS OF INSTITUTION:
State-run, nonprofit university

DATE FOUNDED: 1737

TOTAL ENROLLMENT: 30,000 fulltime students

DEGREES AWARDED:
State examinations in law, medicine and dentistry
State teaching qualification, secondary level
Diplom in various fields
   four–five years required
Magister Artium (arts)
   four–five years required
Doktor in various fields
   approximately nine semesters required
Zahnarztliche Staatsprüfung and Dr.med.dent.
   ten semesters required
Medizinische Staatsprüfung and Dr.med.
   eleven semesters required
Habilitation (teaching qualification, university level)
   a minimum of three years following doctorate required

ACADEMIC PROGRAMS:
Faculty of Agriculture
Faculty of Biology
Faculty of Chemistry
Faculty of Economics
Faculty of Education
Faculty of Forestry
Faculty of Geology
Faculty of History and Philology
Faculty of Law
Faculty of Mathematics
Faculty of Medicine (including dentistry)
Faculty of Physics
Faculty of Social Sciences (including political sci-
   ences and journalism)
Faculty of Theology (Protestant)

SPECIAL PROGRAMS:
Cooperative arrangements with universities from
around the world, including in the United States

LANGUAGE OF INSTRUCTION: German

ADMISSION REQUIREMENTS FOR FOREIGN STUDENTS:
Secondary school certificate *(Reifezeugnis)* or recognized foreign equivalent

TUITION FOR FOREIGN STUDENTS:
None

TOTAL INSTRUCTIONAL FACULTY:
600

LIBRARY COLLECTIONS:
University and state library of lower Saxony—
3,000,000 volumes

MUSEUMS AND GALLERIES:
Museums of Ethnology, Zoology, Chemistry, Ar-
   chaeology
Collections of Musical Instruments and Physical In-
   struments
Art Gallery

UNIVERSITY PUBLICATIONS:
*Vorlesungsverzeichnis, Jahresforschungsbericht, Georgia-
Austria, Nachrichten, Hochschulzeichschift Informationen*

PRESIDENT: Prof. Dr. Norbert Kamp

UNIVERSITÄT ESSEN-GESAMTHOCHSCHULE
(Polytechnic University of Essen)
4300 Essen 1, Universitätsstrasse 2, Postfach 103764,
Germany

CHARACTERISTICS OF INSTITUTION:
State-run, nonprofit university

DATE FOUNDED: 1972

TOTAL ENROLLMENT: 17,500 fulltime students (including 800 foreign students)

DEGREES AWARDED:
State examination in medicine
State teaching qualification, secondary level
   three–four years required
Diplom in various fields
   four years required
Magister Artium (arts)
   four–five required
Doktor, in various fields
   four–five years required

ACADEMIC PROGRAMS:
Department of Architecture, Bio- and Geosciences
Department of Art and Design
Department of Chemistry
Department of Construction Engineering

Department of Economic Sciences
Department of Educational Sciences
Department of Energy, Systems and Electrotechnology
Department of Languages and Literature
Department of Mathematics
Department of Mechanical Engineering
Department of Medicine
Department of Philosophy, Religious Studies and Sociology
Department of Physics
Department of Surveying

SPECIAL PROGRAMS:
Cooperative arrangements with six universities

LANGUAGE OF INSTRUCTION: German

ADMISSION REQUIREMENTS FOR FOREIGN STUDENTS:
Secondary school certificate (Reifezeugnis) or recognized foreign equivalent; technical secondary education (Fachhochschulreife) for some courses

TUITION FOR FOREIGN STUDENTS:
None

TOTAL INSTRUCTIONAL FACULTY:
470

LIBRARY COLLECTIONS:
Central library—317,800 volumes

UNIVERSITY PUBLICATIONS:
Amtliche Bekanntmachungen, GH-Integrale

RECTOR: Prof. Dr. Christian Streffer

UNIVERSITÄT HOHENHEIM
(University of Hohenheim)
7000 Stuttgart 70 (Hohenheim), Postfach 70 05 62, Germany

CHARACTERISTICS OF INSTITUTION:
State-run, nonprofit university

DATE FOUNDED: 1818

TOTAL ENROLLMENT: 5,600 fulltime students (including 340 foreign students)

DEGREES AWARDED:
State teaching qualification, secondary level
Diplom in various fields
    five–six years required
Doktor in various fields
    six years required

ACADEMIC PROGRAMS:
Faculty of Agricultural Sciences I (plant production and ecology)
Faculty of Agricultural Sciences II (agricultural economics, agricultural technology and animal production)
Faculty of Biology
Faculty of Economics and Social Sciences
Faculty of General Natural Sciences

SPECIAL PROGRAMS:
Cooperative arrangements with 13 other universities, including the University of Oregon, the University of Georgia, the University of California at Los Angeles, State University of Massachusetts, the University of Rhode Island and the University of Nebraska

LANGUAGE OF INSTRUCTION: German

ADMISSION REQUIREMENTS FOR FOREIGN STUDENTS:
Secondary school certificate (Reifezeugnis) or recognized foreign equivalent

TUITION FOR FOREIGN STUDENTS:
None

TOTAL INSTRUCTIONAL FACULTY:
615

LIBRARY COLLECTIONS:
Total collection—327,000 volumes

MUSEUMS AND GALLERIES:
Museums of Zoology, Veterinary Medicine and Agriculture

UNIVERSITY PUBLICATIONS:
Hohenheimer Arbeiten, Daten und Dokumente zum Umweltschutz, Rechenschaftsbericht, Universitätsfuhrer, Vorlesungsverzeichnis, Forschungsbericht, Amtliche Mitteilungen

RECTOR: Prof. Dr. W. Haubold

UNIVERSITÄT KAISERLAUTERN
(University of Kaiserlautern)
6750 Kaiserlautern, Erwin-Schrodinger-Strasse, Postfach 3049, Germany

CHARACTERISTICS OF INSTITUTION:
State-run, nonprofit university

DATE FOUNDED: 1970

TOTAL ENROLLMENT: 8,350 fulltime students

DEGREES AWARDED:
State teaching qualification, secondary level
    four–six years required
Diplom in various fields
    four–six years required
Magister Artium (arts)
    four–five years required
Doktor in various fields

four–five years required

Habilitation (teaching qualification, university level) a minimum of three years following doctorate following

ACADEMIC PROGRAMS:

Faculty of Architecture, Environmental Studies, Education

Faculty of Biology

Faculty of Chemistry

Faculty of Computer Science

Faculty of Electrical Engineering

Faculty of Mathematics

Faculty of Mechanical Engineering

Faculty of Physics

Faculty of Social and Economic Sciences

SPECIAL PROGRAMS:

Cooperative arrangements with 80 other universities, including the Universities of: Duke, Louisiana State, California (Berkeley), Michigan, Utah, Vanderbilt, Philadelphia, Harvard, Missouri, Wisconsin, Temple, Arizona State, Lehigh, Texas A&M, Nebraska, Northeastern, New York State at Stony Brook, Washington State, Kansas, Connecticut, Rockefeller at New York, Carnegie-Mellon, Texas at Austin, Pennsylvania State, Southern Methodist and Illinois, and the Massachusetts Institute of Technology

LANGUAGE OF INSTRUCTION: German

ADMISSION REQUIREMENTS FOR FOREIGN STUDENTS:

Secondary school certificate (Reifezeugnis) or recognized foreign equivalent

TUITION FOR FOREIGN STUDENTS:

None

TOTAL INSTRUCTIONAL FACULTY:

500

LIBRARY COLLECTIONS:

Total collection—270,000 volumes

PRESIDENT: Prof. Dr.phil. Klaus Landfried

GESAMTHOCHSCHULE KASSEL
(Polytechnic University of Kassel)
Präsidialverwaltung, 3500 Kassel, Möncheberqstrasse 19, Germany

CHARACTERISTICS OF INSTITUTION:

State-run, nonprofit university

DATE FOUNDED: 1970

TOTAL ENROLLMENT: 11,900 fulltime students (including 800 foreign students)

DEGREES AWARDED:

State teaching qualification, secondary level

four–five years required

Graduierung in various fields

three years required

Diplom in various fields

three–five years required

Magister Artium (arts)

four–five years required

Doktor in various fields

four–five years required

Habilitation (teaching qualification, university level) a minimum of three years following doctorate required

ACADEMIC PROGRAMS:

Department of Agriculture

Department of Architecture

Department of Art

Department of Applied Social Sciences and Applied Law

Department of Biology and Chemistry

Department of Civil Engineering

Department of Economics

Department of Electrical Engineering

Department of Ergonomics, Vocational Education, Polytechnics

Department of German Language and Literature

Department of History, Social and Political Sciences

Department of Humanities and Education

Department of International Agriculture

Department of Mathematics

Department of Mechanical Engineering

Department of Philology, Romance, English and Anglo-American Studies

Department of Physics

Department of Product Design

Department of Psychology, Physical Education, Music

Department of Visual Communication

SPECIAL PROGRAMS:

Research Center on Profession and University Education

Research Center on Psychoanalysis, Psychotherapy and Mental Health

Cooperative arrangements with eight other universities, including the University of Reading in England, the University of Wisconsin and the University of Delaware

LANGUAGE OF INSTRUCTION: German

ADMISSION REQUIREMENTS FOR FOREIGN STUDENTS:

Secondary school certificate (Reifezeugnis) or recognized foreign equivalent; technical secondary education (Fachhochschulreife) for certain courses

TUITION FOR FOREIGN STUDENTS:
None

TOTAL INSTRUCTIONAL FACULTY:
367 professors

LIBRARY COLLECTIONS:
Central library—1,000,000 volumes

UNIVERSITY PUBLICATIONS:
Prisma, GhK-Publik, Fragmente, Schriftenreihe fur Psychoanalyse, Arbeitshefte zur Kinderpsychologie, Preciosa Casselana und Studia Casselana

PRESIDENT: Prof. Dr. Hans Brinckmann

UNIVERSITÄT KONSTANZ
(University of Constance)
7750 Konstanz, Postfach 5560, Germany

CHARACTERISTICS OF INSTITUTION:
State-run, nonprofit university

DATE FOUNDED: 1966

TOTAL ENROLLMENT: 8,800 fulltime students (including 450 foreign students)

DEGREES AWARDED:
State examination in law
   six and one-half years required
State teaching qualification, secondary level
   four–five years required
Diplom in various fields
   four years required
Magister Artium (arts)
   four years required
Licentiates
   an additional two years required
Doktor in various fields
   four–six years required
Habilitation (teaching qualification, university level)
   a minimum of two years following doctorate required

ACADEMIC PROGRAMS:
Faculty of Arts (including philosophy, history, literature and languages)
Faculty of Biology
Faculty of Chemistry
Faculty of Economics and Statistics
Faculty of Law
Faculty of Mathematics
Faculty of Physics
Faculty of Social Sciences (including political science, education, physical education, sociology, information science and psychology)

SPECIAL PROGRAMS:
Cooperative arrangements with 21 other universities, including Rutgers—The State University of New Jersey, St. Olaf College, Oregon State University, University of Massachusetts, Susquehanna University, Wellesley University, and the University of Oregon

LANGUAGE OF INSTRUCTION: German

ADMISSION REQUIREMENTS FOR FOREIGN STUDENTS:
Secondary school certificate *(Reifezeugnis)* or recognized foreign equivalent

TUITION FOR FOREIGN STUDENTS:
None

TOTAL INSTRUCTIONAL FACULTY:
171

LIBRARY COLLECTIONS:
Central library—1,300,000 volumes

UNIVERSITY PUBLICATIONS:
Personal- und Veranstaltungsverzeichnis, Konstanzer Blatter für Hochschulfragen, Konstanzer Universitätzeitung und Hochschulnachrichten, Uni-info, Studienfuhrer

RECTOR: Prof. Dr. H. Sund

UNIVERSITÄT MANNHEIM
(University of Mannheim)
6800 Mannheim 1, Schloss, Postfach 103462, Germany

CHARACTERISTICS OF INSTITUTION:
State-run, nonprofit university

DATE FOUNDED: 1907

TOTAL ENROLLMENT: 9,800 fulltime students (including 660 foreign students)

DEGREES AWARDED:
State examination in law
Diplom in various fields
   eight–ten semesters required
Magister Artium (arts)
   eight semesters required
Doktor in various fields
   four–five years required
Habilitation (teaching qualification, university level)
   a minimum of three years following doctorate required

ACADEMIC PROGRAMS:
Faculty of Economics
Faculty of History and Geography (including archaeology)
Faculty of Languages and Literature
Faculty of Law
Faculty of Mathematics and Information Sciences

Faculty of Philosophy, Psychology and Pedagogy
Faculty of Political Economy and Statistics
Faculty of Social Sciences (including political science)

SPECIAL PROGRAMS:
Institute of Communications Studies
Computer Center
Cooperative arrangements with 14 other universities, including the State University of New York at Stony Brook, Washington University and Georgetown University

LANGUAGE OF INSTRUCTION: German

ADMISSION REQUIREMENTS FOR FOREIGN STUDENTS:
Secondary school certificate (Reifezeugnis) or recognized foreign equivalent

TUITION FOR FOREIGN STUDENTS:
None

TOTAL INSTRUCTIONAL FACULTY:
165

LIBRARY COLLECTIONS:
Total collection—1,600,000 volumes

UNIVERSITY PUBLICATIONS:
Veroffentlichungen der Universität Mannheim, Amtliche Mitteilungen, Mannheimer Berichte

RECTOR: Prof. Dr. Otto H. Jacobs

TECHNISCHE UNIVERSITÄT MÜNCHEN
(Technical University of Munich)
8000 Munich 2, Arcisstrasse 21, Germany

CHARACTERISTICS OF INSTITUTION:
State-run, nonprofit university

DATE FOUNDED: 1868

TOTAL ENROLLMENT: 24,000 fulltime students

DEGREES AWARDED:
State examinations in various fields
    four–six years required
State teaching qualification, secondary level
Diplom in various fields
    two–five years required
Doktor in various fields
    a minimum of two years required following Diplom
Habilitation (teaching qualification, university level)
    at least two years scientific research after doctorate required

ACADEMIC PROGRAMS:
Faculty of Agriculture and Horticulture
Faculty of Architecture
Faculty of Brewing, Food Technology and Dairy Science

Faculty of Chemistry, Biology and Geosciences
Faculty of Civil Engineering and Surveying
Faculty of Economics and Social Sciences
Faculty of Electrical Engineering
Faculty of Mathematics and Informatics
Faculty of Mechanical Engineering
Faculty of Medicine
Faculty of Physics

SPECIAL PROGRAMS:
Institute of Environmental Planning and Research Center for Physical Education
Cooperative arrangements with four universities, including the University of Illinois

LANGUAGE OF INSTRUCTION: German

ADMISSION REQUIREMENTS FOR FOREIGN STUDENTS:
Secondary school certificate (Reifezeugnis) or recognized foreign equivalent

TUITION FOR FOREIGN STUDENTS:
None

TOTAL INSTRUCTIONAL FACULTY:
3,406

LIBRARY COLLECTIONS:
University library—1,250,000 volumes

UNIVERSITY PUBLICATIONS:
Personen- und Vorlesungsverzeichnis, Jahrbuch

PRESIDENT: Prof. Dr.Ing. Otto Meitinger

UNIVERSITÄT-GESAMHOCHSCHULE PADERBORN
(Polytechnic University of Paderborn)
4790 Paderborn, Warburger Strasse 100, Germany

CHARACTERISTICS OF INSTITUTION:
State-run, nonprofit university

DATE FOUNDED: 1972

TOTAL ENROLLMENT: 14,500 fulltime students (including 500 foreign students)

DEGREES AWARDED:
State examinations in various fields
    four–six years required
State teaching qualification, primary and secondary level
Diplom in various fields
    seven–ten semesters required
Magister Artium (arts)
    nine semesters required
Doktor in various fields
    eight–ten semesters required
Habilitation (teaching qualification, university level)
    at least four–six semesters after Doktor required

ACADEMIC PROGRAMS:
Department of Agriculture (Soest)
Department of Architecture and Landscape Design (Hoxter)
Department of Chemistry and Chemical Engineering
Department of Construction Engineering (Hoxter)
Department of Economics
Department of Education, Psychology and Physical Education
Department of Electrical Engineering
Department of Electrical Power Engineering (Soest)
Department of Environmental Protection Technology
Department of Fine Arts and Music
Department of Languages and Literature
Department of Mathematics and Computer Science
Department of Mechanical Engineering I
Department of Mechanical Engineering II (Meschede)
Department of Mechanical Engineering III (Soest)
Department of Philosophy, History, Geography, Religious and Social Sciences
Department of Physics
Department of Telecommunications Technology (Meschede)

SPECIAL PROGRAMS:
Cooperative arrangements with 16 other universities, including Saint Olaf College in Minnesota, State University of Illinois, Howard University in Washington, D.C., and Lock Haven University of Pennsylvania

LANGUAGE OF INSTRUCTION: German

ADMISSION REQUIREMENTS FOR FOREIGN STUDENTS:
Secondary school certificate (*Reifezeugnis*) or recognized foreign equivalent

TUITION FOR FOREIGN STUDENTS:
None

TOTAL INSTRUCTIONAL FACULTY:
850

LIBRARY COLLECTIONS:
Central library—800,000 volumes

UNIVERSITY PUBLICATIONS:
Paderborner Universitätsreden, Paderborner Universitätszeitung, Amtliche Mitteilungen

RECTOR: Prof. Dr.rer.nat. Hans-Dieter Rinkins

UNIVERSITÄT DES SAARLANDES
(University of the Saar)
6600 Saarbrucken, Im Stadtwald, Germany

CHARACTERISTICS OF INSTITUTION:
State-run, nonprofit university

DATE FOUNDED: 1948

TOTAL ENROLLMENT: 20,000 fulltime students (including 1,300 foreign students)

DEGREES AWARDED:
State examinations in various fields
State teaching qualification, secondary level
Diplom in various fields
  six–eight semesters required
Magister Artium (arts)
  eight semesters required
Doktor in various fields
  approximately eight semesters required
Dolmetscher, Diplom-Ubersetzer, Dr.rer.pol.
  six semesters required
Dr.med.dent.
  ten semesters required
Medizinische Staatsprüfung and Dr.med.
  eleven semesters required
Habilitation (teaching qualification, university level)
  at least three years after doctorate required
Certificate and Diploma in European Studies

ACADEMIC PROGRAMS:
Faculty of Law and Economics (including political science and European studies)
Faculty of Medicine (Homburg/Saar) (including dentistry)
Faculty of Natural Sciences (including mathematics and computer science)
Faculty of Philosophy (including social studies, theology and modern languages)
Institute of Physical Education

SPECIAL PROGRAMS:
Cooperative arrangements with 25 other universities, including the University of Maryland, the University of Michigan, the University of California (Los Angeles) and Columbia University in New York

LANGUAGE OF INSTRUCTION: German

ADMISSION REQUIREMENTS FOR FOREIGN STUDENTS:
Secondary school certificate (*Reifezeugnis*) or recognized foreign equivalent

TUITION FOR FOREIGN STUDENTS:
None

TOTAL INSTRUCTIONAL FACULTY:
810

LIBRARY COLLECTIONS:
University library—1,118,000 volumes
Medicine (Homburg)—191,000 volumes
Institute libraries—1,000,000 volumes

UNIVERSITY PUBLICATIONS:
Annales Universitätis Saraviensis, Rechts und Wirtschaftswissenschaften, Philosophie, Medizin, Scientia, Vorlesungsverzeichnis, Jahresbibliographie, Campus

PRESIDENT: Prof. Dr. Richard J. Meiser

UNIVERSITÄT-GESAMTHOCHSCHULE SIEGEN
(Polytechnic University of Siegen)
5900 Siegen, Am Herrengarten 3, Germany

CHARACTERISTICS OF INSTITUTION:
State-run, nonprofit university

DATE FOUNDED: 1972

TOTAL ENROLLMENT: 8,500 fulltime students (including 600 foreign students)

DEGREES AWARDED:
State teaching qualification
    three–five years required
Diplom in various fields
    three-and-a-half–five years required
Magister Artium (arts)
    four-and-a-half years required
Doktor in various fields
    four–five years required
Habilitation (teaching qualification, university level)
    at least two–three years after Doktor required

ACADEMIC PROGRAMS:
Department of Architecture
Department of Art and Design
Department of Construction Engineering
Department of Economics
Department of Education, Psychology and Physical
    Education
Department of Electrical Engineering
Department of Languages and Literature
Department of Mathematics
Department of Mechanical Engineering
Department of Natural Sciences I (physics)
Department of Natural Sciences II (chemistry, biology)
Department of Philosophy, Religion and History

SPECIAL PROGRAMS:
Cooperative arrangements with nine other universities, including the University of Houston in Texas and the University of British Columbia

LANGUAGE OF INSTRUCTION: German

ADMISSION REQUIREMENTS FOR FOREIGN STUDENTS:
Secondary school certificate *(Reifezeugnis)* or recognized foreign equivalent; technical secondary education *(Fachhochschulreife)* for certain courses

TUITION FOR FOREIGN STUDENTS:
None

TOTAL INSTRUCTIONAL FACULTY:
555

LIBRARY COLLECTIONS:
Central library—750,000 volumes

UNIVERSITY PUBLICATIONS:
Research Report, Reihe Siegen, Siegener Hochschulblatter, Siegener Padagogische Studien

PRESIDENT: Prof. Dr. Klaus Sturm

UNIVERSITÄT STUTTGART
(University of Stuttgart)
7000 Stuttgart 1, Keplerstrasse 7, Germany

CHARACTERISTICS OF INSTITUTION:
State-run, nonprofit university

DATE FOUNDED: 1829

TOTAL ENROLLMENT: 21,150 fulltime students

DEGREES AWARDED:
State teaching qualification, secondary and technical
schools
    four–five years required
Diplom in various fields
    four–five years required
Magister Artium (arts)
    four–five years required
Doktor in various fields
    a further three–five years required
Habilitation (teaching qualification, university level)
    at least three years after doctorate required

ACADEMIC PROGRAMS:
Faculty of Architecture and Town Planning
Faculty of Aviation and Aerospace Engineering
Faculty of Biological and Geosciences
Faculty of Chemical Engineering
Faculty of Chemistry
Faculty of Civil Engineering and Surveying
Faculty of Computer Science
Faculty of Design and Production Engineering
Faculty of Electrical Engineering
Faculty of Energy Techniques
Faculty of History, Social Sciences and Economics
Faculty of Mathematics
Faculty of Philosophy
Faculty of Physics

SPECIAL PROGRAMS:
Center for Infrastructure Planning
Institute of Biomedical Technology
Institute for Computer Applications
Institute for Textile Research

Computer Center
Language Center
Cooperative arrangements with 38 other universities, including Oregon State University, University of Arizona, Arizona State University, University of Colorado at Boulder, University of Kansas, University of Massachusetts, George Washington University, Northwestern University, University of Cincinnati, University of Wisconsin, University of Missouri, University of Washington, Michigan Technological University, Georgia Institute of Technology and Rose-Hulman Institute of Technology in Indiana

LANGUAGE OF INSTRUCTION: German

ADMISSION REQUIREMENTS FOR FOREIGN STUDENTS:
Secondary school certificate *(Reifezeugnis)* or recognized foreign equivalent

TUITION FOR FOREIGN STUDENTS:
None

TOTAL INSTRUCTIONAL FACULTY:
2,400 (including 450 professors)

LIBRARY COLLECTIONS:
University library—700,000 volumes
Institute libraries

UNIVERSITY PUBLICATIONS:
Stuttgarter Uni-Kurier, Forschungsbericht, Wechselwirkungen-Aus Lehre und Forschung der Universität Stuttgart, Forschung-Entwicklung-Beratung

RECTOR: Prof. Dr.-Ing.habil. J. Giesecke

UNIVERSITÄT-GESAMTHOCHSCHULE WUPPERTAL
(Polytechnic University of Wuppertal)
W5600 Wuppertal 1, Gauss-Strasse 20, Germany

CHARACTERISTICS OF INSTITUTION:
State-run, nonprofit university

DATE FOUNDED: 1972

TOTAL ENROLLMENT: 15,700 fulltime students (including 800 foreign students)

DEGREES AWARDED:
State teaching qualification, primary and secondary levels
   three–four years required
Diplom in various fields
   seven–ten semesters required
Magister Artium (arts)
   eight semesters required
Doktor in various fields
   eight–ten semesters required
Habilitation (teaching qualification, university level)
   at least four–six semesters after Doktor required

ACADEMIC PROGRAMS:
Faculty I (sociology)
Faculty II (philosophy and theology)
Faculty III (education)
Faculty IV (languages and literature)
Faculty V (art and design, music)
Faculty VI (economics)
Faculty VII (mathematics)
Faculty VIII (Sciences I: physics)
Faculty IX (Sciences II: chemistry, biology)
Faculty X (architecture)
Faculty XI (construction engineering)
Faculty XII (mechanical engineering)
Faculty XIII (electrical engineering)
Faculty XIV (safety and accident prevention)

SPECIAL PROGRAMS:
Computer Center
Cooperative arrangements with four universities

LANGUAGE OF INSTRUCTION: German

ADMISSION REQUIREMENTS FOR FOREIGN STUDENTS:
Secondary school certificate *(Reifezeugnis)* or recognized foreign equivalent; technical secondary education *(Fachhochschulreife)* for certain courses

TUITION FOR FOREIGN STUDENTS:
None

TOTAL INSTRUCTIONAL FACULTY:
325

LIBRARY COLLECTIONS:
Central library—770,000 volumes
Departmental libraries

RECTOR: Prof. Dr.phil. Siegfried Maser

SCHILLER INTERNATIONAL UNIVERSITY
6900 Heidelberg, Friedrich Ebert Anlage 4, Germany

CHARACTERISTICS OF INSTITUTION:
Private, independent university chartered by the State of Delaware, U.S.A.

DATE FOUNDED: 1964

TOTAL ENROLLMENT: 1,500 foreign students from 98 different countries enrolled at various study centers

DEGREES AWARDED:
Associate of Arts (AA and AAS)
Bachelor of Arts (BA)
Associate of Business Administration (ABA)
Bachelor of Business Administration (BBA)
Bachelor of Public Administration (BPA)
Master of Arts (MA)
Master of Business Administration (MBA)
Master of International Management (MIM)

ACADEMIC PROGRAMS:
Department of Business Administration
Department of Law/Public Administration
Department of Applied Sciences (including premedicine, preengineering and preveterinary sciences)
Department of General Studies (including economics, languages and arts courses)
Department of International Relations and Diplomacy
Department of Hotel Management

SPECIAL PROGRAMS:
Study centers located in:
England—London and West Wickham
France—Paris and Strasbourg
Germany—Heidelberg
Spain—Madrid
Switzerland—Engelberg
Hotel Management Internships

LANGUAGE OF INSTRUCTION: English

ADMISSION REQUIREMENTS FOR FOREIGN STUDENTS:
Any foreign secondary school diploma recognized as equivalent to the high school diploma issued in the State of Delaware, U.S.A.

TUITION FOR FOREIGN STUDENTS:
Undergraduate—$8,700 US
Postgraduate—$9,050 US

TOTAL INSTRUCTIONAL FACULTY:
190 teachers and lecturers

LIBRARY COLLECTION:
Total collection—36,000 volumes

UNIVERSITY PUBLICATIONS:
Schiller Newsletter, Hotel Management Newsletter

PRESIDENT: Prof. Dr. W. W. Leibrecht

HUMBOLT-UNIVERSITÄT ZU BERLIN
(Humbolt University of Berlin)
Unter den Linden 6, 1086 Berlin, Germany

CHARACTERISTICS OF INSTITUTION:
State-run, nonprofit university

DATE FOUNDED: 1809

TOTAL ENROLLMENT: 19,000 full-time students (including 7,000 correspondence students)

DEGREES AWARDED:
Diplom in various fields
four years (except for medicine, six years) required
Doktor (Dr.) (doctorate, first level)
by thesis an additional three–four years required

Doktor der wissenschaften (Dr. sc.) (doctorate, second level)
by thesis, four–five years after Doktor, first level

ACADEMIC PROGRAMS:
Department of Aesthetics and Arts
Department of Animal Husbandry and Veterinary Medicine
Department of Asian Studies
Department of Biology
Department of Chemistry
Department of Criminology
Department of Economics
Department of Education
Department of Electronics
Department of English and American Studies
Department of Foreign Languages
Department of Geography
Department of German Studies
Department of History
Department of Horticulture
Department of Law
Department of Marxism-Leninism
Department of Marxist-Leninist Philosophy
Department of Mathematics
Department of Medicine (including dentistry)
Department of Nutrition and Food Technology
Department of Physical Education
Department of Physics
Department of Plant Production
Department of Psychology
Department of Rehabilitation and Communications Science
Department of Romance Studies
Department of Slavonic Studies
Department of Theology (Protestant)
Department of Theory and Organization of Science

SPECIAL PROGRAMS:
Control and Computer Center
Institute of Library Science
Institute of Marxist-Leninist Sociology
Cooperative arrangements with over 75 universities throughout the world

LANGUAGE OF INSTRUCTION: German

ADMISSION REQUIREMENTS FOR FOREIGN STUDENTS:
Secondary school certificate *(Reifezeugnis)* or recognized foreign equivalent

TUITION FOR FOREIGN STUDENTS:
None

TOTAL INSTRUCTIONAL FACULTY:
5,000

LIBRARY COLLECTIONS:
University library—4,100,000 volumes
25 specialized libraries—1,700,000 volumes

MUSEUMS AND GALLERIES:
Natural History Museum

UNIVERSITY PUBLICATIONS:
Wissenschaftliche Zeitschrift der Humboldt Universität zu Berlin and Zeitschrift für Germanistik

RECTOR: Prof. Heinrich Fink

TECHNISCHE UNIVERSITÄT DRESDEN
(Technical University of Dresden)
Mommsenstrasse 13, 8027 Dresden, Germany

CHARACTERISTICS OF INSTITUTION:
State-run, nonprofit university

DATE FOUNDED: 1828

TOTAL ENROLLMENT: 14,700 fulltime students (including 1,200 correspondence students)

DEGREES AWARDED:
Diplom or Diplom-ingenieur in various fields
  four–five years required
Doktor (Dr. or Dr.-Ing) (doctorate, first level)
  by thesis, an additional three–four years required
Doktor der Wissenschaften (Dr.sc.) (Doctorate, second level)
  by thesis, four–five years after Doktor, first level

ACADEMIC PROGRAMS:
Faculty of Civil Engineering, Hydraulics and Forestry
Faculty of Electrical Engineering and Electronics
Faculty of Mechanical Engineering
Faculty of Natural Sciences and Mathematics
Faculty of Social Science

SPECIAL PROGRAMS:
Cooperative arrangements with 36 other universities

LANGUAGE OF INSTRUCTION: German

ADMISSION REQUIREMENTS FOR FOREIGN STUDENTS:
Secondary school certificate *(Reifezeugnis)* or recognized foreign equivalent

TUITION FOR FOREIGN STUDENTS:
None

TOTAL INSTRUCTIONAL FACULTY:
2,700

LIBRARY COLLECTIONS:
University library and section libraries—1,250,000 volumes

MUSEUMS AND GALLERIES:
Forestry Botanical Garden
International Commemorative Monument
Museum of Geology; Forestry Hunting Exhibition

UNIVERSITY PUBLICATIONS:
Wissenschaftliche Zeitschrift der Technischen Universität Dresden, Gesellschaftswissenschaften, Sozialistische Betriebswirtschaft, Naturwissenschaften und Mathematik, Datenverarbeitung, Elektrotechnik, Maschinenwesen, Forstwesen

RECTOR: Prof. Dr. Hans-Jürgen Jacobs

ERNST-MORITZ-ARNDT-UNIVERSITÄT GREIFSWALD
(Ernst Moritz Arndt University of Greifswald)
Domstrasse 11, 2200 Greifswald, Germany

CHARACTERISTICS OF INSTITUTION:
State-run, nonprofit university

DATE FOUNDED: 1456

TOTAL ENROLLMENT: 3,500 students

DEGREES AWARDED:
Diplom in various fields
  four–five years (except medicine, six years) required
Doktor (Dr.) (doctorate, first level)
  by thesis, an additional three–four years required
Doktor der Wissenschaften (Dr.sc.) (doctorate, second level)
  by thesis, four–five years after Doktor, first level

ACADEMIC PROGRAMS:
Department of Biology
Department of Chemistry
Department of Education and Psychology
Department of Geography
Department of Geology
Department of German Studies
Department of History
Department of Languages
Department of Marxism-Leninism
Department of Mathematics
Department of Medicine (including dentistry)
Department of Pharmacy
Department of Physical Education
Department of Physics and Electronics
Department of Scandinavian Studies
Department of Theology (Protestant)
Medical School

SPECIAL PROGRAMS:
Computer Center
Cooperative arrangements with university institutions in Africa and Europe

LANGUAGE OF INSTRUCTION: German

ADMISSION REQUIREMENTS FOR FOREIGN STUDENTS:
Secondary school certificate *(Reifezeugnis)* or recognized foreign equivalent

TUITION FOR FOREIGN STUDENTS:
None

TOTAL INSTRUCTIONAL FACULTY:
1,375 (including 294 professors)

LIBRARY COLLECTIONS:
University library—2,000,000 volumes
Section libraries—700,000 volumes

MUSEUMS AND GALLERIES:
Museums of Anatomy and Zoology
Geological Collection

UNIVERSITY PUBLICATIONS:
Wissenschaftliche Zeitschrift der Ernst-Moritz-Arndt- Universität Greifswald mit Mathematisch-naturwissenschaftliche Reihe, Gesellschafts- und Sprachwissenschaftliche Reihe, Medizinische Reihe, Greifswalder Universitätsreden

RECTOR: Prof. Dr.sc.nat. Peter Richter

MARTIN-LUTHER-UNIVERSITÄT-HALLE-WITTENBERG
(Martin Luther University of Halle-Wittenberg)
Universitätsplatz 10, 4010 Halle (Saale), Germany

CHARACTERISTICS OF INSTITUTION:
State-run, nonprofit university

DATE FOUNDED: 1817, upon merging of Universität Wittenberg, founded 1502, and Universität Halle, founded 1694

TOTAL ENROLLMENT: 8,600 fulltime students

DEGREES AWARDED:
Diplom in various fields
    five years (except medicine and dentistry, six years) required
Doktor (Dr.) (doctorate, first level)
    by thesis, an additional three–four years required
Doktor der Wissenschaften (Dr.sc.) (doctorate, second level)
    by thesis, four–five years after Doktor, first level

ACADEMIC PROGRAMS:
Department of Agriculture
Department of Biological Sciences
Department of Chemistry
Department of Classical and Oriental Studies
Department of Dentistry
Department of Economics
Department of Education
Department of Foreign Languages
Department of German Language and Literature and Fine Arts
Department of History and Political Science
Department of Law
Department of Marxism-Leninism
Department of Marxist and Leninist Philosophy

Department of Mathematics
Department of Medicine
Department of Modern Languages and Literature
Department of Pharmacy
Department of Physical Education
Department of Physics
Department of Teacher Training
Department of Theology

SPECIAL PROGRAMS:
Computer Center
Cooperative arrangements with 31 other universities, including the University of Kansas

LANGUAGE OF INSTRUCTION: German

ADMISSION REQUIREMENTS FOR FOREIGN STUDENTS:
Secondary school certificate (*Reifezeugnis*) or recognized foreign equivalent

TUITION FOR FOREIGN STUDENTS:
None

TOTAL INSTRUCTIONAL FACULTY:
2,522 (including 455 professors)

LIBRARY COLLECTIONS:
University and regional library—3,850,000 volumes
Institute libraries—1,100,000 volumes
Franconian Foundation (library and archives)—300,000 volumes
Library of the German-Oriental Society—52,600 volumes

MUSEUMS AND GALLERIES:
Archaeological Museum, Museum fur Mitteldeutsche Erdgeschichte mit Geiseltalsammlung
Zoological collections
Botanical garden, Julius-Kuhn-Sammlung

UNIVERSITY PUBLICATIONS:
Zeitschrift der Martin-Luther-Universität, Universitätszeitung, Zeitschrift Hercynia, Hallesches Jahrbuch für Geowissenschaften

RECTOR: Prof. Dr. Horst Zaschke

FRIEDRICH-SCHILLER-UNIVERSITÄT JENA
(Friedrich Schiller University of Jena)
Goethe-Allee 1, 6900 Jena, Germany

CHARACTERISTICS OF INSTITUTION:
State-run, nonprofit university

DATE FOUNDED: 1548

TOTAL ENROLLMENT: 5,700 fulltime students (including 1,000 correspondence students)

DEGREES AWARDED:
Diplom in various fields
    five years (except medicine, six years) required

Doktor, (Dr.) (doctorate, first level)
by thesis, an additional three–four years required

Doktor der Wissenschaften (Dr.sc.) (doctorate, second level)
by thesis, an additional four–five years after Doktor, first level

ACADEMIC PROGRAMS:
Department of Biology
Department of Chemistry
Department of Economics
Department of Education
Department of History
Department of Instrument Technology
Department of Languages and Philology
Department of Law
Department of Literature and Art
Department of Marxism-Leninism
Department of Marxist and Leninist Philosophy
Department of Mathematics
Department of Medicine (including dentistry)
Department of Physical Education
Department of Physics
Department of Psychology
Department of Theology (Protestant)
Medical Care Training School

SPECIAL PROGRAMS:
Institute of History of Medicine and Natural Sciences
Institute of Languages
Computer Center
Cooperative arrangements with 12 other universities

LANGUAGE OF INSTRUCTION: German

ADMISSION REQUIREMENTS FOR FOREIGN STUDENTS:
Secondary school certificate (Reifezeugnis) or recognized foreign equivalent

TUITION FOR FOREIGN STUDENTS:
None

TOTAL INSTRUCTIONAL FACULTY:
2,280 (including 596 professors)

LIBRARY COLLECTIONS:
University library—2,576,000 volumes

MUSEUMS AND GALLERIES:
Museums of Phylogenetics, History of Medicine, Natural Science
Botanical garden with Goethe Memorial and Schiller Memorial

UNIVERSITY PUBLICATIONS:
Wissenschaftliche Zeitschrift der Friedrich-Schiller-Universität, Jenaer Reden und Schriften, Jenaer Beitrage zur Parteiengeschichte, Bibliographische Mitteilungen der Universitätsbibliothek, Jena

RECTOR: Prof. Dr.sc.techn. Hans Schmigalla

TECHNISCHE UNIVERSITÄT (KARL-MARX-STADT) CHEMITZ
(Technical University of Karl-Marx-Stadt) Chemitz
Strasse de Nationen 62, 9010 (Karl-Marx-Stadt) Chemitz, Germany

CHARACTERISTICS OF INSTITUTION:
State-run, nonprofit university

DATE FOUNDED: 1836

TOTAL ENROLLMENT: 8,100 students

DEGREES AWARDED:
Diplom or Diplom Ingenieur in various fields
four years required

Diplom Ingenieur Okonom
four years required

Doktor (Dr. or Dr.-Ing) (doctorate, first level)
by thesis an additional three–four years required

Doktor der Wissenschaften (Dr.sc.) (Doctorate, second level)
by thesis, four–five years after Doktor, first level

ACADEMIC PROGRAMS:
Department of Automation Technology
Department of Chemistry and Materials Technology
Department of Computer Sciences
Department of Economics
Department of Information Processing
Department of Machine and Component Engineering
Department of Marxism-Leninism
Department of Mathematics
Department of Metal-Cutting and Industrial Metal-Processing Technology
Department of Metal Production Engineering
Department of Physics and Electronic Engineering
Department of Processing Technology
Department of Teaching Training
Department of Teacher Training (vocational)
Department of Textile and Leather Technology

SPECIAL PROGRAMS:
Cooperative arrangements with 13 other universities

LANGUAGE OF INSTRUCTION: German

ADMISSION REQUIREMENTS FOR FOREIGN STUDENTS:
Secondary school certificate (Reifezeugnis), graduation from technical college (Fachschule, Ingenieurschule) or recognized foreign equivalent

TUITION FOR FOREIGN STUDENTS:
None

TOTAL INSTRUCTIONAL FACULTY:
1,500

LIBRARY COLLECTIONS:
University library—700,000 volumes

UNIVERSITY PUBLICATIONS:
Wissenschaftliche Zeitschrift der Technischen Hochscule Karl-Marx-Stadt

RECTOR: Prof. Dr.sc.techn. Friedmar Erfurt

KARL-MARX-UNIVERSITÄT LEIPZIG
(Karl Marx University of Leipzig)
Karl-Marx Platz, PSF 920, 7010 Leipzig, Germany

CHARACTERISTICS OF INSTITUTION:
State-run, nonprofit university

DATE FOUNDED: 1409

TOTAL ENROLLMENT: 15,000 fulltime students (including 1,200 foreign students)

DEGREES AWARDED:
Diplom in various fields
    four years (except medicine, dentistry, veterinary medicine, Germanic studies and theology, five years) required
Doktor (Dr. or Dr.-Ing) (doctorate, first level)
    by thesis, an additional three–four years required
Doktor der Wissenschaften (Dr.sc.) (doctorate, second level)
    by thesis, four–five years after Doktor, first level

ACADEMIC PROGRAMS:
Department of African and Middle East Studies
Department of Animal Husbandry and Veterinary Medicine
Department of Biology
Department of Chemistry
Department of Cultural Sciences
Department of Dentistry
Department of Economics
Department of Education
Department of Germany Philology
Department of History
Department of Journalism
Department of Law
Department of Marxism-Leninism
Department of Marxist and Leninist Philosophy
Department of Mathematics
Department of Medicine
Department of Physics
Department of Psychology
Department of Scientific Communism
Department of Theology (Protestant)
Department of Theoretical and Applied Linguistics

SPECIAL PROGRAMS:
Institute of Foreign Studies
Institute of International Studies
Institute of Interpreter Training
Institute of Physical Education
Institute of Teacher Training (Marxism-Leninism)

Institute of Teacher Training (Russian)
Institute of Tropical Agriculture and Veterinary Medicine
Department for Lifelong Education
Cooperative arrangements with over 25 other universities

LANGUAGE OF INSTRUCTION: German

ADMISSION REQUIREMENTS FOR FOREIGN STUDENTS:
Secondary school certificate *(Reifezeugnis)* or recognized foreign equivalent

TUITION FOR FOREIGN STUDENTS:
None

TOTAL INSTRUCTIONAL FACULTY:
3,000 (including 350 professors)

LIBRARY COLLECTIONS:
University library—3,340,000 volumes

MUSEUMS AND GALLERIES:
Museum of Egyptology
Collection of musical instruments

UNIVERSITY PUBLICATIONS:
Wissenschaftliche Zeitschrift, Beitrage zur Tropischen Landwirtschaft und Veterinarmedizin, Leipziger Universitätsreden-Neue Folge, Schriftenreihe zum Veteranenkolleg der Karl-Marx-Universitat Leipzig, Linguistische Arbeitsberichte, Theorie und Praxis des Sozialistischen Journalismus, Geophysik und Geologie, Deutsch als Fremdsprache, Index Seminum, Uz Karl-Marx-Universität

RECTOR: Prof. Dr. H. Hennig

WILHELM-PIECK-UNIVERSITÄT ROSTOCK
(Wilhelm-Pieck University of Rostock)
Universitätsplatz 1, 2500 Rostock, Germany

CHARACTERISTICS OF INSTITUTION:
State-run, nonprofit university

DATE FOUNDED: 1419

TOTAL ENROLLMENT: 6,500 students

DEGREES AWARDED:
Diplom in varous fields
    four–five years required
Doktor (Dr. or Dr.-Ing) (doctorate, first level)
    by thesis an additional three–four years required
Doktor der Wissenschaften (Dr.sc.) (doctorate, second level)
    by thesis, four–five years after Doktor, first level

ACADEMIC PROGRAMS:
Department of Agricutural Technology
Department of Animal Husbandry
Department of Biology

Department of Chemistry
Department of Electronic Engineering
Department of History
Department of Latin American Studies
Department of Land Development and Plant Production
Department of Linguistics and Literature
Department of Marine Technology
Department of Marxism-Leninism
Department of Mathematics
Department of Medicine (including dentistry)
Department of Pedagogics and Psychology
Department of Physical Education
Department of Physics
Department of Socialist Business Administration
Department of Theology

SPECIAL PROGRAMS:
Institute of Foreign Languages
Institute of Industry
Institute of Socialist Economic Management
Computer Center
Cooperative arrangements with universities in over 20 countries, including the United States

LANGUAGE OF INSTRUCTION: German

ADMISSION REQUIREMENTS FOR FOREIGN STUDENTS:
Secondary school certificate (Reifezeugnis) or recognized foreign equivalent

TUITION FOR FOREIGN STUDENTS:
None

TOTAL INSTRUCTIONAL FACULTY:
1,950 (430 professors)

LIBRARY COLLECTIONS:
University library—1,641,250 volumes
Specialized libraries—127,175 volumes

UNIVERSITY PUBLICATIONS:
Wissenschaftliche Zeitschrift der Universität Rostock, Rostocker Philosophische Manuskripte, Archiv der Freunde der Naturgeschichte Mecklenburgs, Wissenschaftliche Veroffentlichungen, Rostocker Universitätsreden

RECTOR: Prof. Dr.sc.nat. G. Maess

HOCHSCHULE FÜR RECHT UND VERWALTUNG (College of Law and Administration) August-Bebel-Strasse 89, 1502 Potsdam-Babelsberg, Germany

CHARACTERISTICS OF INSTITUTION:
State-run, nonprofit university

DATE FOUNDED: 1948

TOTAL ENROLLMENT: 2,300 students

DEGREES AWARDED:
Diplom in various fields
    four–five years required
Doktor (Dr.) (doctorate, first level)
    by thesis, an additional three–four years required
Doktor der Wissenschaften (Dr.sc.) (doctorate, second level)
    by thesis, four–five years after Doktor, first level

ACADEMIC PROGRAMS:
Department of Agricultural, Civil, Labor and Penal Law
Department of Economic and Administrative Law
Department of Marxism-Leninism
Department of State Law and Management

SPECIAL PROGRAMS:
Institute of Administration Studies
Institute of International Relations
Institute of Theory of Law

LANGUAGE OF INSTRUCTION: German

ADMISSION REQUIREMENTS FOR FOREIGN STUDENTS:
Secondary school certificate (Reifezeugnis) or recognized foreign equivalent

TUITION FOR FOREIGN STUDENTS:
None

TOTAL INSTRUCTIONAL FACULTY:
450

LIBRARY COLLECTIONS:
University library—335,000 volumes

UNIVERSITY PUBLICATIONS:
Deutsche Aussenpolitik, Organisation, Staat und Recht

RECTOR: Prof. Dr.sc. Horst Steeger

THE UNIVERSITIES OF GREECE

**ATHINISIN ETHNIKON KAI KAPODISTRIAKON
PANEPISTIMION**
(National and Capodistrian University of Athens)
Odos Panepistmiou 30, 10679 Athens, Greece

CHARACTERISTICS OF INSTITUTION:
State-run, nonprofit university

DATE FOUNDED: 1837

TOTAL ENROLLMENT: 45,000 students (including 450
foreign students)

DEGREES AWARDED:
Ptychion (diploma) in various fields
    four–six years required
Didaktoriko (doctorate)
    by thesis

ACADEMIC PROGRAMS:
Faculty of Arts
Faculty of Health Sciences
Faculty of Law, Economic and Political Sciences
Faculty of Sciences
Faculty of Theology
Department of Physical Education and Athletics
Department of Teacher Training for Preschool Edu-
    cation
Department of Teacher Training for Primary Educa-
    tion

LANGUAGE OF INSTRUCTION: Greek

ADMISSION REQUIREMENTS FOR FOREIGN STUDENTS:
Secondary school certificate *(Apolytirion Lykiou)*, or
recognized foreign equivalent, and entrance examination

TUITION FOR FOREIGN STUDENTS:
Between Dr 72,000 and Dr 110,000 per year

TOTAL INSTRUCTIONAL FACULTY:
1,710

LIBRARY COLLECTIONS:
Department libraries

MUSEUMS AND GALLERIES:
Museums of Anthropology, Criminology, Geology
and Paleontology, Hygienics, Petrology, Zoology

RECTOR: Prof. Michael P. Stathopoulos

ARISTOTELEIO PANEPISTIMIO THESSALONIKIS
(Aristotelian University of Thessaloniki)
University Campus, 54006 Thessaloniki, Greece

CHARACTERISTICS OF INSTITUTION:
State-run, nonprofit unversity

DATE FOUNDED: 1925

TOTAL ENROLLMENT: 56,000 students (including 3,500
foreign students)

DEGREES AWARDED:
Ptychion (diploma) in various fields
    four–six years required
Didaktoriko (doctorate)
    by thesis (one–three years required)

ACADEMIC PROGRAMS:
Faculty of Earth Sciences and Technology
Faculty of Fine Arts
Faculty of Health Sciences
Faculty of Law and Economics
Faculty of Philosophy
Faculty of Sciences
Faculty of Technology
Faculty of Theology
School of Education
School of Sport Science and Athletics
School of Primary Education

SPECIAL PROGRAMS:
Byzantine Research Center
Institute of Contemporary Greek
Institute of Foreign Languages and Literature

LANGUAGE OF INSTRUCTION: Greek

ADMISSION REQUIREMENTS FOR FOREIGN STUDENTS:
Secondary school certificate *(Apolytirion Lykiou)*, or
recognized foreign equivalent, and entrance examination

TUITION FOR FOREIGN STUDENTS:
Between Dr 72,000 and Dr 98,000 per year

TOTAL INSTRUCTIONAL FACULTY:
2,280

LIBRARY COLLECTIONS:
Central library—800,000 volumes

RECTOR: Prof. A. Trakateilis

ETHNIKO METSOVIO POLYTECHNEIO
(National Technical University of Athens)
University Campus, 54006 Thessaloniki, Greece

CHARACTERISTICS OF INSTITUTION:
State-run, nonprofit university

DATE FOUNDED: 1836

TOTAL ENROLLMENT: 8,000 students

DEGREES AWARDED:
Ptychion (diploma) in engineering
    five years required
Didaktoriko (doctorate) in engineering
    by thesis

ACADEMIC PROGRAMS:
Department of Architecture
Department of Chemical Engineering
Department of Civil Engineering
Department of Electrical Engineering
Department of Engineering Science
Department of Mechanical Engineering
Department of Mining and Metallurgy
Department of Naval Architecture and Marine Engineering
Department of Surveying

LANGUAGE OF INSTRUCTION: Greek

ADMISSION REQUIREMENTS FOR FOREIGN STUDENTS:
Secondary school certificate (*Apolytirion Lykiou*), or recognized foreign equivalent, and entrance examination

TUITION FOR FOREIGN STUDENTS:
Between Dr 72,000 and Dr 110,000 per year

TOTAL INSTRUCTIONAL FACULTY:
500

LIBRARY COLLECTIONS:
Central library—150,000 volumes
Department libraries

RECTOR: G. N. Noutsopoulos

**PANEPISTIMION KRITIS
(University of Crete)
Rethymnon, Crete, Greece**

CHARACTERISTICS OF INSTITUTION:
State-run, nonprofit university

DATE FOUNDED: 1973

TOTAL ENROLLMENT: 1,040 students

DEGREES AWARDED:
Ptychion (diploma) in various fields
    four–six years required
Didaktorio (doctorate)
    by thesis (one–three years required)

ACADEMIC PROGRAMS:
Faculty of Medicine
Faculty of Philosophy
Faculty of Physics and Mathematics

Department of Preschool Education
Department of Primary Education

SPECIAL PROGRAMS:
Research Center of Crete:
    Institute of Applied and Computational Mathematics
    Institute of Computer Science
    Institute of Electronic Structure and Lasers
    Institute of Mediterranean Studies
    Institute of Molecular Biology and Biotechnology

LANGUAGE OF INSTRUCTION: Greek

ADMISSION REQUIREMENTS FOR FOREIGN STUDENTS:
Secondary school certificate (*Apolytirion Lykiou*) or recognized foreign equivalent

TUITION FOR FOREIGN STUDENTS:
Between Dr 72,000 and Dr 98,000 per year

TOTAL INSTRUCTIONAL FACULTY:
105

LIBRARY COLLECTIONS:
Central library—125,000 volumes

UNIVERSITY PUBLICATIONS:
Ariadne

RECTOR: Prof. D. Markis

**PANEPISTIMION PATRON
(University of Patras)
26110 Patras, Greece**

CHARACTERISTICS OF INSTITUTION:
State-run, nonprofit university

DATE FOUNDED: 1964

TOTAL ENROLLMENT: 9,000 students (including 130 foreign students)

DEGREES AWARDED:
Ptychion (diploma) in various fields
    four–six years required
Didaktoriko (doctorate)
    by thesis (one–three years required)

ACADEMIC PROGRAMS:
School of Engineering
School of Health Science
School of Natural Science
Department of Economics
Department of Education
Department of Preschool Economics

SPECIAL PROGRAMS:
Cooperative arrangements with several other universities in Europe

LANGUAGE OF INSTRUCTION: Greek

ADMISSION REQUIREMENTS FOR FOREIGN STUDENTS:
Secondary school certificate *(Apolytirion Lykiou)* or recognized foreign equivalent

TUITION FOR FOREIGN STUDENTS:
Between Dr 72,000 and Dr 98,000 per year

TOTAL INSTRUCTIONAL FACULTY:
700

LIBRARY COLLECTIONS:
Central library—10,000 volumes

UNIVERSITY PUBLICATIONS:
Bulletin

RECTOR: Prof. Alexios Lycourghiotis

ANOTATI SCHOLI ECONOMIKON KAI EMBORIKON EPISTIMON
(Athens School of Economics and Business Science)
Odos Patission 76, 10434 Athens, Greece

CHARACTERISTICS OF INSTITUTION:
State-run, nonprofit, university-level school

DATE FOUNDED: 1920

TOTAL ENROLLMENT: 4,300 students (including 130 foreign students)

DEGREES AWARDED:
Ptychion (diploma) in business administration and economics
   four years required
Metaptychiako (master)
   two years after Ptychion required
Didaktoriko (doctorate)
   by thesis (one–three years required)

ACADEMIC PROGRAMS:
Department of Business Administration
Department of Economics
Department of Statistics and Information Science

LANGUAGE OF INSTRUCTION: Greek

ADMISSION REQUIREMENTS FOR FOREIGN STUDENTS:
Secondary school certificate *(Apolytirion Lykiou)*, or recognized foreign equivalent, and entrance examination

TUITION FOR FOREIGN STUDENTS:
None

TOTAL INSTRUCTIONAL FACULTY:
60

LIBRARY COLLECTIONS:
Total collection—60,000 volumes

RECTOR: Prof. Theodore P. Lianos

ANOTATI VIOMICHANIKI SCHOLI THESSALONIKIS
(Graduate Industrial School of Thessaloniki)
Odos Tsimiski 45, POB 10380, 54110 Thessaloniki, Greece

CHARACTERISTICS OF INSTITUTION:
State-run, nonprofit, university-level school

DATE FOUNDED: 1957

TOTAL ENROLLMENT: 6,500 students (including 140 foreign students)

DEGREES AWARDED:
Ptychion (diploma) in various fields
   four years required
Didaktoriko (doctorate)
   by thesis

ACADEMIC PROGRAMS:
Department of Business Administration
Department of Economics

LANGUAGE OF INSTRUCTION: Greek

ADMISSION REQUIREMENTS FOR FOREIGN STUDENTS:
Secondary school certificate *(Apolytirion Lykiou)*, or recognized foreign equivalent, and entrance examination

TUITION FOR FOREIGN STUDENTS:
None

TOTAL INSTRUCTIONAL FACULTY:
65

LIBRARY COLLECTIONS:
Total collection—20,000 volumes

RECTOR: Prof. Demetrios Papadopoulos

THE UNIVERSITY OF ICELAND

HÁSKÓLÍ ISLANDS
(University of Iceland)
Sudurgarta, 101 Reykjavik, Iceland

CHARACTERISTICS OF INSTITUTION:
State-run, nonprofit university

DATE FOUNDED: 1911

TOTAL ENROLLMENT: 4,500 students

DEGREES AWARDED:
Candidate in various fields
Bachelor of Arts (BA)
Bachelor of Science (BS)

ACADEMIC PROGRAMS:
Faculty of Arts
Faculty of Dentistry
Faculty of Economics
Faculty of Engineering and Science
Faculty of Law
Faculty of Medicine
Faculty of Nursing
Faculty of Physiotherapy
Faculty of Social Science
Faculty of Theology

LANGUAGE OF INSTRUCTION: Icelandic

ADMISSION REQUIREMENTS FOR FOREIGN STUDENTS:
Secondary school certificate or recognized foreign equivalent

TUITION FOR FOREIGN STUDENTS:
None

TOTAL INSTRUCTIONAL FACULTY:
350 fulltime faculty
400 parttime faculty

LIBRARY COLLECTIONS:
University library—250,000 volumes

UNIVERSITY PUBLICATIONS:
Árbók Háskóla Islands

RECTOR: Prof. Sigmundur Gudbjarnason

THE UNIVERSITIES OF THE REPUBLIC OF IRELAND

GENERAL UNIVERSITY INFORMATION

The universities of Ireland are state-financed, non-profit institutions. There are two universities in the Republic of Ireland: the National University of Ireland and Dublin University. The colleges of the National University of Ireland reviewed in this chapter are: the Royal College of Surgeons in Ireland; University College, Dublin; University College, Cork; and University College, Galway. The only college of Dublin University is Trinity College, Dublin.

The colleges of the National University of Ireland follow similar rules and regulations concerning admission requirements, expenses, degree requirements and application procedures. Dublin University's Trinity College is autonomous and sets its own organizational stipulations. Nevertheless, the general information given is relevant to all the institutions mentioned in this chapter.

ADMISSION REQUIREMENTS FOR FOREIGN STUDENTS:

Foreign students applying to an Irish university must be able to enroll in at least five or six courses of an academic program offered by the university in question. The regulations regarding the applicants's ability to enroll are that the applicant must have passed the highest secondary school final examinations in at least five or six subjects. The secondary school diploma awarded to such students is not simply a leaving certificate but, rather, a certificate that entitles the holder to matriculate into a university-level program of studies. (The Irish certificate is actually called a matriculation certificate. The British Advanced Level General Certificate of Education [GCE] and Scottish Certificate of Education [SCE] are also recognized.) Therefore, a foreign student must be able to prove that his secondary school qualification entitles him to enroll at a university in the country of the qualification's origin. If unable to prove this, the student must take and pass at least five or six matriculation examinations in the Republic of Ireland in order to be considered for admission to an Irish University.

Fulfilling the admission regulations set by the universities of Ireland does not guarantee a student a place in an academic program at a prospective institution. The number of applicants usually exceeds the number of places available in most academic programs, and admission is subject to competitive review by the admissions department of the respective university. In general, the admissions competition is based on academic achievement.

Foreign students applying to the first year of an undergraduate program or as transfer students should contact the admissions department of the prospective Irish Universities for all specific admission requirements. Competitive admissions may require an entrance examination in the academic program in question, an interview with the department or faculty to which the foreign student has applied or some other method of evaluating the candidate's potential to excel within the framework of an Irish university education.

Postgraduate applicants who are foreign nationals must fulfill the following requirements in order to be considered for admission to a postgraduate program at an Irish university:

- recommendation for postgraduate research and course work by a professor of the discipline in question at the university from which the applicant has graduated
- a First Class or Upper Second Class Honors degree, or a foreign equivalent, in a discipline that corresponds to the academic program to which the student has applied
- a Lower Second Class Honors degree, or foreign equivalent, with a satisfactory performance on a postgraduate entrance examination, set by the prospective Irish institution, in the discipline in question

Foreign students applying for recognition of their secondary school, high school or university qualifications should contact the National Academic Recognition Information Center (NARIC) (Higher Education Authority, 21 Fitzwilliam Square, Dublin 1, Ireland; tel. #: 01-761-545). The actual recognition of foreign qualifications is ultimately the responsibility of the registrars' offices at the respective universities; NARIC is simply an information bureau. Foreign students should always apply directly to the university in question for the recognition of qualifications obtained abroad.

The universities of Ireland often restrict enrollment of undergraduate foreign students to the first year of studies because the total number of university applicants usually exceeds the number of places available for students. In such instances, admission is awarded based on the academic achievement of applicants during their secondary school or high school educations.

The universities of Ireland do not, as a rule, conduct entrance examinations for foreign students. However, as mentioned, if an academic program has too many foreign applicants, the respective university may institute an entrance examination for competitive admissions. In addition, postgraduate admissions may require an entrance examination of foreign applicants whose foreign qualifications are not recognized as equivalent to an Irish or British First Class or Upper Second Class Honors degree.

The Language of instruction at Irish universities is English. All foreign students must be proficient in the English language before being fully admitted to an Irish university. Any foreign applicant uncertain of his or her proficiency in the English language should learn English prior to the commencement of a university academic program. English language courses are available to foreign students at Irish universities as well as other educational institutions in Ireland. A foreign student who is unable to provide the prospective Irish university's admissions department with certified proof of proficiency in the English language must pass a language examination before enrolling in an academic program.

APPLICATION PROCEDURE FOR FOREIGN STUDENTS

All foreign student applications for undergraduate studies, including transfer studies, at the universities of Ireland must be sent to the Central Applications Office (CAO) in Galway (CAO, Tower House, Eglinton Street, Galway; Tel.#: 091-63318). The CAO is an information bureau and also serves as a clearing house for foreign student applications. Foreign students are encouraged to contact the admissions departments of any prospective Irish universities for specific application requirements, but the formal application must go through the CAO.

Foreign students applying to Trinity College in Dublin for admission only to the first year of an undergraduate academic program or for only one term must apply directly to the college's admissions office. The application procedure includes a recommendation from a professor or tutor at the university from which the foreign student is applying or from the principal of the student's secondary school.

Postgraduate applicants to the National University of Ireland should apply directly to the registrar's office at the specific college in question. Postgraduate applicants to Trinity College, Dublin, should send their applications to the dean of graduate studies.

The specific application procedure for undergraduate and transfer students is specified by the CAO. These procedures depend upon the academic program in question, the number of applicants for prospective academic programs and whether or not one's

foreign qualifications are recognized as directly equivalent to the corresponding Irish qualifications. Postgraduate applications vary from university to university and from one discipline to another. In order to be accepted by the National University for postgraduate studies, applicants must satisfy the procedures of the relevant faculty. Trinity College, Dublin, puts postgraduate applications before the graduate studies committee before making admissions decisions about foreign students.

APPLICATION DEADLINES

Foreign student applications that must be sent through the CAO should be completed and returned by February 1 of the year in which the applicant hopes to enroll.

Postgraduate applicants for all Irish universities and foreign students wishing to enroll at Trinity College, Dublin, for only the first year of an undergraduate program should begin the application process as early as possible in the year prior to the the prospective academic year. Each individual institution may have its own application deadline. Foreign students should contact the institutions in question directly.

ACADEMIC PROGRAMS AND DEGREE REQUIREMENTS

The academic programs and degree requirements of the universities of Ireland are, for the most part, uniformly arranged. In order to receive a degree, a student must complete the assigned course work in an acceptable manner and then pass a final examination in his or her subject area. The academic programs vary from one discipline to another. However, the undergraduate and postgraduate degrees offered by the National University of Ireland and Dublin University's Trinity College can be generally described.

The Bachelor of Arts (BA) undergraduate degree differs in length between the National University and Dublin University's Trinity College. The National University's Bachelor of Arts degree is offered in many arts subjects and involves three years of course work with each course concluded by a final examination offered in many arts subjects; Trinity's College's Bachelor of Arts degree is also offered in many arts subjects but requires four years of course work with each course concluded by a final examination.

For most of the other undergraduates degrees, the National University and Dublin University have the same requirements:

- Bachelor of Education (BEd)—three years of course work for an ordinary degree; four years of course work for an honors degree
- Bachelor of Theology (BTh)—three or four years of course work in a variety of theological subjects

- Bachelor of Science (BSc)—four years of course work offered in many science subjects
- Law Degree (LLB)—four years of course work in law subjects
- Bachelor of Engineering (BAI)—four years of course work in a variety of engineering science subjects
- Bachelor of Science (BDentSc, BVetSc or BSc)—five years of course work in dentistry, veterinary medicine or architecture
- Bachelor of Medicine (MB, BCh or BOA)—six years of course work in medicine. At the end of the third year, the student is awarded the ordinary Bachelor of Arts degree.

At the postgraduate level, a number of degrees are offered with varying requirements:

- The Master's degree (MA) is awarded following either three years of course work including a minor thesis and concluded by a Master's examination or three years of course work including a major thesis. The MA is offered in a multitude of disciplines.
- The Doctor of Philosophy (PhD) is awarded following another two years of independent research after obtaining a Master's degree. The PhD is offered in a multitude of disciplines.
- The Higher Doctorate (LittD, ScD, DD, LLD or MusD) is awarded following another four years of independent research at a very high level of scholarship after having obtained the Master's degree. The Higher Doctorate is a degree by published research and is awarded only to those students whose scholarly endeavor makes a definitive contribution to academic knowledge.

Temporary students who attend Trinity College or one of the colleges of the National University of Ireland for a single term or the first year of an undergraduate academic program are granted a certificate of attendance by the institution in question. This certificate lists the courses taken and the results of any assessed course work completed during the program.

ACCREDITATION

All degrees awarded by the National University of Ireland are accredited by the Republic of Ireland. The degrees awarded by Trinity College are endorsed by the good name of Dublin University. In certain circumstances, university degrees in law, medicine, education, veterinary medicine and pharmacy may count toward the qualification for professional practice.

REGISTRATION REQUIREMENTS

All registration requirements are conveyed to the foreign student with the notification of admission to an Irish University. Formal registration and matriculation take place during the two weeks prior to the commencement of the academic year. Foreign students must present all information and documents specified by the notification of admission at this time. In addition, foreign students must pay their tuition fees. Some colleges allow foreign students to pay half of the full charge at registration/matriculation and save the remaining amount for payment at the second term.

VISA REQUIREMENTS AND RESIDENCE REGULATIONS

Foreign students who are European Community member state nationals must obtain a temporary residence permit from Irish immigration authorities upon entering the country. The documents required are

- a passport
- the notification of admission by an Irish University
- proof of financial solvency equivalent to the tuition fees for Irish students and E.C. nationals and the cost of living as a foreign student while in Ireland

The temporary residence permit is usually issued for three months at a time. When the original permit expires, foreign students from the European Community are expected to register with the police department (Garda Síochána) of the district in which their university is located. The permanent student residence permit is usually issued for one year at a time and is renewable every academic year a foreign student has been granted admission to an Irish University.

Foreign students who are not European Community member state nationals must follow the same residence regulations as citizens of the European Community. However, they must meet the financial solvency provision for overseas student tuition fees when first registering with the immigration authorities.

Foreign students who were born in the United Kingdom of Great Britain and Northern Ireland do not have to register with the immigration authorities when entering Ireland and do not need a permanent student residence permit for the duration of academic studies at an Irish university.

TUITION FEES FOR FOREIGN STUDENTS

Foreign students who are European Community nationals are subject to the same tuition fees as Irish nationals, about £1,678 per year in 1990. Foreign students who are not citizens of the European Community must pay full overseas student tuition fees.

1991 foreign student fees for the constituent colleges of the National University of Ireland ranged as follows:

- Arts—£3,575–3,600 per year
- Science—£4,910–5,000 per year

Students applying to Dublin University's Trinity College should contact the admissions office for information regarding foreign student tuition fees required by that institution.

EXPENSES

The cost of living for a foreign student is about the same from university to university. Foreign students should expect to pay between £3,200 and £3,500 per academic year for housing, food, clothing and laundry, books and supplies, transportation, health care and miscellaneous expenses. These figures do not include registration or capitation fees and may have been inflated during 1990.

FOREIGN STUDENT SCHOLARSHIPS

Scholarships provided by the government of the Republic of Ireland are generally reserved for students who are permanent residents of Ireland. European Community member state nationals may obtain financial assistance or a scholarship from the Irish government under the framework of agreements on university education within the European Community.

A foreign student may be able to obtain a scholarship from the respective Irish university while enrolled in a program of studies. Scholarships provided by international organizations or foreign governments may also be available. Foreign students should contact the Irish embassy or consulate in their home countries for information. All scholarships provided by international organizations or foreign governments must be arranged prior to the student's arrival at the Irish university in question for the academic year.

UNIVERSITY CALENDAR

The academic year at the universities of Ireland is divided into three terms, beginning in early October and ending in mid-June:

- fall term: October to December
- winter term: January to March
- spring term: April to June

FOREIGN STUDENTS IN IRELAND

Foreign students from the European Community and overseas are considered important to the universities of Ireland. In 1986, roughly 6% of the total student enrollment was made up of foreigners, nearly half of whom came from the European Community. The majority of the remaining foreign student enrollment was made up of Asians and North Americans.

Overseas students from Canada and the United States of America often come to Ireland to study for one year as part of the extensive Junior Year Abroad programs set up by universities on both sides of the Atlantic Ocean. Also, Trinity College allows North American students to attend the university for one term or for the first year of an undergraduate academic program. Traditionally, postgraduate programs at the universities of Ireland are composed of international student bodies.

Dublin University's Trinity College habitually attracts a more international contingent of students than the colleges of the National University of Ireland. However, all the institutions mentioned in this chapter have foreign student enrollment.

DUBLIN UNIVERSITY, TRINITY COLLEGE
Dublin 2, Ireland

CHARACTERISTICS OF INSTITUTION:
Independent, privately controlled university

DATE FOUNDED: 1592

TOTAL ENROLLMENT: 8,650 fulltime students (including 500 foreign students)

DEGREES AWARDED:
Bachelor of Arts honors (BA.hon)
Bachelor of Business Studies (BBS)
Bachelor of Computer Science (BScComp)
Bachelor of Dental Science (BDentSc)
Bachelor of Divinity (BD)
Bachelor of Education honors (BEd.hon)
Bachelor of Engineering (BAI)
Bachelor of Law (LLB)
Bacholor of Medicine (MB)
Bachelor of Music (BMus)
Bachelor of Obstetrics (BAO)
Bachelor of Science (BSc)
Bachelor of Science in Pharmacy (BScPharm)
Bachelor of Science Physiotherapy (BScPhysio)
Bachelor of Social Studies (BSS)
Bachelor of Surgery (BCh)
Bachelor of Theology honors (BTheol.hon)
Master of Agriculture (MAgr)
Master of Agriculture (Forestry) (MAgrForest)
Master of Arts (MA)
Master of Dentistry (MDentSc)
Master of Education (MEd)
Master of Engineering (MAI)
Master of Philosophy (MPhil)
Master of Science (MSc)
Master of Surgery (MCh)

Master of Veterinary Medicine (MVM)
Doctor of Divinity (DD)
Doctor of Law (LLD)
Doctor of Letters (DLitt)
Doctor of Music (DMus)
Doctor of Philosophy (PhD)
Doctor of Science (DSc)

ACADEMIC PROGRAMS:
Faculty of Arts—Humanities
Faculty of Arts—Letters
Faculty of Business, Economic and Social Studies
Faculty of Engineering and Systems Sciences
Faculty of Health Sciences
Faculty of Science

SPECIAL PROGRAMS:
Center of Theology
Graduate School of Engineering Studies
Institute of Management Studies
School of Ecumenics
Cooperative arrangements with universities in several countries

RECOGNIZED COLLEGES OF THE UNIVERSITY:
Church of Ireland College of Education
Froebel College of Education
St. Catherine's College of Home Economics
St. Mary's College, Marino

LANGUAGE OF INSTRUCTION: English

ADMISSION REQUIREMENTS FOR FOREIGN STUDENTS:
Secondary school certificate (Irish matriculation certificate, GCE, SCE; Baccalauréat Européen, international baccalaureate, U.S. or Canadian high school diploma or recognized foreign equivalent)
See GENERAL UNIVERSITY INFORMATION.

TUITION FOR FOREIGN STUDENTS:
See GENERAL UNIVERSITY INFORMATION.

TOTAL INSTRUCTIONAL FACULTY:
460 (including 75 professors)

MUSEUMS AND GALLERIES:
Museums of Anatomy, Geology and Zoology
Weingreen Museum of Biblical Antiquities
The Hugh Lane Municipal Gallery of Modern Art

LIBRARY COLLECTIONS:
Total collection—3,000,000 volumes
Current periodicals—5,000

UNIVERSITY PUBLICATIONS:
Hermathena, Introduction to Trinity College, Long Room

CHANCELLOR: F. J. C. O'Reilly

THE NATIONAL UNIVERSITY OF IRELAND
(Ollscoil Na Heireann)
49 Merrion Square, Dublin 2, Ireland

CHARACTERISTICS OF INSTITUTION:
Independent, staterun university

DATE FOUNDED: 1908

TOTAL ENROLLMENT: See the total enrollment sections of the constitutent colleges of the university.

DEGREES AWARDED:
Bachelor of Agricultural Science (BAgrSc)
Bachelor of Architecture (BArc)
Bachelor of Arts general and honors (BA.gen & hon)
Bachelor of Commerce (BComm)
Bachelor of Civil Law (BCL)
Bachelor of Dairy Science (BDairySc)
Bachelor of Dental Surgery (BDS)
Bachelor of Engineering (BE)
Bachelor of Medicine (MB)
Bachelor of Music (BMus)
Bachelor of Nursing (BN)
Bachelor of Nursing Science (BNSc)
Bachelor of Obstetrics (BAO)
Bachelor of Physiotherapy (BPhysio)
Bachelor of Public Administration (BPA)
Bachelor of Radiography (BRadiog)
Bachelor of Science honors (BSc.hon)
Bachelor of Social Studies (BSS)
Bachelor of Surgery (BCh)
Bachelor of Technology (BTech)
Bachelor of Veterinary Medicine (BVM)
Master of Agricultural Science (MAgrSc)
Master of Animal Science (MAnSc)
Master of Architecture (MArch)
Master of Arts (MA)
Master of Business Administration (MBA)
Master of Business Studies (MBS)
Master of Commerce (MComm)
Master of Counseling (MCouns)
Master of Dental Surgery (MDS)
Master of Economic Science (MEconSc)
Master of Education (MEd)
Master of Engineering (ME)
Master of Engineering Design (MEngDesign)
Master of Engineering Science (MEngSc)
Master of Industrial Engineering (MIndEng)
Master of Law (LLM)
Master of Library and Information Studies (MLIS)
Master of Management Science (MManSc)
Master of Medical Science (MMedSc)
Master of Obstetrics (MAO)
Master of Philosophy (MPhil)
Master of Psychological Science (MPsychSc)
Master of Public Administration (MPA)
Master of Public Health (MPH)
Master of Regional and Urban Planning (MRUP)
Master of Rural Development (MRD)
Master of Science (MSc)

Master of Social Science (MSocSc)
Master of Surgery (MCh)
Master of Veterinary Medicine (MVM)
Doctor of Divinity (DD)
Doctor of Economic Science (DEconSc)
Doctor of Law (LLD)
Doctor of Letters (DLitt)
Doctor of Music (DMus)
Doctor of Philosophy (PhD)
Doctor of Science (DSc)
Medical Doctor (MD)

ACADEMIC PROGRAMS:
Faculty of Arts
Faculty of Celtic Studies
Faculty of Commerce
Faculty of Engineering and Architecture
Faculty of General Agriculture
Faculty of Law
Faculty of Medicine
Faculty of Philosophy and Sociology
Faculty of Science
Faculty of Veterinary Medicine

SPECIAL PROGRAMS:
See the special programs section of the constituent colleges of the university.

RECOGNIZED COLLEGES OF THE UNIVERSITY:
Carysfort College, Blackrock, County Dublin
Mary Immaculate College, Limerick
St. Angela's College of Education for Home Economics, Sligo
St. Patrick's College, Drumcondra, Dublin
St. Patrick's College, Maynooth
The Royal College of Surgeons in Ireland, Dublin 2

CONSTITUENT COLLEGES OF THE UNIVERSITY:
University College, Cork (Colaiste Na Hollscoile, Corcaigh)
University College, Dublin
University College, Galway (Colaiste Na Hollscoile, Gaillimh)

LANGUAGES OF INSTRUCTION: English and Gaelic

ADMISSION REQUIREMENTS FOR FOREIGN STUDENTS:
Secondary school certificate (Irish matriculation certificate, GCE, SCE, Baccalauréat Européen, international baccalaureate, U.S. or Canadian high school diploma, or recognized foreign equivalent)
See GENERAL UNIVERSITY INFORMATION.

TUITION FOR FOREIGN STUDENTS:
See GENERAL UNIVERSITY INFORMATION.

TOTAL INSTRUCTIONAL FACULTY:
Sum of the total instructional faculty of the constituent colleges of the University

MUSEUMS AND GALLERIES:
The National Museum of Ireland
The National Gallery of Ireland

LIBRARY COLLECTIONS:
Sum of the library collections of the constituent colleges of the University

CHANCELLOR: T. K. Whitaker

UNIVERSITY COLLEGE, CORK (COLAISTE NA HOLLSCOILE)
Cork, Ireland

CHARACTERISTICS OF INSTITUTION:
Constituent college of the National University of Ireland

DATE FOUNDED: 1849 (became a constituent college of the National University in 1908)

TOTAL ENROLLMENT: 6,000 fulltime students

DEGREES AWARDED:
Degrees of the college's respective academic programs corresponding to the degrees awarded by the National University

ACADEMIC PROGRAMS:
Faculty of Arts, various disciplines (including education and social sciences)
Faculty of Celtic Studies
Faculty of Commerce
Faculty of Engineering
Faculty of Food Science and Technology (including dairy science)
Faculty of Law
Faculty of Medicine (including dentistry and surgery)
Faculty of Science, various disciplines (including mathematics)

SPECIAL PROGRAMS:
College of Education, Limerick
Department for Lifelong Education
EEC (European Economic Community) Documentation Centre
Irish Manuscript Collection
Cooperative arrangements with universities in several countries

LANGUAGES OF INSTRUCTION: English and Gaelic

ADMISSION REQUIREMENTS FOR FOREIGN STUDENTS:
Secondary school certificate (Irish matriculation certification, GCE, SCE, Baccalauréat Européen, international baccalaureate, U.S. or Canadian high school diploma or recognized foreign equivalent)
See GENERAL UNIVERSITY INFORMATION.

TUITION FOR FOREIGN STUDENTS:
See GENERAL UNIVERSITY INFORMATION.

TOTAL INSTRUCTIONAL FACULTY:
265

MUSEUMS AND GALLERIES:
Cork Public Museum

LIBRARY COLLECTIONS:
Total collection—450,000 volumes

COLLEGE PUBLICATIONS:
Undergraduate Prospectus, Postgraduate Prospectus, several student publications

PRESIDENT: M. P. Mortell

UNIVERSITY COLLEGE, DUBLIN
Belfield, Dublin 4, Ireland

CHARACTERISTICS OF INSTITUTION:
Constituent college of the National University of Ireland

DATE FOUNDED: 1851 (became a constituent college of the National University in 1908)

TOTAL ENROLLMENT: 10,750 fulltime students (including 425 foreign students)

DEGREES AWARDED:
Degrees of the college's respective academic programs corresponding to the degrees awarded by the National University

ACADEMIC PROGRAMS:
Faculty of General Agriculture (including forestry)
Faculty of Arts, various disciplines (including education)
Faculty of Celtic Studies
Faculty of Commerce
Faculty of Engineering and Architecture (including regional and urban planning)
Faculty of Law
Faculty of Medicine (including surgery)
Faculty of Philosophy and Sociology
Faculty of Science, various disciplines
Faculty of Veterinary Medicine

SPECIAL PROGRAMS:
Baron Palles Law Collection in University College Dublin Library
Celtic Collection in University College Dublin Library
C. P. Curran Irish Literature Collection
Department of Extramural Studies
Cooperative arrangements with universities in several countries

LANGUAGES OF INSTRUCTION: English and Gaelic

ADMISSION REQUIREMENTS FOR FOREIGN STUDENTS:
Secondary school certificate (Irish matriculation certificate, GCE, SCE, Baccalauréat Européen, international baccalaureate, U.S. or Canadian high school diploma or recognized foreign equivalent)
See GENERAL UNIVERSITY INFORMATION.

TUITION FOR FOREIGN STUDENTS:
See GENERAL UNIVERSITY INFORMATION.

TOTAL INSTRUCTIONAL FACULTY:
630

MUSEUMS AND GALLERIES:
Civic Museum
Hugh Lane Municipal Gallery of Modern Art
James Joyce Museum

LIBRARY COLLECTIONS:
Total collection—850,000 volumes
Current periodicals—7,300

COLLEGE PUBLICATIONS:
Undergraduate Prospectus, Postgraduate Prospectus, Guide for Overseas Applicants, several student publications

PRESIDENT: Patrick Masterson

UNIVERSITY COLLEGE, GALWAY
(COLAISTE NA HOLLSCOILE, GAILLIMH)
Galway, Ireland

CHARACTERISTICS OF INSTITUTION:
Constitutent college of the National University of Ireland

DATE FOUNDED: 1845 (became a constituent college of the National University in 1908)

TOTAL ENROLLMENT: 5,050 fulltime students (including 190 foreign students)

DEGREES AWARDED:
Degrees of the college's respective academic programs corresponding to the degrees awarded by the National University

ACADEMIC PROGRAMS:
Faculty of Arts, various disciplines (including philosophy)
Faculty of Celtic Studies
Faculty of Commerce
Faculty of Engineering
Faculty of Law
Faculty of Medicine, various disciplines (including pharmacy and surgery)
Faculty of Science, various disciplines (including agriculture)

SPECIAL PROGRAMS:
Board of Extramural Studies

EEC (European Economic Community) Documentation Centre

University College Galway James Hardiman Library Irish Literature Collection

Cooperative arrangements with universities in several countries

LANGUAGES OF INSTRUCTION: English and Gaelic

ADMISSION REQUIREMENTS FOR FOREIGN STUDENTS:
Secondary school certificate (Irish matriculation certificate, GCE, SCE, Baccalauréat Européen, international baccalaureate, U.S. or Canadian high school diploma or recognized foreign equivalent)
See GENERAL UNIVERSITY INFORMATION.

TUITION FOR FOREIGN STUDENTS:
See GENERAL UNIVERSITY INFORMATION.

TOTAL INSTRUCTIONAL FACULTY:
250

MUSEUMS AND GALLERIES:
James Mitchell Museum of Geology

LIBRARY COLLECTIONS:
Total collection—185,000 volumes

COLLEGE PUBLICATIONS:
Undergraduate Prospectus, Postgraduate Prospectus, several student publications

PRESIDENT: Colm ÓhEocha

THE UNIVERSITIES OF ITALY

GENERAL UNIVERSITY INFORMATION

Italian universities are either state-run, nonprofit institutions or are private universities. The private institutions must follow the same rules and regulations regarding admission, language and degree requirements as the state-run universities in order to be recognized and accredited by the Italian government. The general information given is relevant to all the universities mentioned in this chapter.

ADMISSION REQUIREMENTS FOR FOREIGN STUDENTS

Foreign students applying to an Italian university must hold either an Italian secondary school certificate *(diploma di maturità)* or a recognized foreign equivalent:

- a foreign secondary school certificate qualifying the holder for admission to the academic program applied for at an Italian university in the country of the certificate's origin
- a secondary school certificate issued by competent authorities in the United Kingdom or at a foreign secondary school based on the secondary education system of the United Kingdom. Foreign applicants with a British-style secondary school certificate must have completed at least two secondary examinations (A-Levels) and have applied to an academic program that corresponds to the education verified by their A-Levels
- proof of a full 12-year education, ranging from elementary school to secondary school, while in his or her home country, from a foreign applicant whose home country does not have a university offering the academic program applied for at an Italian University

Foreign students applying for full recognition of their secondary school certificates, high school diplomas or university degrees must make their applications to the rector's offices at the prospective Italian universities. Transfer applicants wishing to have their previous university education recognized by a prospective Italian university must also apply to the rector's office. If the foreign student's previous university studies are recognized as equivalent to the corresponding studies at the Italian university in question, the foreign student may be admitted into the level of the studies corresponding to a continuation of the course work completed abroad.

Limitations on the admission of foreign students to Italian universities for academic programs leading to an undergraduate degree *(Corsi di Laurea)* are not regulated by the state. However, some Italian universities have restrictions on the amount of foreign students admitted to certain programs due to the fixed capacities of facilities. Academic programs such as medicine, surgery, dentistry, pharmacy and veterinary medicine have student admission quotas *(Numero programmato)* whereby preference is given to Italian nationals and European Community member state nationals over all other foreigners. Foreign students who are nationals of developing countries or whose home countries do not have the academic programs to which they have applied receive preference over all other foreign applicants.

The following Italian university academic programs hold entrance examinations that effectively restrict the admission of foreign students:

- short-term programs *(Scuole Dirette a Fini Speciali)*. Admission requirements for short-term studies are the same as for undergraduate programs. However, if the number of applicants exceeds the *Numerus Clausus* (admissions capacities), then all foreign applicants must take an entrance examination to be used in determining who will be admitted. An interview might also be required when the student's application is being evaluated.
- doctoral research programs *(Dottorato di ricerca)*. Admissions to doctoral research studies at an Italian university are baased upon entrance examinations due to the limited *Numerus Clausus* of the institutions in question. The foreign student admissions quota is 50% of the total student enrollment at the respective institutions.
- postgraduate programs *(Scuole di Specializzazione)*. Foreign students can be admitted to postgraduate studies after successfully completing a *Corsi di Laurea* or a recognized foreign undergraduate degree in a subject that corresponds to the desired postgraduate studies. Postgraduate studies are subject to strict *Numerus Clausus* at the Italian universities that offer them. If the number of applicants exceeds the specified student capacity at the respective institutions, the foreign applicants must take a competitive entrance examination. The admission quota for foreign students is restricted to 20% of total student enrollment in the respective postgraduate studies.

Admission requirements for foreign students applying for temporary student academic programs *(Corsi Singoli)* are the same as the requirements for *Corsi di Laurea*. Temporary student applicants may be admitted to more than one academic program for the purpose of studying a variety of subjects for a limited amount of time. The duration of temporary student status varies from one university to another.

The language of instruction at Italian universities is Italian. Most foreign students must take a language proficiency examination in order to be admitted. Foreign applicants will be informed by the Italian ministry of foreign affairs of when and at which university the examination will be given. Foreign students who perform unsatisfactorily or do not take the examination at all will not be allowed to retake the examination until the following academic year. Those who complete the examination satisfactorily are admitted to the academic programs for which they applied according to the admission quota of the university in question.

The following foreign students are exempted from both the language proficiency examination and any entrance examination a particular Italian University may use to restrict admission to certain academic programs:

- any foreign student who has completed his or her secondary education in an Italian border area where the language of instruction was Italian (as, southeastern Switzerland)
- any foreign student who honorably completed his or her secondary education at the German schools in Rome or at the Cervantes Spanish school
- any foreign student whose secondary school certificate was issued by a European school
- any foreign student who has completed five years of secondary level education at either an Italian school in Italy or a recognized Italian school abroad and whose secondary school certificate enables the student to undertake a university-level program of studies

The following foreign students are exempt from any *Numero Programmato* at an Italian university but are still required to perform satisfactorily on the language proficiency examination in order to be fully admitted to a university academic program:

- any political refugee accorded that status by the *Servizio Sociale Internazionale* in Rome
- any foreign student whose parent (or parents) is a member of Italy's foreign embassy diplomatic staff
- any European Community member state national who has legal residence in Italy

APPLICATION PROCEDURE FOR FOREIGN STUDENTS

The general application procedure for foreign students at Italian universities is the submission of an application for registration (*Domanda di Iscrizione*). This application specifies the required documents and insists on certified Italian translations of all transcripts and qualifications.

Foreign applicants hoping to gain admission to a *Corsi di Laurea* or *Corsi Singoli* academic program must specify four Italian universities, in order of preference, each from a different geographic location. The following regulations must also be fulfilled:

1. Foreign applicants must sign a formal declaration stating that upon completion of studies the foreign student will return to his or her home country. Foreign students whose student visas have not expired upon completion of their studies are allowed to stay in Italy until the expiration of that visa.
2. Foreign applicants must apply to take at least three university-level examinations during the first two years of studies, followed in the subsequent years by at least three examinations per year.
3. Foreign applicants must register for any required entrance examinations at the authority responsible for the foreign university applicant's visa (a visa that allows foreign university applicants admission into Italy for the purpose of taking entrance examinations, language proficiency examinations and any admission interview that may be required by the prospective Italian universities).
4. Foreign applicants must provide proof of financial solvency for university tuition fees and the cost of living while studying at an Italian University.

Foreign student applications for undergraduate (*Corsi di Laurea*), short-term (*Scuole Dirette a Fini Speciali*) and temporary student (*Corsi Singori*) programs must be admitted to the cultural office of the Italian embassy or consulate in the applicant's home country from where all information will be forwarded on to the prospective universities' admissions departments.

Foreign student applicatioins for doctoral research (*Dottorato di Ricera*) and postgraduate (*Scuole di Specializzazione*) programs must be addressed to the prospective institutions in Italy via the cultural office of the Italian embassy or consulate in the foreign applicant's home country. The applications will be forwarded on to the prospective Italian universities' admissions departments.

APPLICATION DEADLINES

All foreign applicants except temporary students must complete and return the *Domanda di Inscrizione* or the postgraduate applications to the cultural office of the Italian embassy or consulate in their home countries before March 1 of the year in which they hope to commence studies.

Foreign applicants for temporary student status must complete and return their applications to the cultural office of the Italian embassy or consulate in their home countries by November 5 of the year prior to the academic year in which they hope to commence studies.

Foreign applicants for academic programs offered at private universities in Italy must complete and return their formal applications to the cultural office of the Italian embassy or consulate in their home countries by June 1 of the year in which they hope to commence studies. (The respective private institutions must have received the formal applications by June 30.)

ACADEMIC PROGRAMS AND DEGREE REQUIREMENTS

The degrees issued by the universities of Italy are arranged around examination regulations that must be fulfilled within academic programs of stipulated durations. Examinations covering the course work of an academic program must be taken at the end of every course in the curriculum. The curriculum may be set by the university or, at some institutions, proposed by the student, provided that the proposal is accepted by the relevant faculty council (Consiglio di Facoltà).

The passing of the set course examinations is the most important part of the academic program at an Italian university for foreign students. Foreign students' examination results are registered with the authorities responsible for foreign student residence permits in Italy. If a foreign student does not pass the course examinations in two attempts, then his or her residence permit automatically expires.

Examinations take place during the summer examination period, the fall examination period or in February for certain courses. Examinations can be taken only once in any given examination period and twice in any given academic year. After completing a course, students who do not take the course examination are considered to have failed the examination.

Two types of undergraduate degrees are offered by the universities of Italy: the Diploma and the Laurea.

Diploma degrees are obtained after two or three years, depending upon the subject, of an undergraduate program and the passing of all examinations required by the curriculum. The Diploma confers upon the holder the right to practice certain professions.

Laurea (doctor) degrees are awarded after four or five years, depending upon the discipline, of an un-

dergraduate program, the passing of all examinations required by the curriculum and the submission and defense of a written thesis (Tesi Scritta). The topic of the Tesi Scritta must be proposed by the student and accepted by either the professor responsible for the student's course work or the Consiglio di Facoltà. The duration of the academic program for the Laurea degree in medicine and surgery is six years.

Two types of postgraduate degrees are offered at Italian universities: the Dottorato di Ricerca degree and the Post-Laurea degree.

Dottorato di Ricerca (doctorate of research) degrees are awarded following the completion of a research project within a specified or interdisciplinary subject area. The Dottorato di Ricerca is granted by the Italian Ministry of Education to exceptional students who submit original and valuable research results after completing the required academic program. The research results are reviewed by an educational commission set up by the national government of Italy for the assessment of postgraduate studies.

Post-Laurea degrees are available to accomplished students who have obtained the Laurea degree. The Post-Laurea degree is offered at universities with an affiliated Scuole di Specializzazione. The postgraduate program of studies required by students enrolled in such institutes is the Corsi di Perfezionamento. The Post-Laurea is not a true postgraduate academic degree; rather, it is a second diploma awarded after highly intensive training in a specific discipline. Post-Laurea graduates are regarded in Italy as specialists in their respective fields.

The academic program for temporary students results in an examinations certificate granted by the Consiglio di Facoltà of the Italian university in question. The requirements for a Corsi Singoli are attendance at the lectures prescribed by the student's program proposal followed by either the examination required by the respective curriculum for Laurea students or a multidisciplinary examination set by the relevant Consiglio di Facoltà. The Corsi Singoli proposal must be accepted by the relevant Consiglio di Facoltà before the temporary student can commence a program of studies. Due to the differences in admission requirements for foreign students, the examination certificate awarded upon completion of a Corsi Singoli cannot be considered equivalent to the Laurea degree, even if the temporary student's curriculum proposal corresponded to the Laurea academic program in the respective discipline.

ACCREDITATION

All Italian university degrees awarded by either state-run universities or private universities must be recognized and accredited by the State of Italy.

REGISTRATION REQUIREMENTS

Foreign students are notified of registration regulations after the processing of the language proficiency examination and any other entrance examination held for selective admissions purposes by prospective Italian universities. If a foreign applicant is accepted to an academic program at an Italian university, the general registration requirements are as follows:

- Foreign students must possess a health insurance policy that is valid in Italy.
- Foreign students must be financially solvent and able to prove funds of about Lit 1,000,000 per month for tuition fees and living expenses while studying at an Italian university.
- Foreign students must sign a guarantee that they will not pursue remunerative employment while studying at an Italian university.

Any other registration requirements will be fully explained with the admission notification from a prospective Italian university.

VISA REQUIREMENTS AND RESIDENCE REGULATIONS

Foreign students who are not European Community member state nationals must obtain student visas from the Italian embassy or consulate in their home countries before leaving for Italy. Once in Italy, the foreign applicant must obtain a temporary foreign student residence permit that permits legal residence in Italy for the period of time required for the language proficiency and entrance examinations as well as any other admissions procedure. The temporary permit is issued by the *Questura* of the region in which the university holding the foreign applicant's language proficiency examination is located. To obtain the temporary student residence permit, the foreign applicant must have a valid passport, a student visa and a certificate verifying the language proficiency examination test center and the date of the examination. Temporary permits are valid until December 31 of the year in which they were issued and expire automatically if a foreign applicant fails the language proficiency examination or receives a notification of denial from the prospective Italian university.

If a foreign applicant receives a notification of admission to an Italian university, then he or she must report to the *Questura* of the region in which the prospective university is located. The authority that issues permanent foreign student residence permits is the *Autorità Provinciale di Pubblica Sicurezza*. Permanent foreign student residence permits are valid for the duration of the academic year.

TUITION FEES

Foreign student tuition fees vary from university to university and from one academic program to an-

other. Generally, at the staterun universities in Italy, tuition fees for foreign students range between Lit 400,000 and Lit 600,000 per academic year.

Foreign students who are European Community member state nationals pay lower foreign student tuition fees although their fees are not as low as the fees paid by Italian students. Foreign students who are European Community member state nationals and whose parents or legal guardians have legal residence and are employed in Italy are subject to the same tuition fees as Italian students. These students (European Community member state nationals) should provide proof of citizenship when submitting their formal applications for admission to an Italian university.

EXPENSES

The costs of living vary from city to city and especially if the university to which one is applying has a rural campus. The Italian immigration authorities specify that foreign students must be able to guarantee finances of between Lit 1,500,000 to 1,600,000 per month during the academic year for housing, food, clothing and laundry, health and hygiene, books and supplies, entertainment, transportation and miscellaneous expenses.

FOREIGN STUDENT SCHOLARSHIPS

The Italian government only offers scholarships in the form of an academic subsidy to Italian students studying in Italy. Italian nationals who hold permanent residence in a foreign country are eligible for academic subsidy if they apply for financial assistance to the rector's office at the Italian university in question during formal application for admission.

Foreign students are eligible for scholarships from governmental and private institutions in Italy. Information regarding foreign student scholarships can be obtained from the Italian Ministry of Foreign Affairs (Ministero delgi Affari Esteri, Ufficio IX, DGRC, Piazzale Farnesina 1 00184 Roma, Italia).

Foreign students who have arranged scholarships through the Italian government or an international organization may be exempt from paying foreign student tuition fees. In order to insure that a foreign scholarship student's exemption from tuition fees is recognized, foreign students should include the following documents when submitting their formal applications for admission to an Italian university:

1. Document of citizenship from home country
2. Certificate of scholarship from the Italian government or from an international organization
3. Document of permanent residence in a country other than Italy

UNIVERSITY CALENDAR

The academic year begins on November 1 and ends the following October. Academic programs are in process from the beginning of November until the end of May. Degree course examinations take place in the summer and fall with the exception of certain examinations that take place in February. The academic year is not divided into terms or semesters.

FOREIGN STUDENTS IN ITALY

In 1987, about 26,500 foreign students were enrolled at Italian universities—roughly 2.5% of the total student enrollment. In 1990, Italian universities expected about 30,000 foreign students to enroll. Part of the reason for this rapid growth in the admission of foreign students is the proliferation of postgraduate degree programs in the form of Dottorato di Ricerca degrees since 1986. Foreigners regularly compose 50% of Dottorato de Ricerca degree students.

In 1986, almost half of all foreign students enrolled at Italian universities were European Community member state nationals. Many of the foreign students at Italian universities are North Americans who are children of Italian emigrants to the United States of America and Canada. The majority of these students take part in the extensive Junior Year Abroad programs. Certain institutions attract more foreign students than others; the Universities of Rome, Milan, Bologna, Florence, Naples, Padua and Perugia appear to be particularly attractive to foreigners and contain large international student bodies. Nevertheless, most Italian universities are enlarging their foreign student enrollment.

UNIVERSITÀ DEGLI STUDI DI BOLOGNA
(University of Bologna)
Via Zamboni 33, 40126 Bologna, Italy

CHARACTERISTICS OF INSTITUTION:
State-run, nonprofit university

DATE FOUNDED: 11th Century

TOTAL ENROLLMENT: 60,000 fulltime students (including 2,200 foreign students)

DEGREES AWARDED:
Laurea in various fields
  four–five years required
Laurea in medicine
  six years required
Diploma in statistics
  two years required
Postgraduate diplomas of specialization

ACADEMIC PROGRAMS:
Faculty of Agriculture
Faculty of Arts and Philosophy
Faculty of Economics and Commerce
Faculty of Education
Faculty of Engineering
Faculty of Industrial Chemistry
Faculty of Jurisprudence
Faculty of Mathematics, Physics and Natural Sciences
Faculty of Medicine
Faculty of Pharmacy
Faculty of Political Science
Faculty of Veterinary Medicine

SPECIAL PROGRAMS:
Institute of Music and Drama
Language Center
Research Center for Medieval Texts
Cooperative arrangements with the University of Lodz and the University of Montpellier

LANGUAGE OF INSTRUCTION: Italian

ADMISSION REQUIREMENTS FOR FOREIGN STUDENTS:
Secondary school certificate (*maturità*) or recognized foreign equivalent

TUITION FOR FOREIGN STUDENTS:
See GENERAL UNIVERSITY INFORMATION.

TOTAL INSTRUCTIONAL FACULTY:
2,500

LIBRARY COLLECTIONS:
Central library—660,000 volumes
Faculty libraries

MUSEUMS AND GALLERIES:
Museums of Astronomy, Geology and Paleontology, History, Zoology; Naval Museum

UNIVERSITY PUBLICATIONS:
Bollettino ufficiale

RECTOR: Prof. Fabio Roversi Monaco

UNIVERSITÀ DI CAGLIARI
(University of Cagliari)
Via Università 40, 09100 Cagliari, Italy

CHARACTERISTICS OF INSTITUTION:
State-run, nonprofit university

DATE FOUNDED: 1606

TOTAL ENROLLMENT: 18,000 fulltime students

DEGREES AWARDED:
Laurea in various fields
  four years requried
Laurea in engineering
  five years required
Laurea in medicine and surgery

six years required
Diploma of School Inspector
three years required
Postgraduate diplomas of specialization

ACADEMIC PROGRAMS:
Faculty of Economics and Commerce
Faculty of Education
Faculty of Engineering
Faculty of Law
Faculty of Letters and Philosophy
Faculty of Medicine
Faculty of Pharmacy
Faculty of Political Science
Faculty of Science

LANGUAGE OF INSTRUCTION: Italian

ADMISSION REQUIREMENTS FOR FOREIGN STUDENTS:
Secondary school certificate (*maturità*) or recognized
foreign equivalent

TUITION FOR FOREIGN STUDENTS:
See GENERAL UNIVERSITY INFORMATION.

TOTAL INSTRUCTIONAL FACULTY:
1,000

LIBRARY COLLECTIONS:
Faculty libraries

MUSEUMS AND GALLERIES:
Museums of Anthropology, Geology, Natural Sciences

UNIVERSITY PUBLICATIONS:
Studi economico-giuridici, Studi Sardi, Rendiconti Seminario Scienze, Annali Facolta di Lettere e Filosofia, Annali Facolta Economia e Commercio, Rassegna Medica Sarda

RECTOR: Prof. Duilio Casula

UNIVERSITÀ DEGLI STUDI DI FERRARA
(University of Ferrara)
Via Savonarola 9, 44100 Ferrara, Italy

CHARACTERISTICS OF INSTITUTION:
State-run, nonprofit university

DATE FOUNDED: 1391

TOTAL ENROLLMENT: 5,500 fulltime students

DEGREES AWARDED:
Laurea in various fields
four years required
Laurea in chemistry
five years required
Laurea in medicine and surgery
six years required

ACADEMIC PROGRAMS:
Faculty of Education
Faculty of Jurisprudence
Faculty of Mathematical, Physical and Natural Sciences
Faculty of Medicine
Faculty of Pharmacy

LANGUAGE OF INSTRUCTION: Italian

ADMISSION REQUIREMENTS FOR FOREIGN STUDENTS:
Secondary school certificate (*maturità*) or recognized
foreign equivalent

TUITION FOR FOREIGN STUDENTS:
See GENERAL UNIVERSITY INFORMATION.

TOTAL INSTRUCTIONAL FACULTY:
332 (including 115 professors)

MUSEUMS AND GALLERIES:
Museums of Mineralogy and Geology, Natural History

UNIVERSITY PUBLICATIONS:
Annali dell' Università, Annuario

RECTOR: Prof. Antonio Rossi

UNIVERSITÁ DEGLI STUDI DI FIRENZE
(University of Florence)
Piazza San Marco 4, 50121 Florence, Italy

CHARACTERISTICS OF INSTITUTION:
State-run, nonprofit university

DATE FOUNDED: 1321

TOTAL ENROLLMENT: 46,500 fulltime students

DEGREES AWARDED:
Lauea in various fields
four years required
Laurea in engineering
five years required
Laurea in medicine and surgery
six years required
Diploma of School Inspector (elementary level)
Postgraduate diplomas of specialization

ACADEMIC PROGRAMS:
Faculty of Architecture
Faculty of Agriculture and Forestry
Faculty of Economics and Commerce
Faculty of Education
Faculty of Engineering
Faculty of Jurisprudence
Faculty of Letters and Philosophy
Faculty of Medicine and Surgery
Faculty of Pharmacology

Faculty of Political Sciences
Faculty of Science

SPECIAL PROGRAMS:
Cooperative arrangements with 10 universities, including Rutgers—The State University of New Jersey, Johns Hopkins University in Maryland, Virginia Polytechnical Institute and Cornell University in New York

LANGUAGE OF INSTRUCTION: Italian

ADMISSION REQUIREMENTS FOR FOREIGN STUDENTS:
Secondary school certificate (maturità) or recognized foreign equivalent; technical and industrial school qualifications accepted for entry into the Faculty of Economics and Commerce and the Faculty of Agriculture and Forestry

TUITION FOR FOREIGN STUDENTS:
See GENERAL UNIVERSITY INFORMATION.

TOTAL INSTRUCTIONAL FACULTY:
1,332

LIBRARY COLLECTIONS:
Faculty libraries—280,000 volumes

MUSEUMS AND GALLERIES:
Museums of Anthropology, Botany, Geology and Paleontology, Mineralogy

UNIVERSITY PUBLICATIONS:
Caryologo, Monitore Zootecnico Italiano, Ortoflorofrutti-coltura, La Sperimentale, Webbia

RECTOR: Prof. Franco Scaramuzzi

UNIVERSITÀ DEGLI STUDI DI MACERATA
(University of Macerata)
Piaggia Università 2, 62100 Macerata, Italy

CHARACTERISTICS OF INSTITUTION:
State-run, nonprofit university

DATE FOUNDED: 1290

TOTAL ENROLLMENT: 6,300 fulltime students

DEGREES AWARDED:
Laurea in various fields
  four years required

ACADEMIC PROGRAMS:
Faculty of Law (including political science)
Faculty of Letters and Philosophy

LANGUAGE OF INSTRUCTION: Italian

ADMISSION REQUIREMENTS FOR FOREIGN STUDENTS:
Secondary school certificate (maturità) or recognized foreign equivalent

TUITION FOR FOREIGN STUDENTS:
See GENERAL UNIVERSITY INFORMATION.

TOTAL INSTRUCTIONAL FACULTY:
200

LIBRARY COLLECTIONS:
Central library—19,550 volumes
Institute libraries—152,700 volumes

UNIVERSITY PUBLICATIONS:
Annali e Pubblicazioni della Facolta di Giurisprudenza, Annali e Pubblicazioni della Facolta di Lettere e Filosofia

RECTOR: Prof. Giovanni Ferretti

UNIVERSITÀ DEGLI STUDI DI MESSINA
(University of Messina)
Piazza Salvatore Pugliatti, 98100 Messina, Italy

CHARACTERISTICS OF INSTITUTION:
State-run, nonprofit university

DATE FOUNDED: 1548

TOTAL ENROLLMENT: 22,000 fulltime students
6,700 parttime students

DEGREES AWARDED:
Laurea in various fields
  four years required
Laurea in medicine and surgery
  six years required
Diploma of School Inspector (elementary level)
Postgraduate diplomas of specialization

ACADEMIC PROGRAMS:
Faculty of Economics
Faculty of Education
Faculty of Jurisprudence
Faculty of Letters and Philosophy
Faculty of Mathematics, Physics and Natural Sciences
Faculty of Medicine
Faculty of Pharmacy
Faculty of Politics
Faculty of Veterinary Medicine

LANGUAGE OF INSTRUCTION: Italian

ADMISSION REQUIREMENTS FOR FOREIGN STUDENTS:
Secondary school certificate (maturità) or recognized foreign equivalent

TUITION FOR FOREIGN STUDENTS:
See GENERAL UNIVERSITY INFORMATION.

TOTAL INSTRUCTIONAL FACULTY:
1,255

RECTOR: Prof. Guglielmo Stagno d'Alcontres

UNIVERSITÀ DEGLI STUDI DI MILANO
(University of Milan)
Via Festa del Perdono 7, 20122 Milan, Italy

CHARACTERISTICS OF INSTITUTION:
State-run, nonprofit university

DATE FOUNDED: 1924

TOTAL ENROLLMENT: 79,000 full-time students

DEGREES AWARDED:
Laurea in various fields
    four–five years required
Laurea in medicine and surgery
    six years required
Dottorato di ricerca
    an additional three–four years following Laurea
    required
Postgraduate diplomas of specialization

ACADEMIC PROGRAMS:
Faculty of Agriculture
Faculty of Law
Faculty of Letters and Philosophy
Faculty of Medicine
Faculty of Pharmacy
Faculty of Political Sciences
Faculty of Sciences
Faculty of Veterinary Medicine

LANGUAGE OF INSTRUCTION: Italian

ADMISSION REQUIREMENTS FOR FOREIGN STUDENTS:
Secondary school certificate (*maturità*) or recognized
foreign equivalent; technical school certificate for
certain fields of study

TUITION FOR FOREIGN STUDENTS:
See GENERAL UNIVERSITY INFORMATION.

TOTAL INSTRUCTIONAL FACULTY:
1,428

LIBRARY COLLECTIONS:
Agriculture—31,450 volumes
Law, letters and philosophy—612,500 volumes
Political science—30,700 volumes
Veterinary medicine—21,400 volumes

UNIVERSITY PUBLICATIONS:
*Annuario, Guida della Studente, Guida alle scuole di spe-
cializzazione e di perfezionamento, Ricerca Scientifica ed
Educazione, Statuto dell' Università*

RECTOR: Prof. P. Mantegazza

UNIVERSITÀ DEGLI STUDI DI NAPOLI
(University of Naples)
Corso Umberto 1, 80138 Naples, Italy

CHARACTERISTICS OF INSTITUTION:
State-run, nonprofit university

DATE FOUNDED: 1224

TOTAL ENROLLMENT: 100,000 fulltime students

DEGREES AWARDED:
Laurea in various fields
    four–five years required
Laurea in medicine and surgery
    six years required
Postgraduate diplomas of specialization

ACADEMIC PROGRAMS:
Faculty of Agriculture
Faculty of Architecture
Faculty of Economics
Faculty of Engineering
Faculty of Law
Faculty of Letters and Philosophy
Faculty of Mathematics and Natural Sciences
Faculty of Medicine I
Faculty of Medicine II
Faculty of Pharmacy
Faculty of Political Science
Faculty of Veterinary Medicine

LANGUAGE OF INSTRUCTION: Italian

ADMISSION REQUIREMENTS FOR FOREIGN STUDENTS:
Secondary school certificate (*maturità*) or recognized
foreign equivalent; technical school certificate for
certain fields of study

TUITION FOR FOREIGN STUDENTS:
See GENERAL UNIVERSITY INFORMATION.

TOTAL INSTRUCTIONAL FACULTY:
7,555

LIBRARY COLLECTIONS:
Faculty and institute libraries—290,000 volumes

MUSEUMS AND GALLERIES:
Museums of Geology and Earth Sciences, Mineral-
    ogy, Paleontology, Zoology
Picture Gallery

UNIVERSITY PUBLICATIONS:
Annuario, Statuto

RECTOR: Prof. Carlo Ciliberto

UNIVERSITÀ DEGLI STUDI DI PADOVA
(University of Padua)
Via 8 Febbraio 2, 35122 Padua, Italy

CHARACTERISTICS OF INSTITUTION:
State-run, nonprofit university

DATE FOUNDED: 1222

TOTAL ENROLLMENT: 50,000 fulltime students (including 1,500 foreign students)

DEGREES AWARDED:
Laurea in various fields
.four–five years required
Laurea in medicine and surgery
six years required
Diploma in statistics
two years required
Diploma of School Inspector (elementary level)
Postgraduate diplomas of specialization

ACADEMIC PROGRAMS:
Faculty of Agriculture
Faculty of Education
Faculty of Engineering
Faculty of Jurisprudence
Faculty of Letters and Philosophy
Faculty of Mathematics, Physics and Natural Sciences
Faculty of Medicine and Surgery
Faculty of Pharmacy
Faculty of Political Science
Faculty of Statistical Sciences, Demography and Actuarial Science

SPECIAL PROGRAMS:
Cooperative arrangements with 13 universities, including the University of California at Santa Barbara

LANGUAGE OF INSTRUCTION: Italian

ADMISSION REQUIREMENTS FOR FOREIGN STUDENTS:
Secondary school certificate (*maturità*) or recognized foreign equivalent

TUITION FOR FOREIGN STUDENTS:
See GENERAL UNIVERSITY INFORMATION.

TOTAL INSTRUCTIONAL FACULTY:
2,350

LIBRARY COLLECTIONS:
Central library
American library
Faculty libraries

MUSEUMS AND GALLERIES:
Museums of Anthropology, Ethnology

UNIVERSITY PUBLICATIONS:
Annuario, Bollettino-Notiziario, Guida della Studente

RECTOR: Mario Bonsembiante

UNIVERSITÀ DEGLI STUDI DI PALERMO
(University of Palermo)
Piazza Marina 61, 90133 Palermo, Italy

CHARACTERISTICS OF INSTITUTION:
State-run, nonprofit university

DATE FOUNDED: 1777

TOTAL ENROLLMENT: 20,000 full-time students (including 500 foreign students)

DEGREES AWARDED:
Laurea in various fields
four–five years required
Laurea in medicine and surgery
six years required
Dottorato di ricerca
an additional three–four years following Laurea required

ACADEMIC PROGRAMS:
Faculty of Agriculture
Faculty of Architecture
Faculty of Economics
Faculty of Education
Faculty of Engineering
Faculty of Law
Faculty of Letters and Philosophy
Faculty of Mathematics
Faculty of Medicine
Faculty of Pharmacy

SPECIAL PROGRAMS:
Cooperative arrangements with the National University of San Agustin (Arequipa) in Peru, Huazhong Normal University in China and Moscow State University in the U.S.S.R.

LANGUAGE OF INSTRUCTION: Italian

ADMISSION REQUIREMENTS FOR FOREIGN STUDENTS:
Secondary school certificate (*maturità*) or recognized foreign equivalent

TUITION FOR FOREIGN STUDENTS:
See GENERAL UNIVERSITY INFORMATION.

TOTAL INSTRUCTIONAL FACULTY:
1,300

LIBRARY COLLECTIONS:
Faculty libraries—470,800 volumes

MUSEUMS AND GALLERIES:
Museum of Paleontology

UNIVERSITY PUBLICATIONS:
Annali della Facolta di Economia e Commercio, Annali del Seminario Giuridico, Circolo Giuridico L. Sampolo

RECTOR: Prof. I. M. Giambertoni

UNIVERSITÀ DEGLI STUDI DI PAVIA
(University of Pavia)
Corso Strada Nuovo 65, 27100 Pavia, Italy

CHARACTERISTICS OF INSTITUTION:
State-run, nonprofit university

DATE FOUNDED: 1361

TOTAL ENROLLMENT: 21,850 fulltime students (including 1,000 foreign students)

DEGREES AWARDED:
Laurea in various fields
   four years required
Laurea in medicine and surgery
   six years required
Dottorato di ricerca
   three–four years required after Laurea
Postgraduate diplomas of specialization in medicine and surgery

ACADEMIC PROGRAMS:
Faculty of Economics and Commerce
Faculty of Engineering
Faculty of Jurisprudence
Faculty of Letters and Philosophy
Faculty of Medicine
Faculty of Musical Paleography Philology
Faculty of Pharmacy
Faculty of Political Sciences
Faculty of Science

SPECIAL PROGRAMS:
Cooperative arrangements with nine universities, including the University of Missouri

LANGUAGE OF INSTRUCTION: Italian

ADMISSION REQUIREMENTS FOR FOREIGN STUDENTS:
Secondary school certificate *(maturità)* or recognized foreign equivalent

TUITION FOR FOREIGN STUDENTS:
See GENERAL UNIVERSITY INFORMATION.

TOTAL INSTRUCTIONAL FACULTY:
7,555

LIBRARY COLLECTIONS:
Central library—480,000 volumes
Chemistry—30,000 volumes
Economics—20,000 volumes
Engineering—5,000 volumes
Letters and philosophy—125,000 volumes
Medicine—60,000 volumes
Mathematics—25,000 volumes
Musicology—10,000 volumes
Physics—13,000 volumes

MUSEUMS AND GALLERIES:
Museums of Anatomy, Archaeology, Geology, History, Mineralogy, Zoology

UNIVERSITY PUBLICATIONS:
Annuario, Atheneum, Autografo, Il Confronto Letterario, Il Politico, Epidemiologica e Scienze della Terra, Guido della Studente, Haematologica, Microbiologica, Studi della Scienze guiridiche sociali, Selecta Paediatrica

RECTOR: Prof. Roberto Schmid

UNIVERSITÀ DEGLI STUDI DI PISA
(University of Pisa)
Lungarno Pacinotti 43-45, 56100 Pisa, Italy

CHARACTERISTICS OF INSTITUTION:
State-run, nonprofit university

DATE FOUNDED: 1343

TOTAL ENROLLMENT: 28,000 fulltime students (including 400 foreign students)

DEGREES AWARDED:
Laurea in various fields
   four–five years required
Laurea in medicine and surgery
   six years required
Dottorato di ricerca
   an additional three–four years following Laurea required
Postgraduate diplomas of specialization
   three years required

ACADEMIC PROGRAMS:
Faculty of Agrarian Science
Faculty of Economics and Commerce
Faculty of Engineering
Faculty of Foreign Languages and Literature
Faculty of Law
Faculty of Letters and Philosophy
Faculty of Mathematical, Physical and Natural Sciences
Faculty of Medicine
Faculty of Pharmacy
Faculty of Political Science
Faculty of Veterinary Medicine
School of Computer Sciences
School of Social Work

SPECIAL PROGRAMS:
Cooperative arrangements with seven universities, including the University of California at San Francisco and Syracuse University in New York

LANGUAGE OF INSTRUCTION: Italian

ADMISSION REQUIREMENTS FOR FOREIGN STUDENTS:
Secondary school certificate *(maturità)* or recognized foreign equivalent

TUITION FOR FOREIGN STUDENTS:
See GENERAL UNIVERSITY INFORMATION.

TOTAL INSTRUCTIONAL FACULTY:
1,500

LIBRARY COLLECTIONS:
Faculty libraries—138,600 volumes
Institute libraries—100,000 volumes

MUSEUMS AND GALLERIES:
Museums of Geology and Paleontology, History of Art, Natural History

RECTOR: Prof. Gianfranco Elia

UNIVERSITÀ DEGLI STUDI DI ROMA "LA SAPIENZA"
(University of Rome "La Sapienza")
Piazzale Aldo Moro 5, 00185 Rome, Italy

CHARACTERISTICS OF INSTITUTION:
State-run, nonprofit university

DATE FOUNDED: 1303

TOTAL ENROLLMENT: 180,000 fulltime students (including 5,000 foreign students)

DEGREES AWARDED:
Laurea in various fields
    two–five years required
Laurea in medicine and surgery
    six years required
Diploma of School Inspector (elementary level)
    three years required
Diploma of statistics
    two years required
Dottorato di ricerca
    (an additional three–four years following Laurea
    required
Postgraduate diplomas of specialization

ACADEMIC PROGRAMS:
Faculty of Aerospace Engineering
Faculty of Architecture
Faculty of Economics and Commerce
Faculty of Education
Faculty of Engineering
Faculty of Jurisprudence
Faculty of Letters and Philosophy
Faculty of Mathematics, Physics and Natural Sciences
Faculty of Medicine
Faculty of Pharmacy
Faculty of Political Science
Faculty of Statistics, Demography and Actuarial Science
School of Librarianship and Archivists
National Institute of Higher Mathematics

SPECIAL PROGRAMS:
Cooperative arrangements with 45 universities, including Brandeis University, New York University, Columbia University, Cornell University, University of Montreal, University of Pittsburgh, University of Virginia, University of Washington, New York Institute of Technology and Jefferson Medical College

LANGUAGE OF INSTRUCTION: Italian

ADMISSION REQUIREMENTS FOR FOREIGN STUDENTS:
Secondary school certificate (maturità) or recognized foreign equivalent

TUITION FOR FOREIGN STUDENTS:
See GENERAL UNIVERSITY INFORMATION.

TOTAL INSTRUCTIONAL FACULTY:
4,060 (including 900 professors)

LIBRARY COLLECTIONS:
Library of Little Alexandra—1,000,000 volumes
Faculty libraries

MUSEUMS AND GALLERIES:
Museums of Anthropology, Classical Art, Geology, Mineralogy, Paleontology, Physics, Zoology, History of Medicine
Institute museums

UNIVERSITY PUBLICATIONS:
Annuario, Notiziario, Quaderni di Informazione

RECTOR: Prof. Giorgio Tecce

UNIVERSITÀ DEGLI STUDI DI ROMA "TOR VERGATA"
(University of Rome "Tor Vergata")
Via Orazio Raimondo, 00173 Rome, Italy

CHARACTERISTICS OF INSTITUTION:
State-run, nonprofit university

DATE FOUNDED: 1985

TOTAL ENROLLMENT: Not available

DEGREES AWARDED:
Not available. See GENERAL UNIVERSITY INFORMATION.

ACADEMIC PROGRAMS:
Faculty of Economics and Commerce
Faculty of Engineering
Faculty of Law
Faculty of Literature and Philosophy
Faculty of Mathematics, Physics and Natural Sciences
Faculty of Medicine and Surgery

LANGUAGE OF INSTRUCTION: Italian

ADMISSION REQUIREMENTS FOR FOREIGN STUDENTS:
See GENERAL UNIVERSITY INFORMATION.

TUITION FOR FOREIGN STUDENTS:
See GENERAL UNIVERSITY INFORMATION.

TOTAL INSTRUCTIONAL FACULTY:
Not available

RECTOR: Prof. Enrico Garaci

UNIVERSITÀ DEGLI STUDI DI SIENA
(University of Siena)
Banchi di Sotto 55, 53100 Siena, Italy

CHARACTERISTICS OF INSTITUTION:
State-run, nonprofit university

DATE FOUNDED: 1240

TOTAL ENROLLMENT: 11,000 fulltime students (including 350 foreign students)

DEGREES AWARDED:
Laurea in various fields
   four–five years required
Laurea in medicine and surgery
   six years required
Diploma of School Inspector (elementary level)
   three years required
Diploma in social work
   three years required
Postgraduate diplomas of specialization in medicine
   three years after Laurea required

ACADEMIC PROGRAMS:
Faculty of Economics and Banking
Faculty of Education
Faculty of Jurisprudence
Faculty of Letters and Philosophy
Faculty of Mathematics, Physics and Natural Sciences
Faculty of Medicine and Surgery
Faculty of Pharmacy

SPECIAL PROGRAMS:
Cooperative arrangements with 10 universities, including New York University, the University of Massachusetts, the State University of New York at Buffalo and the University of Toronto in Canada

LANGUAGE OF INSTRUCTION: Italian

ADMISSION REQUIREMENTS FOR FOREIGN STUDENTS:
Secondary school certificate *(maturità)* or recognized foreign equivalent

TUITION FOR FOREIGN STUDENTS:
See GENERAL UNIVERSITY INFORMATION.

TOTAL INSTRUCTIONAL FACULTY:
873

LIBRARY COLLECTIONS:
Faculty libraries—143,600 volumes
Institute libraries—223,250 volumes

MUSEUMS AND GALLERIES:
Academy of Physiocracy

UNIVERSITY PUBLICATIONS:
Albi della Facolta Medica Senese, Annuario Accademico, Studi Senesi

RECTOR: Prof. Luigi Berlinguer

UNIVERSITÀ DEGLI STUDI DI TORINO
(University of Turin)
Via Verdi 8, 10124 Turin, Italy

CHARACTERISTICS OF INSTITUTION:
State-run, nonprofit university

DATE FOUNDED: 1404

TOTAL ENROLLMENT: 50,100 fulltime students

DEGREES AWARDED:
Laurea in various fields
   four–five years required
Laurea in medicine and surgery
   six years required
Diploma of School Inspector (elementary level)
   three years required

ACADEMIC PROGRAMS:
Faculty of Agriculture
Faculty of Arts and Philosophy
Faculty of Economics
Faculty of Education
Faculty of Law
Faculty of Mathematics, Physics and Natural Sciences
Faculty of Medicine
Faculty of Pharmacy
Faculty of Political Sciences
Faculty of Veterinary Medicine

LANGUAGE OF INSTRUCTION: Italian

ADMISSION REQUIREMENTS FOR FOREIGN STUDENTS:
Secondary school certificate *(maturità)* or recognized foreign equivalent

TUITION FOR FOREIGN STUDENTS:
See GENERAL UNIVERSITY INFORMATION.

TOTAL INSTRUCTIONAL FACULTY:
1,256

LIBRARY COLLECTIONS:
Faculty libraries

MUSEUMS AND GALLERIES:
Museums of Anthropology, Criminal Anthropology, Geology, Zoology

RECTOR: Prof. Mario Umberto Dianzani

UNIVERSITÀ DEGLI STUDI DI URBINO
(University of Urbino)
Via Saffi 2, 61029 Urbino, Italy

CHARACTERISTICS OF INSTITUTION:
State-run, nonprofit university

DATE FOUNDED: 1506

TOTAL ENROLLMENT: 15,000 fulltime students

DEGREES AWARDED:
Laurea in various fields
four years required
Diploma of School Inspector (elementary level)
three years required
Postgraduate diplomas of specialization
two–three years required

ACADEMIC PROGRAMS:
Faculty of Economics and Commerce
Faculty of Education
Faculty of Jurisprudence
Faculty of Letters and Philosophy
Faculty of Mathematics, Physics and Natural Sciences
Faculty of Pharmacy
School of Business Administration

LANGUAGE OF INSTRUCTION: Italian

ADMISSION REQUIREMENTS FOR FOREIGN STUDENTS:
Secondary school certificate (maturità) or recognized foreign equivalent

TUITION FOR FOREIGN STUDENTS:
See GENERAL UNIVERSITY INFORMATION.

TOTAL INSTRUCTIONAL FACULTY:
750 (including 483 professors)

LIBRARY COLLECTIONS:
Central library—46,000 volumes
Economic and commerce—40,000 volumes
Law—85,000 volumes

UNIVERSITY PUBLICATIONS:
Annuario, Notizie da Palazza Albani, Studi Urbinati-A, Studi-Urbinati-B, Studi-Urbinati-C, L'Università Urbinate

RECTOR: Prof. Dott. Carlo Bo

UNIVERSITÀ DEGLI STUDI DI VENEZIA
(University of Venice)
Dorsoduro 3246, Ca' Foscari, 30123 Venice, Italy

CHARACTERISTICS OF INSTITUTION:
State-run, nonprofit university

DATE FOUNDED: 1868

TOTAL ENROLLMENT: 17,600 fulltime students

DEGREES AWARDED:
Laurea in various fields
four years required

ACADEMIC PROGRAMS:
Faculty of Economics and Commerce
Faculty of Foreign Languages and Literature
Faculty of Industrial Chemistry
Faculty of Letters and Philosophy

SPECIAL PROGRAMS:
Cooperative arrangements with seven universities, including Columbia University in New York and the University of California

LANGUAGE OF INSTRUCTION: Italian

ADMISSION REQUIREMENTS FOR FOREIGN STUDENTS:
Secondary school certificate (maturità) or recognized foreign equivalent

TUITION FOR FOREIGN STUDENTS:
See GENERAL UNIVERSITY INFORMATION.

TOTAL INSTRUCTIONAL FACULTY:
450

LIBRARY COLLECTIONS:
Central library—300,000 volumes
Specialized libraries—25,000 volumes

UNIVERSITY PUBLICATIONS:
Annali di Ca' Foscari, Richerche economiciche

RECTOR: Prof. G. Castellani

UNIVERSITÀ DEGLI STUDI DI BARI
(University of Bari)
Palazzo Ateneo, 70121 Bari, Italy

CHARACTERISTICS OF INSTITUTION:
State-run, nonprofit university

DATE FOUNDED: 1924

TOTAL ENROLLMENT: 42,450 fulltime students

DEGREES AWARDED:
Laurea in various fields
four–five years required
Laurea in medicine and surgery
six years required
Diploma in statistics
two years required
Diploma of School Inspector (elementary level)
three years required

ACADEMIC PROGRAMS:
Faculty of Agriculture
Faculty of Economics and Commerce
Faculty of Education
Faculty of Engineering
Faculty of Foreign Languages
Faculty of Jurisprudence
Faculty of Letters and Philosophy
Faculty of Medicine
Faculty of Pharmacology
Faculty of Science
Faculty of Veterinary Medicine

LANGUAGE OF INSTRUCTION: Italian

ADMISSION REQUIREMENTS FOR FOREIGN STUDENTS:
Secondary school certificate *(maturità)* or recognized foreign equivalent

TUITION FOR FOREIGN STUDENTS:
See GENERAL UNIVERSITY INFORMATION.

TOTAL INSTRUCTIONAL FACULTY:
700

LIBRARY COLLECTIONS:
Agriculture library—8,000 volumes
Economics and commerce library—60,000 volumes
Engineering library—12,000 volumes
Law library—120,000 volumes
Letters and philosophy library—35,000 volumes
Medicine library—5,000 volumes
Science library—18,000 volumes

MUSEUMS AND GALLERIES:
Museum of Archaeology

RECTOR: Prof. Attilio Alto

UNIVERSITÀ DEGLI STUDI DI CAMERINO
(University of Camerino)
Via del Bastione, 62032 Camerino, Italy

CHARACTERISTICS OF INSTITUTION:
State-run, nonprofit university

DATE FOUNDED: 1336

TOTAL ENROLLMENT: 5,200 fulltime students

DEGREES AWARDED:
Laurea in various fields
    four–five years required
Postgraduate diplomas of specialization

ACADEMIC PROGRAMS:
Faculty of Jurisprudence
Faculty of Pharmacy
Faculty of Science

SPECIAL PROGRAMS:
Cooperative arrangements with nine universities, including the University of Maryland and Boston University

LANGUAGE OF INSTRUCTION: Italian

ADMISSION REQUIREMENTS FOR FOREIGN STUDENTS:
Secondary school certificate *(maturità)* or recognized foreign equivalent

TUITION FOR FOREIGN STUDENTS:
See GENERAL UNIVERSITY INFORMATION.

TOTAL INSTRUCTIONAL FACULTY:
200

LIBRARY COLLECTIONS:
Law library—101,000 volumes
Department and institute libraries

RECTOR: Prof. Mario Giannella

UNIVERSITÀ DEGLI STUDI DI CATANIA
(University of Catania)
Piazza dell' Università, 95124 Catania, Italy

CHARACTERISTICS OF INSTITUTION:
State-run, nonprofit university

DATE FOUNDED: 1434

TOTAL ENROLLMENT: 35,500 fulltime students

DEGREES AWARDED:
Laurea in various fields
    four years required
Laurea in medicine and surgery
    six years required

ACADEMIC PROGRAMS:
Faculty of Agriculture
Faculty of Economics and Commerce
Faculty of Engineering
Faculty of Jurisprudence
Faculty of Letters and Philosophy
Faculty of Mathematics, Physics, Chemistry and
    Natural Sciences
Faculty of Medicine
Faculty of Pharmacy
Faculty of Political Science

LANGUAGE OF INSTRUCTION: Italian

ADMISSION REQUIREMENTS FOR FOREIGN STUDENTS:
Secondary school certificate *(maturità)* or recognized foreign equivalent

TUITION FOR FOREIGN STUDENTS:
See GENERAL UNIVERSITY INFORMATION.

TOTAL INSTRUCTIONAL FACULTY:
1,000

LIBRARY COLLECTIONS:
Faculty libraries

RECTOR: Prof. Gaspare Rodolico

UNIVERSITÀ DEGLI STUDI DI GENOVA
(University of Genoa)
Via Balbi 5, 16126 Genoa, Italy

CHARACTERISTICS OF INSTITUTION:
State-run, nonprofit university

DATE FOUNDED: 1471

TOTAL ENROLLMENT: 30,500 fulltime students

DEGREES AWARDED:
Laurea in various fields
four–five years required
Laurea in medicine and surgery
six years required
Diploma of School Inspector (elementary level)
three years required
Diploma in optometry
at least six years required
Postgraduate diplomas of specialization

ACADEMIC PROGRAMS:
Faculty of Architecture
Faculty of Economics and Commerce
Faculty of Education
Faculty of Engineering
Faculty of Jurisprudence
Faculty of Letters and Philosophy
Faculty of Mathematics, Physics and Natural Sciences
Faculty of Medicine
Faculty of Pharmacy
Faculty of Political Science

LANGUAGE OF INSTRUCTION: Italian

ADMISSION REQUIREMENTS FOR FOREIGN STUDENTS:
Secondary school certificate (maturità) or recognized foreign equivalent

TUITION FOR FOREIGN STUDENTS:
See GENERAL UNIVERSITY INFORMATION.

TOTAL INSTRUCTIONAL FACULTY:
1,098

LIBRARY COLLECTIONS:
Central library
Faculty libraries

RECTOR: Prof. E. Beltrametti

UNIVERSITÀ DEGLI STUDI DI MODENA
(University of Modena)
Via Università 4, 41100 Modena, Italy

CHARACTERISTICS OF INSTITUTION:
State-run, nonprofit university

DATE FOUNDED: 1175

TOTAL ENROLLMENT: 8,150 fulltime students (including 200 foreign students)

DEGREES AWARDED:
Laurea in various fields
four years required
Laurea in medicine and surgery
six years required
Dottorato di ricerca

an additional three–four years following Laurea required
Postgraduate diplomas of specialization

ACADEMIC PROGRAMS:
Faculty of Economics and Commerce
Faculty of Jurisprudence
Faculty of Mathematics, Physics, Chemistry and Natural Sciences
Faculty of Medicine
Faculty of Pharmacy

SPECIAL PROGRAMS:
Computer Center
Electron-Microscopy Center
Marine Biology Center

LANGUAGE OF INSTRUCTION: Italian

ADMISSION REQUIREMENTS FOR FOREIGN STUDENTS:
Secondary school certificate (maturità) or recognized foreign equivalent

TUITION FOR FOREIGN STUDENTS:
See GENERAL UNIVERSITY INFORMATION.

TOTAL INSTRUCTIONAL FACULTY:
600 (including 139 professors)

LIBRARY COLLECTIONS:
Economics and commerce—23,000 volumes
Law—60,800 volumes
Institute of mathematics—8,900 volumes

MUSEUMS AND GALLERIES:
Museums and Anatomy, Mineralogy, Zoology

UNIVERSITY PUBLICATIONS:
Annuario, Notiziario

RECTOR: Prof. M. Vellani

UNIVERSITÀ DEGLI STUDI DI PARMA
(University of Parma)
Via Università 12, 43100 Parma, Italy

CHARACTERISTICS OF INSTITUTION:
State-run, nonprofit university

DATE FOUNDED: 1064

TOTAL ENROLLMENT: 17,000 fulltime students (including 300 foreign students)

DEGREES AWARDED:
Laurea in various fields
four–five years required
Laurea in medicine and surgery
six years required
Diplomas in various fields
Dottorato di ricerca

an additional three–four years following Laurea required
Postgraduate diplomas of specialization
two years after Laurea required

ACADEMIC PROGRAMS:
Faculty of Economics and Commerce
Faculty of Education
Faculty of Engineering
Faculty of Jurisprudence
Faculty of Medicine
Faculty of Pharmacy
Faculty of Physical, Mathematical and Natural Sciences
Faculty of Veterinary Medicine

LANGUAGE OF INSTRUCTION: Italian

ADMISSION REQUIREMENTS FOR FOREIGN STUDENTS:
Secondary school certificate (*maturità*) or recognized foreign equivalent

TUITION FOR FOREIGN STUDENTS:
Lit 400,000–524,000 per year depending on academic program

TOTAL INSTRUCTIONAL FACULTY:
1,000

LIBRARY COLLECTIONS:
Economics and commerce—60,000 volumes
Historical library of medicine—9,000 volumes
Medicine—45,000 volumes
Law—57,000 volumes
Science and pharmacy—50,000 volumes
Teacher training—35,000 volumes
Veterinary medicine—25,000 volumes

MUSEUMS AND GALLERIES:
Center for the Study of Communication Archives
Museum of Natural History

UNIVERSITY PUBLICATIONS:
Annali dell'Instituto di Lingue e Letterature Germanische, Annali di Economia e Commercio, Annali di Magistero, Rassegna di Stoia della Filosofia, Revista di Chemica, Revista di Matematica, Revista di Sociologia

RECTOR: Prof. Nicola Occhiocupo

UNIVERSITÀ DEGLI STUDI DI PERUGIA
(University of Perugia)
Piazza dell'Università, 06100 Perugia, Italy

CHARACTERISTICS OF INSTITUTION:
State-run, nonprofit university

DATE FOUNDED: 1200

TOTAL ENROLLMENT: 20,000 fulltime students (including 1,100 foreign students)

DEGREES AWARDED:
Laurea in various fields
four years required
Laurea in medicine and surgery
six years required
Dottorato di ricerca
an additional three–four years following Laurea required
Postgraduate diplomas of specialization

ACADEMIC PROGRAMS:
Faculty of Agrarian Science
Faculty of Economic Science
Faculty of Education
Faculty of Engineering
Faculty of Jurisprudence
Faculty of Letters and Philosophy
Faculty of Mathematical, Physical and Natural Sciences
Faculty of Medicine
Faculty of Pharmacy
Faculty of Political Science
Faculty of Veterinary Medicine

SPECIAL PROGRAMS:
Cooperative arrangements with 12 universities, including Mississippi State University and Florida State University

LANGUAGE OF INSTRUCTION: Italian

ADMISSION REQUIREMENTS FOR FOREIGN STUDENTS:
Secondary school certificate (*maturità*) or recognized foreign equivalent

TUITION FOR FOREIGN STUDENTS:
See GENERAL UNIVERSITY INFORMATION.

TOTAL INSTRUCTIONAL FACULTY:
250

LIBRARY COLLECTIONS:
Central library—150,000 volumes
Faculty libraries—230,500 volumes

UNIVERSITY PUBLICATIONS:
La Salute Umana, L'Universita, Revista di Biologia, Revista di Dermatologia

RECTOR: Prof. Giancarlo Dozza

POLITECNICO DI MILANO
(Polytechnic Institute of Milan)
Piazza Leonardo da Vinci 32, 20133 Milan, Italy

CHARACTERISTICS OF INSTITUTION:
State-run, nonprofit university

DATE FOUNDED: 1863

TOTAL ENROLLMENT: 34,350 fulltime students (including 800 foreign students)

DEGREES AWARDED:
Laurea in various fields
five years required
Dottorato di ricerca
an additional three–four years following Laurea required
Postgraduate diplomas of specialization
two years after Laurea required

ACADEMIC PROGRAMS:
Faculty of Architecture
Faculty of Engineering

LANGUAGE OF INSTRUCTION: Italian

ADMISSION REQUIREMENTS FOR FOREIGN STUDENTS:
Secondary school certificate (maturità) or recognized foreign equivalent

TUITION FOR FOREIGN STUDENTS:
See GENERAL UNIVERSITY INFORMATION.

TOTAL INSTRUCTIONAL FACULTY:
715

LIBRARY COLLECTIONS:
Architecture library—24,350 volumes
Engineering library—151,500 volumes
Institute libraries—340,900 volumes

RECTOR: Prof. Emilio Massa

POLITECNICO DI TORINO
(Polytechnic Institute of Turin)
Corsa Duca degli Abruzzi 24, 10129 Turin, Italy

CHARACTERISTICS OF INSTITUTION:
State-run, nonprofit university

DATE FOUNDED: 1859

TOTAL ENROLLMENT: 11,000 fulltime students

DEGREES AWARDED:
Laurea in various fields
five years required
Laurea in aeronautical engineering
two years after Laurea in engineering required
Diploma in graphic arts
two years required

ACADEMIC PROGRAMS:
Faculty of Architecture
Faculty of Engineering
School of Graphic Arts
Postgraduate School of Aerospace Engineering

LANGUAGE OF INSTRUCTION: Italian

ADMISSION REQUIREMENTS FOR FOREIGN STUDENTS:
Secondary school certificate (maturità) or recognized foreign equivalent

TUITION FOR FOREIGN STUDENTS:
See GENERAL UNIVERSITY INFORMATION.

TOTAL INSTRUCTIONAL FACULTY:
626

LIBRARY COLLECTIONS:
Total collection—130,000 volumes

MUSEUMS AND GALLERIES:
Museum of Mineralogy

RECTOR: Prof. R. Zich

EUROPEAN UNIVERSITY INSTITUTE
Via Dei Roccettini 5, 50016 San Domenico di Fiesole, Florence, Italy

CHARACTERISTICS OF INSTITUTION:
Private; founded by the European Community member states

DATE FOUNDED: 1972

TOTAL ENROLLMENT: 180 fulltime postgraduate students

DEGREES AWARDED:
Postgraduate degrees only (MA, MPhil, PhD)

ACADEMIC PROGRAMS:
Department of Economics
Department of History and Civilization
Department of Law
Department of Political and Social Sciences

LANGUAGES OF INSTRUCTION: Danish, Dutch, English, French, German and Italian

ADMISSION REQUIREMENTS FOR FOREIGN STUDENTS:
See GENERAL UNIVERSITY INFORMATION.

TUITION FOR FOREIGN STUDENTS:
See GENERAL UNIVERSITY INFORMATION.

TOTAL INSTRUCTIONAL FACULTY:
30 fulltime faculty

LIBRARY COLLECTIONS:
Total collection—310,000 volumes

UNIVERSITY PUBLICATIONS:
Activities Report, EUI Working Papers, Yearly Information Booklet

PRESIDENT: Emile Noël

ISTITUTO UNIVERSITARIO DI STUDI EUROPEI
(University Institute of European Studies)
Via Sacchi 28 bis, 10128 Turin, Italy

CHARACTERISTICS OF INSTITUTION:
Private university

DATE FOUNDED: 1952

TOTAL ENROLLMENT: Not available

DEGREES AWARDED:
Not available

ACADEMIC PROGRAMS:
Postgraduate courses of international economics and
law

LANGUAGE OF INSTRUCTION: Italian

ADMISSION REQUIREMENTS FOR FOREIGN STUDENTS:
See GENERAL UNIVERSITY INFORMATION.

TUITION FOR FOREIGN STUDENTS:
See GENERAL UNIVERSITY INFORMATION.

TOTAL INSTRUCTIONAL FACULTY:
Not available

LIBRARY COLLECTIONS:
Total collection—12,000 volumes
(also 20,000 official documents of international organizations)

PRESIDENT: Prof. Andrea Comba

UNIVERSITÀ CATTOLICA DEL SACRO CUORE
(Catholic University of the Sacred Heart)
Largo Agostino Gemelli I., 20123 Milan, Italy

CHARACTERISTICS OF INSTITUTION:
Private Catholic university

DATE FOUNDED: 1920

TOTAL ENROLLMENT: 28,200 fulltime students

DEGREES AWARDED:
Laurea in various fields
   four–five years required
Laurea in medicine and surgery
   six years required
Diploma in statistics
   two years required
Diploma of School Inspector (elementary level)
   three years required
Postgraduate diplomas of specialization

ACADEMIC PROGRAMS:
Faculty of Agrarian Sciences
Faculty of Economics and Commerce
Faculty of Higher Education
Faculty of Jurisprudence

Faculty of Letters and Philosophy
Faculty of Mathematical, Physical and Natural Sci-
   ences
Faculty of Medicine
Faculty of Political Sciences

LANGUAGE OF INSTRUCTION: Italian

ADMISSION REQUIREMENTS FOR FOREIGN STUDENTS:
Secondary school certificate *(maturità)* or recognized
foreign equivalent

TUITION FOR FOREIGN STUDENTS:
See GENERAL UNIVERSITY INFORMATION.

TOTAL INSTRUCTIONAL FACULTY:
1,881

LIBRARY COLLECTIONS:
University library—951,150 volumes
Other libraries—281,150 volumes

UNIVERSITY PUBLICATIONS:
*Acta Medica Romana; Aegyptus; Aevum; Archivo di Psi-
cologia, Neurologia e Psichiatria; Giovanni amici; Revista
di Filosopfia Neoscolastica; Revista Internazionale di Scienze
Sociali; Studi di Sociologia; Vita e Peniero*

RECTOR: Prof. Adriano Bausola

UNIVERSITÀ COMMERCIALE "LUIGI BOCCONI"
(Luigi Bocconi University of Commerce)
Via R. Sarfatti 25, 20136 Milan, Italy

CHARACTERISTICS OF INSTITUTION:
Private university

DATE FOUNDED: 1902

TOTAL ENROLLMENT: 10,000 fulltime students (including 100 foreign students)

DEGREES AWARDED:
Laurea in various fields
   four years required
Dottorato di ricerca
   an additional three–four years following Laurea
   required

ACADEMIC PROGRAMS:
Department of Business Administration
Department of Economics
Graduate School of Business Administration

SPECIAL PROGRAMS:
Center for Economic and Business Research
Center for the Study and Processes of International-
ization

LANGUAGE OF INSTRUCTION: Italian

ADMISSION REQUIREMENTS FOR FOREIGN STUDENTS:
Secondary school certificate *(maturità)* or recognized foreign equivalent

TUITION FOR FOREIGN STUDENTS:
See GENERAL UNIVERSITY INFORMATION.

TOTAL INSTRUCTIONAL FACULTY:
533

LIBRARY COLLECTIONS:
Central library 480,000 volumes

UNIVERSITY PUBLICATIONS:
Economia Internazionale delle fonti di energia, Finanza Marketing e Produzione, Giornale degli Economisti e Annali di Economia

PRESIDENT: Sen. Prof. G. Spadolini

BOLOGNA CENTER OF THE JOHNS HOPKINS UNIVERSITY SCHOOL OF ADVANCED INTERNATIONAL STUDIES
Via Belmeloro 11, 40126 Bologna, Italy

CHARACTERISTICS OF INSTITUTION:
Private

DATE FOUNDED: 1955

TOTAL ENROLLMENT: 130 fulltime postgraduate students

DEGREES AWARDED:
Not available

ACADEMIC PROGRAMS:
Postgraduate courses in international studies

LANGUAGE OF INSTRUCTION: English

ADMISSION REQUIREMENTS FOR FOREIGN STUDENTS:
Not available

TUITION FOR FOREIGN STUDENTS:
Not available

TOTAL INSTRUCTIONAL FACULTY:
25

LIBRARY COLLECTIONS:
Total collection—70,000 volumes

UNIVERSITY PUBLICATIONS:
Bologna Center Catalogue, Occasional Papers series, *Revista*

DIRECTOR: Stephen Low

THE UNIVERSITIES OF LUXEMBOURG

**CENTRE UNIVERSITAIRE DE LUXEMBOURG
(University Center of Luxembourg)
162A ave de la Faiencerie, 1511 Luxembourg**

CHARACTERISTICS OF INSTITUTION:
State-run, nonprofit university

DATE FOUNDED: 1848

TOTAL ENROLLMENT: 700 fulltime students (including 100 foreign students)

DEGREES AWARDED:
Candidat
Diplôme d'etudes universitaires practiques en economie et en droit (DEUPED)
Diplôme de Gradue en gestion

ACADEMIC PROGRAMS:
Department of Education
Department of Law
Department of Law and Economics
Department of Letters and Human Sciences
Department of Science

SPECIAL PROGRAMS:
Cooperative arrangements with universities in several countries, including Canada

LANGUAGES OF INSTRUCTION: English, French and German

ADMISSION REQUIREMENTS FOR FOREIGN STUDENTS:
Secondary school certificate or recognized foreign equivalent

TUITION FOR FOREIGN STUDENTS:
None

TOTAL INSTRUCTIONAL FACULTY:
140 faculty (including 70 professors)

LIBRARY COLLECTIONS:
Total collection—160,000 volumes

PRESIDENT: Pierre Seck

**CONSERVATOIRE DE MUSIQUE D'ESCH-SUR-ALZETTE
(Esch-Sur-Alzette Conservatory of Music)
10 rue de l'Eglise, BP 145, Esch-Sur-Alzette,
Luxembourg**

CHARACTERISTICS OF INSTITUTION:
Independent music conservatory

DATE FOUNDED: 1969

TOTAL ENROLLMENT: 1,200 fulltime students

DEGREES AWARDED:
Not available

ACADEMIC PROGRAMS:
Not available

LANGUAGES OF INSTRUCTION: French and English

ADMISSION REQUIREMENTS FOR FOREIGN STUDENTS:
Not available

TUITION FOR FOREIGN STUDENTS:
Not available

TOTAL INSTRUCTIONAL FACULTY:
50 faculty

UNIVERSITY PUBLICATIONS:
Annuaire

PRINCIPAL:
Prof. Fred Harles

THE UNIVERSITIES OF THE NETHERLANDS

GENERAL UNIVERSITY INFORMATION

The universities of the Netherlands are state-run, nonprofit institutions and, as such, follow similar rules and regulations regarding admission, language and degree requirements, tuition fees and application procedures. The general information given is relevant to all the institutions mentioned in this chapter.

ADMISSION REQUIREMENTS FOR FOREIGN STUDENTS

Foreign students are eligible for admission to a university of the Netherlands if they are graduates (Abituriënten) of the Voorbereidend Wetenschappelijk Onderwijs program at a Dutch secondary school or if they hold a foreign secondary school certificate or high school diploma deemed equivalent to the Dutch secondary school certificate (Gymnasium and Atheneum). The academic level required for a Dutch secondary school certificate is very high by international standards, though all European secondary school certificates from countries which acceded to the European Convention on the Equivalence of Diplomas Leading to a University Education are accepted as equivalent. A foreign applicant whose home country does not have an international agreement with the Netherlands on the equivalence of educational certificates and university degrees may find it difficult to gain recognition from the Dutch Ministry of Education.

All foreign students must submit their foreign qualifications to the National Equivalence Information Center (NEIC) (Postbus 90734, 2509 LS's Gravenhage, Netherlands). The NEIC does not make final judgements regarding equivalence but instead presents the foreign qualifications for an equivalency review to the Dutch Ministry of Education, which makes the final decision.

Postgraduate applicants must undergo the same procedure for attaining recognition of equivalence of university degrees obtained abroad. However, the individual Dutch institutions may admit postgraduate applicants regardless of the ministry's decision. Postgraduate applicants should contact the universities directly for specific admission requirements for their particular academic programs, as these requirements may vary from one university to another.

Temporary students (Toehoorder) are allowed to attend the Dutch universities for one year. The admission requirements for temporary students may vary from one program to another. All temporary student applicants must be students in good standing at their home universities and have the full support of those institutions when making the formal application to the Dutch university. Junior Year Abroad students are considered temporary students by Dutch universities.

Admission of foreign students to Dutch universities may be limited by the total number of applicants for particular academic programs. Most Dutch universities have strict facility capacities (Numerus Fixus), and the government of the Netherlands regulates admission accordingly. Numerus Fixus exists for the following subjects at most Dutch institutions: industrial design, business administration, theatrical studies, Chinese language, Japanese language, linguistic and literature studies, Japanology, medicine, dentistry, veterinary medicine, experimental medicine, medical biology, social health theory and general health welfare. In addition, the Dutch Ministry of Education issues a foreign student limit in the subjects of medicine, dentistry and veterinary medicine. If the number of foreign applicants exceeds the Numerus Fixus in these subjects, admission is decided by lottery.

The language of instruction at the universities of the Netherlands is Dutch. Certain international courses are taught in English and, in some instances, French or Spanish. Foreign students must be proficient in the Dutch language before they are granted full admission to a university academic program. A foreign applicant who has fulfilled all the admission requirements but is not proficient in the Dutch language must take a Dutch language course in the Netherlands before commencing a university level program, and most universities insist the language course last roughly six months. It is estimated that foreign applicants require at least six months of training in the Dutch language prior to taking the language proficiency examination, offered only in September of the academic year. Foreign students are encouraged to continue Dutch language courses while enrolled in Dutch universities.

Most universities have Dutch language courses available to foreign students. There are also other educational institutions that offer Dutch language courses for prospective foreign students. In July and August, the Dutch Ministry of Education holds a three-week language and culture course open to foreign applicants who wish to enhance their Dutch before taking the language proficiency examination.

APPLICATION PROCEDURE FOR FOREIGN STUDENTS

Foreign students applying to Dutch universities must be authorized to take examinations in their academic programs. They should obtain an application from the *Ministerie van Onderwijs en Wetenschappen, Directie Algemene Studiezaken.* This application must be submitted to the university admissions departments and should include the following information and documentation:

- authorized copies of secondary school certificate or high school diploma along with all transcripts from previous institutions
- authorized description of foreign applicant's previous education (courses, examinations, extracurricular activities, standardized tests, etc.)
- all personal information (nationality, address, state of health, birth date and birth place, etc.)
- for transfer or postgraduate applicants, any university degrees or certificates obtained abroad and a statement of honorable dismissal from the previous institutions

Furthermore, foreign applicants for an undergraduate program must also register with the Central Bureau of Applications and Placings, (*Centraal Bureau Aanmelding en Plaatsing* [CBAP]) in Groningen for inclusion in the state of Netherlands records. The application for the CBAP can be obtained from either the Dutch Ministry of Education, the respective university or the CBAP itself each November prior to the year in which the applicant hopes to commence an academic program. Postgraduate and transfer applicants need not apply to the CBAP.

Temporary student applicants should contact the prospective Dutch institution for information regarding temporary student applications. These applications may vary from one university to another and may not require contact with CBAP or the Dutch Ministry of Education. Such applicants should start the application process as early as possible in the year prior to the academic year in which they plan to attend.

APPLICATION DEADLINES

Foreign student applications to the CBAP must be received in Groningen by December of the year prior to the desired academic year. The formal application to the university's admissions department must be completed and submitted at least 10 months in advance of the academic year for which the foreign student is applying.

Foreign students should prepare and submit both applications as early as possible, especially if the foreign applicant is not proficient in the Dutch language and requires training from a Dutch language school.

ACADEMIC PROGRAMS AND DEGREE REQUIREMENTS

The academic program at the universities of the Netherlands is divided into two stages: undergraduate and postgraduate.

The undergraduate stage is usually four years in duration but can take up to six years, depending upon the field of study. It is divided into two distinct cycles.

The first cycle is either one or two years in duration and is concluded by the *Propaedeutisch Examen*. This cycle serves as the basic orientation and training for further university level studies. The student must pass the *Propaedeutisch Examen* in order to gain admission to the second cycle.

The second cycle is three or four years in duration and is concluded by the *Doctoraal Examen*. This cycle provides the student with rigorous undergraduate training in the discipline(s) of the student's choice and prepares the student for the continuation of the academic program in the postgraduate stage. Upon passing the *Doctoraal Examen*, and thereby completing the undergraduate stage, the student is awarded a *Doctoraal Examen* certificate. This undergraduate degree (*Doctorandus*) qualifies the holder to enter a profession in the Netherlands.

The postgraduate stage is available to students who have passed the *Doctoraal Examen* and have proven themselves capable of preparing a doctoral thesis. The academic program in the postgraduate stage (*Post-Doctorale Opleiding*) is made up of highly specialized or professional training. The duration of the postgraduate stage ranges between six months and two years, and the academic programs generally fall into the following categories:

- teacher training, six months
- medical training (medicine, dentistry, veterinary medicine, pharmacy, medical biology or experimental medicine), two years
- specialized research (a multitude of disciplines), two years
- professional training (several disciplines, including law, engineering, architecture), two years

The postgraduate degree awarded to students upon the honorable completion of the postgraduate stage and the doctoral thesis is the Promotie (equivalent to the PhD).

ACCREDITATION

The degrees granted by Dutch universities are accredited, both regionally and professionally, by the government of the Netherlands.

REGISTRATION REQUIREMENTS

Foreign students who have been authorized to take university examinations by CBAP and have been notified of admission to a Dutch university will learn of all registration requirements upon notifying the institution of their intentions to enroll in the coming academic year. Foreign students must be prepared to pay both registration and tuition fees for the academic year at the formal matriculation session in the fall of the academic year.

VISA REQUIREMENTS AND RESIDENCE REGULATIONS

Foreign students who are European Community member state nationals do not need a visa or a temporary residence permit. These students should register for permanent student residence permits with the police department of the districts in which their respective universities' are located.

Foreign students who are not citizens of the European Community must obtain temporary residence permits from the Dutch embassy or consulate in their home countries in order to gain entrance into the Netherlands. Upon arrival and matriculation, the foreign student should register with the district police department for a permanent student residence permit. The requirements for obtaining such a permit are:

- a valid passport
- the notification of admission to a dutch university
- proof of financial capability for both the foreign student tuition fee and living expenses while attending a Dutch university
- a health insurance policy valid in the Netherlands

TUITION FEES FOR FOREIGN STUDENTS

Tuition fees for foreign students enrolled in a 1990–91 undergraduate program ranged from Fl 1,200 to Fl 3,500 per year, depending on the university and the particular field of study. Tuition fees for postgraduate foreign students ranged from Fl 5,000 to Fl 6,500 per year.

EXPENSES

The estimates for a foreign student's living expenses (housing, food, clothing and laundry, books and supplies, transportation, entertainment and other miscellaneous expenses) while attending a Dutch university ranged from Fl 1,400 to Fl 1,850 per month in 1990. Foreign students should inquire with the registration authorities of the district police department about the specific amount required to prove financial solvency.

FOREIGN STUDENT SCHOLARSHIPS

The universities of the Netherlands do not offer scholarships to foreign students—financial assistance from the respective universities is usually reserved for Dutch nationals. However, the Ministry of Education and Science does offer foreign students scholarship opportunities. Information on these scholarships can be obtained from the Dutch embassy or consulate in a foreign student's home country. There is also available a useful booklet describing foreign student scholarship opportunities in the Netherlands published by the Netherlands Organization for International Cooperation in Higher Education (NUFFIC) (P.O. Box 90734, 2509 LS The Hague, Netherlands).

UNIVERSITY CALENDAR

The academic year at Dutch universities runs from September until July. The year is divided into two semesters:

- fall semester: September to January
- spring semester: February to July

FOREIGN STUDENTS IN THE NETHERLANDS

Foreign students are not as numerous at the universities of the Netherlands as in most other European countries though the Ministry of Education was responsible for inaugurating the Erasmus Program (a foreign student exchange program within the European Community). In 1987, foreign students made up only 2% of the total student population in the Netherlands with roughly half of that number coming from other European Community member states. Nevertheless, foreign students from all over the world, particularly Asians, North Americans and non-EC Europeans, are enrolled in Dutch universities. In 1990, the estimated number of foreign students was higher than ever before—around 8,000. Extensive Junior Year Abroad programs as well as many international postgraduate programs exist between the universities of the Netherlands and North America. Though some Dutch universities attract more foreign students than others, each university mentioned in this chapter has an international student body.

UNIVERSITEIT VAN AMSTERDAM
(University of Amsterdam)
Spui 21, 1012 WX Amsterdam, Netherlands

CHARACTERISTICS OF INSTITUTION:
State-run, nonprofit university

DATE FOUNDED: 1632

TOTAL ENROLLMENT: 27,000 fulltime students

DEGREES AWARDED:
Meester in de Rechten (law)
    four years required
Doctorandus in various fields
    five years required
Professional qualifications in various fields

a minimum of two years following Doctorandus required
Doctorate
  by thesis

ACADEMIC PROGRAMS:
Faculty of Arts
Faculty of Biology
Faculty of Chemistry
Faculty of Dentistry
Faculty of Economics
Faculty of Education
Faculty of Geography and Archaeology
Faculty of Law
Faculty of Mathematics and Information Science
Faculty of Medicine
Faculty of Philosophy
Faculty of Physics and Astronomy
Faculty of Political and Social Science
Faculty of Psychology
Faculty of Theology

SPECIAL PROGRAMS:
Economic Research Institute
Institute of Atomic and Molecular Physics
Institute of Education Research
Institute of Nuclear Physics
Mathematics Center
Cooperative arrangements with universities around the world

LANGUAGE OF INSTRUCTION: Dutch

ADMISSION REQUIREMENTS FOR FOREIGN STUDENTS:
Secondary school certificate or recognized foreign equivalent

TUITION FOR FOREIGN STUDENTS:
Fl 1,600 per year. *See* GENERAL UNIVERSITY INFORMATION.

TOTAL INSTRUCTIONAL FACULTY:
3,000 (including 400 professors)

LIBRARY COLLECTIONS:
Central library—3,000,000 volumes
Faculty libraries

MUSEUMS AND GALLERIES:
Museums of Archaeology, Geology, Literature, University History, Zoology; Van Eeden Museum

UNIVERSITY PUBLICATIONS:
School en Universiteit, Studiegids van de Universiteit van Amsterdam

RECTOR: Prof. Dr. P. de Meijer

VRIJE UNIVERSITEIT, AMSTERDAM
(Free University, Amsterdam)
De Boelelaan, 1105, 1081 HV Amsterdam, Netherlands

CHARACTERISTICS OF INSTITUTION:
Private university

DATE FOUNDED: 1880

TOTAL ENROLLMENT: 12,000 fulltime students (including 350 foreign students)

DEGREES AWARDED:
Meester in de Rechten (law)
  four years required
Doctorandus in various fields
  five years required
Professional qualifications in various fields
  a minimum of two years following Doctorandus required
Doctorate
  by thesis

ACADEMIC PROGRAMS:
Faculty of Arts
Faculty of Biology
Faculty of Chemistry
Faculty of Dentistry
Faculty of Economics and Econometry
Faculty of Geophysics
Faculty of Law
Faculty of Mathematics and Computer Science
Faculty of Medicine
Faculty of Philosophy
Faculty of Physical Education
Faculty of Physics and Astronomy
Faculty of Psychology and Pedagogic Science
Faculty of Socio-Cultural Sciences
Faculty of Theology

SPECIAL PROGRAMS:
Cooperative arrangements with universities around the world

LANGUAGE OF INSTRUCTION: Dutch

ADMISSION REQUIREMENTS FOR FOREIGN STUDENTS:
Secondary school certificate or recognized foreign equivalent

TUITION FOR FOREIGN STUDENTS:
Fl 1,600 per year. *See* GENERAL UNIVERSITY INFORMATION.

TOTAL INSTRUCTIONAL FACULTY:
2,400

LIBRARY COLLECTIONS:
Total collection—550,000 volumes

MUSEUMS AND GALLERIES:
Museums of Art, University History

UNIVERSITY PUBLICATIONS:
Ad Valvas, Vrije Universiteitsblad

RECTOR: Prof. Dr. C. Datema

RIJKSUNIVERSITEIT TE GRONINGEN
(State University of Groningen)
Broerstraat 5, POB 72, 9700 AB Groningen, Netherlands

CHARACTERISTICS OF INSTITUTION:
State-run, nonprofit university

DATE FOUNDED: 1614

TOTAL ENROLLMENT: 17,500 fulltime students

DEGREES AWARDED:
Meester in de Rechten (law)
  four years required
Doctorandus in various fields
  five years required
Ingenieur
  five years required
Professional qualifications in various fields
  a minimum of two years following Doctorandus
  required
Doctorate
  by thesis

ACADEMIC PROGRAMS:
Faculty of Arts
Faculty of Economics
Faculty of Geography and Prehistory
Faculty of Law
Faculty of Medicine
Faculty of Organization and Management
Faculty of Philosophy
Faculty of Science
Faculty of Social Sciences
Faculty of Theology

SPECIAL PROGRAMS:
Cooperative arrangements with universities around the world

LANGUAGE OF INSTRUCTION: Dutch

ADMISSION REQUIREMENTS FOR FOREIGN STUDENTS:
Secondary school certificate or recognized foreign equivalent

TUITION FOR FOREIGN STUDENTS:
Fl 1,600 per year. See GENERAL UNIVERSITY INFORMATION.

TOTAL INSTRUCTIONAL FACULTY:
1,700 (including 350 professors)

LIBRARY COLLECTIONS:
University library—1,200,000 volumes
Faculty libraries

MUSEUMS AND GALLERIES:
Museums of Ethnography, University History
Botanical garden

UNIVERSITY PUBLICATIONS:
Algemeen Verslag, Broerstraat 5, Financieel Verslag, Gids voor adspirant studenten, Informatiegids, Onderwijsverslag, Wetenschappelijk Verslag, Universiteitskrant

PRESIDENT: Prof. Dr. E. Bleumink

RIJKSUNIVERSITEIT TEV LEIDEN
(State University of Leiden)
Stationsweg 46, POB 9500, 2300 RA Leiden, Netherlands

CHARACTERISTICS OF INSTITUTION:
State-run, nonprofit university

DATE FOUNDED: 1575

TOTAL ENROLLMENT: 18,000 fulltime students (including 600 foreign students)

DEGREES AWARDED:
Meester in de Rechten (law)
  four years required
Doctorandus in various fields
  five years required
Professional qualifications in various fields
  a minimum of two years following Doctorandus
  required
Doctorate
  by thesis

ACADEMIC PROGRAMS:
Faculty of Arts
Faculty of Geography and Prehistory
Faculty of Law
Faculty of Medicine
Faculty of Organization and Management
Faculty of Philosophy
Faculty of Science
Faculty of Social Sciences
Faculty of Theology

SPECIAL PROGRAMS:
Observatory

LANGUAGE OF INSTRUCTION: Dutch

ADMISSION REQUIREMENTS FOR FOREIGN STUDENTS:
Secondary school certificate or recognized foreign equivalent

TUITION FOR FOREIGN STUDENTS:
See GENERAL UNIVERSITY INFORMATION.

TOTAL INSTRUCTIONAL FACULTY:
1,700

LIBRARY COLLECTIONS:
University library—2,000,000 volumes
Faculty libraries

MUSEUMS AND GALLERIES:
Museums of Archaeology, Ethnology, Geology and Mineralogy, History, Natural History, Natural Science
Botanical garden

UNIVERSITY PUBLICATIONS:
Almanak, Leidse Plein, Leidse Universiteitsgids, Studeren in Leiden, Studiegids, Vademecum

PRESIDENT: Mr. C. P. C. M. Oomen

ERASMUS UNIVERSITEIT ROTTERDAM
(Erasmus University of Rotterdam)
Burgemeester Oudlaan 50, POB 1738, 3000 DR Rotterdam, Netherlands

CHARACTERISTICS OF INSTITUTION:
State-run, nonprofit university

DATE FOUNDED: 1973

TOTAL ENROLLMENT: 19,000 fulltime students

DEGREES AWARDED:
Meester in de Rechten (law)
    four years required
Doctorandus in various fields
    four years required
Professional qualifications in various fields
    a minimum of two years following Doctorandus required
Master of Business Administration
    a minimum of two years following Doctorandus required
Doctorate
    by thesis

ACADEMIC PROGRAMS:
Business School
Faculty of Economics
Faculty of Law
Faculty of Medicine
Faculty of Philosophy
Subfaculty of Social-Cultural Sciences
Subfaculty of Social History

SPECIAL PROGRAMS:
Center of Business Economics
Economic Research Institute
Fiscal Economics Institute
Institute of Econometrics
Institute of Economic Geography
Cooperative arrangements with 24 universities, including Indiana University, University of Pennsylvania, Michigan State University, Northwestern University in Illinois and the University of Western Ontario

LANGUAGE OF INSTRUCTION: Dutch

ADMISSION REQUIREMENTS FOR FOREIGN STUDENTS:
Secondary school certificate or recognized foreign equivalent

TUITION FOR FOREIGN STUDENTS:
Fl 1,600 per year. *See* GENERAL UNIVERSITY INFORMATION.

TOTAL INSTRUCTIONAL FACULTY:
1,000 fulltime faculty

LIBRARY COLLECTIONS:
Central library—500,000 volumes
Faculty libraries

MUSEUMS AND GALLERIES:
Economic Archives
Museum of History
Historic Picture Gallery

UNIVERSITY PUBLICATIONS:
Quod Novum

RECTOR: Prof. Dr. C. J. Rijnvos

KATHOLIEKE UNIVERSITEIT BRABANT
(Catholic Univ. of Brabant)
(Tilburg University)
Hogeschoollaan 225, POB 90153, 5000 LE Tilburg, Netherlands

CHARACTERISTICS OF INSTITUTION:
Private, state-supported university

DATE FOUNDED: 1927

TOTAL ENROLLMENT: 8,000 fulltime students

DEGREES AWARDED:
Meester in de Rechten (law)
    four years required
Doctorandus in various fields
    four years required
Doctorate
    by thesis

ACADEMIC PROGRAMS:
Faculty of Economics
Faculty of Law
Faculty of Letters
Faculty of Philosophy
Faculty of Social Science
Faculty of Theology

SPECIAL PROGRAMS:
Economic Institute
Fiscal Institute
Institute of Social Research
Cooperative arrangements with eight universities, including Indiana University and University of Connecticut

LANGUAGE OF INSTRUCTION: Dutch

ADMISSION REQUIREMENTS FOR FOREIGN STUDENTS:
Secondary school certificate or recognized foreign equivalent

TUITION FOR FOREIGN STUDENTS:
Fl 1,600 per year. *See* GENERAL UNIVERSITY INFORMATION.

TOTAL INSTRUCTIONAL FACULTY:
400 fulltime faculty

LIBRARY COLLECTIONS:
Total collection—400,000 volumes

UNIVERSITY PUBLICATIONS:
Economie, Informatie, Jaarverslag, Social Wetenschappen, UNIVERS

RECTOR: Prof. Dr. R. A. de Moor

RIJKSUNIVERSITEIT TE UTRECHT
(State University of Utrecht)
Heidelberglaan 8, POB 80125, 3508 TC Utrecht, Netherlands

CHARACTERISTICS OF INSTITUTION:
State-run, nonprofit university

DATE FOUNDED: 1636

TOTAL ENROLLMENT: 23,000 fulltime students (including 350 foreign students)

DEGREES AWARDED:
Meester in de Rechten (law)
    four years required
Doctorandus in various fields
    four years required
Professional qualifications in various fields
    a minimum of two years following Doctorandus required
Doctorate
    by thesis

ACADEMIC PROGRAMS:
Faculty of Arts
Faculty of Biology
Faculty of Chemistry
Faculty of Geographical Sciences
Faculty of Geology and Geophysics
Faculty of Law
Faculty of Mathematics and Information Science
Faculty of Medicine
Faculty of Pharmacy
Faculty of Philosophy
Faculty of Physics and Astronomy
Faculty of Social Sciences
Faculty of Theology
Faculty of Veterinary Medicine

SPECIAL PROGRAMS:
Center of Business Economics
Economic Research Institute
Fiscal Economic Institute
Institute of Econometrics
Institute of Economic Geography
Cooperative arrangements with 15 universities, including the University of Florida

LANGUAGE OF INSTRUCTION: Dutch

ADMISSION REQUIREMENTS FOR FOREIGN STUDENTS:
Secondary school certificate or recognized foreign equivalent

TUITION FOR FOREIGN STUDENTS:
Fl 1,600 per year. *See* GENERAL UNIVERSITY INFORMATION.

TOTAL INSTRUCTIONAL FACULTY:
2,000 fulltime faculty

LIBRARY COLLECTIONS:
Central library

MUSEUMS AND GALLERIES:
University museum

UNIVERSITY PUBLICATIONS:
Gids, Jaarverslag, Universiteitsblad

RECTOR: Prof. J. G. F. Veldhuis

NIJENRODE, UNIVERSITEIT VOOR BEDRIJFSKUNDE
(The Netherlands School of Business)
Straatweg 25, 3621 BG Breukelen, Netherlands

CHARACTERISTICS OF INSTITUTION:
State-run, nonprofit university

DATE FOUNDED: 1946

TOTAL ENROLLMENT: 650 fulltime students (including 40 foreign students [25 North Americans])

DEGREES AWARDED:
Bachelor of Business Administration
    three years required
Master of Business Administration
    one year after Bachelor required
Diplomas

ACADEMIC PROGRAMS:
Faculty of Business Administration

SPECIAL PROGRAMS:
Management Development Center
Management Research Center
Cooperative arrangements with several universities in the United States

LANGUAGES OF INSTRUCTION: Dutch and English

ADMISSION REQUIREMENTS FOR FOREIGN STUDENTS:
University degree and entrance examination

TUITION FOR FOREIGN STUDENTS:
Fl 15,000–42,000 per year.

TOTAL INSTRUCTIONAL FACULTY:
75

LIBRARY COLLECTIONS:
Total collection—40,000 volumes

UNIVERSITY PUBLICATIONS:
Gids, Nieuwsbrief

RECTOR: F. J. Schijff

INSTITUTE OF SOCIAL STUDIES
POB 90733, 2509 LS The Hague, Netherlands

CHARACTERISTICS OF INSTITUTION:
Private, independent institution

DATE FOUNDED: 1952

TOTAL ENROLLMENT: 225 fulltime students (almost all are foreign students)

DEGREES AWARDED:
Master of Arts, (MA) in development studies
Master of Philosophy (MPhil) in development studies
Doctor of Philosophy (PhD) in development studies

ACADEMIC PROGRAMS:
Not available

LANGUAGE OF INSTRUCTION: English

ADMISSION REQUIREMENTS FOR FOREIGN STUDENTS:
Not available

TUITION FOR FOREIGN STUDENTS:
As a private institution, tuition fees will be considerably higher than those charged to foreign students attending a public, state-run university. Prospective students are advised to contact the university directly regarding exact tuition fees.

TOTAL INSTRUCTIONAL FACULTY:
82 faculty

LIBRARY COLLECTIONS:
Total collection—30,000 volumes

UNIVERSITY PUBLICATIONS:
Development and Change, Occasional Papers, Working Papers

RECTOR: Prof. G. Lycklama à Nijehot

TECHNISCHE UNIVERSITEIT TE DELFT
(Delft University of Technology)
Julianalaan 134, POB 5, Delft, Netherlands

CHARACTERISTICS OF INSTITUTION:
State-run, nonprofit university

DATE FOUNDED: 1842

TOTAL ENROLLMENT: 14,500 fulltime students (including 800 foreign students)

DEGREES AWARDED:
Diploma
   four–six years required
Doctorates
   by thesis following diploma

ACADEMIC PROGRAMS:
Faculty of Aerospace Engineering
Faculty of Applied Physics
Faculty of Architecture
Faculty of Chemical, Metallurgical and Materials Engineering
Faculty of Civil Engineering
Faculty of Electrical Engineering
Faculty of Geodesy
Faculty of Industrial Design Engineering
Faculty of Mathematics and Computer Science
Faculty of Mechanical and Marine Engineering
Faculty of Mining Engineering
Faculty of Philosophy and Humanities

SPECIAL PROGRAMS:
Computer Center
Nuclear Reactor Institute
Cooperative arrangements with universities around the world

LANGUAGE OF INSTRUCTION: Dutch

ADMISSION REQUIREMENTS FOR FOREIGN STUDENTS:
Secondary school certificate or recognized foreign equivalent

TUITION FOR FOREIGN STUDENTS:
Fl 1,700 per year. *See* GENERAL UNIVERSITY INFORMATION.

TOTAL INSTRUCTIONAL FACULTY:
4,000 fulltime faculty (including 160 professors)

LIBRARY COLLECTIONS:
Central library—500,000 volumes
Faculty libraries

UNIVERSITY PUBLICATIONS:
Delft Integraal, Delta, Jaarboek, Studiegids

RECTOR: Prof. P. A. Schenck

THE UNIVERSITIES OF NORWAY

UNIVERSITETET I BERGEN
(University of Bergen)
POB 25, 5027 Bergen Universitetet, Norway

CHARACTERISTICS OF INSTITUTION:
State-run, nonprofit university

DATE FOUNDED: 1948

TOTAL ENROLLMENT: 12,000 (including 800 foreign students)

DEGREES AWARDED:
Candidatis Magisterii in various fields
   four–seven years required
Doctoral degree in various fields

ACADEMIC PROGRAMS:
Faculty of Arts
Faculty of Dentistry
Faculty of Law
Faculty of Mathematics and Natural Sciences
Faculty of Medicine
Faculty of Psychology
Faculty of Social Sciences

SPECIAL PROGRAMS:
Biological Station (including the research vessels
   Fridtjof Nansen, Hakon Mosby and *August Brinkman)*
Center for Developmental Studies
Center for Feminist·Research in the Humanities
Computer Science Program (within the Faculty of
   Mathematics)
LOS Center (Norwegian Center for Research in Or-
   ganization and Management)
Milde Arboretum
Nansen Remote Sensing Center
Norwegian Social Science Data Services
Nursing Program (within the Faculty of Medicine)
Research Center for Health Promotion, Environment
   and Life Style
Cooperative arrangements with the University of
   California, the University of Minnesota and the
   University of Washington in Seattle

LANGUAGE OF INSTRUCTION: Norwegian

ADMISSION REQUIREMENTS FOR FOREIGN STUDENTS:
Secondary school certificate *(examen artium)* or recognized foreign equivalent

TUITION FOR FOREIGN STUDENTS:
None. Nominal registration fee ranging from NOK
200–NOK 500 per semester

TOTAL INSTRUCTIONAL FACULTY:
800 faculty

LIBRARY COLLECTIONS:
University library—1,400,000 volumes

MUSEUMS AND GALLERIES:
Bryggen Museum of Medieval Archaeology
Historical Museum, Museum of Theater and Drama,
   Natural History Museum

UNIVERSITY PUBLICATIONS:
Bulletin (an English language journal published twice
yearly), *Naturen, Skrifter, Sarsia, UOB News, Småskif-
ter*

RECTOR: Prof. Dr. O. D. Laerum

UNIVERSITETET I OSLO
(University of Oslo)
P.O. Box 1072, Blindern, 0316 Oslo 3, Norway

CHARACTERISTICS OF INSTITUTION:
State-run, nonprofit university

DATE FOUNDED: 1811

TOTAL ENROLLMENT: 22,000

DEGREES AWARDED:
Candidatis Magisterii in various fields
   four–eight years required
Licentiatius in various fields
   five–seven years required
Magister Artium in liberal arts and social sciences
   six–seven years required
Doctoral degree in various fields
   two–three years following Magister Artium required

ACADEMIC PROGRAMS:
Faculty of Dentistry
Faculty of Law
Faculty of Liberal Arts
Faculty of Mathematics and Natural Sciences
Faculty of Medicine
Faculty of Social Sciences

SPECIAL PROGRAMS:
International summer school
Summer session for school teachers

LANGUAGE OF INSTRUCTION: Norwegian

ADMISSION REQUIREMENTS FOR FOREIGN STUDENTS:
Secondary school certificate *(examen artium)* or recognized foreign equivalent

TUITION FOR FOREIGN STUDENTS:
None. Nominal registration fee ranging from NOK
200–NOK 600 per semester

TOTAL INSTRUCTIONAL FACULTY:
1,600 faculty

LIBRARY COLLECTIONS:
University library—4,000,000 volumes

MUSEUMS AND GALLERIES:
Botanical Garden
Collectional of National Antiquities
Museums of Botany, Ethnography, Geology, Pa-
leontology, Zoology

RECTOR: Prof. Dr. Inge Lønning

UNIVERSITETET I TROMSØ
(University of Tromsø)
Post Boks 635, 9001 Tromsø, Norway

CHARACTERISTICS OF INSTITUTION:
State-run, nonprofit university

DATE FOUNDED: 1968

TOTAL ENROLLMENT: 4,000

DEGREES AWARDED:
Candidatis Magisterii in various fields
    four–six years required
Magister Artium
    five–six years required
Doctoral degree in various fields
    two–three years following Magister Artium re-
    quired

ACADEMIC PROGRAMS:
Department of Education
Institute of Biology and Geology
Institute of Mathematics, Physics and Chemistry
Institute of Museology
Institute of Museum Activity
Institute of Social Sciences
School of Fisheries
School of Languages and Literature
School of Law
School of Medicine

LANGUAGE OF INSTRUCTION: Norwegian

ADMISSION REQUIREMENTS FOR FOREIGN STUDENTS:
Secondary school certificate (examen artium) or recognized foreign equivalent

TUITION FOR FOREIGN STUDENTS:
None. Nominal registration fee ranging from NOK
200–NOK 600 per semester

TOTAL INSTRUCTIONAL FACULTY:
310 fulltime faculty
45 parttime faculty

LIBRARY COLLECTIONS:
University library—400,000 volumes

MUSEUMS AND GALLERIES:
Museum of Museology

RECTOR: Prof. Ole D. Mjøs

UNIVERSITETET I TRONDHEIM
(University of Trondheim)
Sverres Gt. 1, 7030 Trondheim, Norway

CHARACTERISTICS OF INSTITUTION:
State-run, nonprofit university

DATE FOUNDED: 1968

TOTAL ENROLLMENT: 9,700. (See also the total enrollment sections of the constituent colleges of the
university.)

DEGREES AWARDED:
Siviingeniør
    four–five years required
Candidatis Magisterii in various fields
    four–six years required
Doctoral degree in various fields
    two–six years required

ACADEMIC PROGRAMS:
College of Arts and Sciences
Faculty of Medicine
Institute of Technology
Society of Sciences and Letters

CONSTITUENT COLLEGES OF THE UNIVERSITY:
Allmennvitenskapelige Høfgskolen
Medisinske Fakultet
Norges Tekniske Høgskole

LANGUAGE OF INSTRUCTION: Norwegian

ADMISSION REQUIREMENTS FOR FOREIGN STUDENTS:
Secondary school certificate (examen artium) or recognized foreign equivalent

TUITION FOR FOREIGN STUDENTS:
None. Nominal registration fee ranging from NOK
200–NOK 600 per semester

TOTAL INSTRUCTIONAL FACULTY:
1,100. (See also the total instructional faculty sections in the constituent colleges of the university.)

LIBRARY COLLECTIONS:
Total of university libraries—940,000 volumes and
    8,000 current periodicals

(See the library collections sections for the constituent colleges of the university.)

RECTOR: Prof. Dr. Rolf Lenschow

ALLMENNVITENSKAPELIGE HØGSKOLEN
(College of Arts and Science)
University Center, 7055 Dragvoll, Trödheim, Norway

CHARACTERISTICS OF INSTITUTION:
State-run, nonprofit college of the University of Trondheim

DATE FOUNDED: 1922

TOTAL ENROLLMENT: 3,500 students

ACADEMIC PROGRAMS:
Faculty of Arts
Faculty of Science
Faculty of Social Sciences

SPECIAL PROGRAMS:
Institute of Teacher Training

LANGUAGE OF INSTRUCTION: Norwegian

ADMISSION REQUIREMENTS FOR FOREIGN STUDENTS:
Secondary school certificate (examen artium) or recognized foreign equivalent

TUITION FOR FOREIGN STUDENTS:
None. Nominal registration fee ranging from NOK 200–NOK 600 per semester

TOTAL INSTRUCTIONAL FACULTY:
300 faculty

RECTOR: Prof. Dr. Eiliv Steinnes

NORGES TEKNISKE HØGSKOLE
(Norwegian Institute of Technology)
7034 Trodheim, NTH, Norway

CHARACTERISTICS OF INSTITUTION:
State-run, nonprofit college of the University of Trondheim

DATE FOUNDED: 1948

TOTAL ENROLLMENT: 8,500

ACADEMIC PROGRAMS:
Department of Architecture
Department of Applied Earth Sciences and Metallurgy
Department of Chemical Engineering
Department of Civil Engineering
Department of Electrical Engineering and Computer Sciences
Department of Economics and Industrial Management

Department of Marine Technology
Department of Mechanical Engineering

LANGUAGE OF INSTRUCTION: Norwegian

ADMISSION REQUIREMENTS FOR FOREIGN STUDENTS:
Secondary school certificate (examen artium) or recognized foreign equivalent

TUITION FOR FOREIGN STUDENTS:
None. Nominal registration fee ranging from NOK 200–NOK 600 per semester

TOTAL INSTRUCTIONAL FACULTY:
700 faculty

RECTOR: Prof. Dr. Dag Kavlie

NORGES HANDELSHØGSKOLE
(Norwegian School of Economics and Business Administration)
Helleveien 30, 5035 Bergen-Sandviken, Norway

CHARACTERISTICS OF INSTITUTION:
State-run, nonprofit university

DATE FOUNDED: 1936

TOTAL ENROLLMENT: 2,700

DEGREES AWARDED:
Various degrees in disparate professional disciplines
    four–seven years required
Licentiatus
    three–four years required
Doctoral degree in economics (Dr.oecon)
    thesis based on independent research required

ACADEMIC PROGRAMS:
Department of Economics and Business Administration
Department of General Studies

SPECIAL PROGRAMS:
Administrative Research Foundation
Center for Applied Research
Center for International Business
Executive Development and Adult Education Foundation

LANGUAGE OF INSTRUCTION: Norwegian

ADMISSION REQUIREMENTS FOR FOREIGN STUDENTS:
Secondary school certificate (examen artium) or recognized foreign equivalent

TUITION FOR FOREIGN STUDENTS:
None. Nominal registration fee ranging from NOK 200–NOK 600 per semester

TOTAL INSTRUCTIONAL FACULTY:
150 faculty

LIBRARY COLLECTIONS:
Library—200,000 volumes

RECTOR: Leif B. Methlie

HØGSKOLESENTERET I NORDLAND
(Nordland University Center)
P.O. BOX 6003, 8016 Mørkved, Norway

CHARACTERISTICS OF INSTITUTION:
State-run, nonprofit university

DATE FOUNDED: 1970

TOTAL ENROLLMENT: 1,100 students

DEGREES AWARDED:
Not available

ACADEMIC PROGRAMS:
Graduate School of Business Administration
School of Business Administration
School of Fisheries and Aquaculture
School of Social Science

LANGUAGE OF INSTRUCTION: Norwegian

ADMISSION REQUIREMENTS FOR FOREIGN STUDENTS:
Secondary school certificate (examen artium) or recognized foreign equivalent

TUITION FOR FOREIGN STUDENTS:
None. Nominal registration fee ranging from NOK 200–NOK 600 per semester

TOTAL INSTRUCTIONAL FACULTY:
100 faculty

RECTOR: Prof. Dr. Audun Sandberg

AGDER DISTRIKTSHØGSKOLE
(Agder College)
Post Boks 407, 4601 Kristiansand, Norway

CHARACTERISTICS OF INSTITUTION:
State-run, nonprofit professional college providing short courses in areas not covered by the universities

DATE FOUNDED: 1948

TOTAL ENROLLMENT: 2,200 students

DEGREES AWARDED:
Høgskolekandidat
   two–three years required
Candidatis Magisterii in various fields
   four years required

ACADEMIC PROGRAMS:
Department of Chemistry
Department of Computer Sciences
Department of Economics and Business Administration
Department of Languages

Department of Mathematics
Department of Public Administration
Department of Translation (English, French, Norwegian)

SPECIAL PROGRAMS:
Cooperative arrangements with the University of California at Santa Barbara, Monterey Institute of International Studies in California, Luther College in Iowa and Pacific Lutheran University at Tacoma

LANGUAGE OF INSTRUCTION: Norwegian

ADMISSION REQUIREMENTS FOR FOREIGN STUDENTS:
Secondary school certificate (examen artium) or recognized foreign equivalent

TUITION FOR FOREIGN STUDENTS:
None. Nominal registration fee ranging from NOK 200–NOK 600 per semester

TOTAL INSTRUCTIONAL FACULTY:
60 faculty

LIBRARY COLLECTIONS:
College library—25,000 volumes

TELEMARK DISTRIKTCHØGSKOLE
(Telemark College)
3800 Bo i Telemark, Norway

CHARACTERISTICS OF INSTITUTION:
State-run, nonprofit regional college providing professional courses

DATE FOUNDED: 1970

TOTAL ENROLLMENT: 1,000 students

DEGREES AWARDED:
Høgskolekandidat
   two–three years required
Candidatis Magisterii in various fields
   four years required

ACADEMIC PROGRAMS:
Department of Cultural Development and Sports Administration
Department of Economics and Administration Studies
Department of English
Department of Environmental Studies
Department of History
Department of Mathematics
Department of Norwegian Studies

SPECIAL PROGRAMS:
Cooperative arrangement with the Luther College in Iowa

LANGUAGE OF INSTRUCTION: Norwegian

ADMISSION REQUIREMENTS FOR FOREIGN STUDENTS:
Secondary school certificate *(examen artium)* or recognized foreign equivalent

TUITION FOR FOREIGN STUDENTS:
None. Nominal registration fee ranging from NOK 200–NOK 600 per semester

TOTAL INSTRUCTIONAL FACULTY:
60 faculty

LIBRARY COLLECTIONS:
College library—50,000 volumes

RECTOR: Prof. Dr. Nils Rottingen

THE UNIVERSITIES OF PORTUGAL

GENERAL UNIVERSITY INFORMATION

Portuguese universities are state-run, nonprofit institutions and, as such, follow similar rules and regulations regarding admission language and degree requirements and tuition fees and expenses. The general information given is relevant for all the universities mentioned in this chapter.

ADMISSION REQUIREMENTS FOR FOREIGN STUDENTS

Admission of foreign students to Portuguese Universities is regulated by a national admission procedure *(Concurso Nacional)*. Under the present regulations, a foreign applicant must hold a secondary school certificate proving the honorable completion of a 12-year preparatory school education. Equivalent foreign qualifications include

- Baccalauréat Européen
- international baccalaureate
- U.S. or Canadian high school diploma
- General Certificate of Education or Scottish Certificate of Education from the United Kingdom
- secondary school certificate awarded by the competent educational authorities in any of the European Community member states

In addition, all foreign students must pass an entrance examination *(Prova de Aferição)*. This examination is in Portuguese; therefore, the admissions requirements for foreign students presupposes proficiency in Portuguese.

Foreign students should apply for recognition *(reconhecimento)* of their qualifications directly to the universities. Specific information regarding equivalency *(equivâlencia)* of foreign academic qualifications can be obtained from the *Direcção-Geral do Ensino Superior* of the *Centro de Informação e Reconhecimento Académico de Diplomas* (CIRAD) (Av. 5 de Outubro, 107, 9. andar, 1051 Lisbon Codex, Portugal). Applicants must provide all their secondary school documents and must specify the Portuguese qualification to which the application for recognition is proposed. Applications for equivalency must be made during the month of April prior to the academic year for which the foreign applicant has applied.

The admissions procedure is competitive, and foreign students are admitted to Portuguese universities based on their standings during the final three years of secondary school education, as well as their performances on the *Prova de Aferição*. Because there

are few postgraduate applicants, they do not face such rigid admission limitations.

APPLICATION PROCEDURE FOR FOREIGN STUDENTS

Foreign students must submit their applications for admission to the *Gabiente Coordenador do Ingresso no Ensino Superior* (GCIES) (Ab. Elias Garcia, 137, 1000 Lisbon, Portugal). The application form can be obtained from Portuguese embassies and consulates abroad. The application provides for the selection of up to 12 universities in order of the applicant's preference. The GCIES does not make decisions concerning foreign student applications but rather serves as a clearing house and forwards all relevant application information to the admissions departments of the respective universities.

APPLICATION DEADLINES

Foreign students must have completed and returned the formal application to GCIES by July or August. The date is set annually by the Ministry of Education and Culture *(Ministério da Educação e Cultura)*. The foreign applicant will learn the application deadline when he or she obtains a formal application from the Portuguese embassy or consulate in his or her home country.

ACADEMIC PROGRAM AND DEGREE REQUIREMENTS

There are three university degrees offered by the universities of Portugal:

- Licenciado degree: awarded following acceptable completion of an academic program, usually between four and six years in duration
- Mestre degree: awarded following the acceptable completion of an academic program that is usually two years in duration after having obtained the Licenciado degree. It requires the submission of and public defense of an independently researched dissertation *(Dissertação)*
- Doutor degree: the Portuguese equivalent of the British Higher Doctorate. The Doutor Degree does not have a specified academic program. However, candidates for the Doutor must submit an original, independently researched thesis that is of scholarly standards and which must make a definitive contribution to the academic knowledge of that particular discipline.

ACCREDITATION

All university degrees awarded by the universities of Portugal are accredited by the Portuguese government.

REGISTRATION REQUIREMENTS

Foreign students who are notified of admission to a Portuguese university will be told of all registration requirements at that time.

VISA REQUIREMENTS AND RESIDENCE REGULATIONS

Foreign students must obtain student visas from the Portuguese embassy or consulate in their home countries prior to arriving in Portugal. Foreign students must provide the following documents in order to be granted a student visa:

• notification of admission to a Portuguese university
• proof of financial solvency for the duration of the academic program to which the foreign student has been admitted
• valid passport

All relevant information regarding visa requirements and residence regulations can be obtained from the Portuguese diplomatic missions abroad and the Central Office for Foreigners (Direcção-Geral do Serviço de Estrangeiros e Fronteiras, Av. Antonio Augusto de Aguiar, 18, 1000 Lisbon, Portugal).

TUITION FEES FOR FOREIGN STUDENTS

Tuition fees for foreign students vary from one university to another and between disciplines. Every university charges a matriculation fee (Matrícula) of roughly Esc 200–250. Tuition fees (Propinas de Inscrição) are paid per semester and range from Esc 1,500 to Esc 3,000.

EXPENSES

For foreign students, costs vary from one city to another. In general, the cost of living in Lisbon is greater than in other areas of Portugal. Nevertheless, the average monthly cost for housing, food, clothing and laundry, books and supplies, entertainment and other miscellaneous expenses is between Esc 125,000 and Esc 200,000.

FOREIGN STUDENT SCHOLARSHIPS

The Portuguese government offers foreign student scholarships based on the applicant's ability to pay foreign student tuition fees. Since tuition fees are relatively inexpensive in Portugal, there are very few foreign student scholarships.

UNIVERSITY CALENDAR

The academic year at the universities of Portugal is divided into two semesters:

• fall semester: October to February
• spring semester: March to July

FOREIGN STUDENTS IN PORTUGAL

Historically, the universities of Portugal have not attracted as many foreign students as the universities in other European countries. In 1986, of a total enrollment of 75,000 students, only 1,775 were foreign (roughly 2%). The vast majority of this small number of foreign students were from the Portuguese-speaking countries of Africa or from Brazil. Less than 100 foreign students were European, and only about 50 foreign students were from North America. Now that Portugal has joined the European Community, the national authorities are expecting a greater number of foreign applicants. Foreign students who are interested in studying at a Portuguese university should apply as early as possible prior to the prospective academic year due to limitations on foreign student enrollment.

UNIVERSIDADE DOS AÇORES
(University of the Azores)
Rua da Mãe De Deus, 9502 Ponta Delgada
Codex, Azores, Portugal

CHARACTERISTICS OF INSTITUTION:
State-run, nonprofit university

DATE FOUNDED: 1976

TOTAL ENROLLMENT: 1,150

DEGREES AWARDED:
Bacharel
    three years required
Licenciado in various fields
    four–five years required
Doutor
    by examination and thesis after Licenciado

ACADEMIC PROGRAMS:
Department of Agriculture
Department of Biology
Department of Economics and Administration
Department of Education
Department of Earth Sciences
Department of History, Philosophy and Social Sciences
Department of Mathematics
Department of Modern Languages and Literature
Department of Oceanography and Fisheries

LANGUAGE OF INSTRUCTION: Portuguese

ADMISSION REQUIREMENTS FOR FOREIGN STUDENTS:
Secondary school certificate, or recognized foreign equivalent, and entrance examination

TUITION FOR FOREIGN STUDENTS:
See GENERAL UNIVERSITY INFORMATION.

TOTAL INSTRUCTIONAL FACULTY:
185

LIBRARY COLLECTIONS:
Documentation Center—181,000 volumes

UNIVERSITY PUBLICATIONS:
Archipelago

RECTOR: Prof. Dr. Antonio M. Bettencourt

UNIVERSIDADE DO ALGARVE
(University of Algarve)
Qt. de Penha, 8000 Faro, Portugal

CHARACTERISTICS OF INSTITUTION:
State-run, nonprofit university

DATE FOUNDED: 1979

TOTAL ENROLLMENT: 500

DEGREES AWARDED:
Licenciado in various fields
    about five years required
Doutor
    by examination and thesis after Licenciado

ACADEMIC PROGRAMS:
Department of Agricultural Science and Technology
Department of Aquatic Science and Technology
Department of Economics and Administration
Department of Exact Sciences and Humanities

SPECIAL PROGRAMS:
Arab Studies Center
Archaeology Center

LANGUAGE OF INSTRUCTION: Portuguese

ADMISSION REQUIREMENTS FOR FOREIGN STUDENTS:
Secondary school certificate or recognized foreign equivalent, and entrance examination

TUITION FOR FOREIGN STUDENTS:
See GENERAL UNIVERSITY INFORMATION.

TOTAL INSTRUCTIONAL FACULTY:
110

LIBRARY COLLECTIONS:
Total collection—7,500 volumes

RECTOR: Carlos Lloyd Braga

UNIVERSIDADE AUTÓNOMA DE LISBOA "LUÍS DE CAMÕES"
(Luis de Camões Autonomous University of Lisbon)
Rua de Santa Marta 56, 1100 Lisbon, Portugal

CHARACTERISTICS OF INSTITUTION:
Private university

DATE FOUNDED: 1986

TOTAL ENROLLMENT: 5,000

DEGREES AWARDED:
Not available

ACADEMIC PROGRAMS:
Department of Applied Mathematics
Department of Business Studies
Department of Economics
Department of History
Department of Law
Department of Modern Languages

LANGUAGE OF INSTRUCTION: Portuguese

ADMISSION REQUIREMENTS FOR FOREIGN STUDENTS:
See GENERAL UNIVERSITY INFORMATION.

TUITION FOR FOREIGN STUDENTS:
See GENERAL UNIVERSITY INFORMATION.

TOTAL INSTRUCTIONAL FACULTY:
500

LIBRARY COLLECTIONS:
Total collection—3,000 volumes

RECTOR: Prof. Dr. Justino Mendes de Almeida

UNIVERSIDADE DE AVEIRO
(University of Aveiro)
Rua Dr. Mário Sacramento, 3800 Aveiro, Portugal

CHARACTERISTICS OF INSTITUTION:
State-run, nonprofit university

DATE FOUNDED: 1973

TOTAL ENROLLMENT: 4,400 (including 30 foreign students)

DEGREES AWARDED:
Licenciado in various fields
    five years required

ACADEMIC PROGRAMS:
Department of Biology
Department of Ceramics and Glass Technology
Department of Chemistry
Department of Earth Sciences
Department of Education
Department of Electronics and Telecommunications
Department of Environmental Studies

Department of Mathematics
Department of Modern Languages and Cultures
Department of Physics

SPECIAL PROGRAMS:
Research centers
Cooperative arrangements with 29 universities, including Université du Québec, Indiana University and the University of Nebraska

LANGUAGE OF INSTRUCTION: Portuguese

ADMISSION REQUIREMENTS FOR FOREIGN STUDENTS:
Secondary school certificate, or recognized foreign equivalent, and entrance examination

TUITION FOR FOREIGN STUDENTS:
Esc 1,500 per year. *See* GENERAL UNIVERSITY INFORMATION.

TOTAL INSTRUCTIONAL FACULTY:
90

LIBRARY COLLECTIONS:
Total collection—45,000 volumes

UNIVERSITY PUBLICATIONS:
Documentação Corrente-boletim biliografico, Guia, Lista de Aquisicoes, Revista (4 series)

RECTOR: Prof. Dr. Joaquim Renato Ferreira de Araujo

UNIVERSIDADE DE COIMBRA
(University of Coimbra)
Paço das Escolas, 3000 Coimbra, Portugal

CHARACTERISTICS OF INSTITUTION:
State-run, nonprofit university

DATE FOUNDED: 1290

TOTAL ENROLLMENT: 13,100

DEGREES AWARDED:
Licenciado in various fields
   four–six years required
Doutor
   By examination and thesis after Licenciado

ACADEMIC PROGRAMS:
Faculty of Arts
Faculty of Economics
Faculty of Law
Faculty of Medicine
Faculty of Pharmacy
Faculty of Psychology
Faculty of Science

SPECIAL PROGRAMS:
Botanical Institute
Institute of Climatology and Hydrology

Geophysical Institute
Observatory
Cooperative arrangements with nine universities, including the University of Illinois

LANGUAGE OF INSTRUCTION: Portuguese

ADMISSION REQUIREMENTS FOR FOREIGN STUDENTS:
Secondary school certificate, or recognized foreign equivalent, and entrance examination

TUITION FOR FOREIGN STUDENTS:
See GENERAL UNIVERSITY INFORMATION.

TOTAL INSTRUCTIONAL FACULTY:
1,015 (including 300 professors)

LIBRARY COLLECTIONS:
Total collection 1,418,000 volumes

MUSEUMS AND GALLERIES:
Museums of Anthropology, Botany, Mineralogy and Geology, Physics, Sacred Art, Zoology

UNIVERSITY PUBLICATIONS:
Acta Universitatis Conimbrigensis, Anuario da Universidade, Biblos, Brasilia, Conimbriga, Humanitas, various faculty publications

RECTOR: Prof. Dr. Rui Nogueira Lobo de Alarcao e Silva

UNIVERSIDADE DE LISBOA
(University of Lisbon)
Alameda da Universidade, 1699 Lisbon Codex, Portugal

CHARACTERISTICS OF INSTITUTION:
State-run, nonprofit university

DATE FOUNDED: 1288

TOTAL ENROLLMENT: 17,200

DEGREES AWARDED:
Licenciado in various fields
   four–six years required
Doutor
   by examination and thesis after Licenciado
Diploma in pharmacy
   three years required

ACADEMIC PROGRAMS:
Faculty of Arts
Faculty of Law
Faculty of Medicine
Faculty of Pharmacy
Faculty of Psychology and Educational Science
Faculty of Science

LANGUAGE OF INSTRUCTION: Portuguese

ADMISSION REQUIREMENTS FOR FOREIGN STUDENTS:
Secondary school certificate, or recognized foreign equivalent, and entrance examination

TUITION FOR FOREIGN STUDENTS:
See GENERAL UNIVERSITY INFORMATION.

TOTAL INSTRUCTIONAL FACULTY:
1,700

LIBRARY COLLECTIONS:
Faculty libraries—378,000 volumes

MUSEUMS AND GALLERIES:
Museums of Archaeology and Ethnology, Anthropology and Zoology, Botany, Mineralogy and Geology

UNIVERSITY PUBLICATIONS:
Anuario, Arquivos, Bloetim, Revista da Fauldade di Letras, Revista de Faculdade di Direito, Arquivo do Anatomia e Antropologia, Arquivo do Instituto Bacteriologico Camara Pestana, Anais do Insituto Geofisco, Portugalie Phisica, Portgugalia Revista de Biologica, Boletim da Faculdade de Famacia, Estudos sobre a fauna poruguesa, Trabalhos do Instituto di Fisiologia.

RECTOR: Prof. Dr. Virgilio A. de Meira Soares

UNIVERSIDADE LUSÍADA
(University of Lusiada)
Rua da Junqueira 194, 1300 Lisbon, Portugal

CHARACTERISTICS OF INSTITUTION:
Private university

DATE FOUNDED: 1986

TOTAL ENROLLMENT: 3,200

ACADEMIC PROGRAMS:
Faculty of Applied Mathematics
Faculty of Architecture
Faculty of Business Management
Faculty of Economics
Faculty of History
Faculty of International Relations
Faculty of Law

SPECIAL PROGRAMS:
Archaeology Center
Computer Center
Drug Dependency Research Center
Legal Studies Center
Linguistic Studies Center

LANGUAGE OF INSTRUCTION: Portuguese

TUITION FOR FOREIGN STUDENTS:
See GENERAL UNIVERSITY INFORMATION.

TOTAL INSTRUCTIONAL FACULTY:
298 fulltime faculty

LIBRARY COLLECTIONS:
Total collection—14,700 volumes

UNIVERSITY PUBLICATIONS:
Boletim Informativo, Revista Lusíada de Ciencia e Cultura

RECTOR: Prof. Dr. António J. Martins da Motta Vega

UNIVERSIDADE DO MINHO
(University of Minho)
Largo do Paço, 4719 Braga Codex, Portugal

CHARACTERISTICS OF INSTITUTION:
State-run, nonprofit university

DATE FOUNDED: 1973

TOTAL ENROLLMENT: 5,500

DEGREES AWARDED:
Licenciado in various fields
    four–six years required
Pos-graduaçao in various fields
    an additional two years required
Doutor
    by examination and thesis after Licenciado

ACADEMIC PROGRAMS:
Faculty of Arts
Faculty of Economics and Management
Faculty of Education
Faculty of Engineering (computer science included)
Faculty of Sciences
Faculty of Social Sciences
Faculty of Psychology

LANGUAGE OF INSTRUCTION: Portuguese

ADMISSION REQUIREMENTS FOR FOREIGN STUDENTS:
Secondary school certificate, or recognized foreign equivalent, and entrance examination

SPECIAL PROGRAMS:
Adult education
Archeology unit
Public archives

TUITION FOR FOREIGN STUDENTS:
See GENERAL UNIVERSITY INFORMATION.

TOTAL INSTRUCTIONAL FACULTY:
450 faculty

LIBRARY COLLECTIONS:
Total collection—34,000 volumes

MUSEUMS AND GALLERIES:
Nogueira da Silva Museum

UNIVERSITY PUBLICATIONS:
Boletim

RECTOR: Prof. Dr. Sergio Machado dos Santos

UNIVERSIDADE NOVA DE LISBOA
(New University of Lisbon)
Praça Do Principe Real 25 r/c, 1200 Lisbon,
Portugal

CHARACTERISTICS OF INSTITUTION:
State-run, nonprofit university

DATE FOUNDED: 1973

TOTAL ENROLLMENT: 6,100

DEGREES AWARDED:
Licenciado in various fields
    four–six years required
Pos-graduaçao in various fields
    an additional two years required following com-
    pletion of the Licenciado
Doutor
    by examination and thesis after Licenciado

ACADEMIC PROGRAMS:
Faculty of African Studies
Faculty of Economics
Faculty of Hygiene and Tropical Medicine
Faculty of Medical Sciences
Faculty of Science and Technology
Faculty of Social and Human Sciences

SPECIAL PROGRAMS:
Institute of African Studies
Cooperative arrangements with the University of São
    Paulo in Brazil

LANGUAGE OF INSTRUCTION: Portuguese

ADMISSION REQUIREMENTS FOR FOREIGN STUDENTS:
Secondary school certificate, or recognized foreign
equivalent, and entrance examination

TUITION FOR FOREIGN STUDENTS:
Esc 1,200 per year. *See* GENERAL UNIVERSITY INFOR-
MATION.

TOTAL INSTRUCTIONAL FACULTY:
600 fulltime professors
350 parttime professors

LIBRARY COLLECTIONS:
Total collection—80,000 volumes

UNIVERSITY PUBLICATIONS:
Boletim (quarterly)

RECTOR: Prof. Dr. J. A. Esperanca Piña

UNIVERSIDADE DO PORTO
University of Porto
Rua D. Manuel II, 4003 Porto Codex, Portugal

CHARACTERISTICS OF INSTITUTION:
State-run, nonprofit university

DATE FOUNDED: 1911

TOTAL ENROLLMENT: 17,000

DEGREES AWARDED:
Licenciado in various fields
    four–six years required
Doutor
    by examination and thesis after Licenciado

ACADEMIC PROGRAMS:
Faculty of Architecture
Faculty of Biomedical Sciences
Faculty of Engineering
Faculty of Humanities
Faculty of Medicine
Faculty of Pharmacy
Faculty of Physical Training
Faculty of Psychology and Educational Sciences
Faculty of Science

SPECIAL PROGRAMS:
College of Nutrition
Cooperative arrangements with State University of
    Virginia and Virginia Polytechnic Institute

LANGUAGE OF INSTRUCTION: Portuguese

ADMISSION REQUIREMENTS FOR FOREIGN STUDENTS:
Secondary school certificate, or recognized foreign
equivalent, and entrance examination

TUITION FOR FOREIGN STUDENTS:
See GENERAL UNIVERSITY INFORMATION.

TOTAL INSTRUCTIONAL FACULTY:
2,100

RECTOR: Prof. Dr. Alberto M. S. C. Amaral

UNIVERSIDADE TÉCHNICA DE LISBOA
(Technical University of Lisbon)
Alameda Santo Antonio dos Capuchos 1, 1100
Lisbon, Portugal

CHARACTERISTICS OF INSTITUTION:
State-run, nonprofit university

DATE FOUNDED: 1930

TOTAL ENROLLMENT: 15,000

DEGREES AWARDED:
Licenciado in various fields
    four–six years required

Doutor
  by examination and thesis after Licenciado

ACADEMIC PROGRAMS:
Faculty of Architecture
Institute of Agriculture
Institute Economics and Management
Institute of Physical Education
Institute of Social and Political Sciences

SPECIAL PROGRAMS:
60 associated research centers
Cooperative arrangements with many universities, including the Massachusettes Institute of Technology (MIT)

LANGUAGE OF INSTRUCTION: Portuguese

ADMISSION REQUIREMENTS FOR FOREIGN STUDENTS:
Secondary school certificate, or recognized foreign equivalent, and entrance examination

TUITION FOR FOREIGN STUDENTS:
Esc 1,500–3,000 per year. *See* GENERAL UNIVERSITY INFORMATION.

TOTAL INSTRUCTIONAL FACULTY:
1,900

LIBRARY COLLECTIONS:
Total collection of school and institute libraries—245,000 volumes

MUSEUMS AND GALLERIES:
Museums of Geology and Zoology

UNIVERSITY PUBLICATIONS:
Ludens, various faculty publications from the institutes

RECTOR: Prof. Dr. Antonio Simões Lopes

UNIVERSIDADE DE TRAS-OS-MONTES E ALTO DOURO
P.O. Box 202, 5001 Vila Real, Portugal

CHARACTERISTICS OF INSTITUTION:
State-run, nonprofit university

DATE FOUNDED: 1973

TOTAL ENROLLMENT: 3,000

DEGREES AWARDED:
Licenciado in various fields

five years required
Doutor
  by examination and thesis after Licenciado

ACADEMIC PROGRAMS:
Department of Animal Pathology and Hygiene
Department of Animal Science
Department of Arts and Workmanship
Department of Biology
Department of Crop Science and Rural Engineering
Department of Earth Sciences
Department of Economics and Sociology
Department of Educational Sciences
Department of Engineering
Department of Food Technology
Department of Forestry
Department of Literature
Department of Mathematics
Department of Physics
Department of Plant Protection
Department of Rural Extension
Department of Sports

SPECIAL PROGRAMS:
Botanical Institute
Institute of Climatology and Hydrology
Geophysical Institute
Observatory
Cooperative arrangements with the University of Georgia, the University of Illinois, the University of Iowa, Purdue University and the University of Wisconsin

LANGUAGE OF INSTRUCTION: Portuguese

ADMISSION REQUIREMENTS FOR FOREIGN STUDENTS:
Secondary school certificate, or recognized foreign equivalent, and entrance examination

TUITION FOR FOREIGN STUDENTS:
See GENERAL UNIVERSITY INFORMATION.

TOTAL INSTRUCTIONAL FACULTY:
250

LIBRARY COLLECTIONS:
Documentation center—9,000 volumes

MUSEUMS AND GALLERIES:
Museum of Geology

RECTOR: Prof. Dr. Fernando Nunes Ferreira Real

THE UNIVERSITIES OF SPAIN

GENERAL UNIVERSITY INFORMATION

Spanish universities are state-run, nonprofit institutions and, as such, follow similar rules regarding admission, language and degree requirements, and tuition and expenses. The general information given is relevant to all the universities mentioned in this chapter.

ADMISSION REQUIREMENTS FOR FOREIGN STUDENTS

Foreign students applying to a Spanish university must either hold the Spanish secondary school certificate (*Bachillerato Unificado y Polivalente* [BUP]) and have completed the one year university introductory course (*Curso de orientación universitaria [COU]*) or hold a recognized foreign equivalent of both requirements. The regulations regarding the recognition of foreign secondary school certificates and university degrees are as follows:

- Admission to the first year of an undergraduate program requires a secondary school certificate sufficient for admission to a comparable academic program in the country of the certificate's origin.
- Admission as a transfer student or to a postgraduate program requires the recognition of past studies and/or university degrees by the Spanish university in question. Transfer students must have a statement of honorable dismissal from their previous institutions in order to be granted recognition of past studies.
- Recognition of awarded degrees and certificates is the responsibility of the Spanish national Government's Ministry of Education and Science.

Admission to the universities of Spain varies depending upon the academic program to which the foreign student has applied. Admission requirements may also vary from one program to another within the same university, depending upon the number of applicants and the capacity for students of the program in question. For example, medicine, dentistry, veterinary science and engineering usually receive many more applications than the facilities available are able to handle, thus making admission requirements to those programs more competitive than to others.

Limitations on foreign applicants admitted to Spanish universities are based on the respective capacities of each institution and vary from university to university. In programs in which capacity limitations do exist, foreign students may not amount to more than 5% of the total number of students enrolled. Foreign students who are European Community member state nationals are considered equal to Spanish students for the purpose of student admission quotas.

All university applicants, including Spanish and E.C. nationals, must take the general entrance examination (*Prueba de Acceso* or *Selectividad*). This examination is offered in July and September of every year at each respective university. Foreign applicants to the National Open University (*Universidad Nacional de Educación a Distancia*) may take the general entrance examination at the Spanish embassy in their home countries. This option is not available at all Spanish embassies. Foreign students should inquire about its availability at the cultural office of the embassy or consulate in their home countries.

The language of instruction at the universities of Spain is Spanish, but in the autonomous communities of Spain (Catalonia, the Basque Provinces, Galicia, Valencia and the Baleares), the indigenous language of the community may be used at the university. Foreign students must be proficient in Spanish in order to be admitted to a university academic program. Many Spanish courses are available to foreign students through the universities and through other educational institutions in Spain. The language and literature courses offered at the Menéndez Palayo International University are a special facility for foreign students.

APPLICATION PROCEDURE FOR FOREIGN STUDENTS

All applicants—Spanish, E.C. nationals and other foreigners—must submit formal applications to the universities to which they hope to gain admission. This formal application must include a first choice academic program as well as alternative programs (because of the existing quotas or limitations on enrollment to certain courses of study). The universities' admissions departments are responsible for giving appropriate consideration to the preference orders.

Foreign applicants should contact the respective universities' admissions departments for specific application requirements as the necessary qualifications may differ from one institution to another.

APPLICATION DEADLINES

For most Spanish universities, the formal application, including certified Spanish translations of all required documents, must be submitted before March 31 of the year in which the student hopes to gain admission. However, since the application deadline may vary from one university to another, foreign students are advised to inquire about the specific deadline when making the initial contact with the university in question.

ACADEMIC PROGRAMS AND DEGREE REQUIREMENTS

Spanish universities offer many different certificates and degrees. The type of degree awarded to graduates of an academic program depends upon the subject studied, the duration of the program and the institution at which the student was enrolled. The types of universities in Spain are as follows:

- *Escuelas Universitarias*—institutions that offer short-term, multidisciplinary programs
- *Facultades*—institutions that offer long-term, multidisciplinary programs
- *Escuelas Técnicas Universitarias*—institutions that offer short-term, technical programs
- *Escuelas Técnicas Superiores*—institutions that offer long-term, technical programs

Spanish universities operate under a strict three-cycle *(ciclo)* system in which the first two cycles compose the undergraduate level academic programs and the third cycle is composed of the postgraduate level program. Short-term degrees are awarded at the end of the first cycle; long-term degrees are then awarded at the end of the second cycle.

Undergraduate Degrees

The first cycle lasts three years and is a short-term academic program resulting in the following university degrees:

- The Diplomado is offered at *Escuelas Universitarias* in a multitude of disciplines and is obtained following the completion of a three-year program.
- Ingeniero Técnico and Arquitecto Técnico are degrees offered at *Escuelas Técnicas Universitarias* in a variety of technical disciplines and are obtained following the completion of three-year programs.

The second cycle includes the first cycle and two to three additional years and is a long-term academic program resulting in the following university degrees:

- The Licenciado is offered at *Facultades* in a multitude of disciplines and is obtained following the completion of a five- to six-year undergraduate program.
- Ingeniero Superior and Arquitecto Superior are degrees offered at *Escuelas Técnicas Superiores* in a variety of technical disciplines and are obtained

following the completion of a six-year undergraduate program.

Postgraduate Degree

The third cycle includes the second cycle and one to three years of postgraduate studies and results in the university degree of Doctor. The academic program for this degree includes independent research and the presentation of an original thesis. Admissions to postgraduate programs are highly competitive, and very few students are accepted into the third cycle.

ACCREDITATION

All degrees obtained at the state-run universities of Spain are accredited by the government of Spain, as are most private university degrees.

REGISTRATION REQUIREMENTS

The respective university will contact the foreign applicant upon reaching a decision about admission into the academic program to which he or she applied. If the foreign applicant is accepted by the university, then he or she will be informed of the registration requirements and the registration/matriculation date set by the university in question. Registration requirements usually specify the presentation, in person, of all documents involved in the formal application. They are typically presented during matriculation *(Matrícula)* prior to the advent of the academic year.

VISA REQUIREMENTS AND RESIDENCE REGULATIONS

Most foreign students must obtain student visas from the Spanish embassy or consulate in their home countries in order to enroll in studies at a Spanish university. New regulations in 1990 made it impossible for foreign students to arrive in Spain with a tourist visa and then convert the document to a student visa upon enrollment at a Spanish university.

Foreign students who are nationals of European Community member states may stay in Spain for up to three months before arranging a student visa or obtaining a residence permit. All European Community regulations regarding the free movement of E.C. nationals will come into effect in Spain in 1992.

Residence permits must be obtained from the Ministry of the Interior or from the police commissioner's department of the region in which the university in question is located. In order to be permitted residence in Spain, the foreign student must have documented proof of financial solvency for the duration of the academic program in which he or she is enrolled.

TUITION FEES FOR FOREIGN STUDENTS

Tuition fees vary from one academic program to another and also from university to university. The governmental University Council of the autonomous communities determines the tuition fees charged by the universities of that region. The Ministry for Education and Science sets the tuition for the national universities. Also, some private universities and institutions under the jurisdiction of the Roman Catholic Church are entirely autonomous regarding Spanish state regulations on tuition fees charged to foreign students.

In general, tuition fees range from Pta 200,000 to Pta 2,000,000 per year. The average annual tuition fee charged a foreign student in 1989 was Pta 360,000.

EXPENSES

Living expenses for a foreign student at a Spanish University vary from location to location. As a rule, student expenses in Madrid and Barcelona are higher than in any other university centers in Spain. Foreign students in these cities can expect to spend roughly Pta 75,000–100,000 per month on housing, food, clothing and laundry, health care and hygiene, books and supplies, transportation, entertainment and miscellaneous expenses.

FOREIGN STUDENT SCHOLARSHIPS

Scholarships from Spain's Ministry of Education and Science are generally reserved for Spanish students or for foreign students who have legal residence in Spain. Financial assistance is available for foreign students through the competent authorities in the foreign student's home country if Spain and the nation in question have reached a bilateral agreement on university studies and/or research.

If foreign students are interested in financial assistance, they must contact the cultural office of the Spanish embassy or consulate in their home countries regarding the opportunities available. Foreign students will not be able to arrange this type of financial assistance after beginning an academic program at a Spanish university.

Foreign students from Latin America should inquire about the opportunities for scholarship or financial assistance at the Spanish Ministry of Foreign Affairs' *Instituto de Cooperación Iberoamericana.*

UNIVERSITY CALENDAR

The academic year runs from early October until late June and is divided into either two semesters:

- fall semester: October to January
- spring semester: February to June

or three terms:

- fall term: October to December
- winter term: January to March
- spring term: April to June

FOREIGN STUDENTS IN SPAIN

In the past, Spanish universities have not attracted as many foreign students as most of the institutions of higher learning in other European countries. In 1987, of the total number of students enrolled at Spanish universities (about 650,000), only about 9,000 were foreign nationals. However, since Spain became a member of the European Community, the number of foreign students attending the universities of Spain has increased dramatically. By 1992, the year in which the Single European Act comes into force, Spain will probably have a far more international student body within its universities than it does now. The majority of North American nationals currently enrolled in the universities of Spain are engaged in Junior Year Abroad programs. However, the number of fulltime foreign students from Canada and the United States of America is increasing. All Spanish universities have foreign students enrolled and are expanding their international contingent of students.

UNIVERSIDAD DE BARCELONA
(University of Barcelona)
Gran Via de Las Cortes Catalanes 585, 08007 Barcelona, Spain

CHARACTERISTICS OF INSTITUTION:
State-run, nonprofit university

DATE FOUNDED: 1450

TOTAL ENROLLMENT: 83,500 fulltime students

DEGREES AWARDED:
Diplomado
   three years required
Licenciado
   five years required
Licenciado in Medicine
   six years required
Doctorado
   by thesis

ACADEMIC PROGRAMS:
Department of Education
Department of Experimental Studies and Mathematics
Department of General Studies at Lerida
Department of Health Sciences
Department of Human and Social Sciences
Department of Law, Economics and Social Sciences

LANGUAGES OF INSTRUCTION: Spanish and Valenciano

ADMISSION REQUIREMENTS FOR FOREIGN STUDENTS:
Secondary school certificate *(bachiller)*, or recognized foreign equivalent, and preuniversity examination *(madurez)*, or entrance examination for adults

TUITION FOR FOREIGN STUDENTS:
See GENERAL UNIVERSITY INFORMATION.

TOTAL INSTRUCTIONAL FACULTY:
3,000

LIBRARY COLLECTIONS:
University library—374,950 volumes
Faculty libraries
Colleges libraries—52,900 volumes

MUSEUMS AND GALLERIES:
Museum of Zoology
Picture Gallery

UNIVERSITY PUBLICATIONS:
Anuario de Filologia, Anuario de Psicologia, Archivos espanoles de Medicina Interna, Archivos de Pediatria, Boletin Americanista, Boletin de estratigrafia, Boletin del Instituto Estudios Helenicos, Boletin de la Sección de Astronomia del Seminario Matematico, Ciencia-Industria farmaceutica, Collecta Mathematica, Convivium, Cuadernos de Arqueologia, Cuadernos de Economia, Cuadernos de Information Economica, Folia botanica miscellanea, Geo-critica, Indice Historico espanol, Logos, Oecologia Aquatica, Publicacions del Departamento de Zoologia, Publicacions de la Universidad de Barcelona, Revista del Departamento de Psiquiatria, Revista de Geografia, Revista del Seminario de la Catedra de Patologia Medica de Barcelona, Studium opthalmologium Fossilia, Temes Monografics Bioestadistica, Trabajos de Antropologia, Universitas Tarraconensis

RECTOR: Josep Maria Bricall Massip

**UNIVERSIDAD AUTÓNOMA DE BARCELONA
(Autonomous University of Barcelona)
Campus Universitario, 08193 Bellaterra
(Barcelona), Spain**

CHARACTERISTICS OF INSTITUTION:
State-run, nonprofit university

DATE FOUNDED: 1968

TOTAL ENROLLMENT: 33,800 fulltime students

DEGREES AWARDED:
Diplomado
   three years required
Licenciado
   an additional two years required
Medicine

an additional three years required after Licenciado required
Doctorado
   An additional two years and thesis after Licenciado required

ACADEMIC PROGRAMS:
Faculty of Economics
Faculty of Information Science
Faculty of Law
Faculty of Letters
Faculty of Medicine
Faculty of Political Sciences
Faculty of Science
Faculty of Veterinary Medicine

LANGUAGES OF INSTRUCTION: Spanish and Catalan

ADMISSION REQUIREMENTS FOR FOREIGN STUDENTS:
Secondary school certificate *(bachiller)*, or recognized foreign equivalent, and preuniversity examination *(madurez)*, or entrance examination for adults

TUITION FOR FOREIGN STUDENTS:
See GENERAL UNIVERSITY INFORMATION.

TOTAL INSTRUCTIONAL FACULTY:
1,852

LIBRARY COLLECTIONS:
Total collection—200,000 volumes

UNIVERSITY PUBLICATIONS:
Administracion Publica, Avances en Terapeutica, Documents d'analisi Metologica en Geografi, Documents d'analisi Urbana, Publicacions de Geologia, Publicacions de Matematique, Quaderns de Psicologia

RECTOR: Dr. Josep M. Vallès

**UNIVERSIDAD DE ALCALÁ DE HENARES
(University of Alcala de Henares)
Apdo 20, Plaza de San Diego, 28801 Alcala de
Henares (Madrid), Spain**

CHARACTERISTICS OF INSTITUTION:
State-run, nonprofit university

DATE FOUNDED: 1977

TOTAL ENROLLMENT: 13,750 fulltime students

DEGREES AWARDED:
Licenciado
   five years required
Medicine
   six years required
Doctorado
   an additional two years and thesis after Licenciado required

ACADEMIC PROGRAMS:
Faculty of Chemical and Biological Sciences
Faculty of Economic and Business Sciences
Faculty of Law
Faculty of Medicine
Faculty of Pharmacy
Faculty of Philosophy and Letters

SPECIAL PROGRAMS:
Center of European Studies
Center for North American Studies
Ibero-American Center for Industrial Relations
Institute of Education
University Institute of Business Administration

LANGUAGE OF INSTRUCTION: Spanish

ADMISSION REQUIREMENTS FOR FOREIGN STUDENTS:
Secondary school certificate *(bachiller)*, or recognized foreign equivalent, and preuniversity examination *(madurez)*

TUITION FOR FOREIGN STUDENTS:
See GENERAL UNIVERSITY INFORMATION.

TOTAL INSTRUCTIONAL FACULTY:
800

LIBRARY COLLECTIONS:
Total collection—120,000 volumes

RECTOR: Manuel Gala Muñoz

UNIVERSIDAD DE ALICANTE
(University of Alicante)
San Vicente del Raspeig, 03690 Alicante, Spain

CHARACTERISTICS OF INSTITUTION:
State-run, nonprofit university

DATE FOUNDED: 1979

TOTAL ENROLLMENT: 11,000 fulltime students

DEGREES AWARDED:
Diplomado
    three years required
Licenciado
    five years required
Medicine
    six years required
Doctorado
    an additional two years following Licenciado required

ACADEMIC PROGRAMS:
Faculty of Economics and Business Administration
Faculty of Law
Faculty of Medicine
Faculty of Philosophy and Letters
Faculty of Sciences

University School of Business Studies
University School of Graduate Social Studies
University School of Nursing
University School of Optics
University School of Professional Studies
University School of Social Work

SPECIAL PROGRAMS:
Cooperative arrangements with Sheffield City Polytechnic University and East Anglia University, both in the United Kingdom

LANGUAGES OF INSTRUCTION: Spanish and Valenciano

ADMISSION REQUIREMENTS FOR FOREIGN STUDENTS:
Secondary school certificate *(bachiller)*, or recognized foreign equivalent, and preuniversity examination *(madurez)*, or entrance examination for adults

TUITION FOR FOREIGN STUDENTS:
See GENERAL UNIVERSITY INFORMATION.

TOTAL INSTRUCTIONAL FACULTY:
530

LIBRARY COLLECTIONS:
College libraries
Faculty libraries

UNIVERSITY PUBLICATIONS:
Annales, Campus, Mediterranea

RECTOR: Ramón Martin Mateo

UNIVERSIDAD DE CANTABRIA
(University of Cantabria)
Avda de los Castros s/n, 39005 Santander, Spain

CHARACTERISTICS OF INSTITUTION:
State-run, nonprofit university

DATE FOUNDED: 1972

TOTAL ENROLLMENT: 11,500 fulltime students (including 50 foreign students)

DEGREES AWARDED:
Diplomado
    three years required
Licenciado in science, law, letters
    five years required
Licenciado in medicine, engineering
    six years required
Ingeniero Técnico Superior de Caminos, Canales y Puertos
    one–two years following Licenciado required
Doctorado
    an additional two years following Licenciado required

ACADEMIC PROGRAMS:
Faculty of Economics and Business Studies
Faculty of Law
Faculty of Medicine
Faculty of Philosophy and Letters
Faculty of Sciences
Higher Engineering School for Industry
Higher Technical School of Civil Engineering
Higher School of the Merchant Navy
University School of Business Studies
University School of Industrial Engineering
University School of Mining Engineering
University School of Nursing
University School of Teacher Training

SPECIAL PROGRAMS:
Cooperative arrangements with eight universities,
including the University of Wisconsin (Madison), the
University of California (Berkeley), the University of
North Carolina and North Carolina State University

LANGUAGE OF INSTRUCTION: Spanish

ADMISSION REQUIREMENTS FOR FOREIGN STUDENTS:
Secondary school certificate (bachiller), or recognized
foreign equivalent, and preuniversity examination
(madurez)

TUITION FOR FOREIGN STUDENTS:
See GENERAL UNIVERSITY INFORMATION.

TOTAL INSTRUCTIONAL FACULTY:
609

LIBRARY COLLECTIONS:
Total collection—200,000 volumes

UNIVERSITY PUBLICATIONS:
Revista

RECTOR: Jose Maria Urena Frances

UNIVERSIDAD PONTIFICIA "COMILLAS"
(Pontifical University Comillas)
Centro Blanco, 28049 Madrid, Spain

CHARACTERISTICS OF INSTITUTION:
Private Catholic university controlled by the Society
of Jesus

DATE FOUNDED: 1892

TOTAL ENROLLMENT: 12,100 fulltime students (including 200 foreign students)

DEGREES AWARDED:
Diplomado in theology, industrial engineering
   three years required
Licenciado
   five years required
Licenciado in medicine

six years required
Doctorado
   an additional two years following Licenciado required
Graduate diploma in business management
   two years required

ACADEMIC PROGRAMS:
Faculty of Canon Law
Faculty of Economics
Faculty of Law
Faculty of Philosophy and Letters
Faculty of Theology
Higher Technical School of Industrial Engineering
University School of Industrial Technical Engineer-
   ing
University School of Social Work
University School of Computer Sciences
University School of Nursing

SPECIAL PROGRAMS:
Institute of Business Administration and Manage-
   ment
Institute of Matrimonial Law
Institute of Modern Languages
Institute of Spiritual Theology

LANGUAGE OF INSTRUCTION: Spanish

ADMISSION REQUIREMENTS FOR FOREIGN STUDENTS:
Secondary school certificate (bachiller), or recognized
foreign equivalent, and preuniversity examination
(madurez)

TUITION FOR FOREIGN STUDENTS:
See GENERAL UNIVERSITY INFORMATION.

TOTAL INSTRUCTIONAL FACULTY:
815

LIBRARY COLLECTIONS:
Total collection—401,350 volumes

UNIVERSITY PUBLICATIONS:
Estudios eclesiásticos, Miscelanea Comillas, Pensamiento

RECTOR: Guillermo Rodriguez-Izquierdo Gavala

UNIVERSIDAD DE CÓRDOBA
(University of Córdoba)
Alfonso XIII, 13, 14071 Córdoba, Spain

CHARACTERISTICS OF INSTITUTION:
State-run, nonprofit university

DATE FOUNDED: 1972

TOTAL ENROLLMENT: 13,000 fulltime students

DEGREES AWARDED:
Licenciado in philosophy and letters, science
   five years required

Licenciado in veterinary medicine
  five years and dissertation required
Professional titles in agriculture and nursing
  five years required
Doctorado in veterinary medicine
  by thesis

ACADEMIC PROGRAMS:
Faculty of Law
Faculty of Medicine
Faculty of Philosophy and Letters
Faculty of Science
Faculty of Veterinary Science
Higher Technical School for Agricultural Engineers
University School of Nursing
University School of Technical Mining Engineering
University Teacher Training School

SPECIAL PROGRAMS:
Institute of Education
Polytechnic University

LANGUAGE OF INSTRUCTION: Spanish

ADMISSION REQUIREMENTS FOR FOREIGN STUDENTS:
Secondary school certificate (bachiller), or recognized foreign equivalent, and preuniversity examination (madurez)

TUITION FOR FOREIGN STUDENTS:
See GENERAL UNIVERSITY INFORMATION.

TOTAL INSTRUCTIONAL FACULTY:
1,000

RECTOR: Prof. Dr. Amador Jover Moyano

UNIVERSIDAD DE DUESTO
(University of Duesto)
Avda de las Universidades s/n, Apdo 1, 48080 Bilbao, Spain

CHARACTERISTICS OF INSTITUTION:
Private Catholic university controlled by the Society of Jesus

DATE FOUNDED: 1886

TOTAL ENROLLMENT: 14,400 fulltime students

DEGREES AWARDED:
Diplomado in tourism and secretarial studies
  three years required
Licenciado
  five years required
Licenciado in theology
  six years required
Professional titles in translation, interpretation, programming and computing
Doctorado

at least one year following Licenciado and thesis required

ACADEMIC PROGRAMS:
Faculty of Economics and Business Studies
Faculty of Economics and Business Studies (San Sebastian)
Faculty of Law
Faculty of Philosophy and Letters
Faculty of Philosophy and Letters (San Sebastian)
Faculty of Philosophy and Education
Faculty of Political Sciences and Sociology
Faculty of Theology
Department of Basque Studies
School of Legal Practice
School of Theology
School of Tourism and Secretarial Studies

SPECIAL PROGRAMS:
Institute of Christian Living and Faith
Institute of Cooperative Studies
Institute of Education
Institute of European Studies
Institute of Languages
International Institute of Business Management
Practice School of the Archeaology of the Basque Country

LANGUAGES OF INSTRUCTION: Spanish and Basque

ADMISSION REQUIREMENTS FOR FOREIGN STUDENTS:
Secondary school certificate (bachiller), or recognized foreign equivalent, and preuniversity examination (madurez)

TUITION FOR FOREIGN STUDENTS:
See GENERAL UNIVERSITY INFORMATION.

TOTAL INSTRUCTIONAL FACULTY:
600

LIBRARY COLLECTIONS:
Central library—125,000 volumes
Basque studies library
European studies library

UNIVERSITY PUBLICATIONS:
Boletin de Estudios Economicos, Estudios de Duesto, Letras de Duesto

CHANCELLOR: R. P. Peter-Hans Kolvenbach

UNIVERSIDAD DE GRANADA
(University of Granada)
Hospital Real, Calle Cuesta del Hospitico s/n, 18701 Granada, Spain

CHARACTERISTICS OF INSTITUTION:
State-run, nonprofit university

DATE FOUNDED: 1526

TOTAL ENROLLMENT: 52,000 fulltime students

DEGREES AWARDED:
Licenciado
  five years required
Licenciado in medicine
  six years required
Doctorado
  an additional two years and thesis required

ACADEMIC PROGRAMS:
Faculty of Fine Arts
Faculty of Law
Faculty of Medicine
Faculty of Pharmacy
Faculty of Philosophy and Letters
Faculty of Science
School of Arabic Studies
Courses in philosophy of law and sacred theology

SPECIAL PROGRAMS:
Anatomy Section of the Federico Oloriz Institute
Experimental Station
Institute of Parasitology

LANGUAGE OF INSTRUCTION: Spanish

ADMISSION REQUIREMENTS FOR FOREIGN STUDENTS:
Secondary school certificate (*bachiller*), or recognized foreign equivalent, and preuniversity examination (*madurez*), or entrance examination for adults

TUITION FOR FOREIGN STUDENTS:
See GENERAL UNIVERSITY INFORMATION.

TOTAL INSTRUCTIONAL FACULTY:
2,500

LIBRARY COLLECTIONS:
University library—78,600 volumes
Faculty libraries—184,000 volumes

UNIVERSITY PUBLICATIONS:
Anales de la catedra Francisco Suarez, Anales del Desarrollo, Ars Pharmaceutica, Miscelanea de Estudios Arabes y Hebraicos

RECTOR: Prof. Pascual Rivas Carrera

UNIVERSIDAD COMPLUTENSE DE MADRID
(University of Madrid at Alcala de Henares)
Ciudad Universitaria, 28040 Madrid, Spain

CHARACTERISTICS OF INSTITUTION:
State-run, nonprofit university

DATE FOUNDED: 1508

TOTAL ENROLLMENT: 105,000 fulltime students

DEGREES AWARDED:
Licenciado
  five–seven years required
Licenciado in medicine
  six years required
Doctorado
  by thesis
Professional title of Ingeniero

ACADEMIC PROGRAMS:
Faculty of Biology
Faculty of Chemistry
Faculty of Economics and Management
Faculty of Fine Arts
Faculty of Geography and History
Faculty of Geology
Faculty of Information Science
Faculty of Law
Faculty of Mathematics
Faculty of Medicine
Faculty of Pharmacy
Faculty of Philology
Faculty of Philosophy and Education
Faculty of Physics
Faculty of Political Science and Sociology
Faculty of Psychology
Faculty of Veterinary Science

LANGUAGE OF INSTRUCTION: Spanish

ADMISSION REQUIREMENTS FOR FOREIGN STUDENTS:
Secondary school certificate (*bachiller*), or recognized foreign equivalent, and preuniversity examination (*madurez*), or entrance examination for adults

TUITION FOR FOREIGN STUDENTS:
See GENERAL UNIVERSITY INFORMATION.

TOTAL INSTRUCTIONAL FACULTY:
4,490

LIBRARY COLLECTIONS:
University library—800,000 volumes

UNIVERSITY PUBLICATIONS:
Boletin Infomativo de la Universidad, Gaceta Complutense, Guia de la Universidad de Madrid, Memoria de la UCM, Revista de la Universidad de Madrid

RECTOR: Prof. Gustavo Villapalos Salas

UNIVERSIDAD DE MÁLAGA
(University of Málaga)
El Ejido s/n, 29071 Málaga, Spain

CHARACTERISTICS OF INSTITUTION:
State-run, nonprofit university

DATE FOUNDED: 1972

TOTAL ENROLLMENT: 23,000 fulltime students

DEGREES AWARDED:
Diplomado
    three years required
Licenciado
    five years required
Doctorado
    two years after Licenciado required
Teaching certificate

ACADEMIC PROGRAMS:
Faculty of Economic and Business Studies
Faculty of Law
Faculty of Medicine
Faculty of Philosophy and Letters
Faculty of Science
University School of Business Studies
University School of Teacher Training

SPECIAL PROGRAMS:
Institute of Education Sciences
University Institute of Applied Economics
University Institute of Mediterranean Ecology
University Institute of Technological Research and
    Control
Polytechnic University

LANGUAGE OF INSTRUCTION: Spanish

ADMISSION REQUIREMENTS FOR FOREIGN STUDENTS:
Secondary school certificate (bachiller), or recognized
foreign equivalent, and preuniversity examination
(madurez)

TUITION FOR FOREIGN STUDENTS:
See GENERAL UNIVERSITY INFORMATION.

TOTAL INSTRUCTIONAL FACULTY:
950

LIBRARY COLLECTIONS:
Central library

UNIVERSITY PUBLICATIONS:
Acta Botanica, Analecta Malacitana, Baetica, Cuadernos
de Ciencias Economicas y Empresariales, Revista de Estudios Regionales

RECTOR: Prof. José M. Martin Delgado

UNIVERSIDAD DE MURCIA
(University of Murcia)
Avda Teniente Flomesta s/n, Edificio
Convalecencia, 30001 Murcia, Spain

CHARACTERISTICS OF INSTITUTION:
State-run, nonprofit university

DATE FOUNDED: 1915

TOTAL ENROLLMENT: 23,000 fulltime students

DEGREES AWARDED:
Diplomado in business administration
    three years required
Licenciado
    five years required
Licenciado in medicine
    six years required
Doctorado
    by thesis

ACADEMIC PROGRAMS:
Faculty of Biology
Faculty of Economics
Faculty of Law
Faculty of Letters
Faculty of Medicine
Faculty of Philosophy
Faculty of Sciences
Faculty of Veterinary Science
University School of Business Studies
University School of Business Studies (Cartagena)
University School of Computer Science
University School of Teacher Training

SPECIAL PROGRAMS:
Polytechnic University

LANGUAGE OF INSTRUCTION: Spanish

ADMISSION REQUIREMENTS FOR FOREIGN STUDENTS:
Secondary school certificate (bachiller), or recognized
foreign equivalent, and preuniversity examination
(madurez)

TUITION FOR FOREIGN STUDENTS:
See GENERAL UNIVERSITY INFORMATION.

TOTAL INSTRUCTIONAL FACULTY:
980

LIBRARY COLLECTIONS:
Main library—80,000 volumes
Faculty libraries—200,000 volumes

UNIVERSITY PUBLICATIONS:
Anales, Boletin Informativo, Monteagudo

RECTOR: Prof. Juan Roca Guillamón

UNIVERSIDAD DE NAVARRA
(University of Navarra)
Ciudad Universitaria, 31080 Pamplona, Spain

CHARACTERISTICS OF INSTITUTION:
Private university

DATE FOUNDED: 1952

TOTAL ENROLLMENT: 15,900 fulltime students (including 600 foreign students)

DEGREES AWARDED:
Bachiller in liberal arts
 four years required
Licenciado in canon law
 two years required
Licenciado in law, philosophy and letters, pharmacy, science
 five years required
Licenciado in medicine
 six years
Professional titles of Enfermera, Ingeniero Téchnico Industrial
 three years required
Professional titles of Ingeniero Superior Industrial, Arquitecto
 six years required
Doctorado in canon law
 by thesis
Doctorado in theology
 an additional year after Licenciado required
Doctorado in business administration
 three additional years after Licenciado required
Doctorado in all other fields
 two additional years after Licenciado required
Diplomas in secretarial sciences and nursing
 three years required
Teaching diploma
 three years required

ACADEMIC PROGRAMS:
Faculty of Arts
Faculty of Canon Law
Faculty of Economics and Business Studies
Faculty of Journalism
Faculty of Law
Faculty of Medicine
Faculty of Pharmacy
Faculty of Sciences
Faculty of Theology
Ecclesiastical Faculty of Philosophy
Higher Technical School of Industrial Engineering
Higher Technical School of Architecture
Graduate School of Business Administration (Barcelona)
School of Nursing
School of Librarianship

SPECIAL PROGRAMS:
Institute of Administration
Institute of Applied Sciences
Institute of Church History
Institute of Education
Institute of Liberal Arts and Sciences
Institute of Modern Languages
Institute of Spanish Language and Culture

Cooperative arrangements with five universities, including Harvard Business School in Massachusetts and Columbia University in New York

LANGUAGE OF INSTRUCTION: Spanish

ADMISSION REQUIREMENTS FOR FOREIGN STUDENTS:
Secondary school certificate (bachiller), or recognized foreign equivalent, and preuniversity examination (madurez)

TUITION FOR FOREIGN STUDENTS:
See GENERAL UNIVERSITY INFORMATION.

TOTAL INSTRUCTIONAL FACULTY:
1,460

LIBRARY COLLECTIONS:
Total collection—471,900 volumes

MUSEUMS AND GALLERIES:
Museum of Zoology

UNIVERSITY PUBLICATIONS:
Anuario de Derecho Internacional, Anuario Filosofico, Excerpta et Dissertationabus in Iure Canonico, Excerpta et Dissertationabus in Sacra Theologica, Ius Canonicum, Nuestro Tiempo, Persona y Derecho, Redacción, Revista de Medicina, Scripta Theologica

CHANCELLOR: Alvaro del Portillo

UNIVERSIDAD DE OVIEDO
(University of Oviedo)
Calle San Francisco 3, 33003 Oviedo, Spain

CHARACTERISTICS OF INSTITUTION:
State-run, nonprofit university

DATE FOUNDED: 1608

TOTAL ENROLLMENT: 29,000 fulltime students

DEGREES AWARDED:
Diplomado in various fields
 three years required
Licenciado
 five years required
Licenciado in medicine
 six years required
Professional titles of Ingeniero Téchnico
 three years required
Professional titles of Ingeniero de Minas, Ingeniero Industrial
 six years required
Doctorado
 an additional two years after Licenciado required

ACADEMIC PROGRAMS:
Faculty of Biology
Faculty of Chemistry
Faculty of Economics and Business Studies

Faculty of Geography and History
Faculty of Geology
Faculty of Law
Faculty of Medicine
Faculty of Philology
Faculty of Philosophy and Education
University School of Business Studies
University School of Business Studies (Gijon)
University School of Computer Science
University School of Computer Science (Gijon)
University School of Industrial Engineering
University School of Mining Engineering
University School of Nursing
University School of Technical Industrial Engineer-
   ing
University School of Stomatology

SPECIAL PROGRAMS:
Cooperative arrangements with five universities

LANGUAGE OF INSTRUCTION: Spanish

ADMISSION REQUIREMENTS FOR FOREIGN STUDENTS:
Secondary school certificate *(bachiller)*, or recognized
foreign equivalent, and preuniversity examination
(madurez)

TUITION FOR FOREIGN STUDENTS:
See GENERAL UNIVERSITY INFORMATION.

TOTAL INSTRUCTIONAL FACULTY:
1,215

LIBRARY COLLECTIONS:
Central library—420,000 volumes
Specialized libraries

UNIVERSITY PUBLICATIONS:
Archivos de la Facultad de Medicina, Asturiensia Medi-
evalia, Brevoria Geologica Asturica, Memorias de Historia
Antigua, Revista de Biologie, Revista de Ciencias, Revista
de Minas, Trabajos de Geologia

RECTOR: Dr. Juan S. Lopez Arranz

UNIVERSIDAD DE SALAMANCA
(University of Salamanca)
Patio de Escuelas 1, Apdo 20, 37008 Salamanca,
Spain

CHARACTERISTICS OF INSTITUTION:
State-run, nonprofit university

DATE FOUNDED: 1218

TOTAL ENROLLMENT: 24,000 fulltime students (including 220 foreign students)

DEGREES AWARDED:
Licenciado
   five years required

Licenciado in medicine
   six years required
Professional titles in various fields
Doctorado
   an additional two years after Licenciado required

ACADEMIC PROGRAMS:
Faculty of Biology
Faculty of Chemistry
Faculty of Fine Arts
Faculty of Geography and History
Faculty of Law
Faculty of Medicine
Faculty of Pharmacy
Faculty of Philology
Faculty of Philosophy and Education
Faculty of Sciences
Teacher Training College
Teacher Training College (Zamora)
Teacher Training College (Avila)
Business Studies School
School of Graduate Social Studies
School of Industrial Engineering (Bejar)
School of Library and Documentation Science
School of Nursing
University School of Social Work

CONSTITUENT COLLEGES:
University College (Avila)
University College (Zamora)

LANGUAGE OF INSTRUCTION: Spanish

ADMISSION REQUIREMENTS FOR FOREIGN STUDENTS:
Secondary school certificate *(bachiller)*, or recognized
foreign equivalent, and preuniversity examination
(madurez)

TUITION FOR FOREIGN STUDENTS:
See GENERAL UNIVERSITY INFORMATION.

TOTAL INSTRUCTIONAL FACULTY:
1,500

LIBRARY COLLECTIONS:
University library—140,300 volumes
Faculty libraries—365,270 volumes

UNIVERSITY PUBLICATIONS:
Colectanea de Jurisprudencia Canonica, Cuadernos Sal-
mantinos de Filosofia, Dialogo Ecumenico, Helmantica,
Hojas Universitarias, Salmanticensis

RECTOR: Julio Fermoso Garcia

UNIVERSIDAD DE SANTIAGO DE COMPOSTELA
(University of Santiago de Compostela)
Plaza del Obradoiro, Palacio de San Geronimo
s/n, Santiago de Compostela, Spain

CHARACTERISTICS OF INSTITUTION:
State-run, nonprofit university

DATE FOUNDED: 1501

TOTAL ENROLLMENT: 53,000 fulltime students (including 2,500 foreign students)

DEGREES AWARDED:
Diplomado in various fields
   three years required
Licenciado
   five years required
Licenciado in medicine
   six years required
Titles of Arquitecto Técnico, Ingeniero Técnico
   six years required
Doctorado
   an additional three–five years required
Teaching qualification
   three years required

ACADEMIC PROGRAMS:
Faculty of Biology
Faculty of Chemistry
Faculty of Economic and Business Science
Faculty of Geography and History
Faculty of Law
Faculty of Mathematics
Faculty of Medicine
Faculty of Pharmacy
Faculty of Philology
Faculty of Philosophy and Education
Faculty of Physics
Faculty of Veterinary Science
Higher Technical School of Architecture
Higher Technical School of Industrial Engineering
Higher Technical School of Telecommunication Engineering

LANGUAGES OF INSTRUCTION: Spanish and Galician

ADMISSION REQUIREMENTS FOR FOREIGN STUDENTS:
Secondary school certificate (bachiller), or recognized foreign equivalent, and preuniversity examination (madurez)

TUITION FOR FOREIGN STUDENTS:
See GENERAL UNIVERSITY INFORMATION.

TOTAL INSTRUCTIONAL FACULTY:
2,400

LIBRARY COLLECTIONS:
General library—1,500,000 volumes
Faculty libraries

MUSEUMS AND GALLERIES:
Museum of Natural History

UNIVERSITY PUBLICATIONS:
Acta Cientifica Compostelana, Anejos de la revista Verba, Anuario Gallego de Filologia, Cursos y Congresos de la Universidad de Santiago de Compostela, Memoria, Monografias, Trabajos Compostelanos de Biologia, Verba

RECTOR: Prof. Carlos Pajares Vales

UNIVERSIDAD DE SEVILLA
(University of Seville)
Calle de San Francisco 4, Seville, Spain

CHARACTERISTICS OF INSTITUTION:
State-run, nonprofit university

DATE FOUNDED: 1502

TOTAL ENROLLMENT: 46,700 fulltime students

DEGREES AWARDED:
Diplomado in business administration
   four years required
Licenciado
   five years required
Licenciado in medicine
   six years required
Professional titles in architecture, industrial engineering and agriculture
   five years required
Doctorado
   by thesis
Postgraduate certificates of specialization in medicine

ACADEMIC PROGRAMS:
Faculty of Biology
Faculty of Chemistry
Faculty of Economics (including business administration)
Faculty of Fine Arts
Faculty of Geography and History
Faculty of Law
Faculty of Mathematics
Faculty of Medicine
Faculty of Pharmacy
Faculty of Philology
Faculty of Philosophy and Education
Faculty of Physics
School of Architecture
School of Engineering

SPECIAL PROGRAMS:
Institute of Education

LANGUAGE OF INSTRUCTION: Spanish

ADMISSION REQUIREMENTS FOR FOREIGN STUDENTS:
Secondary school certificate (bachiller), or recognized foreign equivalent, and preuniversity examination (madurez)

TUITION FOR FOREIGN STUDENTS:
See GENERAL UNIVERSITY INFORMATION.

TOTAL INSTRUCTIONAL FACULTY:
2,300

LIBRARY COLLECTIONS:
University library—101,000 volumes
Law—43,000 volumes
Medicine—2,600 volumes
Philosophy and letters—55,850 volumes
Science—4,300 volumes

UNIVERSITY PUBLICATIONS:
Anales de la Universidad Hispalense

RECTOR: Javier Perez Royo

UNIVERSIDAD DE VALENCIA
(University of Valencia)
Nave 2, 46003 Valencia, Spain

CHARACTERISTICS OF INSTITUTION:
State-run, nonprofit university

DATE FOUNDED: 1500

TOTAL ENROLLMENT: 56,000 fulltime students

DEGREES AWARDED:
Diplomado
   three years required
Licenciado
   five years required
Doctorado
   an additional two years after Licenciado required

ACADEMIC PROGRAMS:
Faculty of Biology
Faculty of Chemistry
Faculty of Economics
Faculty of Geography and History
Faculty of Law
Faculty of Mathematical Sciences
Faculty of Medicine
Faculty of Pharmacy
Faculty of Philology
Faculty of Philosophy and Education
Faculty of Physical Sciences
Faculty of Psychology
Teacher Training College
Teacher Training College (Castellon)
School of Business Studies
School of Nursing
School of Physiotherapy

SPECIAL PROGRAMS:
University College of Sciences

LANGUAGE OF INSTRUCTION: Spanish

ADMISSION REQUIREMENTS FOR FOREIGN STUDENTS:
Secondary school certificate *(bachiller)*, or recognized foreign equivalent, and preuniversity examination *(madurez)*

TUITION FOR FOREIGN STUDENTS:
See GENERAL UNIVERSITY INFORMATION.

TOTAL INSTRUCTIONAL FACULTY:
2,300

LIBRARY COLLECTIONS:
University library—216,200 volumes
Faculty libraries—131,780 volumes

UNIVERSITY PUBLICATIONS:
Anales de la Universidad de Valencia, Anuario de la Facultad de Medicina, Memoria Anual

RECTOR: Prof. Ramon Lapiedra Civera

UNIVERSIDAD DE ZARAGOZA
(University of Zaragoza)
Ciudad Universitaria s/n, 50009 Zaragoza, Spain

CHARACTERISTICS OF INSTITUTION:
State-run, nonprofit university.

DATE FOUNDED: 1583

TOTAL ENROLLMENT: 35,400 fulltime students (including 100 foreign students)

DEGREES AWARDED:
Diplomado
   three years required
Licenciado
   five years required
Licenciado in medicine
   six years required
Doctorado
   an additional two years after Licenciado and thesis required

ACADEMIC PROGRAMS:
Faculty of Economics and Business Studies
Faculty of Law
Faculty of Medicine
Faculty of Philosophy and Letters
Faculty of Science
Faculty of Veterinary Science
Higher School of Industrial Engineering
School of Business Studies
School of Business Studies (Logrono)
School of Business Studies (Pamplona)
School of Industrial Engineering
School of Industrial Engineering (Logrono)
School of Nursing and Physiotherapy
School of Social Studies
Teacher Training College

Teacher Training College (Huesca)
Teacher Training College (Logrono)
Teacher Training College (Pamplona)
Teacher Training College (Teruel)

SPECIAL PROGRAMS:
Institute of Education

CONSTITUENT COLLEGES:
University College (Huesca)
University College (La Rioja)
University College (Teruel)

LANGUAGE OF INSTRUCTION: Spanish

ADMISSION REQUIREMENTS FOR FOREIGN STUDENTS:
Secondary school certificate (bachiller), or recognized foreign equivalent, and preuniversity examination (madurez) or entrance examination for adults

TUITION FOR FOREIGN STUDENTS:
See GENERAL UNIVERSITY INFORMATION.

TOTAL INSTRUCTIONAL FACULTY:
1,690

LIBRARY COLLECTIONS:
University library—600,000 volumes
Faculty libraries

UNIVERSITY PUBLICATIONS:
Archivos de la Facultad de Medicina, Anales de la Facultad de Veterinaria, Boletin Informativo, Guia, Resumenes de Tesis Doctorales, Revista Universidad, Temas

RECTOR: Vicente Camarena Badia

UNIVERSIDAD POLITÉCNICA DE CATALUÑA
(Technical University of Catalonia)
Avda Gregorio Maranon s/n, 08028 Barcelona, Spain

CHARACTERISTICS OF INSTITUTION:
State-run, nonprofit university

DATE FOUNDED: 1971

TOTAL ENROLLMENT: 16,500 fulltime students

DEGREES AWARDED:
Diplomado in Computer Sciences
   three years required
Licenciado in various subjects
   six years required
Professional title of Ingeniero Técnico
   three years required
Professional titles of Ingeniero and Arquitecto
   six years required
Doctorado
   an additional two years after Licenciado and thesis required

ACADEMIC PROGRAMS:
Faculty of Business Administration
Faculty of Computer Science
Faculty of Economics
School of Agricultural Engineering (Lérida)
School of Architecture
School of Architecture (El Valles)
School of Highway Engineering
School of Telecommunication Engineering

SPECIAL PROGRAMS:
Institute of Cybernetics
Institute of Education
Institute of Energetics
Institute of Petrochemistry
Institute of Textile Research
Institute of Transport Research
Center of Agricultural Engineering (Technical)
Center of Agricultural Engineering (Technical) (Lérida)
Center of Architecture (Technical)
Center of Industrial Engineering (Technical)
Center of Industrial Engineering (Technical) (Igualada)
Center of Industrial Engineering (Technical) (Tarragona)
Center of Industrial Engineering (Technical) (Tarrasa)
Center of Industrial Engineering (Technical) (Vilanueva and Geltru)
Center of Knitting and Weaving
Center of Optometry (Tarrasa)
Center of Telecommunication Engineering (Technical) (Vilanueva and Geltru)
Polytechnic Center (Manresa)
Polytechnic Center (Gerona)
Computer Center

LANGUAGES OF INSTRUCTION: Spanish and Catalan

ADMISSION REQUIREMENTS FOR FOREIGN STUDENTS:
Secondary school certificate (bachiller), or recognized foreign equivalent, and preuniversity examination (madurez) or entrance examination for adults

TUITION FOR FOREIGN STUDENTS:
See GENERAL UNIVERSITY INFORMATION.

TOTAL INSTRUCTIONAL FACULTY:
1,620

LIBRARY COLLECTIONS:
Total collection—78,610 volumes

UNIVERSITY PUBLICATIONS:
Cuadernos de Ingenieria, Questio, Revista Technica

RECTOR: Gabriel A. Ferrate Pascual

UNIVERSIDAD POLITÉCNICA DE MADRID
(Technical University of Madrid)
Avda Ramiro de Maeztu s/n, Ciudad Universitaria,
28040 Madrid, Spain

CHARACTERISTICS OF INSTITUTION:
State-run, nonprofit university

DATE FOUNDED: 1971

TOTAL ENROLLMENT: 43,300 fulltime students (including 1,000 foreign students)

DEGREES AWARDED:
Diplomado in computer sciences
   three years required
Licenciado
   six years required
Professional titles of arquitecto técnico, ingeniero técnico
   three years required
Professional titles of arquitecto, ingeniero
   six years required
Doctorado
   an additional two years after Licenciado and thesis required

ACADEMIC PROGRAMS:
Faculty of Computer Science
School of Architecture
School of Aeronautical Engineering
School of Agricultural Engineering
School of Civil Engineering
School of Industrial Engineering
School of Mining
School of Marine Engineering
School of Telecommunications
School of Forestry Engineering

SPECIAL PROGRAMS:
Institute of Aerial Surveying
Institute of Control Systems
Institute of Education
Institute of Environmental Sciences
Institute of New Energy Resources
Institute of Physical Education
Institute of Solar Energy
Institute of Teledetection
Undergraduate Center
Undergraduate Center (architecture)
Center of Aeronautical Engineering (Technical)
Center of Agricultural Engineering (Technical)
Center of Agricultural Engineering (Technical) (Ciudad Real)
Center of Agricultural Engineering (Technical) (Villaba)
Center of Architecture (Technical)
Center of Civil Engineering (Technical)
Center of Computer Sciences (Technical)
Center of Forestry (Technical)
Center of Industrial Engineering (Technical)
Center of Industrial Engineering (Technical) (Almadén)
Center of Industrial Engineering (Technical) (Toledo)
Center of Mining (Technical) (Almadén)
Center of Surveying (Technical)
Center of Telecommunication Engineering (Technical)
Center of Telecommunication Engineering (Technical) (Alcala de Henares)
Cooperative arrangements with over 50 universities in North and South America and Europe

LANGUAGE OF INSTRUCTION: Spanish

ADMISSION REQUIREMENTS FOR FOREIGN STUDENTS:
Secondary school certificate (bachiller), or recognized foreign equivalent, and preuniversity examination (madurez), or entrance examination for adults

TUITION FOR FOREIGN STUDENTS:
See GENERAL UNIVERSITY INFORMATION.

TOTAL INSTRUCTIONAL FACULTY:
2,550

LIBRARY COLLECTIONS:
Total collection—85,000 volumes

MUSEUMS AND GALLERIES:
Museum of Geology

RECTOR: Dr. Rafael Portaencasa Baeza

UNIVERSIDAD INTERNACIONAL MENÉNDEZ PELAYO
(Menéndez Pelayo International University)
Amador de los Ríos 1, Madrid 4, Spain

CHARACTERISTICS OF INSTITUTION:
State-run, nonprofit university

DATE FOUNDED: 1948

TOTAL ENROLLMENT: 6,000 fulltime students

DEGREES AWARDED:
Certificates of aptitude and proficiency in Spanish language and literature and Spanish history
Diploma in Hispanic studies
   three years required
Doctorado
   two years after Licenciado or foreign equivalent required

ACADEMIC PROGRAMS:
Department of Comparative Politics (research)
Department of Development and Social Change (research)
Department of Economics and Energy Resources (research)

Department of European Community Law (research)
Department of Experimental Science (research)
Department of Humanities (research)
Department of Social History (research)
Department of Art and Communication (research)

SPECIAL PROGRAMS:
Center for Foreign Students
Institute of Educational Research
Summer courses
Campuses in Pontevedra, Sitges, La Coruña, Seville, Valencia, Lisbon (Portugal) and Rome (Italy)

LANGUAGE OF INSTRUCTION: Spanish

ADMISSION REQUIREMENTS FOR FOREIGN STUDENTS:
Secondary school certificate (bachiller), or recognized foreign equivalent, and preuniversity examination (madurez)

TUITION FOR FOREIGN STUDENTS:
See GENERAL UNIVERSITY INFORMATION.

TOTAL INSTRUCTIONAL FACULTY:
700

LIBRARY COLLECTIONS:
Total collection—15,200 volumes

RECTOR: Ernest Lluch

SCHILLER INTERNATIONAL UNIVERSITY
Calle de Rodriguez San Pedro 10, 28015 Madrid, Spain

CHARACTERISTICS OF INSTITUTION:
Private, independent university chartered by the State of Delaware, U.S.A.

DATE FOUNDED: 1964

TOTAL ENROLLMENT: 1,500 foreign students from 98 different countries enrolled at the various study centers

DEGREES AWARDED:
Associate of Arts (AA and AAS)
Bachelor of Arts (BA)
Associate of Business Administration (ABA)
Bachelor of Business Administration (BBA)
Bachelor of Public Administration (BPA)
Master of Arts (MA)
Master of Business Administration (MBA)
Master of International Management (MIM)

ACADEMIC PROGRAMS:
Department of Business Administration
Department of Law/Public Administration
Department of Applied Sciences (including premedicine, preengineering and preveterinary sciences)

Department of General Studies (including economics, languages and arts courses)
Department of International Relations and Diplomacy
Department of Hotel Management

SPECIAL PROGRAMS:
Study centers located in:
    England—London and West Wickham
    France—Paris and Strasbourg
    Germany—Heidelberg
    Spain—Madrid
    Switzerland—Engelberg
Hotel management internships

LANGUAGE OF INSTRUCTION: English

ADMISSION REQUIREMENTS FOR FOREIGN STUDENTS:
Any foreign secondary school diploma recognized as equivalent to the high school diploma issued in the State of Delaware, U.S.A.

TUITION FOR FOREIGN STUDENTS:
Undergraduate—$8,700 US
Postgraduate—$9,050 US

TOTAL INSTRUCTIONAL FACULTY:
190 teachers and lecturers

LIBRARY COLLECTIONS:
Total collection—36,000 volumes

UNIVERSITY PUBLICATIONS:
Schiller Newsletter, Hotel Management Newsletter

DIRECTOR: L. Bergunde

ESCUELA SUPERIOR DE ADMINISTRACION Y DIRECCION DE EMPRESAS
(College of Business Administration and Management)
Avda de Pedralbes 60–62, 08034 Barcelona, Spain

CHARACTERISTICS OF INSTITUTION:
Private institution recognized by the Ministry of Education and Science

DATE FOUNDED: 1958

TOTAL ENROLLMENT: 5,300 fulltime students

DEGREES AWARDED:
Diplomas
    one–two years required
Licenciado y Master en Ciencas empresariales (business administration)
    five years required
Master en Direccion y Administracion de Empresas (business administration and management)
    two–three years required
Certificates

ACADEMIC PROGRAMS:
Department of Business Policy
Department of Computer Sciences
Department of Economics
Department of Finance Management
Department of Law
Department of Marketing Management
Department of Personnel Management
Department of Production Management
Department of Quantitative Methods
Department of Social Science

SPECIAL PROGRAMS:
Cooperative arrangements with seven other universities including the Graduate School of Business of the State University of New York, McGill University in Canada, and Brandeis University in Massachusetts

LANGUAGE OF INSTRUCTION: Spanish

ADMISSION REQUIREMENTS FOR FOREIGN STUDENTS:
Secondary school certificate *(bachiller)*, or recognized foreign equivalent, and preuniversity examination *(madurez)*

TUITION FOR FOREIGN STUDENTS:
See GENERAL UNIVERSITY INFORMATION.

TOTAL INSTRUCTIONAL FACULTY:
315

LIBRARY COLLECTIONS:
Total collection—30,000 volumes

UNIVERSITY PUBLICATIONS:
Carta Europea, Coleccion ESADE de Estudios de la Empresa

DIRECTOR: Jaime Filella

THE UNIVERSITIES OF SWEDEN

CHALMERS TEKNISKA HÖGSKOLA
(Chalmers University of Technology)
S-41296 Gothenburg, Sweden

CHARACTERISTICS OF INSTITUTION:
State-run, nonprofit university

DATE FOUNDED: 1829

TOTAL ENROLLMENT: 6,000

DEGREES AWARDED:
Master of Science in various fields
    four and one-half years required
Licenciate
    two years after master's required
Doktor
    six years after Licenciate required

ACADEMIC PROGRAMS:
School of Architecture
School of Chemical Engineering
School of Civil Engineering
School of Electrical Engineering
School of Mathematics
School of Mechanical Engineering
School of Physics

SPECIAL PROGRAMS:
College of Navigation, Marine Engineering and Plant
Operation Observatory

LANGUAGE OF INSTRUCTION: Swedish

ADMISSION REQUIREMENTS FOR FOREIGN STUDENTS:
Secondary school certificate or recognized foreign
equivalent

TUITION FOR FOREIGN STUDENTS:
None. Students must pay a nominal registration fee.

TOTAL INSTRUCTIONAL FACULTY:
500 fulltime faculty (including 110 professors)

LIBRARY COLLECTIONS:
University library—300,000 volumes

UNIVERSITY PUBLICATIONS:
*Forskarutbilding, Laro-och timplaner, Utbildning av Civ-
iling och Arkitekter, Utbilkningsörversike*

RECTOR: Prof. A. Sjoberg

GÖTEBURGS UNIVERISTET
(Göthenburg University)
Vasaparken, S-41124 Göteburg, Sweden

CHARACTERISTICS OF INSTITUTION:
State-run, nonprofit university

DATE FOUNDED: 1891

TOTAL ENROLLMENT: 22,500 fulltime students

DEGREES AWARDED:
Högskoleexamen (professional qualification) in var-
ious fields
    six–eight semesters required
Master's degree in various fields
    three semesters after Högskeleexamen required
Licenciate in philosophy
    two years after master's required
Doktor
    four years after Licenciate required

ACADEMIC PROGRAMS:
Faculty of Arts
Faculty of Dentistry
Faculty of Natural Sciences (including mathematics)
Faculty of Medicine
Faculty of Social Sciences

LANGUAGE OF INSTRUCTION: Swedish

ADMISSION REQUIREMENTS FOR FOREIGN STUDENTS:
Secondary school certificate or recognized foreign
equivalent

TUITION FOR FOREIGN STUDENTS:
None

TOTAL INSTRUCTIONAL FACULTY:
1,800 faculty (including 150 professors)

MUSEUMS AND GALLERIES:
Museum of Biology
Museum of Classical Archaeology

LIBRARY COLLECTIONS:
Central library—2,000,000 volumes
Departmental libraries—450,000 volumes

UNIVERSITY PUBLICATIONS:
*Acta Universitatis Göthoburgensis, Acta Bibliotecae Univ-
ersitatis Göthoburgis, New Literature on Women* and other
departmental publications

RECTOR: Prof. Jan S. Nilsson

KUNGLIGA TEKNISKA HÖGSKOLAN
(The Royal Institute of Technology)
S-10044 Stockholm, Sweden

CHARACTERISTICS OF INSTITUTION:
State-run, nonprofit university

DATE FOUNDED: 1827

TOTAL ENROLLMENT: 9,000

DEGREES AWARDED:
Master of Science in various fields
  four–five years required
Licenciate of technology
  two years after master's required
Doktor of Philosophy
  four years after Licenciate required

ACADEMIC PROGRAMS:
School of Applied Mechanics and Vehicle Technology
School of Architecture
School of Chemical Engineering
School of Civil Engineering
School of Computer Science and Engineering
School of Metallurgy and Materials Technology
School of Mechanical Engineering
School of Physics
School of Surveying

SPECIAL PROGRAMS:
Center for Design and Production Technology
Center for Environmental Sciences
Center for Materials Technology
Computer Center
Institute of Optical Research
Institute of Production Engineering Research
Institute of Technical Audiology

LANGUAGE OF INSTRUCTION: Swedish

ADMISSION REQUIREMENTS FOR FOREIGN STUDENTS:
Secondary school certificate or recognized foreign equivalent

TUITION FOR FOREIGN STUDENTS:
None. Students must pay a nominal registration fee.

TOTAL INSTRUCTIONAL FACULTY:
1,400 fulltime faculty (including 150 professors)

LIBRARY COLLECTIONS:
Institute library—500,000 volumes

UNIVERSITY PUBLICATIONS:
Scientific Reports, Study Handbook

PRESIDENT: Prof. J. Carlsson

LUNDS UNIVERSITET
(Lund University)
POB 117, S-22100 Lund, Sweden

CHARACTERISTICS OF INSTITUTION:
State-run, nonprofit university

DATE FOUNDED: 1666

TOTAL ENROLLMENT: 25,400 students (including 750 foreign students)

DEGREES AWARDED:
Högskoleexamen (professional qualification) in various fields
  six semesters required
Master's degree in various fields
  eight or more semesters required
Doktor
  four years after master's required

ACADEMIC PROGRAMS:
Faculty of Arts
Faculty of Dentistry
Faculty of Law
Faculty of Mathematics and Natural Sciences
Faculty of Medicine
Faculty of Political and Social Sciences
Faculty of Technology
Faculty of Theology

SPECIAL PROGRAMS:
College of Education
College of Music and Theater
Physiotherapy Program
Cooperative arrangements with the University of California and Washington State University

LANGUAGE OF INSTRUCTION: Swedish

ADMISSION REQUIREMENTS FOR FOREIGN STUDENTS:
Secondary school certificate or recognized foreign equivalent

TUITION FOR FOREIGN STUDENTS:
None. Students must pay a nominal registration fee.

TOTAL INSTRUCTIONAL FACULTY:
2,560 (including 250 professors)

MUSEUMS AND GALLERIES:
Museums of Archives, Antiquities, History
Botanical Garden
Lund Art Museum
Zoologiska föreläser (zoological lectures)

LIBRARY COLLECTIONS:
University library—4,000,000 volumes

UNIVERSITY PUBLICATIONS:
LUM, Lunds Universitets Årsskrift, Lunaforskare föreläser, Scripta Academica

RECTOR: Prof. Hakan Westling

STOCKHOLMS UNIVERSITET
(University of Stockholm)
S-10691 Stockholm, Sweden

CHARACTERISTICS OF INSTITUTION:
State-run, nonprofit university

DATE FOUNDED: 1877

TOTAL ENROLLMENT: 27,500 students (including 2,000 foreign students)

DEGREES AWARDED:
Högskoleexamen (professional qualification) in various fields
   six–eight semesters required
Doktor
   four years after Högskoleexamen required

ACADEMIC PROGRAMS:
Faculty of Humanities
Faculty of Law
Faculty of Natural Sciences
Faculty of Social Sciences

SPECIAL PROGRAMS:
Center for Asian Pacific Studies
Center for Baltic Studies
Center for Research on International Migration
Center for Mass Communication Research
Center for the Study of Childhood Culture
Institute for English-speaking Students
Institute for International Economic Studies
Institute of Interpreting and Translation
Institute for Latin American Studies
Institute of Marine Ecology
Swedish Institute for Social Research
Department of International Education

LANGUAGES OF INSTRUCTION: Swedish and English

ADMISSION REQUIREMENTS FOR FOREIGN STUDENTS:
Secondary school certificate or recognized foreign equivalent (All programs and courses have competitive admission.)

TUITION FOR FOREIGN STUDENTS:
None

TOTAL INSTRUCTIONAL FACULTY:
2,200 (including 150 professors)

LIBRARY COLLECTIONS:
Total collection—2,300,000 volumes

MUSEUMS AND GALLERIES:
Botanical garden

UNIVERSITY PUBLICATIONS:
Acta Universitatis Stockholmiensis

PRESIDENT: Prof. I. Jonsson

UMEÅ UNIVERSITET
(Umeå University)
S-90187 Umeå, Sweden

CHARACTERISTICS OF INSTITUTION:
State-run, nonprofit university

DATE FOUNDED: 1965

TOTAL ENROLLMENT: 9,000 students (including 500 foreign students)

DEGREES AWARDED:
Högskoleexamen (professional qualification) in various fields
   six–eleven semesters required
Master's degree (for foreign students)
   one–two years with thesis required
Doktor
   four years after Högskoleexamen required

ACADEMIC PROGRAMS:
Faculty of Arts
Faculty of Dentistry
Faculty of Medicine
Faculty of Mathematics and Natural Sciences
Faculty of Social Sciences

SPECIAL PROGRAMS:
Center for Arctic Cultural Research
Center for Regional Science Research
Computer Center
Kiruna Geophysical Institute
Cooperative arrangements with several universities, including York University in Canada

LANGUAGE OF INSTRUCTION: Swedish

ADMISSION REQUIREMENTS FOR FOREIGN STUDENTS:
Secondary school certificate or recognized foreign equivalent

TUITION FOR FOREIGN STUDENTS:
None. Students must pay a nominal registration fee.

TOTAL INSTRUCTIONAL FACULTY:
1,500 (including 120 professors)

LIBRARY COLLECTIONS:
Total collection—600,000 volumes

UNIVERSITY PUBLICATIONS:
Acta Universitatis Umensis

RECTOR: Prof. Lars Beckman

UPPSALA UNIVERSITET
(Uppsala University)
POB 256, S-75105 Uppsala, Sweden

CHARACTERISTICS OF INSTITUTION:
State-run, nonprofit university

DATE FOUNDED: 1477

TOTAL ENROLLMENT: 20,000 students (including 1,500 foreign students)

DEGREES AWARDED:
Högskoleexamen (professional qualification) in various fields
  six–eleven semesters required
Master's degree 1–2 years with thesis
  three semesters after Högskoleexamen required
Licenciate
  three–four years after master's required
Doktor
  four years after Högskoleexamen required

ACADEMIC PROGRAMS:
Faculty of Arts
Faculty of Law
Faculty of Medicine
Faculty of Pharmacy
Faculty of Sciences
Faculty of Social Sciences
Faculty of Theology

SPECIAL PROGRAMS:
Center for Latin American Studies
Center for Multi-ethnic Research
Center for Research on Women
Institute of African Studies
Institute of Dialect and Folklore Studies

LANGUAGE OF INSTRUCTION: Swedish

ADMISSION REQUIREMENTS FOR FOREIGN STUDENTS:
Secondary school certificate or recognized foreign equivalent

TUITION FOR FOREIGN STUDENTS:
None. Students must pay a nominal registration fee.

TOTAL INSTRUCTIONAL FACULTY:
900 (including 200 professors)

LIBRARY COLLECTIONS:
University library—2,000,000 volumes
Faculty libraries

UNIVERSITY PUBLICATIONS:
Acta Universitatis Upsalienis

CHANCELLOR: G. Brodin

HÖGSKOLAN I VÄXJÖ
(Växjö University)
POB 5035, S-35005 Växjö, Sweden

CHARACTERISTICS OF INSTITUTION:
State-run, nonprofit university

DATE FOUNDED: 1967

TOTAL ENROLLMENT: 3,600 students

DEGREES AWARDED:
Högskoleexamen (professional qualification) in various fields
  three years required

ACADEMIC PROGRAMS:
Department of Art, Physical Education and Music
Department of Chemical Engineering
Department of Civil Engineering
Department of Economics and Law
Department of Educational Methods
Department of Electronic Engineering
Department of Liberal Arts
Department of Mathematics, Statistics and Computer Science
Department of Mechanical Engineering
Department of Natural Science
Department of Social Sciences
Department of Swedish and Social Studies

SPECIAL PROGRAMS:
Center for Labor Market Research
Center for Small Business Development
Center for Transport Economy Research
Unit of Computer Sciences

LANGUAGE OF INSTRUCTION: Swedish (some English)

ADMISSION REQUIREMENTS FOR FOREIGN STUDENTS:
Secondary school certificate or recognized foreign equivalent

TUITION FOR FOREIGN STUDENTS:
None. Students must pay a nominal registration fee.

TOTAL INSTRUCTIONAL FACULTY:
230

LIBRARY COLLECTIONS:
Total collection—90,000 volumes

UNIVERSITY PUBLICATIONS:
Acta Wexionensia, various department publications

RECTOR: Prof. Hans Wieslander

HANDELSHÖGSKOLAN I STOCKHOLM
(Stockholm School of Economics)
POB 6501, S-11383 Stockholm, Sweden

CHARACTERISTICS OF INSTITUTION:
Private university

DATE FOUNDED: 1909

TOTAL ENROLLMENT: 1,300 students

DEGREES AWARDED:
Civilekonom (professional qualification)
  three years required

Ekonomie doktor
four years after Civilekonom required

ACADEMIC PROGRAMS:
Department of Business Administration
Department of Economic Geography
Department of Economics
Department of Languages
Department of Law
Department of Statistics

SPECIAL PROGRAMS:
Center for Marketing Techniques
Economic Research Institute
Institute of International Business
Institute of Management
Institute of Management of Innovation and Technology

LANGUAGE OF INSTRUCTION: Swedish

ADMISSION REQUIREMENTS FOR FOREIGN STUDENTS:
Secondary school certificate or recognized foreign equivalent

TUITION FOR FOREIGN STUDENTS:
None. Students must pay a nominal registration fee.

TOTAL INSTRUCTIONAL FACULTY:
100 (including 20 professors)

LIBRARY COLLECTIONS:
Total collection—180,000 volumes

UNIVERSITY PUBLICATIONS:
Ekonomisk dokumentation

RECTOR: Prof. S. Burenstam Linder

KAROLINSKA INSTITUTET
(Karolinska Institute)
Solnavagen 1, POB 60400, S-10401 Stockholm, Sweden

CHARACTERISTICS OF INSTITUTION:
State-run, nonprofit university

DATE FOUNDED: 1810

TOTAL ENROLLMENT: 2,700 students

DEGREES AWARDED:
Högskoleexamen (professional qualification) in dentistry
nine semesters and one year internship required
Högskoleexamen (professional qualification) in medicine
11 semesters and one year internship required
Doktor
four years after Högskoleexamen required

ACADEMIC PROGRAMS:
Faculty of Dentistry
Faculty of Medicine

LANGUAGE OF INSTRUCTION: Swedish

ADMISSION REQUIREMENTS FOR FOREIGN STUDENTS:
Secondary school certificate or recognized foreign equivalent

TUITION FOR FOREIGN STUDENTS:
None. Students must pay a nominal registration fee.

TOTAL INSTRUCTIONAL FACULTY:
600 (including 170 professors)

LIBRARY COLLECTIONS:
Total collection—250,000 volumes

MUSEUMS AND GALLERIES:
Museum of Medical History

UNIVERSITY PUBLICATIONS:
Forskarutbildningskatalog, Karolinska institutets katalog över lärere och administration, Meddelanden fran Centrala Förvaltningen, Undervisingskatalog

RECTOR: B. I. Samuelsson

THE UNIVERSITIES OF SWITZERLAND

UNIVERSITÄT BASEL
(University of Basel)
Petersplatz 1, 4003 Basel, Switzerland

CHARACTERISTICS OF INSTITUTION:
State-run, nonprofit university

DATE FOUNDED: 1460

TOTAL ENROLLMENT: 6,600 students (including 900 foreign students)

DEGREES AWARDED:
Lizentiat in various fields
   four–five years required
Diploma in various fields
Doktor in various fields
   five–six years (medicine six–seven years) required

ACADEMIC PROGRAMS:
Faculty of Jurisprudence
Faculty of Medicine
Faculty of Philosophy and History
Faculty of Science
Faculty of Theology

SPECIAL PROGRAMS:
Institute of Gerontology
Institute of Physical Education
Institute of Remedial Education and Psychology
Institute of Tropical Medicine
Computer Center

LANGUAGE OF INSTRUCTION: German

ADMISSION REQUIREMENTS FOR FOREIGN STUDENTS:
Secondary school certificate (Maturitatszeugnis) or recognized foreign equivalent

TUITION FOR FOREIGN STUDENTS:
SFr 500–600 per semester

TOTAL INSTRUCTIONAL FACULTY:
700

LIBRARY COLLECTIONS:
Central library—2,500,000 volumes

MUSEUMS AND GALLERIES:
Museums of Anatomy, Ethnology, History, Natural Science, Paleontology, Pharmacy

UNIVERSITY PUBLICATIONS:
Akademische Vortrage, Basler Veitrage zur Ethnologie und Geographie, Basler Studien zur Rechtswissenschaft, Basler Universitatsreden, Schriftenreihen des Instituts fur Inter-nationales Recht, Sozialwissenschaften, Theologische Zeit-schrift

RECTOR: Prof. Dr. K. Pestalozzi

UNIVERSITÄT BERN
(University of Bern)
Hochschulstrasse 4, 3012 Bern, Switzerland

CHARACTERISTICS OF INSTITUTION:
State-run, nonprofit university

DATE FOUNDED: 1528

TOTAL ENROLLMENT: 8,400

DEGREES AWARDED:
Lizentiat in various fields
   four–five years required
State examination in various fields
Doktor in various fields
   five–six years (medicine six–seven years) required

ACADEMIC PROGRAMS:
Faculty of Evangelical Theology
Faculty of Jurisprudence and Economics
Faculty of Medicine
Faculty of Old Catholic Theology
Faculty of Philosophy and History
Faculty of Science
Faculty of Veterinary Science

SPECIAL PROGRAMS:
Institute of Physical Education and Sport
Institute of Medical Research
Language school

LANGUAGE OF INSTRUCTION: German

ADMISSION REQUIREMENTS FOR FOREIGN STUDENTS:
Secondary school certificate (Maturitatszeugnis) or recognized foreign equivalent

TUITION FOR FOREIGN STUDENTS:
SFr 500–600 per semester

TOTAL INSTRUCTIONAL FACULTY:
1,000 (including 450 professors)

LIBRARY COLLECTIONS:
University library

UNIVERSITY PUBLICATIONS:
Vorlesungsverzeichnis

RECTOR: Prof. Pio Caroni

UNIVERSITÉ DE FRIBOURG
(University of Fribourg)
Misericorde, 1700 Fribourg, Switzerland

CHARACTERISTICS OF INSTITUTION:
State-run, nonprofit, Catholic university

DATE FOUNDED: 1889

TOTAL ENROLLMENT: 5,400 students (including 1,350 foreign students)

DEGREES AWARDED:
Licence in various fields
  eight–ten semesters required
Diplome in various fields
  six–eight semesters required
Doctorate in various fields
  10–12 semesters required

ACADEMIC PROGRAMS:
Faculty of Economics and Social Sciences
Faculty of Law
Faculty of Letters
Faculty of Sciences
Faculty of Theology

SPECIAL PROGRAMS:
Institute of Automations and Operations Research
Institute of East European Studies
Institute of Ecclesiastical Law
Institute of Economic and Social Sciences
Institute of Ecumenical Studies
Institute of Federalism
Institute of Journalism and Social Communications
Institute of Medieval Studies
Institute for Missions
Institute of Moral Theology
Institute of Pedagogy
Institute of Physical Education and Sport
Institute of Practical English
Institute of Practical French
Institute of Practical German
Institute of Psychology
Institute of Therapeutic Pedagogy
International Institute of Social and Political Philosophy
Cooperative arrangements with Catholic universities in Europe and the United States

LANGUAGES OF INSTRUCTION: French and German

ADMISSION REQUIREMENTS FOR FOREIGN STUDENTS:
Secondary school certificate (*Baccalauréat*) or recognized foreign equivalent

TUITION FOR FOREIGN STUDENTS:
SFr 420 per semester

TOTAL INSTRUCTIONAL FACULTY:
730 (including 130 professors)

LIBRARY COLLECTIONS:
University library—1,500,000 volumes

MUSEUMS AND GALLERIES:
Museums of Art and History, Natural History

RECTOR: Prof. Augustin Macheret

UNIVERSITÉ DE GENEVE
(University of Geneva)
3 Place de l'Université, 1211 Geneva 4, Switzerland

CHARACTERISTICS OF INSTITUTION:
State-run, nonprofit university

DATE FOUNDED: 1559

TOTAL ENROLLMENT: 11,500 students (including 2,200 foreign students)

DEGREES AWARDED:
Licence in various fields
  six–eight semesters required
Diplôme fédéral in various fields
  eight semesters required
Doctorate in various fields
  10–12 semesters (medicine 12–14 semesters required)
Certificates and state qualifications in various fields

ACADEMIC PROGRAMS:
Faculty of Economics and Social Sciences
Faculty of Law
Faculty of Letters
Faculty of Medicine
Faculty of Protestant Theology
Faculty of Psychology and Educational Sciences
Faculty of Sciences
School of Architecture
School of French Language and Culture
School of Physical Education and Sport
School of Translation and Interpretation

SPECIAL PROGRAMS:
Graduate Institutes:
Institute of Development Studies
Institute of Ecumenical Studies
Institute of European Studies
Institute of International Management
Institute of International Studies

LANGUAGE OF INSTRUCTION: French

ADMISSION REQUIREMENTS FOR FOREIGN STUDENTS:
Secondary school certificate (*Baccalauréat*) or recognized foreign equivalent

TUITION FOR FOREIGN STUDENTS:
SFr 500–600 per semester

TOTAL INSTRUCTIONAL FACULTY:
2,450 (including 650 professors)

LIBRARY COLLECTIONS:
University library—1,660,000 volumes
Faculty libraries—940,000 volumes

UNIVERSITY PUBLICATIONS:
Catalogue des programmes de recherche, Catalogue des publications de l'Université, Dies Académicus, Guide de l'Étudiant, Programme annuel des cours, Reglements et Plans d'Études des diverses Facultés

RECTOR: Prof. Jean-Claude Favez

UNIVERSITÉ DE LAUSANNE
(University of Lausanne)
Batiment du Rectorat et de l'Administration Centrale, 1015 Lausanne, Switzerland

CHARACTERISTICS OF INSTITUTION:
State-run, nonprofit university

DATE FOUNDED: 1537

TOTAL ENROLLMENT: 6,700 students (including 1,600 foreign students)

DEGREES AWARDED:
Licence in various fields
    five–eight semesters required
Diplôme in various fields
    eight semesters required
Medical doctor for foreign students
    12 semesters required
Doctorate in various fields
Certificates in various fields

ACADEMIC PROGRAMS:
Faculty of Law
Faculty of Letters
Faculty of Medicine
Faculty of Science
Faculty of Social and Political Sciences
Faculty of Theology
Institute of Forensic Science
Business School
School of Modern French
School of Pharmacy

SPECIAL PROGRAMS:
Cooperative arrangements with universities in Europe and Africa

LANGUAGE OF INSTRUCTION: French

ADMISSION REQUIREMENTS FOR FOREIGN STUDENTS:
Secondary school certificate *(Baccalauréat)* or recognized foreign equivalent

TUITION FOR FOREIGN STUDENTS:
SFr 450–650 per semester

TOTAL INSTRUCTIONAL FACULTY:
710 (including 200 professors)

LIBRARY COLLECTIONS:
Total collection—2,100,000 volumes

MUSEUMS AND GALLERIES:
Museums of the Institutes

UNIVERSITY PUBLICATIONS:
Annuaire Académique, Cours général public, Dies academicus, Guide de l'Étudiant, Programme des cours, Uni Lausanne

RECTOR: Prof. Pierre Ducrey

UNIVERSITÉ DE NEUCHÂTEL
(University of Neuchâtel)
Avenue du Ier-Mars 26, 2000 Neuchâtel, Switzerland

CHARACTERISTICS OF INSTITUTION:
State-run, nonprofit university

DATE FOUNDED: 1909

TOTAL ENROLLMENT: 2,400 students (including 300 foreign students)

DEGREES AWARDED:
Licence in various fields
    six–ten semesters required
Diplôme in various fields
    four–ten semesters required
Medical doctor for foreign students
    12 semesters required
Doctorate in various fields
    two–three years after Diplôme or Licence
Certificates in various fields

ACADEMIC PROGRAMS:
Faculty of Jurisprudence and Economics
Faculty of Letters
Faculty of Science
Faculty of Theology

SPECIAL PROGRAMS:
Center for Applied Linguistics
Center for Franco-Swiss Studies
Center for Semiological Research
Institute of Botany
Institute of Chemistry
Institute of Ethnology
Institute of Geography
Institute of Geology
Institute of History
Institute of Linguistics
Institute of Mathematics

Institute of Microtechnology
Institute of Physics
Institute of Social and Political Sciences
Institute of Zoology
Computer Center
Seminar of Modern French for foreign students
Cooperative arrangements with several universities
   in Europe

LANGUAGE OF INSTRUCTION: French

ADMISSION REQUIREMENTS FOR FOREIGN STUDENTS:
Secondary school certificate *(Baccalauréat)* or recognized foreign equivalent

TUITION FOR FOREIGN STUDENTS:
SFr 1,100 per semester

TOTAL INSTRUCTIONAL FACULTY:
270

LIBRARY COLLECTIONS:
Central library
Faculty libraries
Institute libraries

MUSEUMS AND GALLERIES:
Museums of Archaeology, Art and History, Ethnology, Natural History

UNIVERSITY PUBLICATIONS:
*Annuales, Domaines et sujets de recherches, Informations,
Recueil de Travaux des Instituts*

RECTOR: Prof. Remy Scheurer

UNIVERSITÄT ZÜRICH
(University of Zürich)
Ramistrasse 71, 8006 Zurich, Switzerland

CHARACTERISTICS OF INSTITUTION:
State-run, nonprofit university

DATE FOUNDED: 1523 (given university status in 1833)

TOTAL ENROLLMENT: 19,300 students (including 2,000
foreign students)

DEGREES AWARDED:
Lizentiat in various fields
   eight semesters required
Diploma in various fields
   seven years required
Doktor in various fields
   10–12 semesters after Lizentiat required
Doktor in medicine

ACADEMIC PROGRAMS:
Faculty of Law and Politics
Faculty of Medicine
Faculty of Philosophy I (Letters)
Faculty of Philosophy II (Sciences)

Faculty of Theology
Faculty of Veterinary Medicine

LANGUAGE OF INSTRUCTION: German

ADMISSION REQUIREMENTS FOR FOREIGN STUDENTS:
Secondary school certificate *(Maturitatszeugnis)* or
recognized foreign equivalent

TUITION FOR FOREIGN STUDENTS:
SFr 450–650 per semester

TOTAL INSTRUCTIONAL FACULTY:
1,670 (including 225 professors)

LIBRARY COLLECTIONS:
Total collection—1,400,000 volumes

MUSEUMS AND GALLERIES:
Museums of Anthropology, Archaeology, Ethnol-
ogy, Medicine, Paleontology
Botanical garden

RECTOR: Prof. Hans Heinrich Schmid

ÉCOLE POLYTECHNIQUE FÉDÉRALE DE LAUSANNE
(Federal Institute of Technology at Lausanne)
Centre-Est, Ecublens, 1015 Lausanne, Switzerland

CHARACTERISTICS OF INSTITUTION:
State-run, nonprofit university

DATE FOUNDED: 1969

TOTAL ENROLLMENT: 3,300 students (including 1,100
foreign students)

DEGREES AWARDED:
Diplôme in various fields
   four years required
Docteur en Sciences and Docteur en Sciences et
Techniques
   three–five years after Diplôme required

ACADEMIC PROGRAMS:
Department of Architecture
Department of Agricultural Engineering and Survey-
ing
Department of Chemistry
Department of Civil Engineering
Department of Electrical Engineering
Department of Mathematics
Department of Materials
Department of Mechanical Engineering
Department of Physics

SPECIAL PROGRAMS:
Affiliated Institutes:
   Federal Forest Research Institute
   Federal Institute for Testing Material and Research
   Federal Institute for Reactor Research

Federal Institute for Water Supply, Sewage Purification and Water Pollution Control
Swiss Institute for Nuclear Research
Interdisciplinary Department of Special Mathematics
Interdepartmental Institute of Metallurgy and Electron Microscopy
Interdepartmental Institute of Microelectronics
Institute of Pedagogy and Didactics
Institute of Plasma Physics Research
Computer Center
Language Laboratory
Cooperative arrangements with nine other universities, including the Carnegie-Mellon Institute of Technology in Pennsylvania

LANGUAGE OF INSTRUCTION: French

ADMISSION REQUIREMENTS FOR FOREIGN STUDENTS:
Secondary school certificate (*Baccalauréat*) or recognized foreign equivalent

TUITION FOR FOREIGN STUDENTS:
SFr 580 per semester

TOTAL INSTRUCTIONAL FACULTY:
1,000 (including 153 professors)

LIBRARY COLLECTIONS:
Main library—264,000 volumes
Department libraries

UNIVERSITY PUBLICATIONS:
Études et Professions, Polyrama, Rapport d'Activité, Rapport scientifique

RECTOR: Prof. Bernard Vittoz

SCHILLER INTERNATIONAL UNIVERSITY
Hôtel Europe, POB 272, 6390 Engelberg, Switzerland

CHARACTERISTICS OF INSTITUTION:
Private, independent university chartered by the State of Delaware, U.S.A.

DATE FOUNDED: 1964

TOTAL ENROLLMENT: 1,500 foreign students from 98 different countries enrolled at the various study centers

DEGREES AWARDED:
Associate of Arts (AA and AAS)
Bachelor of Arts (BA)
Associate of Business Administration (ABA)
Bachelor of Business Administration (BBA)
Bachelor of Public Administration (BPA)
Master of Arts (MA)
Master of Business Administration (MBA)
Master of International Management (MIM)

ACADEMIC PROGRAMS:
Department of Business Administration
Department of Law/Public Administration
Department of Applied Sciences (including premedicine, preengineering and preveterinary Sciences)
Department of General Studies (including economics, languages and arts courses)
Department of International Relations and Diplomacy
Department of Hotel Management

SPECIAL PROGRAMS:
Study centers located in:
England—London and West Wickham
France—Paris and Strasbourg
Germany—Heidelberg
Spain—Madrid
Switzerland—Engelberg
Hotel Management Internships

LANGUAGE OF INSTRUCTION: English

ADMISSION REQUIREMENTS FOR FOREIGN STUDENTS:
Any foreign secondary school diploma recognized as equivalent to the high school diploma issued in the State of Delaware, U.S.A.

TUITION FOR FOREIGN STUDENTS:
Undergraduate—$8,700 US in 1990
Postgraduate—$9,050 US in 1990

TOTAL INSTRUCTIONAL FACULTY:
190 teachers and lecturers

LIBRARY COLLECTION:
Total collection—36,000 volumes

UNIVERSITY PUBLICATIONS:
Schiller Newsletter, Hotel Management Newsletter

DIRECTOR: H. Virtanen

EIDGENOSSISCHE TECHNISCHE HOCHSCHULE ZURICH
(Swiss Federal Institute of Technology at Zurich) Ramistrasse 101, ETH-Zentrum, 8092 Zurich, Switzerland

CHARACTERISTICS OF INSTITUTION:
State-run, nonprofit university

DATE FOUNDED: 1855

TOTAL ENROLLMENT: 11,000 students (including 1,300 foreign students)

DEGREES AWARDED:
Diploma in various fields
four years required
Doctorate in various fields
by thesis

ACADEMIC PROGRAMS:
Department of Architecture
Department of Agriculture
Department of Chemistry
Department of Civil Engineering
Department of Computer Science
Department of Electrical Engineering
Department of Forestry
Department of Liberal Studies
Department of Mathematics and Physics
Department of Materials Science
Department of Mechanical Engineering
Department of Military Science
Department of Natural Sciences
Department of Pharmacy
Department of Rural Engineering and Surveying

SPECIAL PROGRAMS:
Affiliated Institutes:
Federal Forest Research Institute
Federal Institute for Testing Material and Research
Federal Institute for Reactor Research
Federal Institute for Water Supply, Sewage Purification and Water Pollution Control
Swiss Institute for Nuclear Research

LANGUAGES OF INSTRUCTION: German and French

ADMISSION REQUIREMENTS FOR FOREIGN STUDENTS:
Secondary school certificate (*Maturitatszeugnis*) or recognized foreign equivalent

TUITION FOR FOREIGN STUDENTS:
SFr 500 per semester

TOTAL INSTRUCTIONAL FACULTY:
275

LIBRARY COLLECTIONS:
Central library—3,100,000 volumes
Department libraries

UNIVERSITY PUBLICATIONS:
ETHZ Annual Report, ETHZ Bulletin, Semesterprogramm

PRESIDENT: Prof. Jakob Nüesch

HOCHSCULE ST. GALLEN FÜR WIRTSCHAFTS- UND SOZIALWISSENSCHAFTEN
(St. Gallen Graduate School of Economics, Law, Business and Public Administration)
Dufourstrasse 50, 9000 St. Gallen, Switzerland

CHARACTERISTICS OF INSTITUTION:
State-run, nonprofit university

DATE FOUNDED: 1899

TOTAL ENROLLMENT: 3,200 students

DEGREES AWARDED:
Lizentiat in various fields
   eight semesters required
Doctorate in various fields
   by thesis, 10 semesters after Lizentiat required

ACADEMIC PROGRAMS:
Department of Business Administration
Department of Cultural Sciences
Department of Economics
Department of Jurisprudence
Department of Technology and Natural Sciences

SPECIAL PROGRAMS:
Institute of Agricultural Policy and Law
Institute of Banking
Institute of Business Administration
Institute of Economics Research
Institute of European and International Economic and Social Law
Institute of Insurance Economics
Institute of Latin American Research and Development Cooperation
Institute of Operations Research
Institute of Public Finance and Fiscal Law
Institute of Teaching of Economics
Institute for Tourism and Transport Economy
Research Institute for Marketing and Distribution
Swiss Institute of Courses in Public Administration
Swiss Institute for International Economics, Regional Science and Market Research
Swiss Research Institute for Small Business

LANGUAGE OF INSTRUCTION: German

ADMISSION REQUIREMENTS FOR FOREIGN STUDENTS:
Secondary school certificate (*Maturitatszeugnis*), or recognized foreign equivalent, and entrance examination

TUITION FOR FOREIGN STUDENTS:
SFr 400 per semester

TOTAL INSTRUCTIONAL FACULTY:
275

LIBRARY COLLECTIONS:
Central library—74,000 volumes
Institute libraries

UNIVERSITY PUBLICATIONS:
Aulavortrage, Bibliotheksfuhrer, Prüfungsvorschriften, Rektoratsbericht, St. Gallen Hochschulnachrichten, Studentenfuhrer, Studienplane, Vorlesungsverzeichnis

RECTOR: Prof. Dr. R. Dubs

INSTITUT POUR L'ENSEIGNEMENT DES MÉTHODES DE DIRECTION DE L'ENTREPRISE
(International Management Development Institute)

23 Chemin de Bellerive, POB 915, 1001 Lausanne, Switzerland

CHARACTERISTICS OF INSTITUTION:
Independent management development institute

DATE FOUNDED: 1957

TOTAL ENROLLMENT: 2,500 fulltime students (95% foreign)

DEGREES AWARDED:
Master of Business Administration
    one to two years required

ACADEMIC PROGRAMS:
Business Administration
Functional Management
General Management
Specialized Management

SPECIAL PROGRAMS:
Ten-week and shortterm courses in management

LANGUAGE OF INSTRUCTION: English

ADMISSION REQUIREMENTS FOR FOREIGN STUDENTS:
Minimum of two years work experience; satisfactory score on the Graduate Management Admissions Test (GMAT); two references from academics or employers; proven record of academic and/or occupational performance

TUITION FOR FOREIGN STUDENTS:
SFr 34,000 per year

TOTAL INSTRUCTIONAL FACULTY:
40 fulltime faculty
15 parttime faculty

LIBRARY COLLECTIONS:
Total collection—10,000 volumes
Current Periodicals—610
1,550 case studies written by faculty

UNIVERSITY PUBLICATIONS:
Perspectives for Managers series

DIRECTOR: Dr. J. Rada

**JUNG-INSTITUT ZURICH
(Jung Institute of Zurich)
Hornweg 28, CH-8700 Küsnacht, Switzerland**

CHARACTERISTICS OF INSTITUTION:
Private

DATE FOUNDED: 1957

TOTAL ENROLLMENT: 380

DEGREES AWARDED:
Diploma

ACADEMIC PROGRAMS:
Analytical Psychology

SPECIAL PROGRAMS:
Clinical Training Program
Counseling Center
Courses in Child Psychotherapy
International Picture Archive and Library
Professional Training Program

LANGUAGES OF INSTRUCTION: German and English

ADMISSION REQUIREMENTS FOR FOREIGN STUDENTS:
Verification of studies in psychology (degree, professional experience, etc.)

TUITION FOR FOREIGN STUDENTS:
Not available

TOTAL INSTRUCTIONAL FACULTY:
30

LIBRARY COLLECTIONS:
Not available

UNIVERSITY PUBLICATIONS:
Studies from the C. G. Jung Institute

PRESIDENT: Dr. H. Barz

THE UNIVERSITIES OF THE UNITED KINGDOM OF GREAT BRITAIN AND
NORTHERN IRELAND

GENERAL UNIVERSITY INFORMATION

The majority of the universities of the United Kingdom are independent institutions funded by the state. The universities of England, Wales and Northern Ireland share similar rules and regulations regarding admission and degree requirements and other organizational stipulations. The universities of Scotland, however, have their own degree and admissions requirements.

This chapter will provide separate general information for the respective university systems. The information pertaining to foreign students is relevant to all the universities mentioned in this chapter with the exception of private institutions.

ADMISSION REQUIREMENTS FOR FOREIGN STUDENTS

Foreign students applying for admission to a university of the United Kingdom must hold either a British Advanced Level General Certificate of Education (GCE), a Scottish Certificate of Education (SCE) or a recognized foreign equivalent. The GCE and SCE are attained following the passing of examinations called A-Levels in England, Wales and Northern Ireland or Higher Examinations in Scotland. The equivalency of foreign qualifications depends upon the admission requirements of the individual institutions. The following qualifications are generally accepted as equivalent to the GCE and SCE:

- Baccalaureat Européen, issued by a secondary school in Europe
- international baccalaureate, issued by the Office du Baccalauréat International in Geneva, Switzerland
- a secondary school certificate issued by the competent authorities in a European Community member state, provided that the foreign student has documented proof that this prior education entitles one to university admission in the home country and that the student is proficient in English
- a GCE or SCE obtained at a recognized secondary school abroad
- a high school diploma from the United States or Canada
- a secondary school certificate, issued by any foreign secondary school, that has been approved as equivalent to the British qualifications by the university to which the student applies

Foreign students wishing to acquire information regarding their foreign qualifications may contact the National Academic Recognition Information Center (NARIC) (British Council, 10 Spring Gardens, London SW1A 2BN England).

Foreign students possessing the required qualifications for admission to a university-level academic program are by no means guaranteed acceptance. Admissions are very competitive, and foreign students are advised to apply to a number of British institutions.

The admission requirements for foreign students may vary widely from one university to another and also among academic programs. Foreign students applying to a specific academic program are usually required to fulfill certain course requirements, which may vary from one program to another. Course requirements are set by the individual universities and are designed to affirm adequate preparation or aptitude on the part of the applicant. The purpose of this is to insure that those applicants who gain admission to an academic program will be able to cope with the academic rigor of the course work.

Foreign students should contact the prospective British universities for specific admission requirements for the desired academic programs.

Admission requirements also vary for foreign students seeking temporary student status. Foreign students who have already earned an undergraduate degree are often permitted to complete an academic program in two rather than three years in England, Wales or Northern Ireland or in three rather than four years in Scotland.

A foreign student may also be admitted to a British university for one or two years while enrolled in a degree program at his or her original university. Junior Year Abroad programs are available at many British universities for U.S. and Canadian university students, though the number of temporary students accepted by British universities is limited due to enrollment capacity. All British universities who offer temporary student status grant Certificates of Satisfactory Attendance as proof of the acceptable completion of the program of studies.

Admission requirements for foreign students applying for postgraduate studies are subject to the individual policies of the respective universities. However, all institutions require an undergraduate degree of high standard before consideration for postgraduate admission. The undergraduate degree acquired by the foreign applicant need not necessarily be in the same discipline as the postgraduate degree course to which he or she applies, though certain postgraduate courses presuppose extensive prior knowledge of the subject. Foreign postgraduate applicants must also be proficient in the English language as most postgraduate programs require a dissertation. Furthermore, a foreign student must be recommended strongly by his or her previous university's academic faculty as a capable candidate for postgraduate work in the particular academic program. Admissions to postgraduate courses in Britain are highly competitive.

All foreign applicants must be proficient in English, the language of instruction at all universities of the United Kingdom. Some universities require a language proficiency examination for foreign students whose secondary school education was not conducted in English. Foreign applicants uncertain of their proficiency should take an English language course in their home countries or inquire at the prospective British university about available preparatory courses. Many such courses are available to foreign students, ranging from comprehensive year-long courses to week-long refresher courses. Foreign students do not need a notification of admission to a British university in order to enroll in a language course.

APPLICATION PROCEDURE FOR FOREIGN STUDENTS

Foreign students applying to a British university can either correspond with the prospective universities' admission departments directly or write to the Universities Central Council on Admissions (UCCA) for the state-run applications procedure.

Foreign students who prefer to deal directly with the prospective university should direct requests for applications and other necessary information to the admission department. Since regulations vary, foreign students should contact prospective universities as early as possible.

Information on the state-run application procedure for British universities is obtained through the UCCA. The UCCA does not make decisions on foreign student applications but instead serves as a clearing house that forwards university applications to the competent authorities at the respective universities. Foreign students should contact UCCA first, requesting the UCCA handbook and an application form. When the application form has been completed and all necessary qualifications and information have been assembled, the forms should be returned to UCCA for processing.

Temporary student applications should be directed to the universities themselves and not through UCCA. They should include all the relevant qualifications and the desired academic program and its duration. Other requirements may be stipulated by the individual universities or departments within the institutions.

Postgraduate application requirements for foreign students are subject to the regulations of the individual departments of the universities. Foreign applicants should apply directly to the department and address their applications to the chairperson.

APPLICATION DEADLINES

Foreign students who apply through the UCCA for undergraduate programs at either Oxford University or the University of Cambridge must return their completed applications to UCCA by an arranged date in October of the year prior to the commencement of the prospective program. The suggested application dates for schools other than Oxford or Cambridge will be in December. Foreign students may continue to submit university applications until September of the following year, although UCCA suggests that foreign applicants fulfill all application requirements as early as possible.

Foreign students who apply directly to the universities as undergraduate, postgraduate or temporary student applicants do not have application deadlines. However, because of limited enrollment as well as competitive admissions policies, foreign applicants are strongly advised to apply as early as possible in advance of the prospective academic year.

ACADEMIC PROGRAMS AND DEGREE REQUIREMENTS

The undergraduate degrees offered by universities of the United Kingdom are based on an academic program of specified duration concluded by final examinations. The undergraduate course work includes lectures, seminars, laboratory practicals, tutorials and, in some cases, a dissertation.

Undergraduate degrees in England, Wales and Northern Ireland are generally three or four years in duration, excluding Medicine, dentistry and veterinary medicine degrees, which require five to six years of course work preceding final examinations. The following undergraduate degrees are offered by most universities in England, Wales and Northern Ireland:

• Bachelor of Arts (BA)—awarded after three or four years of course work concluded by final examinations in one of the arts disciplines, or two or three other disciplines
• Bachelor of Science (BSc)—awarded after three or four years of course work concluded by final examinations in one of the science disciplines, or two or three other disciplines

There are also a variety of undergraduate degrees that grant the holder the right to practice professionally the subject for which they have been trained at a university. Some of these undergraduate degrees include:

- Bachelor of Medicine (MB)
- Bachelor of Surgery (ChB)
- Bachelor of Education (BEd)
- Bachelor of Laws (LLB)

The undergraduate degrees offered at Scottish universities are different from the degrees at other British universities. Scottish undergraduate programs are either three or four years in duration and are concluded by final examinations, just as in the rest of the United Kingdom. However, Scottish undergraduate degrees fall into two categories of degrees: Acceptable completion of a four-year program results in a degree "with Honours"; acceptable completion of a three-year program results in an "Ordinary" degree. These degrees include:

- Master of Arts with Honours (MA.hon); Bachelor of Science with Honours (BSc.hon)—awarded after a four-year course in which the degree discipline is studied throughout the program of studies. The final two years of the course, the honours program, specializes in one, or a combination of two or three, of the various arts or science disciplines (depending on the program). The final examinations test the student's knowledge of the honours subject(s).
- Ordinary Master of Arts (MA.ord); Ordinary Bachelor of Science (BSc.ord)—awarded after three-year program spanning a broad base of subjects. The course examinations are taken at the end of every year.

The universities of the United Kingdom offer a wide variety of arts, science and professional degrees. All degrees are concluded by an examination period, whether the program stipulates course examinations or final examinations. However, examinations are not necessarily held every year or upon completion of a course.

As indicated earlier, undergraduate students may engage in a program specializing in one discipline or divided between two and sometimes three disciplines. With such programs, the degrees conferred are:

- dual-discipline degrees—joint degrees that specify major/minor subjects
- three-discipline degrees—degrees that specify all subject areas, as Management/Economics/Politics (MEP) or Politics/Philosophy/Economics (PPE)

Temporary students are not eligible for undergraduate degrees unless they transfer to a degree program. Temporary students are awarded a Certificate of Attendance upon acceptable completion of the program of studies in which they are enrolled.

Postgraduate degrees offered are divided into two main types: postgraduate research degrees and postgraduate examination degrees. In addition, postgraduate certificates are available for vocational training and postgraduate diplomas for professional qualifications.

Postgraduate master's degrees are different from the Scottish undergraduate master's degree with honors. The postgraduate master's research degree usually requires two years of course work and the submission of an original thesis. The postgraduate master's examination degree usually requires one year of course work culminating in degree examinations at the end of that year. Numerous postgraduate courses are available in the United Kingdom for master's degrees ranging across a multitude of subjects in both arts and science disciplines. The standard postgraduate master's degrees are:

- Master of Arts (MA)
- Master of Science (MSc)
- Master of Philosophy (MPhil)

Postgraduate research degrees usually result in a Doctor of Philosophy (PhD) degree. The PhD requires the submission of an original doctoral thesis following three years of independent scholarly research. A research doctoral thesis is more demanding than the thesis required for a master's degree and is expected to contribute to the academic knowledge of that particular subject.

ACCREDITATION

The universities of the United Kingdom are not accredited by any national agency. They are endorsed by the institutions themselves. In certain circumstances, university degrees in law, medicine, education, veterinary medicine and pharmacy may count towards the licensing of a professional practice.

REGISTRATION REQUIREMENTS

Foreign students are notified of admission in the spring prior to the Academic year. Admission may be provisional if the foreign applicant's final qualifications were incomplete at the time the formal application was submitted. In such cases, foreign students should contact the universities' admissions departments to finalize their qualifications as soon as possible.

The state-run university application clearing house, UCCA, holds a second applications procedure in

August and September prior to the commencement of the academic year for all foreign students who were not admitted to any universities or who submitted their formal applications too late to be included in the first round clearing. Foreign students are often offered late admission because of vacancies left by British students admitted to several universities.

Specific registration requirements will be sent to the prospective foreign student along with the notification of admission.

VISA REQUIREMENTS AND RESIDENCE REGULATIONS

Foreign students who are European Community member state nationals may enter and remain in the United Kingdom for six months before registering with the Home Office for a residence permit. Residence permits for citizens of the European Community are issued for 12-month periods. To obtain a residence permit, the student must present either the Home Office or British Immigration with the following:

- proof of financial solvency for tuition fees and living expenses for the duration of the academic program at a British university

Foreign students who are not European Community member state nationals must provide the same information upon arrival in the United Kingdom in order to gain entrance to the country as a foreign student.

TUITION FEES

Foreign students who are European Community member state nationals or who have held legal residence in a country of the European Community for at least three years prior to commencing studies at a British university pay the same tuition fees as British nationals:

- undergraduate tuition fee: about £600 per year in 1990
- postgraduate tuition fee: about £1,850 per year in 1990

Foreign students who are not citizens or residents of the European Community must pay the full overseas student tuition fee. In 1990, this fee varied from one university to another and, in some institutions, from one program to another. Generally, overseas student tuition fees ranged as follows:

- Undergraduate: Arts—£4,600–5,000 per year
Science—£6,000–6,500 per year
Medicine—£8,000–11,200 per year
- Postgraduate: Arts—£5,000–6,000 per year
Science—£5,000–6,000 per year
Lab-based Science—£6,500–11,500 per year

EXPENSES

Living expenses for a foreign student at a British university will vary according to location. Universities in London are reputed to be the most expensive.

For 1990, the estimate based on the requirements of financial solvency set by British immigration or the Home Office is £5,000 for 12 months. Undergraduates who stay in the United Kingdom for nine months should expect living expenses totaling between £4,000 and £4,500. This estimate covers housing, food, clothing and laundry, health care, books and supplies, transportation, entertainment and other miscellaneous expenses. Examination fees, college fees (these types of fees include room and board, health services, heating, lighting, etc.), CNAA registration fees and other charges may be included in miscellaneous expenses at certain British universities. Nevertheless, foreign students are advised to request details regarding the cost of living from the university in question before traveling to the United Kingdom.

FOREIGN STUDENT SCHOLARSHIPS

Several scholarships from the British Government, the British Council and many international organizations are available to foreign students. Foreign students who are interested in scholarships or in financial assistance while enrolled at a British university are advised to contact the British embassy, consulate, high commission or council in their home countries for information.

Foreign students who are European Community member state nationals or who have held legal residence in a country of the European Community for at least three years prior to commencing studies at a British university may be eligible for scholarships and/or financial assistance from local authorities in the United Kingdom. These students should contact the prospective university for information on local authority awards.

UNIVERSITY CALENDAR

The academic year in the United Kingdom extends from early October until the following September. Most British universities operate on a three-term calendar:

- fall term: October to December
- winter term: January to March
- spring term: April to June

Undergraduates and postgraduates have long holidays at Christmas and Easter, but only undergraduates have a summer holiday. Terms will vary from one academic program to another.

FOREIGN STUDENTS IN THE UNITED KINGDOM

Foreign student enrollment is an essential part of the universities of the United Kingdom. In 1986, there were roughly 50,000 overseas students enrolled in British Universities—about 12% of total student enrollment. The total estimate for the number of overseas students studying in the United Kingdom in 1990 was almost 60,000.

Only a small percentage of foreign students enrolled in British universities come from the European Community (about 13%). Perhaps because of shared language and heritage, many North Americans come to the United Kingdom for their university educations. A great many come as part of the Junior Year Abroad programs that exist between numerous universities on both sides of the Atlantic. A large percentage of foreign student enrollment comes from British Commonwealth nations.

Exceptional educational facilities are available in the United Kingdom, and these institutions represent the most diverse international gathering for the purposes of university education in Europe and, quite probably, the world. Though some British universities attract more foreign students than others, each university has an international student population.

THE UNIVERSITIES OF ENGLAND

UNIVERSITY OF ASTON
Aston Triangle, Birmingham, B4 7ET, England

CHARACTERISTICS OF INSTITUTION:
Independent, state-funded university

DATE FOUNDED: 1895

TOTAL ENROLLMENT: 3,600 fulltime students (175 foreign students in 1988)

DEGREES AWARDED:
Bachelor of Engineering (BEng)
Bachelor of Science (BSc) in various fields
Master of Business Administration (MBA)
Master of Engineering (MEng)
Master of Philosophy (MPhil)
Master of Science (MSc) in various fields
Doctor of Philosophy (PhD)

ACADEMIC PROGRAMS:
Faculty of Engineering
Faculty of Management and Modern Languages
Faculty of Science

SPECIAL PROGRAMS:
Affiliated Institutes:
    Aston Science Park
    West Midlands Technology Transfer Center

Cooperative arrangements with universities in several countries

LANGUAGE OF INSTRUCTION: English

ADMISSION REQUIREMENTS FOR FOREIGN STUDENTS:
Secondary school certificate (GCE, SCE, Baccalauréat Européen, international baccalaureate, U.S. or Canadian high school diploma or recognized foreign equivalent)

TUITION FOR FOREIGN STUDENTS:
See GENERAL UNIVERSITY INFORMATION.

TOTAL INSTRUCTIONAL FACULTY:
275

LIBRARY COLLECTIONS:
Total collection—225,000 volumes
Current periodicals—1,500
Bound periodicals—100,000

UNIVERSITY PUBLICATIONS:
Guide for Overseas Students, Annual Report and Accounts

CHANCELLOR: Sir Adrian Cadbury

UNIVERSITY OF BATH
Claverton Down, Bath, BA2 7AY, England

CHARACTERISTICS OF INSTITUTION:
Independent, state-funded university

DATE FOUNDED: 1894

TOTAL ENROLLMENT: 3,740 fulltime students (410 foreign students in 1988)

DEGREES AWARDED:
Bachelor of Architecture (BArch)
Bachelor of Arts (BA) in various fields
Bachelor of Engineering (BEng)
Bachelor of Pharmacy (BPharm)
Bachelor of Science (BSc) in various fields
Master of Arts (MA)
Master of Education (MEd)
Master of Engineering (MEng)
Master of Philosophy (MPhil)
Master of Science (MSc) in various fields
Doctor of Letters (DLitt)
Doctor of Philosophy (PhD)
Doctor of Science (DSc)

ACADEMIC PROGRAMS:
School of Architecture and Building Engineering (including aeronautical engineering)
School of Biological Science
School of Chemistry
School of Chemical Engineering
School of Education

School of Electrical Engineering
School of Mechanical Engineering
School of Management
School of Materials Science
School of Mathematical Sciences
School of Mechanical Engineering
School of Modern Languages and International Studies
School of Pharmacy and Pharmacology
School of Physics
School of Social Sciences

SPECIAL PROGRAMS:
Bath Institute of Medical Engineering
Bath University of Computing Services
Centre for the Analysis of Social Policy
Centre for Bibliographic Management
Centre for Continuing Education
Centre for Criminal Justice Societies
Centre for Development Studies
Centre for Economic Psychology
Centre for European Industrial Studies
Centre for Executive Development
Centre for Fiscal Studies
Centre for the History of Technology, Science and Society
Centre for Medical Studies
Centre for Science Studies
Centre for the Study of Organizational Change and Development
Cooperative arrangements with universities in several countries

LANGUAGE OF INSTRUCTION:　English

ADMISSION REQUIREMENTS FOR FOREIGN STUDENTS:
Secondary school certificate (GCE, SCE, Baccalauréat Européen, international baccalaureate, U.S. or Canadian high school diploma or recognized foreign equivalent)

TUITION FOR FOREIGN STUDENTS:
See GENERAL UNIVERSITY INFORMATION.

TOTAL INSTRUCTIONAL FACULTY:
375

LIBRARY COLLECTIONS:
Total collection—200,000 volumes
Current periodicals—3,000

UNIVERSITY PUBLICATIONS:
Annual Report, publications of the various programs within the university

CHANCELLOR:　Lord Kearton of Whitchurch

UNIVERSITY OF BIRMINGHAM
P.O. Box 363, Birmingham, England

CHARACTERISTICS OF INSTITUTION:
Independent, state-funded university

DATE FOUNDED:　1900

TOTAL ENROLLMENT:　9,050 fulltime students (1,300 foreign students in 1988)

DEGREES AWARDED:
Bachelor of Arts (BA) in various fields
Bachelor of Commerce (BComm)
Bachelor of Education (BEd)
Bachelor of Engineering (BEng)
Bachelor of Law (LLB)
Bachelor of Music (BMus)
Bachelor of Science (BSc) in various fields
Bachelor of Social Science (BSocSc)
Master of Arts (MA)
Master of Dental Science (MDentSc)
Master of Education (MEd)
Master of Engineering (MEng)
Master of International Studies (MIS)
Master of Jurisprudence (MJur)
Master of Letters (MLitt)
Master of Medical Science (MMedSc)
Master of Philosophy (MPhil)
Master of Science (MSc) in various fields
Master of Social Science (MSocSc)
Doctor of Divinity (DD)
Doctor of Letters (DLitt)
Doctor of Music (DMus)
Doctor of Philosophy (PhD)
Doctor of Science (DSc)
Doctor of Social Science (DSocSc)

ACADEMIC PROGRAMS:
Faculty of Arts
Faculty of Commerce and Social Science
Faculty of Education and Continuing Studies
Faculty of Engineering
Faculty of Law
Faculty of Medicine and Dentistry
Faculty of Science

SPECIAL PROGRAMS:
Automotive Engineering Centre
Barber Institute of Fine Arts
Cancer Clinical Trials Unit
Cancer Epidemiology Research Unit
Centre for Byzantine, Ottoman and Modern Greek Studies
Centre for Child Studies
Centre for Computer Studies
Centre for Russian and East European Studies
Centre for Urban and Regional Studies
Centre for West African Studies
Dental School
Drama and Theatre Arts

Educational Services Unit (medicine)
Examinations and Assessment Research Unit
Health Services Management Centre
Health Services Research Centre
Institute for Advanced Research in the Humanities
Institute of Child Health
Institute of Judicial Administration
Institute of Local Government Studies
Institute of Occupational Health
Institute for Research and Development
Ironbridge Institute
Research Centre for the Education of the Visually Handicapped
Shakespeare Institute
Cooperation arrangements with universities in several countries

LANGUAGE OF INSTRUCTION: English

ADMISSION REQUIREMENTS FOR FOREIGN STUDENTS:
Secondary school certificate (GCE, SCE, Baccalauréat Européen, international baccalaureate, U.S. or Canadian high school diploma or recognized foreign equivalent)

TUITION FOR FOREIGN STUDENTS:
See GENERAL UNIVERSITY INFORMATION.

TOTAL INSTRUCTIONAL FACULTY:
1,600

LIBRARY COLLECTIONS:
Total collection—1,500,000 volumes
Current periodicals—5,000

MUSEUMS AND GALLERIES:
Museums of Anatomy, Dentistry, Geology, Pathology, Physiology, Zoology
Herbarium

UNIVERSITY PUBLICATIONS:
University of Birmingham Gazette, Report of Residences and Publications, publications of the various programs within the university

CHANCELLOR: Sir Alex Jarratt

UNIVERSITY OF BRISTOL
Senate House, Bristol, BS8 1TH, England

CHARACTERISTICS OF INSTITUTION:
Independent, state-funded university

DATE FOUNDED: 1876 as University College, Bristol; 1909 as University of Bristol

TOTAL ENROLLMENT: 8,000 fulltime students (including 600 foreign students)

DEGREES AWARDED:
Bachelor of Arts (BA) in various fields

Bachelor of Education (BEd)
Bachelor of Engineering (BEng)
Bachelor of Law (LLB)
Bachelor of Science (BSc) in various fields
Master of Arts (MA)
Master of Education (MEd)
Master of Engineering (MEng)
Master of Law (LLM)
Master of Letters (MLitt)
Master of Music (MMus)
Master of Philosophy (MPhil)
Master of Political Science (MPS)
Master of Science (MSc) in various fields
Master of Social Science (MSocSc)
Master of Dental Surgery (MDS)
Medical Doctor (MD)
Doctor of Letters (DLitt)
Doctor of Music (DMus)
Doctor of Philosophy (PhD)
Doctor of Science (DSc)

ACADEMIC PROGRAMS:
Faculty of Arts
Faculty of Engineering
Faculty of Law
Faculty of Medicine and Dentistry
Faculty of Science
Faculty of Social Sciences

SPECIAL PROGRAMS:
AFRC Institute of Food Research
Baptist College
Bath Centre for Criminal Justice Studies
Bath College of Higher Education
Bristol Polytechnic Faculty of Education
Centre for Mediterranean Studies
College of St. Paul and St. Mary
Long Ashton Research Station
Westminster College
Cooperative arrangements with universities in several countries

LANGUAGE OF INSTRUCTION: English

ADMISSION REQUIREMENTS FOR FOREIGN STUDENTS:
Secondary school certificate (GCE, SCE, Baccalauréat Européen, international baccalaureate, U.S. or Canadian high school diploma or recognized foreign equivalent)

TUITION FOR FOREIGN STUDENTS:
See GENERAL UNIVERSITY INFORMATION.

TOTAL INSTRUCTIONAL FACULTY:
900 (including 130 professors)

LIBRARY COLLECTIONS:
Total collection—1,000,000 volumes
Current periodicals—4,700

UNIVERSITY PUBLICATIONS:
Accommodations Newsletter, publications of the various programs within the university

CHANCELLOR: Sir Jeremy Morse

UNIVERSITY OF BUCKINGHAM
Buckingham, MK18 1EG, England

CHARACTERISTICS OF INSTITUTION:
Independent, state-funded university

DATE FOUNDED: 1973

TOTAL ENROLLMENT: 800 fulltime students (including 450 foreign students)

DEGREES AWARDED:
Bachelor of Arts (BA) in various fields
Bachelor of Law (LLB)
Bachelor of Science (BSc) in various fields
Bachelor of Economic Science (BSc [Econ])
Master of Arts (MA)
Master of Law (LLM)
Master of Philosophy (MPhil)
Master of Science (MSc) in various fields
Doctor of Law (LLD)
Doctor of Philosophy (PhD)
Doctor of Science (DSc)

ACADEMIC PROGRAMS:
School of Accounting, Business and Economics
School of Humanities
School of Law
School of Sciences

SPECIAL PROGRAMS:
Cooperative arrangements with universities in several countries

LANGUAGE OF INSTRUCTION: English

ADMISSION REQUIREMENTS FOR FOREIGN STUDENTS:
Secondary school certificate (GCE, SCE, Baccalauréat Européen, international baccalaureate, U.S. or Canadian high school diploma or recognized foreign equivalent)

TUITION FOR FOREIGN STUDENTS:
See GENERAL UNIVERSITY INFORMATION.

TOTAL INSTRUCTIONAL FACULTY:
85

LIBRARY COLLECTIONS:
Total collection—70,000 volumes
Current periodicals—500

UNIVERSITY PUBLICATIONS:
The Independent, Newsletter, Annual Report

CHANCELLOR: Lord Hailsham of St. Marylebone

UNIVERSITY OF CAMBRIDGE
The Old School, Trinity Lane, Cambridge, CB2 1TN, England

CHARACTERISTICS OF INSTITUTION:
Independent, state-funded university

DATE FOUNDED: 13th century

TOTAL ENROLLMENT: 13,000 fulltime students (including 1,800 foreign students)

DEGREES AWARDED:
Bachelor of Arts (BA) in various fields
Bachelor of Education (BEd)
Bachelor of Medicine (MB)
Bachelor of Science (BSc) in various fields
Bachelor of Veterinary Medicine (VetMB)
Master of Arts (MA)
Master of Law (LLM)
Master of Letters (M Litt)
Master of Music (MMus)
Master of Philosophy (MPhil)
Master of Science (MSc) in various fields
Doctor of Divinity (DD)
Doctor of Law (LLD)
Doctor of Letters (DLitt)
Medical Doctor (MD)
Doctor of Music (DMus)
Doctor of Philosophy (PhD)
Doctor of Science (DSc)

ACADEMIC PROGRAMS:
Department of Chemical Engineering
Department of Clinical Veterinary Medicine
Department of History and Philosophy of Science
Department of Land Economy
Faculty of Archaeology and Anthropology
Faculty of Architecture and History of Art
Faculty of Classics
Faculty of Biology (a)
Faculty of Biology (b)
Faculty of Clinical Medicine
Faculty of Divinity
Faculty of Earth Sciences and Geography
Faculty of Economics and Politics
Faculty of Education
Faculty of Engineering
Faculty of English
Faculty of History
Faculty of Law
Faculty of Modern and Medieval Languages
Faculty of Mathematics
Faculty of Music
Faculty of Oriental Studies
Faculty of Philosophy
Faculty of Physics and Chemistry

SPECIAL PROGRAMS:
Audio-Visual Aids Unit
Centre for African Studies
Centre for Biomedical Services
Centre of English as an International Language
Centre of International Studies
Centre of Latin American Studies
Centre for Medical Genetics
Centre of Middle Eastern Studies
Centre of South Asian Studies
Committee for Aerial Photography
Committee for Biotechnology
Superconductivity Research Centre
Wolfson Cambridge Industrial Unit
Cooperative arrangements with universities in several countries

CONSTITUENT COLLEGES:
Christ's College
Churchill College
Clare College
Clare Hall
Corpus Christi College
Darwin College
Downing College
Emmanuel College
Fitzwilliam College
Girton College
Gonville and Cauis College
Homerton College
Hughes Hall
Jesus College
King's College
Lucy Cavendish College
Magdalene College
New Hall
Newnham College
Pembroke College
Peterhouse
Queen's College
Robinson College
St. Catherine's College
St. Edmund's College
St. John's College
Selwyn College
Sidney Sussex College
Trinity College
Trinity Hall
Wolfson College

LANGUAGE OF INSTRUCTION: English

ADMISSION REQUIREMENTS FOR FOREIGN STUDENTS:
Secondary school certificate (GCE, SCE, Baccalauréat Européen, international baccalaureate, U.S. or Canadian high school diploma or recognized foreign equivalent)

TUITION FOR FOREIGN STUDENTS:
See GENERAL UNIVERSITY INFORMATION.

TOTAL INSTRUCTIONAL FACULTY:
1,500

LIBRARY COLLECTIONS:
Total collection—5,000,000 volumes
University library—4,200,000 volumes
Departmental libraries—800,000 combined

MUSEUMS AND GALLERIES:
Fitzwilliam Museum
Kettle's Yard
Museums of Archaeology and Anthropology, Classical Archaeology, Zoology
Sedgwick Museum of Geology
Whipple Museum of the History of Science

UNIVERSITY PUBLICATIONS:
Cambridge University Reporter, Statutes and Ordinances of the University, Varsity Handbook, Varsity publications of the various programs within the university

CHANCELLOR: HRH The Prince Philip, Duke of Edinburgh

CITY UNIVERSITY
Northampton Square, London, EC1V 0HB, England

CHARACTERISTICS OF INSTITUTION:
Independent, state-funded university

DATE FOUNDED: 1896

TOTAL ENROLLMENT: 4,300 fulltime students (including 700 foreign students)

DEGREES AWARDED:
Bachelor of Engineering (BEng)
Bachelor of Science (BSc) in various fields
Master of Arts (MA)
Master of Business Administration (MBA)
Master of Philosophy (MPhil)
Master of Science (MSc) in various fields
Doctor of Philosophy (PhD)
Doctor of Science (DSc)

ACADEMIC PROGRAMS
Business School
School of Engineering
School of Mathematics
Department of Arts Policy and Management
Department of Business Systems Analysis
Department of Chemistry
Department of Clinical Communication Studies
Department of Computer Science
Department of Information Science
Department of Journalism
Department of Law

Department of Music
Department of Optometry and Visual Science
Department of Social Science and Humanities
Department of Systems Science

SPECIAL PROGRAMS:
Centre of Continuing Education
Centre of Property Valuation and Management
Social Statistics Research Unit
Cooperative arrangements with universities in several countries

LANGUAGE OF INSTRUCTION: English

ADMISSION REQUIREMENTS FOR FOREIGN STUDENTS:
Secondary school certificate (GCE, SCE, Baccalauréat Européen, international baccalaureate, U.S. or Canadian high school diploma or recognized foreign equivalent)

TUITION FOR FOREIGN STUDENTS:
See GENERAL UNIVERSITY INFORMATION.

TOTAL INSTRUCTIONAL FACULTY:
300

LIBRARY COLLECTIONS:
Total collection—250,000 volumes
Current periodicals—1,800

UNIVERSITY PUBLICATIONS:
Annual Report, Newsletter, publications of the various programs within the university

CHANCELLOR: The Lord Mayor of London

UNIVERSITY OF DURHAM
Old Shire Hall, Durham, DH1 3HP, England

CHARACTERISTICS OF INSTITUTION:
Independent, state-funded university

DATE FOUNDED: 1832

TOTAL ENROLLMENT: 5,100 fulltime students (including 330 foreign students)

DEGREES AWARDED:
Bachelor of Arts (BA)
Bachelor of Science (BSc) in various fields
Master of Arts (MA)
Master of Business Administration (MBA)
Master of Education (MEd)
Master of Letters (MLitt)
Master of Music (MMus)
Master of Philosophy (MPhil)
Master of Science (MSc) in various fields
Master of Theology (MTheol)
Doctor of Letters (DLitt)
Doctor of Music (DMus)

Doctor of Philosophy (PhD)
Doctor of Science (DSc)

ACADEMIC PROGRAMS:
Faculty of Arts
Faculty of Science
Faculty of Social Sciences

SPECIAL PROGRAMS:
Centre for Middle Eastern Studies
Centre for Overseas Research and Development
Durham Mountjoy Centre
Institute of European Studies Programme
School of Education
University Business School
University of Durham Industrial Research Laboratories
Cooperative arrangements with universities in several countries

CONSTITUENT COLLEGES:
College of St. Hilde and St. Bede
Collingwood College
Grey College
Hatfield College
St. Aidan's College
St. Chad's College
St. Cuthbert's College
St. John's College
St. Mary's College
The Graduate Society
Trevelyan College
University College
Van Mildert College

LANGUAGE OF INSTRUCTION: English

ADMISSION REQUIREMENTS FOR FOREIGN STUDENTS:
Secondary school certificate (GCE, SCE, Baccalauréat Européen, international baccalaureate, U.S. or Canadian high school diploma or recognized foreign equivalent)

TUITION FOR FOREIGN STUDENTS:
See GENERAL UNIVERSITY INFORMATION.

TOTAL INSTRUCTIONAL FACULTY:
430 (including 60 professors)

LIBRARY COLLECTIONS:
Total collection—700,000 volumes
Current periodicals—4,800

MUSEUMS AND GALLERIES:
Botanical Gardens
Museum of Archaeology
Oriental Museum

UNIVERSITY PUBLICATIONS:
Durham University Journal, Durham University gazette, Palatinate, Password, publications of the various programs within the university

UNIVERSITY OF EAST ANGLIA
Norwich, Norfolk, NR4 7TJ, England

CHARACTERISTICS OF INSTITUTION:
Independent, state-funded university

DATE FOUNDED: 1964

TOTAL ENROLLMENT: 5,000 fulltime students (including 600 foreign students)

DEGREES AWARDED:
Bachelor of Arts (BA)
Bachelor of Education (BEd)
Bachelor of Engineering (BEng)
Bachelor of Law (LLB)
Bachelor of Science (BSc) in various fields
Master of Arts (MA)
Master of Education (MEd)
Master of Law (LLM)
Master of Music (MMus)
Master of Philosophy (MPhil)
Master of Social Work (MSW)
Master of Science (MSc) in various fields
Doctor of Letters (DLitt)
Doctor of Philosophy (PhD)
Doctor of Science (DSc)

ACADEMIC PROGRAMS:
School of Art History and Music
School of Biological Sciences
School of Chemical Sciences
School of Development Studies
School of Economic and Social Science
School of Education
School of English and American Studies
School of Environmental Sciences
School of Informational Systems
School of Law
School of Mathematics and Science
School of Modern Languages and European History

SPECIAL PROGRAMS
British Sugar Corporation Research Laboratories
Cambridge Institute of Education
Explosives Research and Development Establishment
Fisheries Laboratory
Institute of Food Research Norwich Laboratories
John Innes Institute
Norfolk and Norwich Institute for Medical Education

Royal Armament Research and Development Establishment
Cooperative arrangements with universities in several countries

LANGUAGE OF INSTRUCTION: English

ADMISSION REQUIREMENTS FOR FOREIGN STUDENTS:
Secondary school certificate (GCE, SCE, Baccalauréat Européen, international baccalaureate, U.S. or Canadian high school diploma or recognized foreign equivalent)

TUITION FOR FOREIGN STUDENTS:
See GENERAL UNIVERSITY INFORMATION.

TOTAL INSTRUCTIONAL FACULTY:
400

LIBRARY COLLECTIONS:
Total collection—600,000 volumes
Current periodicals—2,500

MUSEUMS AND GALLERIES:
Sainsbury Centre for Visual Arts

UNIVERSITY PUBLICATIONS:
University of East Anglia Prospectus, Overseas Student's Guide, Newsletter, Student's Union Handbook, Insight, Ziggurat, publications of the various programs within the university

CHANCELLOR: Rev. Prof. W. O. Chadwick

UNIVERSITY OF ESSEX
Wivenhoe Park, Colchester, CO4 3SQ, England

CHARACTERISTICS OF INSTITUTION:
Independent, state-funded university

DATE FOUNDED: 1961

TOTAL ENROLLMENT: 3,200 fulltime students (including 800 foreign students)

DEGREES AWARDED:
Bachelor of Arts (BA)
Bachelor of Engineering (BEng)
Bachelor of Law (LLB)
Bachelor of Science (BSc) in various fields
Master of Arts (MA)
Master of Law (LLM)
Master of Philosophy (MPhil)
Master of Science (MSc) in various fields
Doctor of Law (LLD)
Doctor of Letters (DLitt)
Doctor of Philosophy (PhD)
Doctor of Science (DSc)

ACADEMIC PROGRAMS:
School of Comparative Studies
School of Law

School of Mathematical and Computer Sciences
School of Social Sciences

SPECIAL PROGRAMS:
Educational Technology Unit
Economic and Social Science Research Council (E.S.R.C.) Data Archive
Cooperative arrangements with universities in several countries

LANGUAGE OF INSTRUCTION: English

ADMISSION REQUIREMENTS FOR FOREIGN STUDENTS:
Secondary school certificate (GCE, SCE, Baccalauréat Européen, international baccalaureate, U.S. or Canadian high school diploma or recognized foreign equivalent)

TUITION FOR FOREIGN STUDENTS:
See GENERAL UNIVERSITY INFORMATION.

TOTAL INSTRUCTIONAL FACULTY:
270

LIBRARY COLLECTIONS:
Total collection—425,000 volumes
Current periodicals—2,500

UNIVERSITY PUBLICATIONS:
Sport's Handbook, Wivenhoe, publications of the various programs within the university

CHANCELLOR: The Rt. Hon. Sir Patrick Nairne

UNIVERSITY OF HULL
Cottingham Road, Hull, HU6 7RX, England

CHARACTERISTICS OF INSTITUTION:
Independent, state-funded university

DATE FOUNDED: 1927 as the University College of Hull; 1954 as the University of Hull

TOTAL ENROLLMENT: 5,300 fulltime students (including 650 foreign students)

DEGREES AWARDED:
Bachelor of Arts (BA)
Bachelor of Engineering (BEng)
Bachelor of Law (LLB)
Bachelor of Music (BMus)
Bachelor of Science (BSc) in various fields
Bachelor of Theology (BTheol)
Master of Arts (MA)
Master of Education (MEd)
Master of Engineering (MEng)
Master of Law (LLM)
Master of Music (MMus)
Master of Philosophy (MPhil)
Master of Science (MSc) in various fields
Doctor of Divinity (DD)

Doctor of Law (LLD)
Doctor of Letters (DLitt)
Doctor of Philosophy (PhD)
Doctor of Science (DSc)
Doctor of Economic Science (DSc [Econ])

ACADEMIC PROGRAMS:
Department of Accounting
Department of American Studies
Department of Applied Biology
Department of Chemistry
Department of Classics
Department of Computer Science
Department of Drama
Department of Economic and Social History
Department of Economics and Commerce
Department of Educational Studies
Department of Electronic Engineering
Department of Engineering and Design
Department of English Language and Literature
Department of European Studies
Department of French
Department of Geography
Department of Geology
Department of German
Department of Hispanic Studies
Department of History
Department of Italian
Department of Law
Department of Linguistics
Department of Management Systems and Science
Department of Mathematics—Applied
Department of Mathematics—Pure
Department of Music
Department of Philosophy
Department of Physics
Department of Physics—Applied
Department of Politics
Department of Psychology
Department of Russian Studies
Department of Scandinavian Studies
Department of Social Policy and Professional Studies
Department of Sociology and Social Anthropology
Department of Statistics
Department of Theology

SPECIAL PROGRAMS:
Audio-Visual Centre
Biomedical Research Unit
Centre for South East Asian Studies
European Community Research Unit
Institute of Education
Institute of Nursing
Language Teaching Centre
Cooperative arrangements with universities in several countries

LANGUAGE OF INSTRUCTION: English

ADMISSION REQUIREMENTS FOR FOREIGN STUDENTS:
Secondary school certificate (GCE, SCE, Baccalauréat
Européen, international baccalaureate, U.S. or Canadian high school diploma or recognized foreign
equivalent)

TUITION FOR FOREIGN STUDENTS:
See GENERAL UNIVERSITY INFORMATION.

TOTAL INSTRUCTIONAL FACULTY:
400 (including 50 professors)

LIBRARY COLLECTIONS:
Total collection—800,000 volumes
Current periodicals—4,700

UNIVERSITY PUBLICATIONS:
*Annual Report, Aspects of Education, Bulletin of Eco-
nomic Research*, publications of the various programs
within the university

CHANCELLOR: The Rt. Hon. Lord Wilberforce

UNIVERSITY OF KENT AT CANTERBURY
Canterbury, Kent, CT2 7NZ, England

CHARACTERISTICS OF INSTITUTION:
Independent, state-funded university

DATE FOUNDED: 1964

TOTAL ENROLLMENT: 5,000 fulltime students (including 950 foreign students)

DEGREES AWARDED:
Bachelor of Arts (BA)
Bachelor of Education (BEd)
Bachelor of Law (LLB)
Bachelor of Science (BSc) in various fields
Master of Arts (MA)
Master of Biotechnology (MBiotech)
Master of Education (MEd)
Master of Engineering (MEng)
Master of Law (LLM)
Master of Philosophy (MPhil)
Master of Science (MSc) in various fields
Doctor of Divinity (DD)
Doctor of Law (LLD)
Doctor of Letters (DLitt)
Doctor of Philosophy (PhD)
Doctor of Science (DSc)

ACADEMIC PROGRAMS:
Faculty of Humanities
Faculty of Information Technology
Faculty of Natural Sciences
Faculty of Social Sciences

SPECIAL PROGRAMS:
Applied Statistics Research Unit
Bibliographical Studies Research Group

Centre for the Study of Cartoons and Caricature
Channel Tunnel Research Unit
Electronic Publishing Research Unit
Health Services Research Unit
Institute for Biotechnological Studies
Institute of Languages and Linguistics
Institute of Management
Institute of Social and Applied Policy
Personal Services Research Unit
School of Continuing Education
Unit for the History, Philosophy and Social Relations
of Science
Urban and Regional Studies Unit
Cooperative arrangements with universities in sev-
eral countries

LANGUAGE OF INSTRUCTION: English

ADMISSION REQUIREMENTS FOR FOREIGN STUDENTS:
Secondary school certificate (GCE, SCE, Baccalauréat
Européen, international baccalaureate, U.S. or Canadian high school diploma or recognized foreign
equivalent)

TUITION FOR FOREIGN STUDENTS:
See GENERAL UNIVERSITY INFORMATION.

TOTAL INSTRUCTIONAL FACULTY:
475

LIBRARY COLLECTIONS:
Total collection—650,000 volumes
Current periodicals—4,000

UNIVERSITY PUBLICATIONS:
Guide for Overseas Students, Newsletter, Kent Bulletin,
publications of the various programs within the university

CHANCELLOR: Robert Horton

UNIVERSITY OF LEEDS
Leeds, LS2 9JT, England

CHARACTERISTICS OF INSTITUTION:
Independent, state-funded university

DATE FOUNDED: 1884, upon merging of Yorkshire
College and the Leeds School of Medicine; 1904 as
the University of Leeds

TOTAL ENROLLMENT: 11,500 fulltime students—9,000
undergraduates, 2,500 postgraduates—(including
1,100 foreign students)

DEGREES AWARDED:
Bachelor of Arts (BA)
Bachelor of Education (BEd)
Bachelor of Engineering (BEng)
Bachelor of Law (LLB)
Bachelor of Medicine (MBChB, BChD)

Bachelor of Science (BSc) in various fields
Master of Arts (MA)
Master of Business Administration (MBA)
Master of Education (MEd)
Master of Engineering (MEng)
Master of Law (LLM)
Master of Medical Science (MMedSc)
Master of Music (MMus)
Master of Philosophy (MPhil)
Master of Science (MSc) in various fields
Medical Doctor (ChM, MD)
Medical Doctor of Science (MDSc)
Doctor of Dental Science (DDSc)
Doctor of Divinity (DD)
Doctor of Engineering (DEng)
Doctor of Law (LLD)
Doctor of Letters (DLitt)
Doctor of Music (DMus)
Doctor of Philosophy (PhD)
Doctor of Science (DSc)

ACADEMIC PROGRAMS:
Faculty of Arts
Faculty of Economic and Social Studies
Faculty of Education
Faculty of Engineering
Faculty of Law
Faculty of Medicine
Faculty of Science

SPECIAL PROGRAMS:
African Studies Unit
Centre for Combustion and Energy Studies
Centre for Developmental Studies
Centre for Medieval Studies
Centre for Studies in Medical Engineering
Centre for Studies in Science and Mathematical Education
Institute for Bibliography and Textual Criticism
Institute of Dialect and Folk Life Studies
Institute for Transport Studies
Institute of Tribology
Overseas Education Unit
Regional Canadian Study Centre
Science Park
University of Leeds Industrial Services, Ltd.
Cooperative arrangements with universities in several countries

LANGUAGE OF INSTRUCTION: English

ADMISSION REQUIREMENTS FOR FOREIGN STUDENTS:
Secondary school certificate (GCE, SCE, Baccalauréat Européen, international baccalaureate, U.S. or Canadian high school diploma or recognized foreign equivalent)

TUITION FOR FOREIGN STUDENTS:
See GENERAL UNIVERSITY INFORMATION.

TOTAL INSTRUCTIONAL FACULTY:
1,050

LIBRARY COLLECTIONS:
Total collection—1,700,000 volumes
Current periodicals—7,000

MUSEUMS AND GALLERIES:
Museums of Dyeing, Education, Forensic Medicine, Pathology, Semitics, Textiles, Zoology

UNIVERSITY PUBLICATIONS:
Leeds University Review; Information for Overseas Students; Troika; Poetry and Audience; This; Blackhole; Mountaineering Journal; Xiao Qiao; publications of the various programs within the university

CHANCELLOR: HRH The Duchess of Kent

UNIVERSITY OF LEICESTER
University Road, Leicester, LE1 7RH, England

CHARACTERISTICS OF INSTITUTION:
Independent, state-funded university

DATE FOUNDED: 1905 as the University College of Leicester; 1957 as the University of Leicester

TOTAL ENROLLMENT: 5,000 fulltime students—63% undergraduate, 27% postgraduate—(including 500 foreign students)

DEGREES AWARDED:
Bachelor of Arts (BA)
Bachelor of Education (BEd)
Bachelor of Law (LLB)
Bachelor of Medicine (MBChB)
Bachelor of Science (BSc) in various fields
Master of Arts (MA)
Master of Arts/Education (MA[Ed])
Master of Education (MEd)
Master of Law (LLM)
Master of Philosophy (MPhil)
Master of Science (MSc) in various fields
Medical Doctor (MD)
Doctor of Law (LLD)
Doctor of Letters (DLitt)
Doctor of Philosophy (PhD)
Doctor of Science (DSc)

ACADEMIC PROGRAMS:
Faculty of Arts
Faculty of Law
Faculty of Medicine
Faculty of Science
Faculty of Social Science

SPECIAL PROGRAMS:
Biological NMR Spectroscopy Centre
Centre for Mass Communication Research

Centre for Urban History
Leicester Biocentre
Office for Humanities Communication
Public Sector Economics Research Centre
School of Education
Sir Norman Chester Centre for Football Research
Victorian Studies Centre
Cooperative arrangements with universities in several countries

LANGUAGE OF INSTRUCTION: English

ADMISSION REQUIREMENTS FOR FOREIGN STUDENTS:
Secondary school certificate (GCE, SCE, Baccalauréat Européen, international baccalaureate, U.S. or Canadian high school diploma or recognized foreign equivalent)

TUITION FOR FOREIGN STUDENTS:
See GENERAL UNIVERSITY INFORMATION.

TOTAL INSTRUCTIONAL FACULTY:
550 (including 70 professors)

LIBRARY COLLECTIONS:
Total collection—800,000 volumes
Current periodicals—4,500

UNIVERSITY PUBLICATIONS:
Annual Report, publications of the various programs within the university

CHANCELLOR: Sir George Porter

UNIVERSITY OF LIVERPOOL
P.O. Box 147, Liverpool, L69 3BX, England

CHARACTERISTICS OF INSTITUTION:
Independent, state-funded university

DATE FOUNDED: 1881 as the University College of Liverpool; 1903 as the University of Liverpool

TOTAL ENROLLMENT: 9,000 fulltime students—2,500 undergraduates, 6,500 postgraduates—(including 700 foreign students)

DEGREES AWARDED:
Bachelor of Architecture (BArch)
Bachelor of Arts (BA)
Bachelor of Dental Surgery (BDS)
Bachelor of Education (BEd)
Bachelor of Engineering (BEng)
Bachelor of Law (LLB)
Bachelor of Medicine (MBChB)
Bachelor of Science (BSc) in various fields
Bachelor of Veterinary Science (BVS)
Master of Animal Science (MAnimSc)
Master of Architecture (MArch)
Master of Archive Administration (MArAd)
Master of Arts (MA)

Master of Business Administration (MBA)
Master of Dental Surgery (MDS)
Master of Education (MEd)
Master of Engineering (MEng)
Master of Law (LLM)
Master of Philosophy (MPhil)
Master of Psychology (MPsych)
Master of Science (MSc) in various fields
Master of Veterinary Science (MVSc)
Medical Doctor (MD) in various fields
Doctor of Engineering (DEng)
Doctor of Law (LLD)
Doctor of Letters (DLitt)
Doctor of Music (DMus)
Doctor of Philosophy (PhD)
Doctor of Science (DSc)
Doctor of Veterinary Science (DVSc)

ACADEMIC PROGRAMS:
Department of College Studies
Department of Dental Studies
Faculty of Arts
Faculty of Education and Extension Studies
Faculty of Engineering
Faculty of Law
Faculty of Medicine
Faculty of Science
Faculty of Social and Environmental Science
Faculty of Veterinary Science

SPECIAL PROGRAMS:
Centre for Marine and Coastal Studies
English Language Unit
Institute of Human Ageing
Institute of Irish Studies
Institute of Latin American Studies
Liverpool School of Tropical Medicine
Marinetech North West
Marine Transport Centre
Merseyside Innovation Centre
Cooperative arrangements with universities in several countries

LANGUAGE OF INSTRUCTION: English

ADMISSION REQUIREMENTS FOR FOREIGN STUDENTS:
Secondary school certificate (GCE, SCE, Baccalauréat Européen, international baccalaureate, U.S. or Canadian high school diploma or recognized foreign equivalent)

TUITION FOR FOREIGN STUDENTS:
See GENERAL UNIVERSITY INFORMATION.

TOTAL INSTRUCTIONAL FACULTY:
850 (including 120 professors)

LIBRARY COLLECTIONS:
Total collection—1,000,000 volumes
Current periodicals—6,000

MUSEUMS AND GALLERIES:
University Art Gallery

UNIVERSITY PUBLICATIONS:
University Diary, Guild and City Gazette, Annual Report, Sphinx, Sphincter, Town Planning Review, Bulletin of Hispanic Studies, Third World Planning Review, Recorder, publications of the various programs within the university

CHANCELLOR: The Rt. Hon. The Viscount Lever-Hulme

UNIVERSITY OF LONDON
Senate House, London, WC1E 7HU, England

CHARACTERISTICS OF INSTITUTION:
Independent, state-funded university

DATE FOUNDED: 1836

TOTAL ENROLLMENT: 54,000 fulltime students—34,000 undergraduates, 20,000 postgraduates—(including 10,000 foreign students) (See the total enrollment sections of the individual constituent colleges of the university.)

DEGREES AWARDED:
See the degrees awarded sections of the individual constituent colleges of the university.

ACADEMIC PROGRAMS:
See the academic programs sections of the individual constituent colleges of the university.

SPECIAL PROGRAMS:
University of London Audio-Visual Centre
University of London Biological Station
University of London Botanic Garden
(See the special programs section of the individual constituent colleges of the university.)

CONSTITUENT COLLEGES OF THE UNIVERSITY:
Colleges reviewed in this chapter:
  Birkbeck College
  Goldsmith's College
  Heythrop College
  Imperial College of Science, Technology and Medicine
  King's College London
  London School of Economics and Political Science
  Queen Mary and Westfield College
  Royal Holloway and Bedford New College
  School of Oriental and African Studies
  University College
  Wye College
Institutes reviewed in this chapter:
  British Institute in Paris
  Courtauld Institute of Art
  Institute of Advanced Legal Studies

  Institute of Classical Studies
  Institute of Commonwealth Studies
  Institute of Education
  Institute of Germanic Studies
  Institute of Historical Research
  Institute of Latin American Studies
  Institute of United States Studies
  School of Slavonic and East European Studies
  Warburg Institute
School reviewed in this chapter:
  London Business School

LANGUAGE OF INSTRUCTION: English

ADMISSION REQUIREMENTS FOR FOREIGN STUDENTS:
Secondary school certificate (GCE, SCE, Baccalauréat Européen, international baccalaureate, U.S. or Canadian high school diploma or recognized foreign equivalent)

TUITION FOR FOREIGN STUDENTS:
See GENERAL UNIVERSITY INFORMATION.

TOTAL INSTRUCTIONAL FACULTY:
1,700 (See the total instructional faculty sections of the individual constituent colleges of the university.)

LIBRARY COLLECTIONS:
Total collection:
  university library—1,250,000 volumes
  depository library—750,000 volumes
Current periodicals:
  university library—5,500
(See the library collections sections of the individual constituent colleges of the university.)

MUSEUMS AND GALLERIES:
See the museums and galleries sections of the individual constituent colleges of the university.

UNIVERSITY PUBLICATIONS:
See the college publications sections of the individual constituent colleges of the university.

CHANCELLOR: HRH The Princess Royal

BIRKBECK COLLEGE
Malet St., London, WC1E 7HX, England

CHARACTERISTICS OF INSTITUTION:
Constituent college of the University of London

DATE FOUNDED: 1823

TOTAL ENROLLMENT: 350 fulltime students, 3,000 parttime students—33% undergraduate, 66% postgraduate

DEGREES AWARDED:
Bachelor of Arts (BA)
Bachelor of Science (BSc)

THE UNIVERSITIES OF THE UNITED KINGDOM OF GREAT BRITAIN AND NORTHERN IRELAND 235

Master of Arts (MA)
Master of Science (MSc)
Doctor of Philosophy (PhD)

ACADEMIC PROGRAMS:
Department of Biology
Department of Chemistry
Department of Classics
Department of Computer Science
Department of Crystallography
Department of Economics
Department of English Language and Literature
Department of French Language and Literature
Department of Geography
Department of Geology
Department of German
Department of History
Department of the History of Art
Department of Linguistics (Applied)
Department of Mathematics
Department of Mathematics (Applied)
Department of Occupational Psychology
Department of Philosophy
Department of Physics
Department of Politics and Sociology
Department of Psychology
Department of Spanish and Italian Language and
   Literature
Department of Statistics

SPECIAL PROGRAMS:
Cooperative arrangements with universities in several countries

LANGUAGE OF INSTRUCTION: English

ADMISSION REQUIREMENTS FOR FOREIGN STUDENTS:
Secondary school certificate (GCE, SCE, Baccalauréat
Européen, international baccalaureate, U.S. or Canadian high school diploma or recognized foreign
equivalent)

TUITION FOR FOREIGN STUDENTS:
See GENERAL UNIVERSITY INFORMATION.

TOTAL INSTRUCTIONAL FACULTY:
182 (including 35 professors)

LIBRARY COLLECTIONS:
Total collection—250,000 volumes
Current periodicals—1,500

MUSEUMS AND GALLERIES:
Access to all museums and galleries of the colleges
of the University of London

UNIVERSITY PUBLICATIONS:
History of Birkbeck College, Haldane Memorial Lectures

MASTER: The Baroness Blackstone

GOLDSMITHS' COLLEGE
**Lewisham Way, New Cross, London, SE14 6NW,
England**

CHARACTERISTICS OF INSTITUTION:
Constituent college of the University of London

DATE FOUNDED: 1904

TOTAL ENROLLMENT: 2,700 fulltime students—1,800
undergraduates, 900 postgraduates—(including 150
foreign students)

DEGREES AWARDED:
Bachelor of Arts (BA)
Bachelor of Education (BEd)
Bachelor of Music (BMus)
Bachelor of Science (BSc)
Master of Arts (MA)
Master of Music (MMus)
Master of Philosophy (MPhil)
Master of Science (MSc)
Doctor of Philosophy (PhD)

ACADEMIC PROGRAMS:
Department of Anthropology and Community Stud-
   ies
Department of Communications
Department of Design and Technology
Department of Drama
Department of Education (advanced studies)
Department of Education (community and continu-
   ing)
Department of Education (postgraduate)
Department of Education (undergraduate)
Department of English
Department of European Languages
Department of Historical and Cultural Studies
Department of Mathematical Sciences
Department of Music
Department of Psychology
Department of Resource and Environmental Man-
   agement
Department of Social Science and Administration
Department of Sociology
Department of Visual Arts

SPECIAL PROGRAMS:
Cooperative arrangements with universities in several countries

LANGUAGE OF INSTRUCTION: English

ADMISSION REQUIREMENTS FOR FOREIGN STUDENTS:
Secondary school certificate (GCE, SCE, Baccalauréat
Européen, international baccalaureate, U.S. or Canadian high school diploma or recognized foreign
equivalent)

TUITION FOR FOREIGN STUDENTS:
See GENERAL UNIVERSITY INFORMATION.

TOTAL INSTRUCTIONAL FACULTY:
175

LIBRARY COLLECTIONS:
Total collection—250,000 volumes
Current periodicals—1,500

MUSEUMS AND GALLERIES:
Access to all museums and galleries of the colleges
of the University of London

UNIVERSITY PUBLICATIONS:
Goldsith's College Association Yearbook, The Forge, Annual Report

WARDEN: Prof. Andrew Rutherford

HEYTHROP COLLEGE
11–13 Cavendish Sq., London, W1M 0AN, England

CHARACTERISTICS OF INSTITUTION:
Constituent college of the University of London

DATE FOUNDED: 1926

TOTAL ENROLLMENT: 200 fulltime students (including 30 foreign students)

DEGREES AWARDED:
Bachelor of Arts in Biblical Studies (BABS)
Bachelor of Arts in Philosophy (BAPhil)
Bachelor of Arts in Theology (BATheo)
Bachelor of Divinity (BD)
Master of Philosophy (MPhil)
Master of Theology (MT)
Doctor of Philosophy (PhD)
Postgraduate diploma in pastoral theology

ACADEMIC PROGRAMS:
Faculty of Philosophy
Faculty of Theology

SPECIAL PROGRAMS:
Cooperative arrangements with universities in several countries

LANGUAGE OF INSTRUCTION: English

ADMISSION REQUIREMENTS FOR FOREIGN STUDENTS:
Secondary school certificate (GCE, SCE, Baccalauréat Européen, international baccalaureate, U.S. or Canadian high school diploma or recognized foreign equivalent)

TUITION FOR FOREIGN STUDENTS:
See GENERAL UNIVERSITY INFORMATION.

TOTAL INSTRUCTIONAL FACULTY:
25

LIBRARY COLLECTIONS:
Total collection—250,000 volumes

MUSEUMS AND GALLERIES:
Access to all museums and galleries of the colleges
of the University of London

UNIVERSITY PUBLICATIONS:
Heythrop Journal of Academic Theology, and The Way and supplements

RECTOR: Rev. B. Callaghan

IMPERIAL COLLEGE OF SCIENCE, TECHNOLOGY AND MEDICINE
South Kensington, London, SW7 2AZ, England

CHARACTERISTICS OF INSTITUTION:
Constituent college of the University of London

DATE FOUNDED: 1907

TOTAL ENROLLMENT: 6,300 fulltime students (including 1,500 foreign students)

DEGREES AWARDED:
Bachelor of Engineering (BEng)
Bachelor of Medicine (MB BChir, MB BS)
Bachelor of Science (BSc) in various fields
Master of Business Administration (MBA)
   (proposed)
Master of Philosophy (MPhil)
Master of Science (MSc) in various fields
Doctor of Philosophy (PhD)

ACADEMIC PROGRAMS:
Centre for Biotechnology
Centre for Environmental Technology
Computer Centre
Department of Aeronautics
Department of Anatomy and Cell Biology
Department of Biochemistry
Department of Biology
Department of Biophysics
Department of Chemical Engineering and Chemical
   Technology
Department of Chemistry
Department of Civil Engineering
Department of Computing
Department of Electrical Engineering
Department of Geology
Department of Humanities
Department of Materials
Department of Mathemetics and Statistics
Department of Mechanical Engineering
Department of Mineral Resource Engineering
Department of Physics
Division of Life Sciences
Physiological Flow Studies Unit

School of Management
School of Medicine (various disciplines)

SPECIAL PROGRAMS:
City and Guilds College
Royal College of Science
Royal School of Mines
St. Mary's Hospital Medical School
Cooperative arrangements with universities in several countries

LANGUAGE OF INSTRUCTION: English

ADMISSION REQUIREMENTS FOR FOREIGN STUDENTS:
Secondary school certificate (GCE, SCE, Baccalauréat Européen, international baccalaureate, U.S. or Canadian high school diploma or recognized foreign equivalent)

TUITION FOR FOREIGN STUDENTS:
See GENERAL UNIVERSITY INFORMATION.

TOTAL INSTRUCTIONAL FACULTY:
725 (including 120 professors)

LIBRARY COLLECTIONS:
Total collection—500,000 volumes (medical school library collection—37,000 volumes)
Current periodicals—400

MUSEUMS AND GALLERIES:
Access to all museums and galleries of the colleges of the University of London

UNIVERSITY PUBLICATIONS:
Publications of the various programs within the college

WARDEN: Prof. E. A. Ash

KING'S COLLEGE LONDON
Strand, London, WC2R 2LS, England

CHARACTERISTICS OF INSTITUTION:
Constituent college of the University of London

DATE FOUNDED: 1829

TOTAL ENROLLMENT: 6,000 fulltime students (including 1,100 foreign students)

DEGREES AWARDED:
Bachelor of Arts (BA)
Bachelor of Dental Surgery (BDS)
Bachelor of Divinity (BD)
Bachelor of Engineering (BEng)
Bachelor of Law (LLB)
Bachelor of Music (BMus)
Bachelor of Medicine (MB BS)
Bachelor of Pharmacy (BPharm)
Master of Arts (MA) in various fields
Master of Education (MEd)

Master of Law (LLM)
Master of Music (MMus)
Master of Philosophy (MPhil) in all faculties
Master of Science (MSc) in various fields
Master of Theology (MTheol)
Doctor of Philosophy (PhD) in all faculties

ACADEMIC PROGRAMS:
Department of Anatomy and Human Biology
Department of Biochemistry
Department of Biology, Botany and Zoology
Department of Biophysics, Cellular and Molecular Biology
Department of Chemical Engineering and Chemical Technology
Department of Chemistry
Department of the Christian Doctrine and History
Department of Civil Engineering
Department of Classics
Department of Computing
Department of Electronic and Electrical Engineering
Department of English Language and Literature
Department of French
Department of Food and Nutritional Sciences
Department of Geography
Department of Geology
Department of German
Department of Greek, Byzantine and Modern Studies
Department of History
Department of History and Philosophy of Science
Department of Human Environmental Science
Department of Laws
Department of Management Studies
Department of Mathematics
Department of Mechanical Engineering
Department of Microbiology
Department of Music
Department of Nursing
Department of Nutrition
Department of Paleography
Department of Pharmacology
Department of Pharmacy
Department of Physics
Department of Philosophy
Department of Portuguese and Brazilian Studies
Department of Spanish and Latin American Studies
Department of War Studies
School of Dentistry
School of Medicine (various disciplines)

SPECIAL PROGRAMS:
Age Concern Institute of Gerontology
Centre for Construction Law and Project Management
Centre for Medical Law
Drug Control and Teaching Centre

Harris Birthright Research Centre for Fetal Medicine
King's College School of Medicine and Dentistry
Monitoring and Assessment Research Centre (MARC)
Cooperative arrangements with universities in several countries

LANGUAGE OF INSTRUCTION: English

ADMISSION REQUIREMENTS FOR FOREIGN STUDENTS:
Secondary school certificate (GCE, SCE, Baccalauréat Européen, international baccalaureate, U.S. or Canadian high school diploma or recognized foreign equivalent

TUITION FOR FOREIGN STUDENTS:
See GENERAL UNIVERSITY INFORMATION.

TOTAL INSTRUCTIONAL FACULTY:
750 (including 130 professors)

LIBRARY COLLECTIONS:
Total collection—850,000 volumes
  (medical school library collection—30,000 volumes)
Current periodicals—2,750

MUSEUMS AND GALLERIES:
Access to all museums and galleries of the colleges of the University of London

UNIVERSITY PUBLICATIONS:
Publications of the various programs within the college

PRINCIPAL: Dr. J. D. E. Beynon

LONDON SCHOOL OF ECONOMICS AND POLITICAL SCIENCE
Houghton St., London, WC2A 2AE, England

CHARACTERISTICS OF INSTITUTION:
Constituent college of the University of London

DATE FOUNDED: 1895

TOTAL ENROLLMENT: 4,000 fulltime students (including 2,300 foreign students)

DEGREES AWARDED:
Bachelor of Arts (BA)
Bachelor of Law (LLB)
Bachelor of Science (BSc) in various fields
Bachelor of Economic Science (BScEcon)
Master of Arts (MA) in various fields
Master of Law (LLM)
Master of Philosophy (MPhil) in all faculties
Master of Science (MSc) in various fields
Doctor of Philosophy (PhD) in all faculties

ACADEMIC PROGRAMS:
Department of Accounting and Finance
Department of Anthropology (Social)
Department of Economics
Department of Economic History
Department of Geography
Department of Government
Department of Industrial Relations
Department of International History
Department of International Relations
Department of Language Studies (English, French, German, Russian and Spanish)
Department of Law
Department of Philosophy, Logic and Scientific Method
Department of Social Psychology
Department of Social Science and Administration
Department of Statistical and Mathematical Sciences (actuarial science, computing, management, mathematics, operational research, population studies, systems analysis)

SPECIAL PROGRAMS:
Business History Unit
Centre for International Studies
Centre for Labour Economics
Centre for Voluntary Organization
Decision Analysis Unit
International Resources Unit
Financial Markets Group
Greater London Group
Population Investigation Committee
Suntory-Toyota International Centre
Cooperative arrangements with universities in several countries

LANGUAGE OF INSTRUCTION: English

ADMISSION REQUIREMENTS FOR FOREIGN STUDENTS:
Secondary school certificate (GCE, SCE, Baccalauréat Européen, international baccalaureate, U.S. or Canadian high school diploma or recognized foreign equivalent)

TUITION FOR FOREIGN STUDENTS:
See GENERAL UNIVERSITY INFORMATION.

TOTAL INSTRUCTIONAL FACULTY:
265 (including 70 professors)

LIBRARY COLLECTIONS:
Total collection—900,000 volumes
Current periodicals—13,000

MUSEUMS AND GALLERIES:
Access to all museums and galleries of the colleges of the University of London

UNIVERSITY PUBLICATIONS:
Research at LSE, Some Facts, LSE Magazine, Beaver, LSE Quarterly, Government and Opposition, Millennium,

publications of the various programs within the university

DIRECTOR: Prof. J. Ashworth

QUEEN MARY AND WESTFIELD COLLEGE
Mile End Road, London, E1 4NS, England

CHARACTERISTICS OF INSTITUTION:
Constituent college of the University of London

DATE FOUNDED: 1989, following the merging of Queen Mary College, founded in 1887, and Westfield College, founded in 1882

TOTAL ENROLLMENT: 4,500 fulltime students (including 850 foreign students)

DEGREES AWARDED:
Bachelor of Arts (BA)
Bachelor of Engineering (BEng)
Bachelor of Law (LLB)
Bachelor of Science (BSc) in various fields
Bachelor of Economic Science (BScEcon)
Master of Arts (MA) in various fields
Master of Law (LLM)
Master of Philosophy (MPhil) in all faculties
Master of Science (MSc) in various fields
Doctor of Philosophy (PhD) in all faculties

ACADEMIC PROGRAMS:
Faculty of Arts
Faculty of Engineering
Faculty of Information and Mathematical Sciences
Faculty of Law
Faculty of Physical and Biological Sciences
Faculty of Social Sciences

SPECIAL PROGRAMS:
Centre for Business Studies
Centre for Commercial Law Studies
Centre for Contemporary Spanish Studies
Centre for East London Studies
Centre for Information Technology
Centre for Research in Aquatic Biology (CRAB)
Economics Research Bureau
Health and Health Care Research Centre
Public Policy Research Unit
Cooperative arrangements with universities in several countries

LANGUAGE OF INSTRUCTION: English

ADMISSION REQUIREMENTS FOR FOREIGN STUDENTS:
Secondary school certificate (GCE, SCE, Baccalauréat Európen, international baccalaureate, U.S. or Canadian high school diploma or recognized foreign equivalent)

TUITION FOR FOREIGN STUDENTS:
See GENERAL UNIVERSITY INFORMATION.

TOTAL INSTRUCTIONAL FACULTY:
350 (including 85 professors)

LIBRARY COLLECTIONS:
Total collection—400,000 volumes
Current periodicals—2,800

MUSEUMS AND GALLERIES:
Access to all museums and galleries of the colleges of the University of London

UNIVERSITY PUBLICATIONS:
Publications of the various programs within the college

PRINCIPAL: Prof. Ian Butterworth

ROYAL HOLLOWAY AND BEDFORD NEW COLLEGE
Egham Hill, Egham, Surrey, TW20 0EX, England

CHARACTERISTICS OF INSTITUTION:
Constituent college of the University of London

DATE FOUNDED: 1985, by the merging of Royal Holloway College, founded in 1886, and Bedford College, founded in 1849

TOTAL ENROLLMENT: 3,000 fulltime students (including 200 foreign students)

DEGREES AWARDED:
Bachelor of Arts (BA)
Bachelor of Music (BMus)
Bachelor of Science (BSc) in various fields
Master of Arts (MA) in various fields
Master of Music (MMus)
Master of Philosophy (MPhil) in all faculties
Master of Science (MSc) in various fields
Doctor of Philosophy (PhD) in all faculties

ACADEMIC PROGRAMS:
Faculty of Arts and Music
Faculty of Science

SPECIAL PROGRAMS:
Centre for the Study of Victorian Art
Cooperative arrangements with universities in several countries

LANGUAGE OF INSTRUCTION: English

ADMISSION REQUIREMENTS FOR FOREIGN STUDENTS:
Secondary school certificate (GCE, SCE, Baccalauréat Européen, international baccalaureate, U.S. or Canadian high school diploma or recognized foreign equivalent

TUITION FOR FOREIGN STUDENTS:
See GENERAL UNIVERSITY INFORMATION.

TOTAL INSTRUCTIONAL FACULTY:
350 (including 85 professors)

LIBRARY COLLECTIONS:
Total collection—450,000 volumes
Current periodicals—1,700

MUSEUMS AND GALLERIES:
University of London Botanic Garden
Picture Gallery with works by Turner, Constable and
    Frith
Access to all museums and galleries of the colleges
    of the University of London

UNIVERSITY PUBLICATIONS:
A publication by the Centre for the Study of Victorian Art, *Junior Year Abroad Catalogue*

PRINCIPAL: Prof. N. Gower

SCHOOL OF ORIENTAL AND AFRICAN STUDIES
**Thornhaugh St., Russell Sq., London, WC1H 0XG,
England**

CHARACTERISTICS OF INSTITUTION:
Constituent college of the University of London

DATE FOUNDED: 1916

TOTAL ENROLLMENT: 1,200 fulltime students (including 300 foreign students)

DEGREES AWARDED:
Bachelor of Arts (BA)
Bachelor of Law (LLB)
Master of Arts (MA) in various fields
Master of Law (LLM)
Master of Philosophy (MPhil) in all faculties
Master of Science (MSc) in various fields
Doctor of Philosophy (PhD) in all faculties

ACADEMIC PROGRAMS:
Department of African Studies
Department of Anthropology and Sociology
Department of Economic and Political Studies
Department of Far Eastern Studies
Department of Geography
Department of History
Department of Indology and Modern Languages and
    Literatures of South Asia
Department of Near and Middle Eastern Studies
Department of Phonetics and Linguistics
Department of the Studies of South East Asia and
    The Islands

SPECIAL PROGRAMS:
Contemporary China Institute

Cooperative arrangements with universities in sev-
    eral countries

LANGUAGE OF INSTRUCTION: English

ADMISSION REQUIREMENTS FOR FOREIGN STUDENTS:
Secondary school certificate (GCE, SCE, Baccalauréat
Européen, international baccalaureate, U.S. or Canadian high school diploma or recognized foreign
equivalent)

TUITION FOR FOREIGN STUDENTS:
See GENERAL UNIVERSITY INFORMATION.

TOTAL INSTRUCTIONAL FACULTY:
150 (including 35 professors)

LIBRARY COLLECTIONS:
Total collection—750,000 volumes
Current periodicals—5,000

MUSEUMS AND GALLERIES:
Percival David Foundation of Chinese Art
Access to all museums and galleries of the colleges
    of the University of London.

UNIVERSITY PUBLICATIONS:
Bulletin, Journal of African Law, The China Quarterly

DIRECTOR: M. D. McWilliam

UNIVERSITY COLLEGE
Gower St., London, WC1E 6BT, England

CHARACTERISTICS OF INSTITUTION:
Constituent college of the University of London

DATE FOUNDED: 1826

TOTAL ENROLLMENT: 8,600 fulltime students (including 1,800 foreign students [280 North Americans])

DEGREES AWARDED:
Bachelor of Arts (BA)
Bachelor of Dental Surgery (BDS)
Bachelor of Engineering (BEng)
Bachelor of Law (LLB)
Bachelor of Science (BSc)
Bachelor of Medicine (MB BS)
Master of Arts (MA) in various fields
Master of Law (LLM)
Master of Philosophy (MPhil) in all faculties
Master of Science (MSc) in various fields
Medical Doctor (MD)
Medical Dental Surgeon (MDS)
Medical Surgeon (MS)
Doctor of Philosophy (PhD) in all faculties

ACADEMIC PROGRAMS:
Faculty of Arts
Faculty of Clinical Science
Faculty of Engineering

Faculty of Environmental Studies
Faculty of Laws
Faculty of Medical Sciences

SPECIAL PROGRAMS:
Blakeney Point Field Station
Botanical Research Garden
Institute of Archaeology
Institute of Biotechnological Studies
Institute of Larynology and Otology
Institute of Orthopaedics
Institute of Urology
Mullard Space Science Laboratory
National Center of Biochemical Engineering
University of London Observatory
Cooperative arrangements with universities in several countries

LANGUAGE OF INSTRUCTION: English

ADMISSION REQUIREMENTS FOR FOREIGN STUDENTS:
Secondary school certificate (GCE, SCE, Baccalauréat Européen, international baccalaureate, U.S. or Canadian high school diploma or recognized foreign equivalent)

TUITION FOR FOREIGN STUDENTS:
See GENERAL UNIVERSITY INFORMATION.

TOTAL INSTRUCTIONAL FACULTY:
1,000 (including 165 professors)

LIBRARY COLLECTIONS:
Total collection—1,250,000 volumes
Current periodicals—7,000

MUSEUMS AND GALLERIES:
Department of Anthropology Museum, Wellcome Collection
Department of Geology Museum, Johnston Lavis Vulcanology Collection
Gustave Tuck Museum of Jewish Antiquities
Museum of Archaeology, Petri Palestinian Collection
Museums of Classical Archaeology, Egyptology, Pathology, Zoology, Comparative Anatomy
Access to all museums and galleries of the colleges of the University of London.

UNIVERSITY PUBLICATIONS:
UCL Union Welfare Handbook, Alternative Prospectus

PROVOST: Dr. Derek H. Roberts

WYE COLLEGE
Wye, Ashford, Kent, TN25 5AH, England

CHARACTERISTICS OF INSTITUTION:
Constituent college of the University of London

DATE FOUNDED: 1447

TOTAL ENROLLMENT: 650 fulltime students (including 185 foreign students)

DEGREES AWARDED:
Bachelor of Science (BSc)
Master of Philosophy (MPhil) in all faculties
Master of Science (MSc) in various fields
Doctor of Philosophy (PhD) in all faculties

ACADEMIC PROGRAMS:
Department of Agricultural Economics
Department of Agriculture, Horticulture and the Environment
Department of Biochemistry and Biological Sciences

SPECIAL PROGRAMS:
Centre for European Agricultural Studies
Centre for Tunnel Research Unit (with Kent University)
Cooperative arrangements with universities in several countries

LANGUAGE OF INSTRUCTION: English

ADMISSION REQUIREMENTS FOR FOREIGN STUDENTS:
Secondary school certificate (GCE, SCE, Baccalauréat Européen, international baccalaureate U.S. or Canadian high school diploma or recognized foreign equivalent)

TUITION FOR FOREIGN STUDENTS:
See GENERAL UNIVERSITY INFORMATION.

TOTAL INSTRUCTIONAL FACULTY:
100 (including 15 professors)

LIBRARY COLLECTIONS:
Total collection—40,000 volumes
Current periodicals—750
European Documentation Centre

MUSEUMS AND GALLERIES:
Museum of Agriculture
Access to all museums and galleries of the colleges of the University of London

PRINCIPAL: J. H. D. Prescott

BRITISH INSTITUTE IN PARIS
11 rue de Constantine, 75007 Paris, France

CHARACTERISTICS OF INSTITUTION:
Senate institute of the University of London

DATE FOUNDED: 1894, incorporated into the University of London in 1969

TOTAL ENROLLMENT: 3,850 fulltime students (including 400 foreign students) and 750 correspondence students

CERTIFICATES AND DIPLOMAS:
Certificates of proficiency in French and English translation and in contemporary written and spoken French
Diploma in contemporary French studies

ACADEMIC PROGRAMS:
Department of English Language and Literature
Department of French Language and Literature

SPECIAL PROGRAMS:
Instructional faculty draws on lecturers from the Universities of France and the United Kingdom.
Cooperative arrangements with universities in several countries

LANGUAGES OF INSTRUCTION: English and French

ADMISSION REQUIREMENTS FOR FOREIGN STUDENTS:
Secondary school certificate (GCE, SCE, Baccalauréat Européen, international baccalaureate, U.S. or Canadian high school diploma or recognized foreign equivalent)

TUITION FOR FOREIGN STUDENTS:
See GENERAL UNIVERSITY INFORMATION.

TOTAL INSTRUCTIONAL FACULTY:
35

LIBRARY COLLECTIONS:
Total collection—40,000 French volumes, 200,000 English volumes
Current periodicals—300

MUSEUMS AND GALLERIES:
Access to all museums and galleries of the colleges of the University of London and the affiliated university museums and galleries in Paris

UNIVERSITY PUBLICATIONS:
Franco-British Studies, Academic Journal

DIRECTOR: Prof. C. L. Campos

COURTAULD INSTITUTE OF ART
Somerset House, Strand, London, WC2R ORN, England

CHARACTERISTICS OF INSTITUTION:
Senate institute of the University of London

DATE FOUNDED: 1932

TOTAL ENROLLMENT: 350 students—190 fulltime, 160 parttime—(including 100 foreign students)

DEGREES AWARDED:
Bachelor of Arts (BA) in history of art
Master of Arts (MA) in history of art and history of dress
Master of Philosophy (MPhil) in history of art

Doctor of Philosophy (PhD) in history of art
Diplomas awarded for all courses on the conservation of paintings, textiles and wall paintings

ACADEMIC PROGRAMS:
Department for the Conservation of Paintings
Department for the Conservation of Textiles
Department for the Conservation of Wall Paintings
Department of Art History
Department of the History of Dress

SPECIAL PROGRAMS:
Somerset House Gallery
Cooperative arrangements with universities in several countries

LANGUAGE OF INSTRUCTION: English

ADMISSION REQUIREMENTS FOR FOREIGN STUDENTS:
Secondary school certificate (GCE, SCE, Baccalauréat Européen, international baccalaureate U.S. or Canadian high school diploma or recognized foreign equivalent)

TUITION FOR FOREIGN STUDENTS:
See GENERAL UNIVERSITY INFORMATION.

TOTAL INSTRUCTIONAL FACULTY:
35

LIBRARY COLLECTIONS:
Total collection—70,000 volumes
Current periodicals—300

MUSEUMS AND GALLERIES:
Somerset House Gallery
Access to all museums and galleries of the colleges of the University of London

UNIVERSITY PUBLICATIONS:
Journal of the Warburg and Courtauld Institutes

DIRECTOR: Prof. C. M. Kauffmann

INSTITUTE OF ADVANCED LEGAL STUDIES
Charles Clore House, 17 Russell Sq., London, WC1B 5DR, England

CHARACTERISTICS OF INSTITUTION:
Senate institute of the University of London

DATE FOUNDED: 1947

TOTAL ENROLLMENT: 850 postgraduate students (including 585 foreign students)

DEGREES AWARDED:
Master of Philosophy (MPhil)
Doctor of Philosophy (PhD)

ACADEMIC PROGRAMS:
Law courses at faculties and departments of law in the constituent colleges of the University of London:

King's College
London School of Economics and Political Science
Queen Mary College
School of Oriental African Studies
University College

SPECIAL PROGRAMS:
Cooperative arrangements with universities in several countries

LANGUAGE OF INSTRUCTION: English

ADMISSION REQUIREMENTS FOR FOREIGN STUDENTS:
Postgraduate admission: university degree recognized as equivalent to the British undergraduate degree
Professional qualifications may also be accepted

TUITION FOR FOREIGN STUDENTS:
See GENERAL UNIVERSITY INFORMATION.

TOTAL INSTRUCTIONAL FACULTY:
The sum of the Departments of Law instructional faculties in the constituent colleges of the University of London

LIBRARY COLLECTIONS:
Total collection—200,000 volumes
Current periodicals—2,500

MUSEUMS AND GALLERIES:
Access to all museums and galleries of the colleges of the University of London

UNIVERSITY PUBLICATIONS:
Legal Research Topics, University of London Legal Series, *A Bibliographical Guide to the Law of the U.K., the Channel Islands and the Isle of Man, The Bulletin*

DIRECTOR: T. C. Daintith

INSTITUTE OF CLASSICAL STUDIES
31–34 Gordon Square, London, WC1H 0PY, England

CHARACTERISTICS OF INSTITUTION:
Senate institute of the University of London

DATE FOUNDED: 1953

TOTAL ENROLLMENT: 250 postgraduate students (including 75 foreign students)

DEGREES AWARDED:
None (All degrees are awarded by the individual constituent college of the University of London attended by the student.)

ACADEMIC PROGRAMS:
Research programs

SPECIAL PROGRAMS:
Hellenic Society
Roman Society

Cooperative arrangements with universities in several countries

LANGUAGE OF INSTRUCTION: English

ADMISSION REQUIREMENTS FOR FOREIGN STUDENTS:
Postgraduate admission: university degree recognized as equivalent to the British undergraduate degree in classics

TUITION FOR FOREIGN STUDENTS:
See GENERAL UNIVERSITY INFORMATION.

TOTAL INSTRUCTIONAL FACULTY:
The sum of the Department of Classics instructional faculties in the constituent colleges of the University of London

LIBRARY COLLECTIONS:
Total collection—75,000 volumes
Current periodicals—500

MUSEUMS AND GALLERIES:
Access to all museums and galleries of the colleges of the University of London

UNIVERSITY PUBLICATIONS:
Classical Handbook

DIRECTOR: Prof. J. P. Barron

INSTITUTE OF COMMONWEALTH STUDIES
27–28 Russell Square, London, WC1B 5DS, England

CHARACTERISTICS OF INSTITUTION:
Senate institute of the University of London

DATE FOUNDED: 1949

TOTAL ENROLLMENT: 1,000 postgraduate students (including 300 foreign students)

DEGREES AWARDED:
Master of Arts (MA) in various fields
Master of Philosophy (MPhil) in in various fields
Doctor of Philosophy (PhD) in various fields

ACADEMIC PROGRAMS:
Various courses, offered by the constituent colleges of the University of London, that offer area studies on the British Commonwealth
Research programs

SPECIAL PROGRAMS:
Sir Robert Menzies Centre for Australian Studies
Cooperative arrangements with universities in several countries

LANGUAGE OF INSTRUCTION: English

ADMISSION REQUIREMENTS FOR FOREIGN STUDENTS:
Postgraduate admission: university degree recognized as equivalent to the British undergraduate degree

TUITION FOR FOREIGN STUDENTS:
See GENERAL UNIVERSITY INFORMATION.

TOTAL INSTRUCTIONAL FACULTY:
The sum of the departments of the constituent colleges of the University of London that offer courses on Area Studies on the British Commonwealth

LIBRARY COLLECTIONS:
Total collection—135,000 volumes
Current periodicals—750

MUSEUMS AND GALLERIES:
Access to all museums and galleries of the colleges of the University of London

UNIVERSITY PUBLICATIONS:
Commonwealth Papers

DIRECTOR: Prof. Shula E. Marks

INSTITUTE OF EDUCATION
20 Bedford Way, London, WC1H 0AL, England

CHARACTERISTICS OF INSTITUTION:
Constituent college of the University of London

DATE FOUNDED: 1902

TOTAL ENROLLMENT: 1,350 fulltime students (including 450 foreign students)

DEGREES AWARDED:
Bachelor of Education (BEd)
Master of Arts (MA) in various fields
Master of Philosophy (MPhil)
Master of Science (MSc) in various fields
Doctor of Philosophy (PhD)

ACADEMIC PROGRAMS:
Department of Art and Design Education
Department of Child Development and Primary Education
Department of Curriculum Studies
Department of Economic, Administrative and Policy Studies in Education
Department of Economics, Geography and Business
Department of Educational Psychology and Special Educational Needs
Department of English and Media Studies
Department of English for Speakers of Other Languages
Department of History and Humanity
Department of In-service Education for Teachers
Department of International and Comparative Education

Department of Mathematics, Statistics and Computing
Department of Modern Languages
Department of Music Education
Department of the Philosophy of Education
Department of Science Education
Department of the Sociology of Education

SPECIAL PROGRAMS:
Centre for Higher Education Studies
Centre for Multicultural Education
Centre for Post Sixteen Education
Centre for Research and Education on Gender
Thomas Coram Research Unit
Cooperative arrangements with universities in several countries

LANGUAGE OF INSTRUCTION: English

ADMISSION REQUIREMENTS FOR FOREIGN STUDENTS:
Secondary school certificate (GCE, SCE, Baccalauréat Européen, international baccalaureate, U.S. or Canadian high school diploma or recognized foreign equivalent)

TUITION FOR FOREIGN STUDENTS:
See GENERAL UNIVERSITY INFORMATION.

TOTAL INSTRUCTIONAL FACULTY:
115 (including 18 professors)

LIBRARY COLLECTIONS:
Total collection—270,000 volumes
Current periodicals—2,100

MUSEUMS AND GALLERIES:
Access to all museums and galleries of the colleges of the University of London

UNIVERSITY PUBLICATIONS:
Studies in Education, Bedford Way Papers, London Educational Studies, publications of the various programs within the college

DIRECTOR: Sir Peter Newsam

INSTITUTE OF GERMANIC STUDIES
29 Russell Square, London, WC1B 5DP, England

CHARACTERISTICS OF INSTITUTION:
Senate institute of the University of London

DATE FOUNDED: 1950

TOTAL ENROLLMENT: 1,050 postgraduate students

DEGREES AWARDED:
Master of Arts (MA) in various fields
Master of Philosophy (MPhil) in various fields
Doctor of Philosophy (PhD) in various fields

ACADEMIC PROGRAMS:
Various courses, offered by the constituent colleges of the University of London, that offer area studies in Germanic languages, literature, history, culture, etc.
Research programs

SPECIAL PROGRAMS:
Cooperative arrangements with universities in several countries

LANGUAGE OF INSTRUCTION: English

ADMISSION REQUIREMENTS FOR FOREIGN STUDENTS:
Postgraduate admission: university degree recognized as equivalent to the British undergraduate degree

TUITION FOR FOREIGN STUDENTS:
See GENERAL UNIVERSITY INFORMATION.

TOTAL INSTRUCTIONAL FACULTY:
The sum of the departments of the constituent colleges of the University of London that offer courses on area studies on Germanic language, literature, history, culture, etc.

LIBRARY COLLECTIONS:
Total collection—75,000 volumes
Current periodicals—500

MUSEUMS AND GALLERIES:
Access to all museums and galleries of the colleges of the University of London

UNIVERSITY PUBLICATIONS:
Research in Germanic Studies at British Universities, Publications, Bithell Series of Dissertations, several other Germanic Studies publications

HONORARY DIRECTOR: Prof. M. W. Swales

INSTITUTE OF HISTORICAL RESEARCH
Senate House, Malet Street, London, WC1E 7HU, England

CHARACTERISTICS OF INSTITUTION:
Senate institute of the University of London

DATE FOUNDED: 1921

TOTAL ENROLLMENT: 2,650 postgraduate students

DEGREES AWARDED:
Master of Arts (MA) in various fields
Doctor of Philosophy (PhD) in various fields

ACADEMIC PROGRAMS:
Research programs

SPECIAL PROGRAMS:
Institute of United States Studies

Cooperative arrangements with universities in several countries

LANGUAGE OF INSTRUCTION: English

ADMISSION REQUIREMENTS FOR FOREIGN STUDENTS:
Postgraduate admission: university degree recognized as equivalent to the British undergraduate degree
Undergraduates are allowed to use library facilities but cannot undertake an academic program.

TUITION FOR FOREIGN STUDENTS:
See GENERAL UNIVERSITY INFORMATION.

TOTAL INSTRUCTIONAL FACULTY:
One professor, 26 research staff

LIBRARY COLLECTIONS:
Total collection—150,000 volumes

MUSEUMS AND GALLERIES:
Access to all museums and galleries of the colleges of the University of London

UNIVERSITY PUBLICATIONS:
Historical Research Bulletin, Victoria History of the Countries of England, Historical Research for University Degrees in the United Kingdom, several historical research publications on specific topics

DIRECTOR: Dr. Patrick O'Brien

INSTITUTE OF LATIN AMERICAN STUDIES
31 Tavistock Square, London, WC1H 9HA, England

CHARACTERISTICS OF INSTITUTION:
Senate institute of the University of London

DATE FOUNDED: 1965

TOTAL ENROLLMENT: 1,250 postgraduate students

DEGREES AWARDED:
Master of Arts (MA) in various fields

ACADEMIC PROGRAMS:
Various courses offered by the constituent colleges of the University of London on Latin American area studies

SPECIAL PROGRAMS:
Cooperative arrangements with universities in several countries

LANGUAGE OF INSTRUCTION: English

ADMISSION REQUIREMENTS FOR FOREIGN STUDENTS:
Postgraduate admission: university degree recognized as equivalent to the British undergraduate degree

TUITION FOR FOREIGN STUDENTS:
See GENERAL UNIVERSITY INFORMATION.

TOTAL INSTRUCTIONAL FACULTY:
10 academic staff at the Institute in addition to the Latin American area studies faculties of the constituent colleges of the University of London

LIBRARY COLLECTIONS:
Total collection—7,700 volumes

MUSEUMS AND GALLERIES:
Access to all museums and galleries of the colleges of the University of London

UNIVERSITY PUBLICATIONS:
Latin American Studies at the Universities of the United Kingdom, Theses in Latin American Studies at the Universities of the United Kingdom, institution monographs, occasional papers

DIRECTOR: Prof. Leslie M. Bethell

INSTITUTE OF UNITED STATES STUDIES
31 Tavistock Square, London, WC1H 9EZ, England

CHARACTERISTICS OF INSTITUTION:
Senate institute of the University of London and an affiliated institution of the Institute of Historical Research

DATE FOUNDED: 1965

TOTAL ENROLLMENT: 20 postgraduate students

DEGREES AWARDED:
Master of Arts (MA) in various fields
Doctor of Philosophy (PhD) in various fields

ACADEMIC PROGRAMS:
Cooperative research programs between U.S. and British universities

LANGUAGE OF INSTRUCTION: English

ADMISSION REQUIREMENTS FOR FOREIGN STUDENTS:
Postgraduate admission: university degree recognized as equivalent to the British undergraduate degree

TUITION FOR FOREIGN STUDENTS:
See GENERAL UNIVERSITY INFORMATION.

TOTAL INSTRUCTIONAL FACULTY:
One professor

LIBRARY COLLECTIONS:
Total collection—3,500 volumes
Current periodicals—25

MUSEUMS AND GALLERIES:
Access to all museums and galleries of the colleges of the University of London

UNIVERSITY PUBLICATIONS:
American Studies at British Universities

DIRECTOR: Prof. P. J. Parish

SCHOOL OF SLAVONIC AND EAST EUROPEAN STUDIES
Senate House, London, WC1E 7HU, England

CHARACTERISTICS OF INSTITUTION:
Senate institute of the University of London

DATE FOUNDED: 1915

TOTAL ENROLLMENT: 350 fulltime students (including 50 foreign students)

DEGREES AWARDED:
Bachelor of Arts (BA) in all disciplines
Master of Arts (MA) in various fields
Master of Philosophy (MPhil)
Doctor of Philosophy (PhD)

ACADEMIC PROGRAMS:
Department of East European Languages and Literature
Department of History
Department of Russian Language and Literature
Department of Social Sciences

SPECIAL PROGRAMS:
Cooperative arrangements with universities in several countries

LANGUAGE OF INSTRUCTION: English

ADMISSION REQUIREMENTS FOR FOREIGN STUDENTS:
Secondary school certificate (GCE, SCE, Baccalauréat Européen, international baccalauréat, U.S. or Canadian high school diploma or recognized foreign equivalent)
Postgraduate admission: university degree recognized as equivalent to the British undergraduate degree

TUITION FOR FOREIGN STUDENTS:
See GENERAL UNIVERSITY INFORMATION.

TOTAL INSTRUCTIONAL FACULTY:
40 (including 7 professors)

LIBRARY COLLECTIONS:
Total collection—285,000 volumes
Current periodicals—1,100

MUSEUMS AND GALLERIES:
Access to all museums and galleries of the colleges of the University of London

UNIVERSITY PUBLICATIONS:
Slavonic and East European Review, Slovo

DIRECTOR: Prof. M. A. Branch

WARBURG INSTITUTE
Woburn Square, London, WC1H 0AB, England

CHARACTERISTICS OF INSTITUTION:
Senate institute of the University of London

DATE FOUNDED: 1921

TOTAL ENROLLMENT: 50 postgraduate students (including 15 foreign students)

DEGREES AWARDED:
Master of Philosophy (MPhil)
Doctor of Philosophy (PhD)

ACADEMIC PROGRAMS:
History of the Classical Tradition
History of Islamic Influence
History of Philosophy
Renaissance Studies

SPECIAL PROGRAMS:
Cooperative arrangements with universities in several countries

LANGUAGE OF INSTRUCTION: English

ADMISSION REQUIREMENTS FOR FOREIGN STUDENTS:
Postgraduate admission: university degree recognized as equivalent to the British undergraduate degree

TUITION FOR FOREIGN STUDENTS:
See GENERAL UNIVERSITY INFORMATION.

TOTAL INSTRUCTIONAL FACULTY:
8 (including 3 professors)

LIBRARY COLLECTIONS:
Total collection—300,000 volumes
Current periodicals—1,100

MUSEUMS AND GALLERIES:
Access to all museums and galleries of the colleges of the University of London

UNIVERSITY PUBLICATIONS:
Corpus Platonicum Medii Avei, Journal of the Warburg and Courtauld Institutes, Medieval & Renaissance Studies, Warburg Institute surveys and texts, *Warburg Studies*

DIRECTOR: Prof. C. N. J. Mann

LONDON BUSINESS SCHOOL
Sussex Place, Regent's Park, London, NW1 4SA, England

CHARACTERISTICS OF INSTITUTION:
Independent school affiliated with the University of London

DATE FOUNDED: 1965

TOTAL ENROLLMENT: 450 postgraduate students

DEGREES AWARDED:
Master of Science (MSc)
Doctor of Philosophy (PhD)

ACADEMIC PROGRAMS:
Department of Accounting
Department of Accounting and Financial Control
Department of Business Administration
Department of Corporate Finance
Department of Economics
Department of Finance
Department of Human Relations
Department of Industrial Policy
Department of Information Management
Department of International Business
Department of Management and Finance
Department of Marketing
Department of Marketing and International Business
Department of Operations Management
Department of Production Management Statistics and Operational Research
Department of Organizational Behavior
Department of Public Sector Management
Department of Quantitative Methods

SPECIAL PROGRAMS:
Access to the library facilities of the University of London
Cooperative arrangements with universities in several countries

LANGUAGE OF INSTRUCTION: English

ADMISSION REQUIREMENTS FOR FOREIGN STUDENTS:
Postgraduate admission: university degree recognized as equivalent to the British undergraduate degree

TUITION FOR FOREIGN STUDENTS:
See GENERAL UNIVERSITY INFORMATION.

TOTAL INSTRUCTIONAL FACULTY:
55

LIBRARY COLLECTIONS:
Business collections of the libraries of the University of London

MUSEUMS AND GALLERIES:
Access to all museums and galleries of the colleges of the University of London

PRINCIPAL: Prof. G. Bain

LOUGHBOROUGH UNIVERSITY OF TECHNOLOGY
Loughborough, Leicester, LE11 3TU, England

CHARACTERISTICS OF INSTITUTION:
Independent, state-funded university

DATE FOUNDED: 1966

TOTAL ENROLLMENT: 6,000 fulltime students (including 720 foreign students)

DEGREES AWARDED:
Bachelor of Arts (BA)
Bachelor of Engineering (BEng)
Bachelor of Science (BSc)
Master of Arts (MA)
Master of Business Administration (MBA)
Master of Library Studies (MLS)
Master of Philosophy (MPhil)
Master of Science (MSc)
Master of Technology (MTech)

ACADEMIC PROGRAMS:
School of Education and Humanities
School of Engineering
School of Human and Environmental Studies
School of Pure and Applied Sciences

SPECIAL PROGRAMS:
Banking Centre
Centre for Extension Studies
Centre for Research in Social Policy
Computer Centre
Engineering Design Institute
Human Sciences and Advanced Technology (HUSAT)
Institute for Consumer Ergonomics
Institute for Polymer Technology and Materials Engineering
Institute for Surface Science and Technology
Institute of Sport and Recreation Planning and Management
Library and Information Statistics
Loughborough Consultants Ltd.
Loughborough Technology Centre
Cooperative arrangements with universities in several countries

LANGUAGE OF INSTRUCTION: English

ADMISSION REQUIREMENTS FOR FOREIGN STUDENTS:
Secondary school certificate (GCE, SCE, Baccalauréat Européen, international baccalaureate, U.S. or Canadian high school diploma or recognized foreign equivalent)

TUITION FOR FOREIGN STUDENTS:
See GENERAL UNIVERSITY INFORMATION.

TOTAL INSTRUCTIONAL FACULTY:
520

LIBRARY COLLECTIONS:
Total collection—620,000 volumes
Current periodicals—3,900

UNIVERSITY PUBLICATIONS:
Gazette, Annual Report

CHANCELLOR: Sir Denis Rooke

UNIVERSITY OF MANCHESTER
Oxford Road, Manchester, M13 9PL, England

CHARACTERISTICS OF INSTITUTION:
Independent, state-funded university

DATE FOUNDED: 1851

TOTAL ENROLLMENT: 16,000 fulltime students (including 3,000 foreign students)

DEGREES AWARDED:
Bachelor of Architecture (BArch)
Bachelor of Arts (BA)
Bachelor of Dental Surgery (BDS)
Bachelor of Divinity (BD)
Bachelor of Engineering (BEng)
Bachelor of Law (LLB)
Bachelor of Linguistics (BLing)
Bachelor of Medicine (MB ChB)
Bachelor of Music (BMus)
Bachelor of Nursing (BNurs)
Bachelor of Science (BSc)
Bachelor of Social Science (BSocSc)
Bachelor of Town Planning (BTP)
Master of Arts (MA)
Master of Business Administration (MBA)
Master of Dental Surgery (MDS)
Master of Education (MEd)
Master of Law (LLM)
Master of Linguistics (MLing)
Master of Music (MMus)
Master of Music Performance (MMusPerf)
Master of Philosophy (MPhil)
Master of Science (MSc)
Master of Town Planning (MTP)
Medical Doctor (MD)
Doctor of Dental Science (DDSc)
Doctor of Law (LLD)
Doctor of Letters (DLitt)
Doctor of Music (DMus)
Doctor of Social Science (DSocSc)
Doctor of Science (DSc)

ACADEMIC PROGRAMS:
Faculty of Arts
Faculty of Business Administration
Faculty of Economic and Social Studies
Faculty of Education
Faculty of Law
Faculty of Medicine
Faculty of Science

Faculty of Technology
Faculty of Theology

SPECIAL PROGRAMS:
Audio-Visual Service
Centre for Adult and Higher Education
Centre for Anglo Saxon Studies
Centre for Business Research
Centre for 19th Century Studies
Centre for the Study of Chronic Rheumatism
Centre for Youth Studies
Computer Graphics Unit
European Institute for the Media
Faculty of Medicine Computational Group
Granada Centre for Visual Anthropology
Hester Adrian Research Centre
Joint Centre for European Studies
Management Services Unit
Manchester Business School
Manchester Science Park
Manchester-Sheffield School of Probability and Statistics
Marinetech North West
Robert Darbishire Practice
University of Manchester of Computer Centre
University Research Reactor
University Theatre
Cooperative arrangements with universities in several countries

LANGUAGE OF INSTRUCTION: English

ADMISSION REQUIREMENTS FOR FOREIGN STUDENTS:
Secondary school certificate (GCE, SCE, Baccalauréat Européen, international baccalaureate, U.S. or Canadian high school diploma or recognized foreign equivalent)

TUITION FOR FOREIGN STUDENTS:
See GENERAL UNIVERSITY INFORMATION.

TOTAL INSTRUCTIONAL FACULTY:
1,300

LIBRARY COLLECTIONS:
Total collection—3,500,000 volumes (750,000 titles on microfilm)
Current periodicals—9,000

MUSEUMS AND GALLERIES:
Manchester Museum
Whitworth Art Gallery

UNIVERSITY PUBLICATIONS:
Overseas Student's Guide, The Medical School Gazette, Mancunion, publications of the various programs within the university

CHANCELLOR: Prof. J. A. G. Griffith

UNIVERSITY OF NEWCASTLE-UPON-TYNE
Newcastle Upon Tyne, NE1 7RU, England

CHARACTERISTICS OF INSTITUTION:
Independent, state-funded university

DATE FOUNDED: 1851

TOTAL ENROLLMENT: 7,750 fulltime students (including 950 foreign students)

DEGREES AWARDED:
Bachelor of Architecture (BArch)
Bachelor of Arts (BA) in various fields
Bachelor of Dental Surgery (BDS)
Bachelor of Engineering (BEng)
Bachelor of Medical Science (BMedSci)
Bachelor of Medicine (MB ChB)
Bachelor of Science (BSc) in various fields
Master of Arts (MA)
Master of Business Administration (MBA)
Master of Dental Surgery (MDS)
Master of Education (MEd)
Master of Fine Arts (MFA)
Master of Law (LLM)
Master of Letters (MLitt)
Master of Music (MMus)
Master of Philosophy (MPhil)
Master of Science (MSc) in various fields
Medical Doctor (MD)
Doctor of Dental Science (DDSc)
Doctor of Engineering (DEng)
Doctor of Law (LLD)
Doctor of Letters (DLitt)
Doctor of Science (DSc)

ACADEMIC PROGRAMS:
Faculty of Agriculture
Faculty of Arts
Faculty of Education
Faculty of Engineering
Faculty of Law
Faculty of Medicine
Faculty of Science

SPECIAL PROGRAMS:
Audio-Visual Centre
Centre for Continuing Education
Computing Laboratory
Design Unit
Newcastle Technology Centre
School of Education
Teaching Hospitals
Cooperative arrangements with universities in several countries

LANGUAGE OF INSTRUCTION: English

ADMISSION REQUIREMENTS FOR FOREIGN STUDENTS:
Secondary school certificate (GCE, SCE, Baccalauréat Européen, international baccalaureate, U.S. or Ca-

nadian high school diploma or recognized foreign equivalent)

TUITION FOR FOREIGN STUDENTS:
See GENERAL UNIVERSITY INFORMATION.

TOTAL INSTRUCTIONAL FACULTY:
850 (including 125 professors)

LIBRARY COLLECTIONS:
Total collection—700,000 volumes
Current periodicals—5,000

MUSEUMS AND GALLERIES:
Museums of Anthropology, Antiquities, Geology, Natural History, Zoology
Departmental Museums of Anatomy, Chemistry, Dentistry, Geology, Greek, Pathology, Zoology
Hatton Gallery

UNIVERSITY PUBLICATIONS:
Overseas Prospectus, Junior Year Abroad Prospectus, various publications of the programs within the university

CHANCELLOR: The Viscount Ridley

UNIVERSITY OF NOTTINGHAM
University Park, Nottingham, NG7 2RD, England

CHARACTERISTICS OF INSTITUTION:
Independent, state-funded university

DATE FOUNDED: 1881

TOTAL ENROLLMENT: 7,500 fulltime students (including 950 foreign students)

DEGREES AWARDED:
Bachelor of Architecture (BArch)
Bachelor of Arts (BA) in various fields
Bachelor of Education (BEd)
Bachelor of Engineering (BEng)
Bachelor of Law (LLB)
Bachelor of Medical Science (BM BS BMedSci)
Bachelor of Medicine (MB ChB)
Bachelor of Philosophy (BPhil)
Bachelor of Science (BSc) in various fields
Bachelor of Theology (BTh)
Master of Arts (MA)
Master of Business Administration (MBA)
Master of Education (MEd)
Master of Law (LLM)
Master of Musical Art (AMMus)
Master of Philosophy (MPhil)
Master of Science (MSc) in various fields
Master of Theology (MTh)
Doctor of Divinity (DD)

Doctor of Engineering (DEng)
Doctor of Law (LLD)
Doctor of Letters (DLitt)
Doctor of Medicine (DM)
Doctor of Music (DMus)
Doctor of Musical Art (ADMus)
Doctor of Philosophy (PhD)
Doctor of Science (DSc)

ACADEMIC PROGRAMS:
Faculty of Agriculture
Faculty of Arts
Faculty of Education
Faculty of Engineering
Faculty of Law
Faculty of Medicine
Faculty of Science

SPECIAL PROGRAMS:
Cripps Computer Centre
Highfields Science Park
Industrial and Business Liaison Office
School of Education
Cooperative arrangements with universities in several countries

LANGUAGE OF INSTRUCTION: English

ADMISSION REQUIREMENTS FOR FOREIGN STUDENTS:
Secondary school certificate (GCE, SCE, Baccalauréat Européen, international baccalaureate, U.S. or Canadian high school diploma or recognized foreign equivalent)

TUITION FOR FOREIGN STUDENTS:
See GENERAL UNIVERSITY INFORMATION.

TOTAL INSTRUCTIONAL FACULTY:
700 (including 120 professors)

LIBRARY COLLECTIONS:
Total collection—910,000 volumes
Current periodicals—5,000

MUSEUMS AND GALLERIES:
Museum of Archaeology
Departmental Museums

UNIVERSITY PUBLICATIONS:
Newsletter, Gazette, Impact, The Week, Union Handbook

CHANCELLOR: Sir Gordon Hobday

UNIVERSITY OF OXFORD
University Offices, Wellington Square, Oxford, OX1 2JD, England

CHARACTERISTICS OF INSTITUTION:
Independent, state-funded university

DATE FOUNDED: 12th century

TOTAL ENROLLMENT: 13,500 fulltime students (including 2,250 foreign students)

DEGREES AWARDED:
Bachelor of Arts (BA) in various fields
Bachelor of Canon Law (BCL)
Bachelor of Divinity (BD)
Bachelor of Education (BEd)
Bachelor of Fine Arts (BFA)
Bachelor of Medicine (MB ChB)
Bachelor of Music (BMus)
Bachelor of Philosophy (BPhil)
Bachelor of Science (BSc) in various fields
Master of Arts (MA)
Master of Letters (MLitt)
Master of Philosophy (MPhil)
Master of Science (MSc) in various fields
Master of Surgery (MCh)
Master of Studies (MST)
Doctor of Divinity (DD)
Doctor of Engineering (DEng)
Doctor of Canon Law (DCL)
Doctor of Letters (DLitt)
Doctor of Medicine (DM)
Doctor of Music (DMus)
Doctor of Philosophy (PhD)
Doctor of Science (DSc)

ACADEMIC PROGRAMS:
Faculty of Anthropology and Geography
Faculty of Archaeology and the History of Art
Faculty of Biological Sciences
Faculty of Clinical Medicine
Faculty of English Language and Literature
Faculty of Fine Arts
Faculty of Japanese Studies
Faculty of Law
Faculty of Literae Humaniores
Faculty of Mathematical Sciences
Faculty of Medieval and Modern Languages
Faculty of Modern History
Faculty of Modern Middle Eastern Studies
Faculty of Music
Faculty of Oriental Studies
Faculty of Physical Sciences
Faculty of Physiological Sciences
Faculty of Psychological Studies
Faculty of Social Studies
Faculty of Slavonic and East European Studies
Faculty of Theology

SPECIAL PROGRAMS:
Botanical Garden
Centre for Postgraduate Hebrew Studies
Centre for Socio-Legal Studies

Ian Ramsey Centre
NERC Institute of Virology
Oxford Centre for Islamic Studies
Oxford Institute for Energy Studies
Oxford University Observatory
Templeton College, Oxford Centre for Management Studies
Cooperative arrangements with universities in several countries

CONSTITUENT COLLEGES OF THE UNIVERSITY:
All Souls College
Balliol College
Brasenose College
Christ Church
Corpus Christi College
Exeter College
Green College
Hertford College
Jesus College
Keble College
Lady Margaret Hall
Linacre College
Lincoln College
Magdalen College
Merton College
New College
Nuffield College
Oriel College
Pembroke College
The Queens College
St. Anne's College
St. Antony's College
St. Catherine's College
St. Cross College
St. Edmund Hall
St. Hilda's College
St. Hugh's College
St. John's College
St. Peter's College
Somerville College
Trinity College
University College
Wadham College
Wolfson College
Worcester College
Private Halls of the University:
Campion Hall
Greyfriars
Mansfield College
Regent's Park College
St. Benet's Hall
Theological Colleges of the University:
Blackfriars College
Manchester College

Ripon College, Cuddesdon
St. Stephen's House
Wycliffe Hall

LANGUAGE OF INSTRUCTION: English

ADMISSION REQUIREMENTS FOR FOREIGN STUDENTS:
Secondary school certificate (GCE, SCE, Baccalauréat
Européen, international baccalaureate, U.S. or Canadian high school diploma or recognized foreign
equivalent)

TUITION FOR FOREIGN STUDENTS:
See GENERAL UNIVERSITY INFORMATION.

TOTAL INSTRUCTIONAL FACULTY:
1,500 (including 150 professors)

LIBRARY COLLECTIONS:
Total collection—6,000,000 volumes

MUSEUMS AND GALLERIES:
Ashmolean Museum
Pitt Rivers Museum
University Museum
Departmental collections

UNIVERSITY PUBLICATIONS:
*Oxford University Gazette; Statutes, Decrees of the Uni-
versity of Oxford; Examination Decrees; Admission of
Overseas Students; Decrees and Regulations*

CHANCELLOR: Lord Jenkins

UNIVERSITY OF READING
Reading, Berkshire, RG6 2AH, England

CHARACTERISTICS OF INSTITUTION:
Independent, state-funded university

DATE FOUNDED: 1926

TOTAL ENROLLMENT: 8,000 fulltime students (including 1,300 foreign students)

DEGREES AWARDED:
Bachelor of Arts (BA) in various fields
Bachelor of Education (BEd)
Bachelor of Engineering (BEng)
Bachelor of Law (LLB)
Bachelor of Music (BMus)
Bachelor of Philosophy (BPhil)
Bachelor of Science (BSc) in various fields
Master of Agricultural Science (MAS)
Master of Arts (MA)
Master of Education (MEd)
Master of Fine Art(s) (MFA)
Master of Law (LLM)
Master of Music (MMus)
Master of Philosophy (MPhil)
Master of Science (MSc) in various fields

Doctor of Letters (DLitt)
Doctor of Music (DMus)
Doctor of Philosophy (PhD)
Doctor of Science (DSc)

ACADEMIC PROGRAMS:
Faculty of Agriculture and Food
Faculty of Education and Community
Faculty of Letters and Social Sciences
Faculty of Science
Faculty of Urban and Regional Studies

SPECIAL PROGRAMS:
AFRC Institute of Food Research, Reading Labora-
tory
Centre for Agricultural Strategy
Centre for Applied Language Studies
Centre for Environmental Education
College of Estate Management
School of Educational Studies
Statistical Services Centre
University Industrial Liaison Committee
Cooperative arrangements with universities in sev-
eral countries

LANGUAGE OF INSTRUCTION: English

ADMISSION REQUIREMENTS FOR FOREIGN STUDENTS:
Secondary school certificate (GCE, SCE, Baccalauréat
Européen, international baccalaureate, U.S. or Canadian high school diploma or recognized foreign
equivalent)

TUITION FOR FOREIGN STUDENTS:
See GENERAL UNIVERSITY INFORMATION.

TOTAL INSTRUCTIONAL FACULTY:
725 (including 100 professors)

LIBRARY COLLECTIONS:
Total collection—500,000 volumes
Current periodicals—4,100

MUSEUMS AND GALLERIES:
Museums of Archaeology, English Rural Life, His-
tory, Zoology
Departmental museums

UNIVERSITY PUBLICATIONS:
*Bulletin, University Diary, Spark, Junior Year Abroad
Prospectus*

CHANCELLOR: The Rt. Hon. Lord Sherfield

UNIVERSITY OF SHEFFIELD
Sheffield, S10 2TN, England

CHARACTERISTICS OF INSTITUTION:
Independent, state-funded university

DATE FOUNDED: 1897

TOTAL ENROLLMENT: 8,050 fulltime students (including 725 foreign students)

DEGREES AWARDED:
Bachelor of Arts (BA) in various fields
Bachelor of Dental Science (BDS)
Bachelor of Education (BEd)
Bachelor of Engineering (BEng)
Bachelor of Law (LLB)
Bachelor of Medicine (MB, ChB)
Bachelor of Metallurgy (BMet)
Bachelor of Music (BMus)
Bachelor of Philosophy (BPhil)
Bachelor of Science (BSc) in various fields
Bachelor of Science Technology (BScTech)
Master of Arts (MA)
Master of Business Administration (MBA)
Master of Dental Surgery (MDS)
Master of Education (MEd)
Master of Law (LLM)
Master of Medical Science (MMedSci)
Master of Metallurgy (MMet)
Master of Music (MMus)
Master of Philosophy (MPhil)
Master of Science (MSc) in various fields
Master of Science Technology (MScTech)
Medical Doctor (MD)
Doctor of Law (LLD)
Doctor of Letters (DLitt)
Doctor of Metallurgy (DMet)
Doctor of Music (DMus)
Doctor of Philosophy (PhD)
Doctor of Science (DSc)
Doctor of Science Technology (DScTech)

ACADEMIC PROGRAMS:
Faculty of Architectural Studies
Faculty of Arts
Faculty of Educational Studies
Faculty of Engineering
Faculty of Law
Faculty of Medicine and Dentistry
Faculty of Social Sciences

SPECIAL PROGRAMS:
Artificial Intelligence Research Unit
Centre for Continuing Vocational Education
Centre for Criminological and Socio-Legal Studies
Centre for Development Planning Studies
Centre for English Cultural Tradition and Language
Centre for Extension Studies
Centre for Japanese Studies
Centre for Statistical Research
Commercial and Industrial Development Bureau
Consultancy and Research Unit
Drama Studio
Educational Research Centre

Harris Birthright Centre of Reproductive Medicine
Institute for Biomolecular Research
Institute for Folklore Studies in Britain and Canada
Institute for Korean Studies
Institute for Space Biomedicine
Joint Unit for Social Services Unit
Medical Care Research Centre
MRC/ESRC Social and Applied Psychology Unit
National Transputer Support Unit
Natural Environmental Research Council Unit of Comparative Plant Ecology
Policy Studies Centre Research Institute for Photosynthesis
SERC Central Facility for III-V Semiconductors
Sheffield Science Park
Structural Integrity Research Unit
Wolfson Institute of Biotechnology
Cooperative arrangements with universities in several countries

LANGUAGE OF INSTRUCTION: English

ADMISSION REQUIREMENTS FOR FOREIGN STUDENTS:
Secondary school certificate (GCE, SCE, Baccalauréat Européen, international baccalaureate, U.S. or Canadian high school diploma or recognized foreign equivalent)

TUITION FOR FOREIGN STUDENTS:
See GENERAL UNIVERSITY INFORMATION.

TOTAL INSTRUCTIONAL FACULTY:
800 (including 115 professors)

LIBRARY COLLECTIONS:
Total collection—965,000 volumes
Current periodicals—5,000

MUSEUMS AND GALLERIES:
Departmental museums

UNIVERSITY PUBLICATIONS:
Newsletter, Pocket Diary, Darts, Arrows, North Wing, publications of the various programs of the university

CHANCELLOR: The Rt. Hon. The Lord Dainton of Hallam Moors

UNIVERSITY OF SOUTHAMPTON
Highfield, Southampton, SO9 5NH, England

CHARACTERISTICS OF INSTITUTION:
Independent, state-funded university

DATE FOUNDED: 1902

TOTAL ENROLLMENT: 6,800 fulltime students (including 625 foreign students)

DEGREES AWARDED:
Bachelor of Arts (BA) in various fields
Bachelor of Education (BEd)
Bachelor of Engineering (BEng)
Bachelor of Law (LLB)
Bachelor of Medicine (MB, ChB)
Bachelor of Nursing (BN)
Bachelor of Science (BSc) in various fields
Bachelor of Theology (BTh)
Master of Arts (MA)
Master of Arts (Education) (MA[Ed])
Master of Law (LLM)
Master of Music (MMus)
Master of Philosophy (MPhil)
Master of Science (MSc) in various fields
Doctor of Law (LLD)
Doctor of Medicine (DM, MS)
Doctor of Letters (DLitt)
Doctor of Music (DMus)
Doctor of Philosophy (PhD)
Doctor of Science (DSc)

ACADEMIC PROGRAMS:
Faculty of Arts
Faculty of Educational Studies
Faculty of Engineering and Applied Science
Faculty of Law
Faculty of Mathematical Studies
Faculty of Medicine
Faculty of Science
Faculty of Social Sciences

SPECIAL PROGRAMS:
Computing Service
Consultancy Units
Language Centre
Postgraduate Medical Education Unit
Science Park teaching hospitals
Teaching Media Department
Cooperative arrangements with universities in several countries

LANGUAGE OF INSTRUCTION: English

ADMISSION REQUIREMENTS FOR FOREIGN STUDENTS:
Secondary school certificate (GCE, SCE, Baccalauréat Européen, international baccalaureate, U.S. or Canadian high school diploma or recognized foreign equivalent)

TUITION FOR FOREIGN STUDENTS:
See GENERAL UNIVERSITY INFORMATION.

TOTAL INSTRUCTIONAL FACULTY:
750 (including 125 professors)

LIBRARY COLLECTIONS:
Total collection—800,000 volumes
Current periodicals—6,600

MUSEUMS AND GALLERIES:
Museum of Geology

UNIVERSITY PUBLICATIONS:
New Reporter, Hartley News, Viewpoint, Wessex News

CHANCELLOR: The Rt. Hon. The Earl Jellicoe

UNIVERSITY OF SUSSEX
Falmer, Brighton, Sussex, BN1 9RH, England

CHARACTERISTICS OF INSTITUTION:
Independent, state-funded university

DATE FOUNDED: 1961

TOTAL ENROLLMENT: 4,850 fulltime students (including 950 foreign students)

DEGREES AWARDED:
Bachelor of Arts (BA) in various fields
Bachelor of Engineering (BEng)
Bachelor of Science (BSc) in various fields
Master of Arts (MA)
Master of Philosophy (MPhil)
Master of Science (MSc) in various fields
Master of Social Work (MSW)
Doctor of Letters (DLitt)
Doctor of Music (DMus)
Doctor of Philosophy (PhD)
Doctor of Science (DSc)

ACADEMIC PROGRAMS:
School of African and Asian Studies
School of Biological Sciences
School of Chemistry and Molecular Sciences
School of Cognitive Sciences
School of Cultural and Community Studies
School of Education
School of Engineering and Applied Sciences
School of English and American Studies
School of European Studies
School of Mathematical and Physical Sciences
School of Social Science

SPECIAL PROGRAMS:
Centre for Medical Research
Computing Service
Gardner Centre for the Arts
International Economics Research Centre
Institute for Development Studies
Institute for Manpower Studies
Media Service Unit
Science Park
Science Policy Research Unit
Unit for Comparative Research on Industrial Relations

Cooperative arrangements with universities in several countries

LANGUAGE OF INSTRUCTION: English

ADMISSION REQUIREMENTS FOR FOREIGN STUDENTS:
Secondary school certificate (GCE, SCE, Baccalauréat Européen, international baccalaureate, U.S. or Canadian high school diploma or recognized foreign equivalent)

TUITION FOR FOREIGN STUDENTS:
See GENERAL UNIVERSITY INFORMATION.

TOTAL INSTRUCTIONAL FACULTY:
400 (including 65 professors)

LIBRARY COLLECTIONS:
Total collection—500,000 volumes
Current periodicals—3,500

MUSEUMS AND GALLERIES:
Barlow Collection of Chinese Ceramics
Tom Harrisson Mass-Observation Archive of British Social History

UNIVERSITY PUBLICATIONS:
Falmer, Bulletin, publications of the various programs within the university

CHANCELLOR:
The Earl of March and Kinrara

UNIVERSITY OF WARWICK
Coventry, CV4 7AL, England

CHARACTERISTICS OF INSTITUTION:
Independent, state-funded university

DATE FOUNDED: 1965

TOTAL ENROLLMENT: 8,000 fulltime students (including 800 foreign students)

DEGREES AWARDED:
Bachelor of Arts (BA) in various fields
Bachelor of Education (BEd)
Bachelor of Engineering (BEng)
Bachelor of Law (LLB)
Bachelor of Science (BSc) in various fields
Master of Arts (MA)
Master of Business Administration (MBA)
Master of Education (MEd)
Master of Law (LLM)
Master of Philosophy (MPhil)
Master of Science (MSc) in various fields
Doctor of Letters (DLitt)
Doctor of Law (LLD)
Doctor of Philosophy (PhD)
Doctor of Science (DSc)

ACADEMIC PROGRAMS:
Faculty of Arts
Faculty of Educational Studies
Faculty of Science
Faculty of Sociology

SPECIAL PROGRAMS:
Austin Rover Advanced Technology Centre
Centre for Advanced Materials Technology
Centre for Caribbean Studies
Centre for Corporate Strategy and Change
Centre for Educational Development, Appraisal and Research
Centre for Education and Industry
Centre for English Language Teaching
Centre for Manufacturing Renewal
Centre for Microengineering and Metrology
Centre for Nuclear Magnetic Resonance
Centre for Research in Ethnic Relations
Centre for Research in Philosophy and Literature
Centre for the Study of Social History
Control and Instrument Systems Centre
Control Theory Centre
Development Economics Research Centre
European Humanities Research Centre
House of Commons Parliamentary Unit
Industrial Relations Research Unit
Institute for Employment Research
Institute for Management Research and Development
Institute for Mass Spectrometry
Legal Research Unit
ESRC Macroeconomic Modelling Bureau
Mathematics Education Research Centre
Mathematics Research Centre
Non-Linear Systems Laboratory
Nursing Policy Studies Centre
Small Business Centre
Science Park
Cooperative arrangements with universities in several countries

LANGUAGE OF INSTRUCTION: English

ADMISSION REQUIREMENTS FOR FOREIGN STUDENTS:
Secondary school certificate (GCE, SCE, Baccalauréat Européen, international baccalaureate, U.S. or Canadian high school diploma or recognized foreign equivalent)

TUITION FOR FOREIGN STUDENTS:
See GENERAL UNIVERSITY INFORMATION.

TOTAL INSTRUCTIONAL FACULTY:
590 (including 95 professors)

LIBRARY COLLECTIONS:
Total collection—675,000 volumes
Current periodicals—4,000

MUSEUMS AND GALLERIES:
Arts Centre
Mead Art Gallery

UNIVERSITY PUBLICATIONS:
Publications of the various programs within the university

CHANCELLOR: Sir Shridath Ramphal

UNIVERSITY OF YORK
Heslington, York, YO1 5DD, England

CHARACTERISTICS OF INSTITUTION:
Independent, state-funded university

DATE FOUNDED: 1963

TOTAL ENROLLMENT: 4,000 fulltime students (including 275 foreign students)

DEGREES AWARDED:
Bachelor of Arts (BA) in various fields
Bachelor of Engineering (BEng)
Bachelor of Science (BSc) in various fields
Master of Arts (MA)
Master of Philosophy (MPhil)
Master of Science (MSc) in various fields
Master of Social Work (MSW)
Doctor of Letters (DLitt)
Doctor of Music (DMus)
Doctor of Philosophy (PhD)
Doctor of Science (DSc)

ACADEMIC PROGRAMS:
Centre for Medieval Studies
Department of Archaeology
Department of Biology
Department of Chemistry
Department of Computer Services
Department of Economics and Related Studies
Department of Education
Department of Electronics
Department of English and Related Literature
Department of History
Department of History of Art
Department of Language and Linguistics
Department of Mathematics
Department of Music
Department of Philosophy
Department of Physics
Department of Politics
Department of Psychology
Department of Social Policy and Social Work
Department of Sociology

SPECIAL PROGRAMS:
Audio-Visual Centre

Beijer Institute Centre for Resource Assessment and Management
Borthwick Institute of Historical Research
Cancer Research Unit
Centre for Cell and Tissue Research
Electronics Service
Environmental Archaeology Unit
Institute of Advanced Architectural Studies
Institute for Applied Biology
Institute for Research in the Social Sciences
Language Teaching Centre
Microtest Research Ltd.
Norwegian Study Centre
Tropical Marine Research Unit
York Electronics Centre
Cooperative arrangements with universities in several countries

LANGUAGE OF INSTRUCTION: English

ADMISSION REQUIREMENTS FOR FOREIGN STUDENTS:
Secondary school certificate (GCE, SCE) Baccalauréat Européen, international baccalaureate, U.S. or Canadian high school diploma or recognized foreign equivalent)

TUITION FOR FOREIGN STUDENTS:
See GENERAL UNIVERSITY INFORMATION.

TOTAL INSTRUCTIONAL FACULTY:
410 (including 60 professors)

LIBRARY COLLECTIONS:
Total collection—350,000 volumes
Current periodicals—2,000

UNIVERSITY PUBLICATIONS:
Publications of the various programs within the university

CHANCELLOR: The Lord Swann

THE UNIVERSITIES OF NORTHERN IRELAND

QUEEN'S UNIVERSITY OF BELFAST
University Road, Belfast, BT7 1NN, Northern Ireland

CHARACTERISTICS OF INSTITUTION:
State-administered, academically autonomous university

DATE FOUNDED: 1845

TOTAL ENROLLMENT: 7,000 fulltime students (including 315 foreign students)

DEGREES AWARDED:
Bachelor of Agriculture (BAgr)
Bachelor of Arts (BA) in various fields
Bachelor of Dental Surgery (BDS)

Bachelor of Divinity (BD)
Bachelor of Education (BEd)
Bachelor of Engineering (BEng)
Bachelor of Law (LLB)
Bachelor of Obstetrics (BAO)
Bachelor of Science (BSc) in various fields
Bachelor of Social Science (BSSc)
Bachelor of Surgery (BCh)
Master of Accounting (MAcc)
Master of Arts (MA)
Master of Dental Surgery (MDS)
Master of Education (MEd)
Master of Law (LLM)
Master of Library Studies (MLS)
Master of Medical Science (MMedSc)
Master of Philosophy (MPhil)
Master of Science (MSc) in various fields
Master of Social Work (MSW)
Master of Surgery (MCh)
Master of Theology (MTh)
Medical Doctor (MD)
Doctor of Divinity (DD)
Doctor of Law (LLD)
Doctor of Literature (DLit)
Doctor of Music (DMus)
Doctor of Philosophy (PhD)
Doctor of Social Science (DSSc)
Doctor of Science (DSc)

ACADEMIC PROGRAMS:
Faculty of Agriculture and Food Science
Faculty of Arts
Faculty of Economics and Social Sciences
Faculty of Education
Faculty of Engineering
Faculty of Law
Faculty of Medicine
Faculty of Science
Faculty of Theology

SPECIAL PROGRAMS:
Arts Centre
Audio-Visual Aids
Centre for Information Management
Institute of Continuing Education
Institute of Irish Studies
Institute for Professional Legal Studies
Northern Ireland Centre for Genetic Engineering (NICGENE)
Northern Ireland Technology Centre
Palaeoecology Centre
QUBIS Ltd.
Teacher Centre
Cooperative arrangements with universities in several countries

RECOGNIZED COLLEGES OF THE UNIVERSITY:
Edgehill Theological College

Irish Baptist College
Loughry College of Agriculture and Food Technology
St. Mary's College
Stranmillis College
Union Theological College

LANGUAGE OF INSTRUCTION: English

ADMISSION REQUIREMENTS FOR FOREIGN STUDENTS:
Secondary school certificate (GCE, SCE, Baccalauréat Européen, international baccalaureate, U.S. or Canadian high school diploma or recognized foreign equivalent)

TUITION FOR FOREIGN STUDENTS:
See GENERAL UNIVERSITY INFORMATION.

TOTAL INSTRUCTIONAL FACULTY:
700 (including 90 professors)

LIBRARY COLLECTIONS:
Total collection—960,000 volumes
Current periodicals—5,100

UNIVERSITY PUBLICATIONS:
Institute of Professioinal Legal Studies Handbook, publications of the various programs within the university

CHANCELLOR: Sir Rowland Wright

UNIVERSITY OF ULSTER
University House, Cromore Road, Coleraine, County Londonderry, BT52 1SA, Northern Ireland

CHARACTERISTICS OF INSTITUTION:
State-administrated, academically autonomous university

DATE FOUNDED: 1984

TOTAL ENROLLMENT: 8,000 fulltime students (including 900 foreign students)

DEGREES AWARDED:
Bachelor of Arts (BA) in various fields
Bachelor of Education (BEd)
Bachelor of Engineering (BEng)
Bachelor of Law (LLB)
Bachelor of Letters (BLitt)
Bachelor of Music (BMus)
Bachelor of Science (BSc) in various fields
Bachelor of Technology (BTech)
Master of Arts (MA)
Master of Business Administration (MBA)
Master of Education (MEd)
Master of Engineering (MEng)
Master of Philosophy (MPhil)
Master of Science (MSc) in various fields
Doctor of Letters (DLitt)

Doctor of Music (DMus)
Doctor of Philosophy (PhD)
Doctor of Science (DSc)

ACADEMIC PROGRAMS:
Adult and Continuing Education
Faculty of Art and Design
Faculty of Business and Management
Faculty of Education
Faculty of Humanities
Faculty of Science and Technology
Faculty of Social and Health Sciences
Institute of Informatics
Women's Studies

SPECIAL PROGRAMS:
Computing Service
Educational Technology
Freshwater Biological Field Station
Industrial Liaison
Interdisciplinary Research Centres
Meteorological Station
Teaching hospitals
Cooperative arrangements with universities in several countries

LANGUAGE OF INSTRUCTION: English

ADMISSION REQUIREMENTS FOR FOREIGN STUDENTS:
Secondary school certificate (GCE, SCE, Baccalauréat Européen, international baccalaureate, U.S. or Canadian high school diploma or recognized foreign equivalent)

TUITION FOR FOREIGN STUDENTS:
See GENERAL UNIVERSITY INFORMATION.

TOTAL INSTRUCTIONAL FACULTY:
760 (including 40 professors)

LIBRARY COLLECTIONS:
Total collection—550,000 volumes
Current periodicals—5,500

UNIVERSITY PUBLICATIONS:
Publications of the various programs within the university

CHANCELLOR: The Rt. Hon. The Lord Grey of Naunton

THE UNIVERSITIES OF SCOTLAND

UNIVERSITY OF ABERDEEN
Aberdeen, AB9 1FX, Scotland

CHARACTERISTICS OF INSTITUTION:
Independent, state-funded university

DATE FOUNDED: 1495

TOTAL ENROLLMENT: 7,250 fulltime students (including 850 foreign students)

DEGREES AWARDED:
Bachelor of Agricultural Science ordinary and honours (BScAgr.ord & hon)
Bachelor of Arts ordinary (BA. ord) in various fields
Bachelor of Divinity (BD)
Bachelor of Engineering ordinary and honours (BEng.ord & hon)
Bachelor of Engineering Science ordinary and honours (BEngSc.ord & hon)
Bachelor of Forestry Science ordinary and honours (BForSc.ord & hon)
Bachelor of Land Economy ordinary and honours (BLE.ord & hon)
Bachelor of Law ordinary and honours (LLB.ord & hon)
Bachelor of Medical Biology (BMedBiol)
Bachelor of Medicine (MB)
Bachelor of Music ordinary and honours (BMus.ord & hon)
Bachelor of Science honours (BSc.hon) in various fields
Bachelor of Surgery (BCh)
Bachelor of Theology ordinary and honours (BTh.ord & hon)
Master of Arts ordinary and honours (MA.ord & hon) in various fields
Master of Education honours (MEd.hon)
Master of Land Economy (MLE)
Master of Law (LLM)
Master of Letters (MLitt)
Master of Medical Science (MMedSci)
Master of Music (MMus)
Master of Philosophy (MPhil)
Master of Science (MSc) in various fields
Master of Surgery (MCh)
Medical Doctor (MD)
Doctor of Law (LLD)
Doctor of Letters (DLitt)
Doctor of Music (DMus)
Doctor of Philosophy (PhD)
Doctor of Science (DSc)

ACADEMIC PROGRAMS:
Faculty of Arts and Divinity
Faculty of Biological Science
Faculty of Clinical Medicine
Faculty of Economic and Social Sciences
Faculty of Engineering, Mathematical and Physical Sciences
Faculty of Law

SPECIAL PROGRAMS:
Aberdeen University Research and Industrial Services Ltd. (AURIS)

Centre of Defence Studies
Centre for the Study of Religions
Computing Centre
Institute of Terrestrial Ecology (NERC)
Interdisciplinary institutes and centres
Language Laboratory
Macaulay Land Use Research Institute
Marine Laboratory of the Department of Agriculture and Fisheries for Scotland
Rowett Research Institute
Science and Technology Regional Organization (SATRO) for North Scotland
Science Park
Scottish Universities Management Services and Efficiency Unit
Scottish Universities Research and Reactor Centre
Torry Research Station (MAFF)
Cooperative arrangements with universities in several countries

LANGUAGE OF INSTRUCTION: English

ADMISSION REQUIREMENTS FOR FOREIGN STUDENTS:
Secondary school certificate (GCE, SCE, Baccalauréat Européen, international baccalaureate, U.S. or Canadian high school diploma or recognized foreign equivalent)

TUITION FOR FOREIGN STUDENTS:
See GENERAL UNIVERSITY INFORMATION.

TOTAL INSTRUCTIONAL FACULTY:
870 (including 85 professors)

LIBRARY COLLECTIONS:
Total collection—1,000,000 volumes
Current periodicals—4,550

MUSEUMS AND GALLERIES:
University Museum, Marischal College (anthropological collections, including Egyptian antiquities, Chinese bronzes and ceramics)
Departmental museums

UNIVERSITY PUBLICATIONS:
Aberdeen University Review, Aberdeen University Study Series, Newsletter, Alma Mater, publications of the various programs within the university

CHANCELLOR: Sir Kenneth Alexander

UNIVERSITY OF DUNDEE
Dundee, DD1 4HN, Scotland

CHARACTERISTICS OF INSTITUTION:
Independent, state-funded university

DATE FOUNDED: 1881

TOTAL ENROLLMENT: 4,000 fulltime students (including 500 foreign students)

DEGREES AWARDED:
Bachelor of Accounting ordinary (BAcc.ord)
Bachelor of Dental Science (BDS)
Bachelor of Engineering honours (BEng.hon)
Bachelor of Law ordinary and honours (LLB.ord & hon)
Bachelor of Medical Science honours (BMSc.hon)
Bachelor of Medicine (MB)
Bachelor of Science ordinary and honours (BSc.ord & hon) in various fields
Bachelor of Surgery (BCh)
Master of Accounting (MAcc)
Master of Arts ordinary and honours (MA.ord & hon) in various fields
Master of Business Administration (MBA)
Master of Dental Science (MDSc)
Master of Education (MEd)
Master of Law (LLM)
Master of Medical Science (MMSc)
Master of Music (MMus)
Master of Philosophy (MPhil)
Master of Public Health (MPH)
Master of Science (MSc) in various fields
Master of Social Science (MSSc)
Master of Social Work (MSW)
Master of Surgery (MCh)
Master of Doctor (MD)
Doctor of Dental Science (DDSc)
Doctor of Law (LLD)
Doctor of Letters (DLitt)
Doctor of Philosophy (PhD)
Doctor of Science (DSc)

ACADEMIC PROGRAMS:
Faculty of Arts and Social Science
Faculty of Environmental Studies
Faculty of Law
Faculty of Medicine and Dentistry
Faculty of Science and Engineering

SPECIAL PROGRAMS:
Botanic Garden
Computing Facilities
Centre for Medical Education
Centre for Petroleum and Mineral Law Studies
Science Park
Scottish Universities Management Services and Efficiency Unit
Teaching hospitals
Cooperative arrangements with universities in several countries

LANGUAGE OF INSTRUCTION: English

ADMISSION REQUIREMENTS FOR FOREIGN STUDENTS:
Secondary school certificate (GCE, SCE, Baccalauréat Européen, international baccalaureate, U.S. or Ca-

nadian high school diploma or recognized foreign equivalent)

TUITION FOR FOREIGN STUDENTS:
See GENERAL UNIVERSITY INFORMATION.

TOTAL INSTRUCTIONAL FACULTY:
340 (including 75 professors)

LIBRARY COLLECTIONS:
Total collection—475,000 volumes
Current periodicals—4,000

MUSUEMS AND GALLERIES:
Departmental Museums of Dentistry, Geology, Medicine
Natural History

UNIVERSITY PUBLICATIONS:
Annual Report, Diary, Annasach, Contact, publications of the various programs within the university

CHANCELLOR: The Rt. Hon. The Earl of Dalhousie

UNIVERSITY OF EDINBURGH
Old College, South Bridge, Edinburgh, EH8 9YL, Scotland

CHARACTERISTICS OF INSTITUTION:
State-funded, private university

DATE FOUNDED: 1583

TOTAL ENROLLMENT: 12,000 fulltime students (including 1,250 foreign students)

DEGREES AWARDED:
Bachelor of Arts (BA) in various fields
Bachelor of Commerce honours (BCom.hon)
Bachelor of Dental Science (BDS)
Bachelor of Divinity ordinary and honours (BD.ord & hon)
Bachelor of Engineering honours (BEng.hon)
Bachelor of Law ordinary and honours (LLB.ord & hon)
Bachelor of Medicine (MB)
Bachelor of Music honours (BMus.hon)
Bachelor of Science ordinary and honours (BSc.ord & hon) in various fields
Bachelor of Surgery (BCh)
Bachelor of Veterinary Medicine and Surgery (BVM&S)
Master of Arts general and honours (MA.gen & hon) in various fields
Master of Business Administration (MBA)
Master of Education (MEd)
Master of Landscape Architecture (MLA)
Master of Law (LLM)
Master of Letters (MLitt)
Master of Music (MMus)

Master of Philosophy (MPhil)
Master of Science (MSc) in various fields
Master of Surgery (MCh)
Master of Theology (MTh)
Medical Doctor (MD)
Doctor of Dental Surgery (DDS)
Doctor of Music (DMus)
Doctor of Law (LLD)
Doctor of Letters (DLitt)
Doctor of Philosophy (PhD)
Doctor of Science (DSc)

ACADEMIC PROGRAMS:
Faculty of Arts
Faculty of Divinity
Faculty of Law
Faculty of Medicine
Faculty of Music
Faculty of Science
Faculty of Social Sciences
Faculty of Veterinary Medicine

SPECIAL PROGRAMS:
Artificial Intelligence Applications Institute
Centre for Canadian Studies
Centre for Cognitive Science
Centre for Criminology and the Social and Philosophical Study of Law
Centre for Speech Technology Research
Centre for the Study of Christianity in the Non-Western World
Computing Service
East Scotland College of Agriculture
Edinburgh School of Environmental Design
Institute for Advanced Studies in the Humanities
Institute for Applied Language
Royal Observatory
Scottish Universities Management Services and Efficiency Unit
Scottish Universities Research and Reactor Centre
Teaching hospitals
UnivEd Technologies, Ltd.
University theatre
Cooperative arrangements with universities in several countries

CONSTITUENT COLLEGE OF THE UNIVERSITY:
New College

LANGUAGE OF INSTRUCTION: English

ADMISSION REQUIREMENTS FOR FOREIGN STUDENTS:
Secondary school certificate (GCE, SCE, Baccalauréat Européen, international baccalaureate, U.S. or Canadian high school diploma or recognized foreign equivalent)

TUITION FOR FOREIGN STUDENTS:
See GENERAL UNIVERSITY INFORMATION.

TOTAL INSTRUCTIONAL FACULTY:
1,350 (including 160 professors)

LIBRARY COLLECTIONS:
Total collection—over 2,000,000 volumes
Current periodicals—over 12,000

MUSEUMS AND GALLERIES:
Museums of Agriculture, Anatomy, Chemistry, Communications, Entomology & Forest Zoology (Waterhouse Collection of Coleoptera), Fine Art (Torrie Collection of 16th and 17th Century Paintings and Sculpture), Forestry, Geology, Material Medicines (Duncan and Christison medicinal and food substances), Music and Musical Instruments (collections include Russell, Galpin and others), Natural History, Natural Philosophy, Obstetrics (Simpson Collection), Pathology, Physiology, Surgery and the Robson Medical archives

UNIVERSITY PUBLICATIONS:
Annual Report, Bulletin, Faculty Programmes, publications of the various programs within the university

CHANCELLOR: HRH The Duke of Edinburgh

UNIVERSITY OF GLASGOW
Glasgow, G12 8QQ, Scotland

CHARACTERISTICS OF INSTITUTION:
Independent, state-funded university

DATE FOUNDED: 1451

TOTAL ENROLLMENT: 13,500 fulltime students (including 1,500 foreign students)

DEGREES AWARDED:
Bachelor of Accounting (BAcc)
Bachelor of Architecture (BArch)
Bachelor of Arts ordinary and honours (BA.ord & hon) in various fields
Bachelor of Dental Science (BDS)
Bachelor of Divinity ordinary and honours (BD.ord & hon)
Bachelor of Education ordinary (BEd.ord)
Bachelor of Engineering honours (BEng.hon)
Bachelor of Law (LLB)
Bachelor of Medicine (MB)
Bachelor of Music (BMus)
Bachelor of Nursing (BN)
Bachelor of Science ordinary and honours (BSc.ord & hon) in various fields
Bachelor of Surgery (BCh)
Bachelor of Technical Education (BTechEd)
Bachelor of Veterinary Medicine and Surgery (BVM&S)
Master of Accounting (MAcc)
Master of Applied Science (MAppSci)

Master of Architecture (MArch)
Master of Arts general and honours (MA.gen & hon) in various fields
Master of Business Administration (MBA)
Master of Education (MEd)
Master of Engineering (MEng)
Master of Law (LLM)
Master of Letters (MLitt)
Master of Music (MMus)
Master of Nursing (MN)
Master of Philosophy (MPhil)
Master of Public Health (MPH)
Master of Science (MSc) in various fields
Master of Theology (MTh)
Master of University Administration (MUA)
Master of Veterinary Medicine (MVM)
Medical Doctor (MD)
Doctor of Dental Surgery (DDS)
Doctor of Music (DMus)
Doctor of Law (LLD)
Doctor of Letters (DLitt)
Doctor of Philosophy (PhD)
Doctor of Science (DSc)
Doctor of Veterinary Medicine (DVM)
Doctor of Veterinary Surgery (DVS)

ACADEMIC PROGRAMS:
Faculty of Arts
Faculty of Divinity
Faculty of Engineering
Faculty of Law and Financial Studies
Faculty of Medicine
Faculty of Science
Faculty of Social Sciences
Faculty of Veterinary Medicine

SPECIAL PROGRAMS:
Beatson Institute for Cancer Research
Building Services Unit
Confederation of Scottish Business Schools
Engineering Research Design Centre
Hetherington Language Centre
Institute of Soviet and East European Studies
John Logie Baird Centre for Research in Television and Film
Medical Research Council of Blood Pressure Unit
Medical Research Council Medical Sociology Unit
Medical Research Council Virology Unit
Science and Engineering Research Council Particle Physics Unit (Physics and Astronomy)
Scottish Science and Technology Forum
Scottish Universities Management Services and Efficiency Unit
Scottish Universities Research and Reactors Centre
Social Paediatric and Obstetric Research Group
Teaching hospitals
University Audio-Visual Services

University Marine Biological Station
Wellcome History of Medicine Unit
Wellcome Surgical Research Institute
West of Scotland Science Park
Cooperative arrangements with universities in several countries

ASSOCIATED COLLEGE OF THE UNIVERSITY:
West of Scotland Agricultural College

LANGUAGE OF INSTRUCTION: English

ADMISSION REQUIREMENTS FOR FOREIGN STUDENTS:
Secondary school certificate (GCE, SCE, Baccalauréat Européen, international baccalaureate, U.S. or Canadian high school diploma or recognized foreign equivalent)

TUITION FOR FOREIGN STUDENTS:
See GENERAL UNIVERSITY INFORMATION.

TOTAL INSTRUCTIONAL FACULTY:
1,250 (including 200 professors)

LIBRARY COLLECTIONS:
Total collection—over 1,500,000 volumes
Current periodicals—over 7,000

MUSEUMS AND GALLERIES:
Hunterian Art Gallery
Hunterian Museum

UNIVERSITY PUBLICATIONS:
Annual Report of the University Court, Bulletin, Glasgow University Guardian, Avenue, Newsletter, publications of the various programs within the university

CHANCELLOR: Sir Alexander Cairncross

HERIOT-WATT UNIVERSITY
Riccarton, Edinburgh, EH14 4AS, Scotland

CHARACTERISTICS OF INSTITUTION:
Independent, state-funded university

DATE FOUNDED: 1821

TOTAL ENROLLMENT: 5,000 fulltime students (including 570 foreign students

DEGREES AWARDED:
Bachelor of Architecture (BArch)
Bachelor of Arts ordinary and honours (BA.ord & hon) in various fields
Bachelor of Engineering honours (BEng.hon)
Bachelor of Science ordinary and honours (BSc.ord & hon) in various fields
Master of Architecture (MArch)
Master of Business Administration (MBA)
Master of Design (MDes)
Master of Engineering (MEng)
Master of Fine Arts (MFA)

Master of Letters (MLitt)
Master of Science (MSc) in various fields
Master of Urban and Regional Planning (MURP)
Doctor of Engineering (DEng)
Doctor of Letters (DLitt)
Doctor of Philosophy (PhD)
Doctor of Science (DSc)

ACADEMIC PROGRAMS:
Faculty of Art and Design
Faculty of Economic and Social Studies
Faculty of Engineering
Faculty of Environmental Studies
Faculty of Science

SPECIAL PROGRAMS:
Computer Application Services
Computer Centre
Confederation of Scottish Business Schools
Engineering Design Research Centre
Esmee Fairbairn Research Centre
Heriot-Watt Business School
International Centre for Brewing and Distilling
Institute for Offshore Engineering
Medical Laser Unit
Orkney Water Test Centre
Research Park
Scottish Human Computer Interaction Centre
Scottish Universities Management Services and Efficiency Unit
Television Centre
Video Course Services International
Unilink
Cooperative arrangements with universities in several countries

ASSOCIATED INSTITUTIONS OF THE UNIVERSITY:
Edinburgh College of Art
Scottish College of Textiles

LANGUAGE OF INSTRUCTION: English

ADMISSION REQUIREMENTS FOR FOREIGN STUDENTS:
Secondary school certificate (GCE, SCE, Baccalauréat Européen, international baccalaureate, U.S. or Canadian high school diploma or recognized foreign equivalent)

TUITION FOR FOREIGN STUDENTS:
See GENERAL UNIVERSITY INFORMATION.

TOTAL INSTRUCTIONAL FACULTY:
410 (including 55 professors)

LIBRARY COLLECTIONS:
Total collection—130,000 volumes
Current periodicals—2,250

UNIVERSITY PUBLICATIONS:
Heriot-Watt University News, Watt's On, publications of the various programs within the university

CHANCELLOR: The Rt. Hon. The Lord Thomson of Monifieth

UNIVERSITY OF ST. ANDREWS
College Gate, North Street, St. Andrews, Fife, KY16 9AJ, Scotland

CHARACTERISTICS OF INSTITUTION:
Independent, state-funded university

DATE FOUNDED: 1411

TOTAL ENROLLMENT: 4,000 fulltime students (including 500 foreign students)

DEGREES AWARDED:
Bachelor of Divinity ordinary and honours (BD.ord & hon) in various fields
Bachelor of Science ordinary and honours (BSc.ord & hon) in various fields
Master of Arts ordinary and honours (MA.ord & hon) in various fields
Master of Letters (MLitt)
Master of Philosophy (MPhil)
Master of Science (MSc) in various fields
Master of Theology ordinary (MTh.ord)
Doctor of Letters (DLitt)
Doctor of Philosophy (PhD)
Doctor of Science (DSc)

ACADEMIC PROGRAMS:
Faculty of Arts
Faculty of Divinity
Faculty of Science

SPECIAL PROGRAMS:
Centre for Philosophy and Public Affairs
Computing Services
Institute of Amerindian Studies
Institute of Maritime Archaeology
School of Abbasid Studies
Science Park
Scottish Universities Management Services and Efficiency Unit
Scottish Universities Research and Reactor Centre
St. John's Centre for Advanced Historical Research
The Central
Wolfson Institute of Luminescence
Cooperative arrangements with universities in several countries

LANGUAGE OF INSTRUCTION: English

ADMISSION REQUIREMENTS FOR FOREIGN STUDENTS:
Secondary school certificate (GCE, SCE, Baccalauréat Européen, international baccalaureate, U.S. or Canadian high school diploma or recognized foreign equivalent)

TUITION FOR FOREIGN STUDENTS:
See GENERAL UNIVERSITY INFORMATION.

TOTAL INSTRUCTIONAL FACULTY:
320 (including 50 professors)

LIBRARY COLLECTIONS:
Total collection—775,000 volumes
Current periodicals—4,200

MUSEUMS AND GALLERIES:
Museums of Anthropology, Anatomy, Geology, Natural History
Crawford Art Centre

UNIVERSITY PUBLICATIONS:
Handbook of Awards for Postgraduate Studies and Research, Mosaics: A Journal of Internationalism, Forum for Modern Language Studies, Research and Industry, The Chronicle, publications of the various programs within the university

CHANCELLOR: Sir Kenneth Dover

UNIVERSITY OF STIRLING
Stirling, FK9 4LA, Scotland

CHARACTERISTICS OF INSTITUTION:
Independent, state-funded university

DATE FOUNDED: 1967

TOTAL ENROLLMENT: 3,800 fulltime students (including 550 foreign students)

DEGREES AWARDED:
Bachelor of Accounting general and honours (BAcc. gen & hon)
Bachelor of Arts general and honours (BA.gen & hon)
Bachelor of Education (BEd)
Bachelor of Science ordinary and honours (BSc.ord & hon) in various fields
Master of Arts (MA) in various fields
Master of Business Administration (MBA)
Master of Education (MEd)
Master of Letters (MLitt)
Master of Philosophy (MPhil)
Master of Science (MSc) in various fields
Doctor of Letters (DLitt)
Doctor of Philosophy (PhD)
Doctor of Science (DSc)

ACADEMIC PROGRAMS:
Centre for English Language Teaching
Centre for Japanese Studies
Department of Accountancy and Business Law
Department of Biochemistry and Cell Biology
Department of Business and Management
Department of Chemistry and Physics
Department of Commonwealth Studies

Department of Computing Science
Department of Ecology
Department of Economics
Department of Education
Department of English Studies
Department of Environmental Science
Department of Film and Media Studies
Department of French
Department of German
Department of History
Department of Mathematics
Department of Music
Department of Philosophy
Department of Political Studies
Department of Psychology
Department of Religious Studies
Department of Sociology and Social Policy
Department of Spanish
Department of Technological Economics
Institute of Aquaculture

SPECIAL PROGRAMS:
Centre for Bibliographical Studies
Centre of Commonwealth Studies
Centre for English Language Teaching
Centre for Japanese Studies
Centre for Physical Education and Sports Development
Centre for Scottish Literature and Culture
Computer Unit
Confederation of Scottish Business Schools
Industrial Projects Service
Innovation Park
Institute of Aquaculture
Institute of Retail Studies
MacRoberts Arts Centre
Research Institute for Film and Media Studies
Scottish Enterprise Foundation
Scottish Universities Management Services and Efficiency Unit
Social Work Research Centre
Technological Economics Research Unit
University Field Station
Cooperative arrangements with universities in several countries

LANGUAGE OF INSTRUCTION: English

ADMISSION REQUIREMENTS FOR FOREIGN STUDENTS:
Secondary school certificate (GCE, SCE, Baccalauréat Européen, international baccalaureate, U.S. or Canadian high school diploma or recognized foreign equivalent)

TUITION FOR FOREIGN STUDENTS:
See GENERAL UNIVERSITY INFORMATION.

TOTAL INSTRUCTIONAL FACULTY:
400 (including 55 professors)

LIBRARY COLLECTIONS:
Total collection—400,000 volumes
Current periodicals—2,500

UNIVERSITY PUBLICATIONS:
Study Abroad brochure, publications of the various programs within the university

CHANCELLOR: Lord Balfour of Burleigh

UNIVERSITY OF STRATHCLYDE
16 Richmond Street, Glasgow, G1 1XQ, Scotland

CHARACTERISTICS OF INSTITUTION:
Independent, state-funded university

DATE FOUNDED: 1796

TOTAL ENROLLMENT: 8,600 fulltime students (including 1,210 foreign students)

DEGREES AWARDED:
Bachelor of Architecture (BArch)
Bachelor of Arts general and honours (BA.gen & hon) in various fields
Bachelor of Education (BEd)
Bachelor of Engineering ordinary and honours (BEng.ord & hon)
Bachelor of Law general and honours (LLB.gen & hon)
Bachelor of Science ordinary and honours (BSc.ord & hon) in various fields
Master of Arts (MA) in various fields
Master of Business Administration (MBA)
Master of Engineering (MEng)
Master of Law (LLM)
Master of Letters (MLitt)
Master of Philosophy (MPhil)
Master of Science (MSc) in various fields
Doctor of Business Administration (DBA)
Doctor of Letters (DLitt)
Doctor of Philosophy (PhD)
Doctor of Science (DSc)

ACADEMIC PROGRAMS:
Faculty of Arts and Social Studies
Faculty of Engineering
Faculty of Science
Strathclyde Business School

SPECIAL PROGRAMS:
ABACUS (Architecture & Building Aids Computer Unit Strathclyde)
Audio-Visual Services
Centre for Professional Legal Studies
Centre for the Study of Public Policy
Computer-Aided Design Centre
Computer Centre

David Livingstone Institute of Overseas Development Studies

Energy Studies Unit

Engineering Applications Centre

Engineering Design Research Centre

European Policies Research Centre

Fraser of Allander Institute for Research on the Scottish Economy

John Logie Baird Centre for Research in Television and Film

National Centre for Training and Education in Prosthetics and Orthotics

Scottish Hotel School

Scottish Human Computer Interaction Centre

Scottish Local Authorities Management Centre

Scottish Universities Management Services and Efficiency Unit

Scottish Universities Research and Reactor Centre

Strathclyde Business School

Strathclyde Institute for Drug Research

Strathclyde Science and Technology Forum

West of Scotland Science Park

Cooperative arrangements with universities in several countries

ASSOCIATED INSTITUTE OF THE UNIVERSITY:
Turing Institute

LANGUAGE OF INSTRUCTION: English

ADMISSION REQUIREMENTS FOR FOREIGN STUDENTS:
Secondary school certificate (GCE, SCE, Baccalauréat Européen, international baccaalaureate, U.S. or Canadian high school diploma or recognized foreign equivalent)

TUITION FOR FOREIGN STUDENTS:
See GENERAL UNIVERSITY INFORMATION.

TOTAL INSTRUCTIONAL FACULTY:
700 (including 110 professors)

LIBRARY COLLECTIONS:
Total collection—400,000 volumes
Current periodicals—4,100

MUSEUMS AND GALLERIES:
Collins Gallery

UNIVERSITY PUBLICATIONS:
Telegraph, Continuing Education Programme, publications of the various programs within the university

CHANCELLOR: The Rt. Hon. Lord Todd of Trumpington

THE UNIVERSITIES OF WALES

UNIVERSITY OF WALES
University Registry, King Edward VII Avenue, Cathay's Park, Cardiff, CF1 3NS, Wales

CHARACTERISTICS OF INSTITUTION:
Independent, state-funded university

DATE FOUNDED: 1893

TOTAL ENROLLMENT: 21,000 fulltime students—total enrollment of the constituent colleges of the University—(including 3,000 foreign students)

DEGREES AWARDED:
Bachelor of Architecture (BArch)
Bachelor of Arts ordinary and honours (BA.ord & hon) in various fields
Bachelor of Dental Surgery (BDS)
Bachelor of Divinity (BD)
Bachelor of Education (BEd)
Bachelor of Engineering (BEng)
Bachelor of Law (LLB)
Bachelor of Medicine and Surgery (MB BCH)
Bachelor of Music (BMus)
Bachelor of Nursing (BN)
Bachelor of Pharmacy (BPharm)
Bachelor in the Faculty of Economic and Social Studies (BScEcon)
Bachelor of Science general, ordinary and honours (BSc.gen, ord & hon) in various fields
Master of Arts (MA) in various fields
Master of Business Administration (MBA)
Master of Dental Science (MScD)
Master of Education (MEd)
Master of Engineering (MEng)
Master in the Faculty of Economic and Social Studies (MScEcon)
Master of Law (LLM)
Master of Librarianship (MLib)
Master of Music (MMus)
Master of Nursing (MN)
Master of Pharmacy (MPharm)
Master of Philosophy (MPhil)
Master of Science (MSc) in various fields
Master of Surgery (MCh)
Master of Theology (MTh)
Medical Doctor (MD)
Doctor of Divinity (DD)
Doctor of Dental Surgery (DChD)
Doctor of Law (LLD)
Doctor of Letters (DLitt)
Doctor of Music (DMus)
Doctor of Philosophy (PhD)
Doctor in the Faculty of Economic and Social Studies (DScEcon)
Doctor of Science (DSc)

ACADEMIC PROGRAMS:
See the academic programs sections of the constituent colleges.

SPECIAL PROGRAMS:
Board of Celtic Studies

Cooperative arrangements with universities in several countries

CONSTITUENT COLLEGES OF THE UNIVERSITY:
University College of Wales, Aberystwyth
University College of North Wales, Bangor
University College of Swansea
University of Wales College of Cardiff
University of Wales College of Medicine
St. David's University College, Lampeter

LANGUAGE OF INSTRUCTION: English

ADMISSION REQUIREMENTS FOR FOREIGN STUDENTS:
Secondary school certificate (GCE, SCE, Baccalauréat Européen, international baccaluareate, U.S. or Canadian high school diploma or recognized foreign equivalent)

TUITION FOR FOREIGN STUDENTS:
See GENERAL UNIVERSITY INFORMATION.

TOTAL INSTRUCTIONAL FACULTY:
The sum of all total instructional faculty of the constituent colleges of the University

LIBRARY COLLECTIONS:
Total collection—the sum of all library collections of the constituent colleges

MUSEUMS AND GALLERIES:
See the Museums and Galleries sections of the individual constituent colleges.

UNIVERSITY PUBLICATIONS:
Studia Celtica, Bulletin, Llen Cymru, Efrydiau Athronyddol, Y Gwyddonydd, Geiriadur Prifysgol Cymru, publications of the constituent colleges

CHANCELLOR: HRH The Prince Charles, The Prince of Wales

UNIVERSITY COLLEGE OF WALES, ABERYSTWYTH
P.O. Box 2, Aberystwyth, Dyfed, SY23 2AX, Wales

CHARACTERISTICS OF INSTITUTION:
Constituent college of the University of Wales

DATE FOUNDED: 1872

TOTAL ENROLLMENT: 3,125 fulltime students—2,600 undergraduate students, 525 postgraduate students—(including 450 foreign students)

DEGREES AWARDED:
Bachelor of Arts honours (BA.hon) in various fields
Bachelor of Divinity (BD)
Bachelor of Education (BEd)
Bachelor of Law (LLB)
Bachelor of Librarianship (BLib)
Bachelor of Music (BMus)

Bachelor in the Faculty of Economic and Social Studies (BScEcon)
Bachelor of Science honours (BSc.hon) in various fields
Master of Arts (MA) in various fields
Master of Education (MEd)
Master of the Faculty of Economic and Social Studies (MScEcon)
Master of Law (LLM)
Master of Librarianship (MLib)
Master of Music (MMus)
Master of Philosophy (MPhil)
Master of Science (MSc) in various fields
Master of Theology (MTh)
Doctor of Law (LLD)
Doctor of Letters (DLitt)
Doctor of Philosophy (PhD)
Doctor of Science (DSc)

ACADEMIC PROGRAMS:
Faculty of Arts
Faculty of Economic and Social Studies
Faculty of Education
Faculty of Law
Faculty of Science

SPECIAL PROGRAMS:
Aberystwyth and Lampeter School of Theology
Cefn Llan Science Park
Centre for Advanced Welsh and Celtic Studies
Welsh Plant Breeding Station
Cooperative arrangements with universities in several countries

LANGUAGE OF INSTRUCTION: English

ADMISSION REQUIREMENTS FOR FOREIGN STUDENTS:
Secondary school certificate (GCE, SCE, Baccalauréat Européen, international baccalaureate, U.S. or Canadian high school diploma or recognized foreign equivalent)

TUITION FOR FOREIGN STUDENTS:
See GENERAL UNIVERSITY INFORMATION.

TOTAL INSTRUCTIONAL FACULTY:
290 (including 45 professors)

LIBRARY COLLECTIONS:
Total collection—475,000 volumes
Current periodicals—2,850

MUSEUMS AND GALLERIES:
Museums of Archaeology, Botany, Chemistry, Ethnography, Geography, Geology, Physics, Zoology
Gallery of Arts and Crafts

UNIVERSITY PUBLICATIONS:
A Guide for Overseas Students at a British University, Courier, Dragon, several departmental publications

PRESIDENT: Sir Melvyn Rosser

UNIVERSITY COLLEGE OF NORTH WALES, BANGOR
Bangor, Gwynedd, LL57 2DG, Wales

CHARACTERISTICS OF INSTITUTION:
Constituent college of the University of Wales

DATE FOUNDED: 1884

TOTAL ENROLLMENT: 3,000 fulltime students—2,450 undergraduate students, 550 postgraduate students—(including 350 foreign students)

DEGREES AWARDED:
Bachelor of Arts ordinary and honours (BA.ord & hon) in various fields
Bachelor of Divinity (BD)
Bachelor of Education (BEd)
Bachelor of Engineering honours (BEng.hon)
Bachelor of Music (BMus)
Bachelor of Science ordinary and honours (BSc.ord & hon) in various fields
Master of Arts (MA) in various fields
Master of Education (MEd)
Master of Engineering (MEng)
Master of Law (LLM)
Master of Librarianship (MLib)
Master of Music (MMus)
Master of Philosophy (MPhil)
Masterof Science (MSc) in various fields
Master of Theology (MTh)
Medical Doctor (MD)
Doctor of Divinity (DD)
Doctor of Letters (DLitt)
Doctor of Philosophy (PhD)
Doctor of Science (DSc)

ACADEMIC PROGRAMS:
Faculty of Arts
Faculty of Science

SPECIAL PROGRAMS:
Applied Computing Technology Unit
Bangor School of Theology
Centre for Applicable Mathematics
Centre for Applied Statistics
Centre for Arid Zone Studies
Centre for Social Policy, Research and Development
Development Trust
Forestry Products Technology Research Unit
Industrial Development Bangor—UNCW
Institute of Economic Research
Institute of European Finance
Institute of Molecular and Biomolecular Electronics
Marinetech North West
Menai Technology Enterprise Centre (MENTEC)
Northwest Universities Management Services Unit
Research Centre Wales
Social Work Practice Centre
Unit for Coastal and Estuarine Studies

Welsh National Centre for Religious Education
Cooperative arrangements with universities in several countries

LANGUAGE OF INSTRUCTION: English

ADMISSION REQUIREMENTS FOR FOREIGN STUDENTS:
Secondary school certificate (GCE, SCE, Baccalauréat Européen, international baccalaureate, U.S. or Canadian high school diploma or recognized foreign equivalent)

TUITION FOR FOREIGN STUDENTS:
See GENERAL UNIVERSITY INFORMATION.

TOTAL INSTRUCTIONAL FACULTY:
275 (including 35 professors)

LIBRARY COLLECTIONS:
Total collection—400,000 volumes
Current periodicals—3,600

MUSEUMS AND GALLERIES:
Museum of Welsh Antiquities
Museum of Zoology
University Art Gallery

UNIVERSITY PUBLICATIONS:
Research Report, Prospectus on Teaching through the Medium of Welsh, Pont, publications of the various programs within the college

CHANCELLOR: HRH The Prince Charles, The Prince of Wales

UNIVERSITY COLLEGE OF SWANSEA
Singleton Park, Swansea, SA2 8PP, Wales

CHARACTERISTICS OF INSTITUTION:
Constituent college of the University of Wales

DATE FOUNDED: 1920

TOTAL ENROLLMENT: 4,500 fulltime students—3,500 undergraduate students, 1,000 postgraduate students—(including 650 foreign students)

DEGREES AWARDED:
Bachelor of Arts honours (BA.hon) in various fields
Bachelor of Engineering (BEng)
Bachelor in the Faculty of Economic and Social Studies (BScEcon)
Bachelor of Science honours (BSc.hon) in various fields
Master of Arts (MA) in various fields
Master of Education (MEd)
Master of Engineering (MEng)
Master in the Faculty of Economics and Social Studies (MScEcon)
Master of Philosophy (MPhil)
Master of Science (MSc) in various fields

Doctor of Letters (DLitt)
Doctor of Philosophy (PhD)
Doctor of Science (DSc)

ACADEMIC PROGRAMS:
Faculty of Arts
Faculty of Economic and Social Studies
Faculty of Educational Studies
Faculty of Engineering
Faculty of Science

SPECIAL PROGRAMS:
Centre for Applied Language Studies
Centre for Development Studies
Centre for East European and Russian Studies
Closed Circuit Television Centre
Computer Centre
Innovation Centre
Institute of Health Care Studies
Swansea Tribology Centre
Taliesan Arts Centre
Cooperative arrangements with universities in several countries

LANGUAGE OF INSTRUCTION: English

ADMISSION REQUIREMENTS FOR FOREIGN STUDENTS:
Secondary school certificate (GCE, SCE, Baccalauréat Européen, international baccalaureate, U.S. or Canadian high school diploma or recognized foreign equivalent)

TUITION FOR FOREIGN STUDENTS:
See GENERAL UNIVERSITY INFORMATION.

TOTAL INSTRUCTIONAL FACULTY:
500 (including 70 professors)

LIBRARY COLLECTIONS:
Total collection—525,000
Periodicals—3,750

MUSEUMS AND GALLERIES:
Department of Classics Museum

UNIVERSITY PUBLICATIONS:
Y Darian, Bad Press, publications of the various programs within the college

PRESIDENT: The Rt. Hon. The Lord Callaghan

UNIVERSITY OF WALES COLLEGE OF CARDIFF
P.O. Box 68, Cardiff, CF1 3XA, Wales

CHARACTERISTICS OF INSTITUTION:
Constituent college of the University of Wales

DATE FOUNDED: 1988

TOTAL ENROLLMENT: 8,000 fulltime students—5,500 undergraduate students, 2,500 postgraduate students—(including 1,250 foreign students)

DEGREES AWARDED:
Bachelor of Architecture (BArch)
Bachelor of Arts ordinary and honours (BA.ord & hon) in various fields
Bachelor of Divinity (BD)
Bachelor of Engineering (BEng)
Bachelor in the Faculty of Economic and Social Studies (BScEcon)
Bachelor of Law (LLB)
Bachelor of Music (BMus)
Bachelor of Pharmacy (BPharm)
Bachelor of Science honours (BSc.hon) in various fields
Master of Arts (MA) in various fields
Master of Business Administration (MBA)
Master of Education (MEd)
Master of Engineering (MEng)
Master of Law (LLM)
Master of Music (MMus)
Master of Philosophy (MPhil)
Master of Science (MSc) in various fields
Master of Theology (MTh)
Doctor of Philosophy (PhD)
Doctor of Science (DSc)

ACADEMIC PROGRAMS:
Faculty of Business Studies and Law
Faculty of Engineering and Environmental Design
Faculty of Health and Life Sciences
Faculty of Humanities
Faculty of Physical Sciences

SPECIAL PROGRAMS:
Cardiff School of Theology
Cardiff University Industry Centre
China Studies Centre
Computing Centre
Cooperative arrangements with universities in several countries

LANGUAGE OF INSTRUCTION: English

ADMISSION REQUIREMENTS FOR FOREIGN STUDENTS:
Secondary school certificaate (GCE, SCE, Baccalauréat Européen, international baccalaureate, U.S. or Canadian high school diploma or recognized foreign equivalent)

TUITION FOR FOREIGN STUDENTS:
See GENERAL UNIVERSITY INFORMATION.

TOTAL INSTRUCTIONAL FACULTY:
750 (including 115 professors)

LIBRARY COLLECTIONS:
Total collection—675,000
Current periodicals—4,650

UNIVERSITY PUBLICATIONS:
Gair Rhydd, publications of the various programs within the university

CHANCELLOR: The Rt. Hon. Lord Crickhowell

UNIVERSITY OF WALES COLLEGE OF MEDICINE
Heath Park, Cardiff, CF4 4XN, Wales

CHARACTERISTICS OF INSTITUTION:
Constituent college of the University of Wales

DATE FOUNDED: 1931

TOTAL ENROLLMENT: 1,100 fulltime students—825 undergraduate students, 275 postgraduate students—(including 120 foreign students)

DEGREES AWARDED:
Bachelor of Dental Surgery (BDS)
Bachelor of Medicine (MB)
Bachelor of Nursing (BN)
Bachelor of Surgery (BCh)
Master of Dental Science (MDSc)
Master of Nursing (MN)
Master of Pharmacy (MPharm)
Master of Science (MSc) in various fields
Master of Surgery (MCh)
Doctor of Dental Surgery (DChD)
Doctor of Philosophy (PhD)
Doctor of Science (DSc)

ACADEMIC PROGRAMS:
Department of Anaesthetics
Department of Basic Dental Science
Department of Cardiology
Department of Child Dental Health
Department of Child Health
Department of Conservative Dentistry
Department of Dermatology
Department of Diagnostic Radiology
Department of Epidemiology and Community Medicine
Department of Forensic Medicine
Department of General Practice
Department of Geriatrics
Department of Haematology
Department of Medical Biochemistry
Department of Medical Computing and Statistics
Department of Medical Illustration
Department of Medical Microbiology
Department of Medicine
Department of Obstetrics and Gynaecology
Department of Ophthalmology
Department of Oral Surgery, Medicine and Pathology
Department of Oto-Rhino-Laryngology
Department of Pathology

Department of Pharmacology and Therapeutics
Department of Physical Medicine
Department of Prosthetic Dentistry
Department of Psychological Medicine
Department of Radiotherapy
Department of Renal Medicine
Department of Surgery
Department of Traumatic and Orthopaedic Surgery
Department of Tuberculosis and Chest Diseases

SPECIAL PROGRAMS:
Teaching hospitals
Tenovus Institute for Cancer Research
Cooperative arrangements with universities in several countries

LANGUAGE OF INSTRUCTION: English

ADMISSION REQUIREMENTS FOR FOREIGN STUDENTS:
Secondary school certificate (GCE, SCE, Baccalauréat Européen, international baccalaureate, U.S. or Canadian high school diploma or recognized foreign equivalent)

TUITION FOR FOREIGN STUDENTS:
See GENERAL UNIVERSITY INFORMATION.

TOTAL INSTRUCTIONAL FACULTY:
225 (including 30 professors)

LIBRARY COLLECTIONS:
Total collection—65,000
Current Periodicals—1,000

UNIVERSITY PUBLICATIONS:
The Leech

PRESIDENT: The Rt. Hon. The Lord Justice Tasker Watkins

ST. DAVID'S UNIVERSITY COLLEGE, LAMPETER
Lampeter, Dyfed, SA48, 7ED, Wales

CHARACTERISTICS OF INSTITUTION:
Constituent college of the University of Wales

DATE FOUNDED: 1822

TOTAL ENROLLMENT: 850 fulltime students—780 undergraduates students, 70 postgraduate students—(including 25 foreign students)

DEGREES AWARDED:
Bachelor of Arts (BA)
Bachelor of Divinity (BD)
Master of Arts (MA)
Master of Philosophy (MPhil)
Master of Theology (MTh)
Doctor of Divinity (DD)
Doctor of Letters (DLitt)
Doctor of Philosophy (PhD)

ACADEMIC PROGRAMS:
Department of Classics
Department of Continuing Education and External Liaison
Department of English
Department of French
Department of Geography
Department of German
Department of History
Department of Informatics
Department of Philosophy
Department of Theology and Religious Studies
Department of Welsh

SPECIAL PROGRAMS:
Aberystwyth and Lampeter School of Theology
Audio-Visual Unit
Computer Unit
Language laboratories
Cooperative arrangements with universities in several countries

LANGUAGE OF INSTRUCTION: English

ADMISSION REQUIREMENTS FOR FOREIGN STUDENTS:
Secondary school certificate (GCE, SCE, Baccalauréat Européen, international baccaluareate, U.S. or Canadian high school diploma or recognized foreign equivalent)

TUITION FOR FOREIGN STUDENTS:
See GENERAL UNIVERSITY INFORMATION.

TOTAL INSTRUCTIONAL FACULTY:
70 (including 7 professors)

LIBRARY COLLECTIONS:
Total collection—125,000
Current Periodicals—1,050

UNIVERSITY PUBLICATIONS:
Trivium, Cambria, DOG

PRINCIPAL: The Rt Hon. Lord Morris of Castle Morris

THE UNIVERSITIES OF EASTERN EUROPE

It would be impossible at this point in time to make general statements about the universities of Czechoslovakia, Hungary, Poland, the U.S.S.R. and Yugoslavia. At the time of this book's proposal, Eastern Europe, including the German Democratic Republic, was firmly within the framework of the Warsaw Pact and the Council for Mutual Economic Assistance (C.M.E.A.) (both organizations were dominated by the Soviet sphere of influence). The political and cultural influence of the Soviet Union would have made it possible to generalize about the respective state systems of education and their policies toward foreign students at the university level. However, recent events saw the aforementioned countries undergoing severe political dislocations, the ultimate effect of which remains undecided.

Only the German Democratic Republic has developed a more coherent university system over the past two years, as it was reunited with its western neighbor to become Germany once again in October, 1990. Thus, the universities of what was the German Democratic Republic (G.D.R.) have been integrated with the universities of what was the Federal Republic of Germany (F.R.G.) in the chapter "Germany."

The aim of the following section on the universities of Eastern Europe is simply to give interested readers an idea of the specific characteristics of the institutions and their academic programs. Much of the information could be subject to change in the near future, especially the tuition fees, living expenses and academic programs. Foreign students who desire further information on higher educational opportunities in Czechoslovakia, Hungary, Poland, the Soviet Union or Yugoslavia are strongly advised to contact the respective individual universities themselves. Additional information can be obtained from the diplomatic mission of the student's home country in the prospective East European state and/or the embassy or consulate of the East European state within the student's home country. Prospective foreign students should consult all of these sources of information in order to obtain the most accurate picture of the academic opportunities available in Eastern Europe.

THE UNIVERSITIES OF CZECHOSLOVAKIA

NOTE ON CZECHOSLOVAKIAN UNIVERSITIES: Czechoslovakian universities have undergone dramatic changes to their ideological orientation since 1990. For instance, the Institutes of Marxism-Leninism at most universities have either been removed or are scheduled for serious restructuring in 1991. The institution that was Univerzita Jana Evangelisty Purkyne has been changed to Univerzita Masarykova. The Vysoká Škole Eckonomiká v Prazé has informed applicants that changes to the administration and the courses available are to take place in 1991. Prospective students are advised to contact Czechoslovakian schools directly.

UNIVERZITA KARLOVA
(Charles University)
116 36 Prague 1, Ovocný trh 5, Czechoslovakia

CHARACTERISTICS OF INSTITUTION:
State-run, nonprofit university

DATE FOUNDED: 1349

TOTAL ENROLLMENT: 26,000

DEGREES AWARDED:
Absolvent, graduate and title of Doctor in various fields
   four–five years by examen rigorosum
Absolvent, graduate and title of doctor in medicine or dentistry (MUDr)
   five–six years required
Candidatus scientiarum
   a minimum of three years of additional study required
Doctor scientiarum (DrSc)
   by thesis after Candidatus scientiarum

ACADEMIC PROGRAMS:
Faculty of Education
Faculty of Journalism
Faculty of Law
Faculty of Mathematics and Physics
Faculty of Medical Hygiene
Faculty of Medicine
Faculty of Pediatrics
Faculty of Pharmacy
Faculty of Philosophy
Faculty of Physical Training and Sport
Faculty of Sciences
Department of Linguistics (for foreign students)

SPECIAL PROGRAMS:
Institute of Slavonic Studies

Institute of Marxism-Leninism (may be removed in 1991)
Cooperative arrangements with 29 other universities

LANGUAGE OF INSTRUCTION: Czech

ADMISSION REQUIREMENTS FOR FOREIGN STUDENTS:
Secondary school certificate, or recognized foreign equivalent, and entrance examination

TUITION FOR FOREIGN STUDENTS:
None

TOTAL INSTRUCTIONAL FACULTY:
2,840

LIBRARY COLLECTIONS:
Faculty libraries—3,350,000 volumes

UNIVERSITY PUBLICATIONS:
Acta Universitatis Carolinae, Historia Universitatis Carolinae Pragensis, Prague Bulletin of Mathematical Linguistics, Psychologie v Ekonomicke Praxi

RECTOR: Prof. Radim Palouš

UNIVERZITA MASARYKOVA
(Masaryk University)
601 77 Brno, Burešova 20, Czechoslovakia

CHARACTERISTICS OF INSTITUTION:
State-run, nonprofit university

DATE FOUNDED: 1919

TOTAL ENROLLMENT: 8,610

DEGREES AWARDED:
Absolvent, graduate and title of doctor in various fields
   four–five years by examen rigorosum
Absolvent, graduate and title of Doctor in medicine or dentistry (MUDr)
   five–six years required
Candidatus scientiarum
   a minimum of three years of additional study required
Doctor scientiarum (DrSc)
   By thesis after Candidatus scientiarum

ACADEMIC PROGRAMS:
Faculty of Education
Faculty of Law
Faculty of Medicine
Faculty of Natural Sciences
Faculty of Pedagogics
Faculty of Philosophy

Department of Languages
Department of Physical Education

SPECIAL PROGRAMS:
Institute of Computer Sciences
Cooperative arrangements with 11 other universities

LANGUAGE OF INSTRUCTION: Czech

ADMISSION REQUIREMENTS FOR FOREIGN STUDENTS:
Secondary school certificate or secondary technical school certificate, or recognized foreign equivalent, and interview

TUITION FOR FOREIGN STUDENTS:
None

TOTAL INSTRUCTIONAL FACULTY:
971

LIBRARY COLLECTIONS:
University library—1,268,000 volumes

UNIVERSITY PUBLICATIONS:
Universitas, Scripta Medica, Archivum Mathematicum

RECTOR: Prof. Dr. Milan Jelínek

UNIVERZITA PALACKÉHO V OLOMOUCI
(Palacký University at Olomouci)
7771 47 Olomouc, Olomouc 10, Czechoslovakia

CHARACTERISTICS OF INSTITUTION:
State-run, nonprofit university

DATE FOUNDED: 1573

TOTAL ENROLLMENT: 7,200 students

DEGREES AWARDED:
Absolvent and graduate in philosophy and science
  five years required
Absolvent and graduate in medicine or dentistry
  five–six years required
Title of Doctor (by examen rigorosum after Absolvent) in various fields
Teaching qualifications
  five years
Candidatus scientiarum (CSc)
  a minimum of three years of additional study required
Doctor scientiarum (DrSc)
  by thesis after Candidatus scientiarum

ACADEMIC PROGRAMS:
Faculty of Education
Faculty of Medicine
Faculty of Natural Sciences
Faculty of Philosophy (including psychology)

SPECIAL PROGRAMS:
Computer Center

Institute of Marxism-Leninism (may be removed in
  1991)
Research Institute of Higher Nervous Activity
Human Reproduction Research Laboratory
Optics Laboratory
Cooperative arrangements with 14 other universities

LANGUAGES OF INSTRUCTION: Czech and Slovak

ADMISSION REQUIREMENTS FOR FOREIGN STUDENTS:
Secondary school certificate, or recognized foreign equivalent, and entrance examination

TUITION FOR FOREIGN STUDENTS:
None

TOTAL INSTRUCTIONAL FACULTY:
690

LIBRARY COLLECTIONS:
Total collection—390,000 volumes

UNIVERSITY PUBLICATIONS:
Acta Universitatis Palackianae

RECTOR: Prof. Ph. Dr. Josef Jařab

ČESKÉ VYSOKÉ UČENÍ TECHNICKÉ PRAZE
(Czech Technical University)
166 35 Prague, Zikova 4, Czechoslovakia

CHARACTERISTICS OF INSTITUTION:
State-run, nonprofit university

DATE FOUNDED: 1707

TOTAL ENROLLMENT: 17,200 students

DEGREES AWARDED:
Professional title of Inzenyr in various fields
  four–five years required
Candidatus scientiarum (CSc)
  a minmum of three years of additional study accompanied by a thesis required
Doctor scientiarum (DrSc)
  by thesis after Candidatus scientiarum

ACADEMIC PROGRAMS:
Faculty of Architecture
Faculty of Civil Engineering
Faculty of Electrical Engineering
Faculty of Mechanical Engineering

SPECIAL PROGRAMS:
Computer Center
Building Research Institute
Engineering Research Institute
Institute of Architectural Planning and Development
Institute of Marxism-Leninism (may be removed in
  1991)

Cooperative arrangements with seven other universities

LANGUAGE OF INSTRUCTION: Czech

ADMISSION REQUIREMENTS FOR FOREIGN STUDENTS:
Secondary school certificate, or recognized foreign equivalent, and entrance examination

TUITION FOR FOREIGN STUDENTS:
None

TOTAL INSTRUCTIONAL FACULTY:
1,526

LIBRARY COLLECTIONS:
Faculty libraries—50,000–70,000 volumes

UNIVERSITY PUBLICATIONS:
Acta Polytechnica, Prace Cvut v Praze, Informacni Zpravodaj Cvut

RECTOR: Prof. Ing. S. Hanzl

VYSOKÁ ŠKOLA EKONOMICKÁ V PRAZE
(Prague School of Economics)
130 67 Prague 3, Nam. Ant. Západockého 4,
Czechoslovakia

CHARACTERISTICS OF INSTITUTION:
State-run, nonprofit university

DATE FOUNDED: 1953

TOTAL ENROLLMENT: 13,000 students

DEGREES AWARDED:
Professional title of Inzenyr

four years required
Candidatus scientiarum (CSc)
a minimum of three years of additional study required
Doctor scientiarum (DrSc)
by thesis after Candidatus scientiarum

ACADEMIC PROGRAMS:
Faculty of Commerce
Faculty of Management
Faculty of Natural Economy
Faculty of Production Economics — all subject to change in 1991

SPECIAL PROGRAMS:
Computer Center
Institute of Marxism-Leninism (may be removed in 1991)
Cooperative arrangements with 13 other universities

LANGUAGE OF INSTRUCTION: Czech

ADMISSION REQUIREMENTS FOR FOREIGN STUDENTS:
Secondary school certificate, or recognized foreign equivalent, and entrance examination

TUITION FOR FOREIGN STUDENTS:
None

TOTAL INSTRUCTIONAL FACULTY:
600

LIBRARY COLLECTIONS:
Central library—760,000 volumes

UNIVERSITY PUBLICATIONS:
Acta Oeconomica Pragensia, Informační Bulletin

RECTOR: Prof. Ing. Antonín Brůžek

THE UNIVERSITIES OF HUNGARY

EÖTVÖS LORÁND TUDOMÁNYEGYETEM
(Loránd Eötvös University)
1364 Budapest V, Egyetem-tér 1–3, POB 109, Hungary

CHARACTERISTICS OF INSTITUTION:
State-run, nonprofit university

DATE FOUNDED: 1635

TOTAL ENROLLMENT: 8,800 students

DEGREES AWARDED:
Professioinal titles in various fields
   five years required
Doctor iuris et rerum politicarum (law and politics)
   four and one-half years required
Teaching certificate (secondary level)
Doctor philosophiae or Doctor rerum naturalum
   by thesis

ACADEMIC PROGRAMS:
Faculty of Arts
Faculty of Law and Political Science
Faculty of Science
Faculty of Teacher Training
Postgraduate Institute of Law and Political Science

SPECIAL PROGRAMS:
Computer Center
Center for Foreign Languages
Institute of Sociology
Cooperative arrangements with 30 other universities, including the University of California at Santa Barbara

LANGUAGE OF INSTRUCTION: Hungarian

ADMISSION REQUIREMENTS FOR FOREIGN STUDENTS:
Secondary school certificate, or recognized foreign equivalent, and entrance examination

TUITION FOR FOREIGN STUDENTS:
Not available and subject to change in the coming year

TOTAL INSTRUCTIONAL FACULTY:
1,522 fulltime faculty
170 parttime faculty

LIBRARY COLLECTIONS:
Central library—1,300,000 volumes
Faculty and departmental libraries—1,000,000 volumes

UNIVERSITY PUBLICATIONS:
Annales, Egyetemi Értestiő, Acta Facultatis Politico-Iuridicae, Dissertationes Archaeologicae, Az Egyetemi Könyvtár Értisitői

RECTOR: Lajos Vékás

BUDAPESTI KÖZGAZDASÁGTUDOMÁNYI EGYETEM
(Budapest University of Economic Sciences)
1093 Budapest IX, Dimitrov-tér 8, Hungary

CHARACTERISTICS OF INSTITUTION:
State-run, nonprofit university

DATE FOUNDED: 1948

TOTAL ENROLLMENT: 4,300 students

DEGREES AWARDED:
Professional title of Economist
   four–five years required
Diploma of engineering
   two years after title of Economist required
Doctorate
   by thesis

ACADEMIC PROGRAMS:
Faculty of General Economics (including political economics and philosophy)
Faculty of Industrial Economics (including agricultural economics)
Faculty of Trade Economics

SPECIAL PROGRAMS:
Institute of Languages
Institute of Mathematics and Computer Science
Institute of Planning

LANGUAGE OF INSTRUCTION: Hungarian

ADMISSION REQUIREMENTS FOR FOREIGN STUDENTS:
Secondary school certificate, or recognized foreign equivalent, and entrance examination

TUITION FOR FOREIGN STUDENTS:
Not available and subject to change in the coming year

TOTAL INSTRUCTIONAL FACULTY:
485 (including 64 professors)

LIBRARY COLLECTIONS:
Central library—300,000 volumes

UNIVERSITY PUBLICATIONS:
Egyetemi Szemle, Kozgazdasz

RECTOR: Cs. Csaki

KOSSUTH LAJOS TUDOMÁNYEGYETEM
(Lajos Kossuth University)
4010 Debrecen, Egyetem tér 1, Hungary

CHARACTERISTICS OF INSTITUTION:
State-run, nonprofit university

DATE FOUNDED: 1912

TOTAL ENROLLMENT: 2,200 students

DEGREES AWARDED:
Professional titles in various fields
    three–five years required
Teaching certificate (secondary level)
Doctorate
    by thesis

ACADEMIC PROGRAMS:
Faculty of Arts
Faculty of Sciences

SPECIAL PROGRAMS:
Institute of Marxism-Leninism

LANGUAGE OF INSTRUCTION: Hungarian

ADMISSION REQUIREMENTS FOR FOREIGN STUDENTS:
Secondary school certificate or recognized foreign equivalent

TUITION FOR FOREIGN STUDENTS:
Not available and subject to change in the coming year

TOTAL INSTRUCTIONAL FACULTY:
492

LIBRARY COLLECTIONS:
University library—1,600,000 volumes

UNIVERSITY PUBLICATIONS:
Évkönyv, Magyar Nyelvjarasok, Nemet Filologiai Tanulmanyok, various departmental publications

RECTOR: Dr. A. Lipták

PÉCSI JANUS PANNONIUS TUDOMÁNYEGYETEM
(Janus Pannonius University of Pécs)
7622 Pécs, Rákóczi u. 80, Hungary)

CHARACTERISTICS OF INSTITUTION:
State-run, nonprofit university

DATE FOUNDED: 1367

TOTAL ENROLLMENT: 4,000 students

DEGREES AWARDED:
Doctor iuris (law)
    four years required
Licence es Sciences economiques (economics)
    four years required
Doctorate
    by thesis

ACADEMIC PROGRAMS:
Faculty of Economics
Faculty of Humanities, Sciences and Education
Faculty of Law and Political Science
Faculty of Teacher Training

SPECIAL PROGRAMS:
Cooperative arrangements with 14 universities

LANGUAGE OF INSTRUCTION: Hungarian

ADMISSION REQUIREMENTS FOR FOREIGN STUDENTS:
Secondary school certificate, or recognized foreign equivalent, and entrance examination

TUITION FOR FOREIGN STUDENTS:
Not available and subject to change in the coming year

TOTAL INSTRUCTIONAL FACULTY:
500

LIBRARY COLLECTIONS:
Central library—700,000 volumes

UNIVERSITY PUBLICATIONS:
Studia Iuridica Auctoritatae Universitatis Pécs Publicata, Studia Oeconomica Auctoritatae Universitatis Pécs Publicata, Studia Philosophica et Sociologica Auctoritatae Universitatis Pécs Publicata, Studia Paedagogica Auctoritatae Universitatis Pécs Publicata (Scientiae Humanae et Naturales Artesque)

RECTOR: Dr. M. Ormos

ATTILA JÓZSEF TUDOMÁNYEGYETEM
(Attila József University)
6701 Szeged, Dugonics-tér 13, Hungary

CHARACTERISTICS OF INSTITUTION:
State-run, nonprofit university

DATE FOUNDED: 1872

TOTAL ENROLLMENT: 3,700 students

DEGREES AWARDED:
Doctor iuris (law)
    four years required
Doctorate in various fields
    five years and thesis reqired

ACADEMIC PROGRAMS:
Faculty of Arts
Faculty of Law and Political Science
Faculty of Science

LANGUAGE OF INSTRUCTION: Hungarian

ADMISSION REQUIREMENTS FOR FOREIGN STUDENTS:
Secondary school certificate, or recognized foreign equivalent, and entrance examination

TUITION FOR FOREIGN STUDENTS:
Not available and subject to change in the coming year

TOTAL INSTRUCTIONAL FACULTY:
523 (including 51 professors)

LIBRARY COLLECTIONS:
Central library—600,000 volumes

UNIVERSITY PUBLICATIONS:
Acta Universitatis Szegediensis de Attila Joszef Nominatae, various departmental publications

RECTOR: Dr. Bela Csakany

THE UNIVERSITIES OF POLAND

UNIWERSYTET GDAŃSKI
(University of Gdansk)
80-952 Gdansk, Ul. Bazynskiego 1A, Poland

CHARACTERISTICS OF INSTITUTION:
State-run, nonprofit university

DATE FOUNDED: 1970

TOTAL ENROLLMENT: 10,500 students

DEGREES AWARDED:
Magister in various fields
 five years required
Doctorate
 by thesis
Teaching qualification (university level)

ACADEMIC PROGRAMS:
Faculty of Biology, Geology and Oceanology
Faculty of Humanities
Faculty of Law and Administration
Faculty of Mathematics, Physics and Chemistry
Faculty of Production Economics
Faculty of Transport Economics
Department of Education

LANGUAGE OF INSTRUCTION: Polish

ADMISSION REQUIREMENTS FOR FOREIGN STUDENTS:
Secondary school certificate, or recognized foreign equivalent, and entrance examination

TUITION FOR FOREIGN STUDENTS:
Not available and subject to change in the coming year

TOTAL INSTRUCTIONAL FACULTY:
1,396

UNIVERSITY PUBLICATIONS:
Prace Habilitaccyjne, Skrypty, Zeszty Naukowe

RECTOR: Prof. Dr hab. Czeslaw Jackowiak

UNIWERSYTET JAGIELLOŃSKI
(Jagiellonian University)
31-007 Cracow, Gołębia 24, Poland

CHARACTERISTICS OF INSTITUTION:
State-run, nonprofit university

DATE FOUNDED: 1364

TOTAL ENROLLMENT: 9,300 students (including 50 foreign students)

DEGREES AWARDED:
Magister in various fields
 five years required
Doctorate
 by thesis
Teaching qualification (university level)

ACADEMIC PROGRAMS:
Faculty of Biology and Earth Sciences
Faculty of Chemistry
Faculty of Law and Management
Faculty of Mathematics and Physics
Faculty of Philology
Faculty of Philosophy and History

SPECIAL PROGRAMS:
Institute of Inventions (Protection of Intellectual Property)
Polish Language and Culture Research Institute
Regional Laboratory of Physico-Chemical Analyses and Structural Research
Department for Evening and Correspondence Studies
Language Center
Cooperative arrangements with 43 other universities, including the University of Connecticut, the University of Wisconsin, Medical College of Wisconsin, Wayne State University in Maryland, Alliance College in Pennsylvania and Johns Hopkins University

LANGUAGE OF INSTRUCTION: Polish

ADMISSION REQUIREMENTS FOR FOREIGN STUDENTS:
Secondary school certificate, or recognized foreign equivalent, and entrance examination

TUITION FOR FOREIGN STUDENTS:
Not available and subject to change in the coming year

TOTAL INSTRUCTIONAL FACULTY:
1,874

LIBRARY COLLECTIONS:
Central library—2,111,100 volumes
Institute libraries—975,500 volumes

MUSEUMS AND GALLERIES;
University Museum
Museums of Anthropology, Geology, Natural History

UNIVERSITY PUBLICATIONS:
Zeszty Naukowe Uniwersytetu Jagiellońskiego, Skrypty

RECTOR: Prof. Dr hab. Aleksander Koj

UNIWERSYTET LÓDZKI
(University of Lodz)
90-131 Lodz, Narutowicza 65, Poland

CHARACTERISTICS OF INSTITUTION:
State-run, nonprofit university

DATE FOUNDED: 1945

TOTAL ENROLLMENT: 10,600 students, (including 140 foreign students)

DEGREES AWARDED:
Magister in various fields
   four–five years required
Doctorate
   by thesis
Teaching qualification (university level)

ACADEMIC PROGRAMS:
Faculty of Biology and Earth Sciences
Faculty of Economics and Sociology
Faculty of Law and Administration
Faculty of Mathematics, Physics and Chemistry
Faculty of Philology
Faculty of Philosophy and History

SPECIAL PROGRAMS:
Institute of Political Science
Center for Polish (for foreign students)
Center for Foreign Languages
Cooperative arrangements with 43 other universities, including North Texas State University

LANGUAGE OF INSTRUCTION: Polish

ADMISSION REQUIREMENTS FOR FOREIGN STUDENTS:
Secondary school certificate, or recognized foreign equivalent, and entrance examination

TUITION FOR FOREIGN STUDENTS:
Not available and subject to change in the coming years

TOTAL INSTRUCTIONAL FACULTY:
300

LIBRARY COLLECTIONS:
Central library—1,258,400 volumes

MUSEUMS AND GALLERIES:
Museum of Evolutionary Biology

UNIVERSITY PUBLICATIONS:
Acta Universitatis Lodzienis

RECTOR: Prof. Dr hab. Leszek Wojtczak

UNIWERSYTET MARII CURIE-SKŁODOWSKIEJ
(Marie Curie-Skłodowska University)
20-031 Lublin, Plac Marii Curie-Skłodowskiej 5, Poland

CHARACTERISTICS OF INSTITUTION:
State-run, nonprofit university

DATE FOUNDED: 1944

TOTAL ENROLLMENT: 13,000 students

DEGREES AWARDED:
Magister in various fields
   five years required
Doctorate
   by thesis
Teaching qualification (university level)

ACADEMIC PROGRAMS:
Faculty of Biology and Earth Sciences
Faculty of Economics
Faculty of Humanities
Faculty of Law and Administration
Faculty of Mathematics, Physics and Chemistry
Faculty of Psychology and Pedagogy
Department of Foreign Languages
Department of Physical Education

SPECIAL PROGRAMS:
Interuniversity Institute of Philosophy and Sociology
Interuniversity Institute of Political Science

LANGUAGE OF INSTRUCTION: Polish

ADMISSION REQUIREMENTS FOR FOREIGN STUDENTS:
Secondary school certificate, or recognized foreign equivalent, and entrance examination

TUITION FOR FOREIGN STUDENTS:
Not available and subject to change in the coming year

TOTAL INSTRUCTIONAL FACULTY:
1,427

LIBRARY COLLECTIONS:
Total collection—1,777,900 volumes

MUSEUMS AND GALLERIES:
Museum of Zoology

UNIVERSITY PUBLICATIONS:
Annales Universitatis Mariae Curie-Skłodowska

RECTOR: Prof. Dr hab. Zdzislaw Cackowski

UNIWERSYTET IM ADAMA MICKIEWICZA W POZNANIU
(Adam Mickiewicz University in Poznan)
67-712 Poznań, Ul. Henryka Wieniawskiego 1, Poland

CHARACTERISTICS OF INSTITUTION:
State-run, nonprofit university

DATE FOUNDED: 1919

TOTAL ENROLLMENT: 11,900 students

DEGREES AWARDED:
Magister in various fields
   five years required
Doctorate
   by thesis
Teaching qualification (university level)

ACADEMIC PROGRAMS:
Faculty of Biology
Faculty of Chemistry
Faculty of Geography and Geosciences
Faculty of History (including Archaeology)
Faculty of Law and Administration
Faculty of Mathematics and Physics (including astronomy)
Faculty of Philology
Faculty of Social Sciences (including philosophy, education and political science)

SPECIAL PROGRAMS:
Cooperative arrangements with 16 other universities, including American University in Washington, D.C., the University of Florida and the State University of New York

LANGUAGE OF INSTRUCTION: Polish

ADMISSION REQUIREMENTS FOR FOREIGN STUDENTS:
Secondary school certificate, or recognized foreign equivalent, and entrance examination

TUITION FOR FOREIGN STUDENTS:
Not available and subject to change in the coming year

TOTAL INSTRUCTIONAL FACULTY:
1,700

LIBRARY COLLECTIONS:
University library—2,350,000 volumes
Faculty and institute libraries—1,300,000 volumes

UNVIERSITY PUBLICATIONS:
Various departmental publications

RECTOR: Prof. Dr hab. Bogdan Marciniec

UNIWERSYTET MIKOŁAJA KOPERNIKA W TORUNIU
(Nicholas Copernicus University of Toruń)
87-100 Toruń, Ul. Gagarina 11, Poland

CHARACTERISTICS OF INSTITUTION:
State-run, nonprofit university

DATE FOUNDED: 1945

TOTAL ENROLLMENT: 7,900 students

DEGREES AWARDED:
Magister in various fields
   five years required
Doctorate

by thesis
Teaching qualification (university level)

ACADEMIC PROGRAMS:
Faculty of Biology and Earth Sciences
Faculty of Economics
Faculty of Fine Arts
Faculty of Humanities (including education and archaeology)
Faculty of Law and Administration
Faculty of Mathematics, Physics and Chemistry
Department for Extramural Studies

SPECIAL PROGRAMS:
Center for Applied Biological Research
Cooperative arrangements with nine other universities

LANGUAGE OF INSTRUCTION: Polish

ADMISSION REQUIREMENTS FOR FOREIGN STUDENTS:
Secondary school certificate, or recognized foreign equivalent, and entrance examination

TUITION FOR FOREIGN STUDENTS:
Not available and subject to change in the coming year

TOTAL INSTRUCTIONAL FACULTY:
1,000

LIBRARY COLLECTIONS:
Central library—1,500,000 volumes

MUSUEMS AND GALLERIES:
Museum of Natural History

UNIVERSITY PUBLICATIONS:
Acta Universitatis Nicolai Copernici, Zeszyty Naukowe Uniwersytetu Mikolaja Kopernika

RECTOR: Prof. Dr hab. Jan Kopcewicz

UNIWERSYTET ŚLASKI
(Silesian University)
40-007 Katowice, Bankowa 12, Poland

CHARACTERISTICS OF INSTITUTION:
State-run, nonprofit university

DATE FOUNDED: 1968

TOTAL ENROLLMENT: 12,000 students

DEGREES AWARDED:
Professional diploma in administration
   three years required
Magister in various fields
   five years required
Doctorate
   by thesis
Teaching qualification (university level)

ACADEMIC PROGRAMS:
Faculty of Artistic Pedagogy
Faculty of Biology and Earth Sciences
Faculty of Geology and Geography
Faculty of Law and Administration
Faculty of Mathematics, Physics and Chemistry
Faculty of Philology
Faculty of Psychology and Education
Faculty of Radio and Television
Faculty of Social Science
Faculty of Technical Education
Foreign Language Unit
Physical Education Unit

SPECIAL PROGRAMS:
Center for French
Center for Lifelong Education
Cooperative arrangements with eight other universities

LANGUAGE OF INSTRUCTION: Polish

ADMISSION REQUIREMENTS FOR FOREIGN STUDENTS:
Secondary school certificate, or recognized foreign equivalent, and entrance examination

TUITION FOR FOREIGN STUDENTS:
Not available and subject to change in the coming year

TOTAL INSTRUCTIONAL FACULTY:
1,590

LIBRARY COLLECTIONS:
Central library—172,900
Faculty libraries
Institute libraries
Branch libraries

UNIVERSITY PUBLICATIONS:
Zeszyty Naukowe Wydziałów

RECTOR: Prof. Dr. Sedzimir Klimaszewski

UNIWERSYTET WARSZAWSKI
(University of Warsaw)
00-325 Warsaw, Krakowskie Przedmiescie 26–28, Poland

CHARACTERISTICS OF INSTITUTION:
State-run, nonprofit university

DATE FOUNDED: 1818

TOTAL ENROLLMENT: 25,000 students

DEGREES AWARDED:
Magister in various fields
    five years required
Doctorate

by thesis
Teaching qualification (university level)

ACADEMIC PROGRAMS:
Faculty of Biology
Faculty of Chemistry
Faculty of Economic Science
Faculty of Geography and Regional Studies
Faculty of Geology
Faculty of History
Faculty of Journalism and Political Science
Faculty of Law and Administration
Faculty of Management
Faculty of Mathematics, Informatics and Mechanics
Faculty of Neophilologies
Faculty of Pedagogy
Faculty of Philsophy and Sociology
Faculty of Physics
Faculty of Polish Philology
Faculty of Psychology
Faculty of Russian Philology and Applied Linguistics
Faculty of Social Prevention and Resocialization

SPECIAL PROGRAMS:
American Study Center
Center for Political Science Studies
Language Teaching Center
Cooperative arrangements with universities around the world, including in Canada and the United States

LANGUAGE OF INSTRUCTION: Polish

ADMISSION REQUIREMENTS FOR FOREIGN STUDENTS:
Secondary school certificate, or recognized foreign equivalent, and entrance examination

TUITION FOR FOREIGN STUDENTS:
Not available and subject to change in the coming year

TOTAL INSTRUCTIONAL FACULTY:
850

LIBRARY COLLECTIONS:
Central library—2,100,000 volumes
Specialized libraries—1,500,000 volumes

MUSEUMS AND GALLERIES:
Museum of Geology

UNIVERSITY PUBLICATIONS:
American Studies, Acta Philologica, Africana Bulletin, Analiza I Synteza Informacji, Biuletyn Geologiczny, Biuletyn Instytutu Jezyka I Kultury Polskiej Dla Cudzoziemców, Ekonomia, Fasciculi Historici, Phytocoenosis, Prace Filologiczne, Przeglad Informacji O Afryce, Quaestiones Medii Aevi Roczniki Uniwersytetu Warszawskiego, Studia

I Materiały Instytutu Archeologii, Studia Palmyrenskie, Swiatowit, Zeszyty Naukowe Instytutu Nauk Politcznych

RECTOR: Prof. Dr hab. Andrzej Wroblewski

UNIWERSYTET WROCŁAWSKI
(Univerisity of Wrocław)
50-137 Wrocław, Plac Uniwersytecki 1, Poland

CHARACTERISTICS OF INSTITUTION:
State-run, nonprofit university

DATE FOUNDED: 1702

TOTAL ENROLLMENT: 11,300 students

DEGREES AWARDED:
Magister in various fields
   five years required
Doctorate
   by thesis
Teaching qualification (university level)

ACADEMIC PROGRAMS:
Faculty of Historical and Pedagogical Sciences
Faculty of Law and Administration
Faculty of Mathematiccs, Physics and Chemistry
Faculty of Natural Sciences
Faculty of Philology
Faculty of Social Sciences

SPECIAL PROGRAMS:
Cooperative arrangements with 10 other universities, including the State University of New York in Stony Brook

LANGUAGE OF INSTRUCTION: Polish

ADMISSION REQUIREMENTS FOR FOREIGN STUDENTS:
Secondary school certificate, or recognized foreign equivalent, and entrance examination

TUITION FOR FOREIGN STUDENTS:
Not available and subject to change in the coming year

TOTAL INSTRUCTIONAL FACULTY:
1,534

LIBRARY COLLECTIONS:
University library—714,000 volumes
Institute libraries

MUSEUMS AND GALLERIES:
Museum of Natural Science

UNIVERSITY PUBLICATIONS:
Acta Universitatis Wratislaviensis and various departmental publications

RECTOR: Prof. Dr. Mieczyslaw Klimowicz

THE UNIVERSITIES OF THE UNION OF SOVIET SOCIALIST REPUBLICS

LENINGRADSKIJ ORDENA LENINA I ORDENA TRUDOVOGO KRASNOGO ZNAMENI GOSUDARSTVENNYJ UNIVERSITET IM. A. A. ZDANOVA
(Leningrad State University)
199034 Leningrad, B-164, Universitetskaya nab. 7/9, U.S.S.R.

CHARACTERISTICS OF INSTITUTION:
State-run, nonprofit university

DATE FOUNDED: 1724

TOTAL ENROLLMENT: 20,000 students

DEGREES AWARDED:
Diploma of Specialist in various fields of study
   five years required
Kandidat Nauk (Candidate of the Sciences)
   an additional three years and thesis required
Doktor Nauk
   by thesis after Kandidat

ACADEMIC PROGRAMS:
Faculty of Applied Mathematics
Faculty of Biology and Soil Science
Faculty of Chemistry
Faculty of Economics
Faculty of Geography
Faculty of Geology
Faculty of History
Faculty of Journalism
Faculty of Law
Faculty of Mathematics and Mechanics
Faculty of Oriental Studies
Faculty of Philology
Faculty of Philosophy
Faculty of Physics
Faculty of Psychology
Faculty of Russian (as a foreign language)

SPECIAL PROGRAMS:
Institute of Biological Research
Institute of Chemical Research
Institute of Geographical and Economic Research
Institute of Geological Research
Institute of Mathematical and Applied Mathematical
   Research
Institute of Physical Research
Institute of Physiological Research
Department for Correspondence Courses
Department for Evening Studies
Department of Interpretation
Astronomical Observatory

Cooperative arrangements with 17 other universities

LANGUAGE OF INSTRUCTION: Russian

ADMISSION REQUIREMENTS FOR FOREIGN STUDENTS:
Competitive entrance examination following general or special secondary school certificate or recognized foreign equivalent

TUITION FOR FOREIGN STUDENTS:
Not available and subject to change in the coming year

TOTAL INSTRUCTIONAL FACULTY:
4,000 (including 1,700 professors)

LIBRARY COLLECTIONS:
Gor'kij Scientific Library—5,000,000 volumes

MUSEUMS AND GALLERIES:
General University Museum, Mendeleyev Museum
Botanical Garden

UNIVERSITY PUBLICATIONS:
Vestnik Leningradskogo Universiteta

RECTOR: Prof. S. P. Merkurev

MOSKOVSKIJ ORDENA LENINA I ORDENA TRUDOVOGO KRASNOGO ZNAMENI ORDENA OKTJABR'SKOI REVOLJUCH GOSUDARSTVENNYJ UNIVERSITET IM. M. V. LOMONOSOVA
(Moscow State University)
117234 Moscow, Leninskie gory, U.S.S.R.

CHARACTERISTICS OF INSTITUTION:
State-run, nonprofit university

DATE FOUNDED: 1755

TOTAL ENROLLMENT: 28,000 students

DEGREES AWARDED:
Diploma of Specialist in various fields of study
   five years required
Kandidat Nauk (Candidate of the Sciences)
   an additional three years and thesis required
Doktor Nauk
   by thesis after Kandidat

ACADEMIC PROGRAMS:
Faculty of Biology and Soil Science
Faculty of Chemistry
Faculty of Computing Mathematics and Cybernetics
Faculty of Economics
Faculty of Geography
Faculty of Geology
Faculty of History

Faculty of Journalism
Faculty of Law
Faculty of Mathematics and Mechanics
Faculty of Philology
Faculty of Philosophy
Faculty of Physics
Faculty of Psychology
Faculty for Teachers in Higher Education Institutions
Preparatory Faculty for Foreign Students

SPECIAL PROGRAMS:
Institute of Anthropological Studies
Institute of Asian and African Studies
Institute of Astronomy
Institute of Mechanics
Institute of Nucelar Physics
Institute of Oriental Languages
Department of Evening Studies
Department of Correspondence Courses
Cooperative arrangements with universities in countries around the world, including Canada and the United States

LANGUAGE OF INSTRUCTION: Russian

ADMISSION REQUIREMENTS FOR FOREIGN STUDENTS:
Entrance examination following general or special secondary school certificate or recognized foreign equivalent

TUITION FOR FOREIGN STUDENTS:
Not available and subject to change in the coming year

TOTAL INSTRUCTIONAL FACULTY:
8,000

LIBRARY COLLECTIONS:
A. M. Gorki Scientific Library—6,600,000 volumes

MUSEUMS AND GALLERIES:
Museums of Anthropology, University History, Soil Science, Zoology

UNIVERSITY PUBLICATIONS:
Vestnik Moskovskogo Universiteta, Byulleten Moskovskogo Obschestva Ispytatelei Prirody, Russkii Yazyk Za Rubezhom

RECTOR: Prof. Viktor Sadovnichy

THE UNIVERSITIES OF YUGOSLAVIA

UNIVERZITET U BEOGRADU
(University of Belgrade)
11001 Belgrade 6, Studentski trg 1, Yugoslavia

CHARACTERISTICS OF INSTITUTION:
State-run, nonprofit university

DATE FOUNDED: 1863

TOTAL ENROLLMENT: 57,000 students (including 3,000 foreign students)

DEGREES AWARDED:
First Degree
   two–three years required
Second Degree
   four–five years required
Third Degree
   up to two years after Second Degree required
Doctorate

ACADEMIC PROGRAMS:
Faculty of Agriculture
Faculty of Architecture (including town planning)
Faculty of Civil Engineering
Faculty of Defectology
Faculty of Dentistry
Faculty of Economics
Faculty of Electrical Engineering
Faculty of Forestry
Faculty of Law
Faculty of Mechanical Engineering
Faculty of Medicine
Faculty of Mining and Geology
Faculty of National Defense
Faculty of Organizational Sciences
Faculty of Pharmacy
Faculty of Philology
Faculty of Philosophy (including education, archeology, history and sociology)
Faculty of Physical Education
Faculty of Political Sciences
Faculty of Sciences
Faculty of Stomatology
Faculty of Technical Engineering
Faculty of Technology and Metallurgy
Faculty of Transport
Faculty of Veterinary Medicine

SPECIAL PROGRAMS:
Institute of Biological Research
Institute of Chemistry, Technology and Metallurgy
Institute of Nuclear Energy
Institute of Nuclear Research
Institute of Social Sciences
Physics Research Institute
Center for Marxism
Center for Multidisciplinary Studies
International University Centre for Social Sciences
Cooperative arrangements with over 30 universities in other countries

LANGUAGE OF INSTRUCTION: Serbo-Croatian

ADMISSION REQUIREMENTS FOR FOREIGN STUDENTS:
Secondary school certificate, recognized foreign equivalent or four years practical experience, and entrance examination

TUITION FOR FOREIGN STUDENTS:
None

TOTAL INSTRUCTIONAL FACULTY:
3,702

LIBRARY COLLECTIONS:
Svetozar Markovic Library—1,500,000 volumes

UNIVERSITY PUBLICATIONS:
Bilten, Dijalektika, Gledista, Univerzitetski Glasnik

RECTOR: Prof. Dr. Slobodan Unkovic

UNIVERZA EDVARDA KARDELJA V LJUBLJANI
(Edward Kardelj University of Ljubljana)
Ljubljani, Trg Osvoboditve 11, Yugoslavia

CHARACTERISTICS OF INSTITUTION:
State-run, nonprofit university

DATE FOUNDED: 1595

TOTAL ENROLLMENT: 24,000 students

DEGREES AWARDED:
First Degree
   two–three years required
Second Degree
   four–five years required
Third Degree
   up to two years after Second Degree required
Doctorate

ACADEMIC PROGRAMS:
Faculty of Architecture, Civil Engineering and Geodesy
Faculty of Arts and Science
Faculty of Biotechnical Engineering
Faculty of Economics
Faculty of Electrical and Electronic Engineering
Faculty of Law
Faculty of Mechanical Engineering

Faculty of Medicine
Faculty of Natural Science and Technology
Faculty of Physical Education
Faculty of Sociology, Political Science and Journalism
Academy of Music
Academy of Theater, Radio, Film and Television
Academy of Fine Arts
Academy of Pedagogy
Higher School of Maritime Engineering
Higher School for Social Workers
Higher School for Health Service Workers
Higher School of Safety Engineering
Higher School of Public Administration
Higher School for Internal Affairs

SPECIAL PROGRAMS:
Computer Center
Cooperative arrangements with 21 other universities, including the University of Seattle in Washington

LANGUAGE OF INSTRUCTION: Slovene

ADMISSION REQUIREMENTS FOR FOREIGN STUDENTS:
Secondary school certificate and entrance examination, or recognized foreign equivalent

TUITION FOR FOREIGN STUDENTS:
None

TOTAL INSTRUCTIONAL FACULTY:
2,167

LIBRARY COLLECTIONS:
National and university library—1,140,600 volumes
Central technical library—112,200 volumes

MUSEUMS AND GALLERIES:
University Museum

UNIVERSITY PUBLICATIONS:
*Biografije in bibliografije univerzitetnih učiteljev in sode-
lavcev, Objave, Poročilo, Seznam predavanj, Vestnik*

RECTOR: Prof. Boris Sket

UNIVERZITET U NIŠU
(University of Nis)
18000 Nis, Trg Bratstva i Jedinstva 2, Yugoslavia

CHARACTERISTICS OF INSTITUTION:
State-run, nonprofit university

DATE FOUNDED: 1965

TOTAL ENROLLMENT: 13,000 students

DEGREES AWARDED:
First Degree
   two–three years required
Second Degree
   four–five years required

Third Degree
   up to two years after Second Degree required
Doctorate

ACADEMIC PROGRAMS:
Faculty of Civil Engineering (including architecture)
Faculty of Economics
Faculty of Electronic Engineering
Faculty of Law
Faculty of Mechanical Engineering
Faculty of Medicine (including pharmacy)
Faculty of Philosophy
Faculty of Safety at Work
Faculty of Technology

SPECIAL PROGRAMS:
Center for Lifelong Education

LANGUAGE OF INSTRUCTION: Serbo-Croatian

ADMISSION REQUIREMENTS FOR FOREIGN STUDENTS:
Secondary school certificate or recognized foreign
equivalent

TUITION FOR FOREIGN STUDENTS:
None

TOTAL INSTRUCTIONAL FACULTY:
938

LIBRARY COLLECTIONS:
Central library
Faculty libraries

UNIVERSITY PUBLICATIONS:
*Bilten referata za izbor nastavnika i fakultetskih saradnika,
Facta Universitatis, Glasnik Univerziteta u Nišu, Pregled
predavanja*

RECTOR: Prof. Dr. Branimir Djordjevic

UNIVERZITET U SARAJEVU
(University of Sarajevo)
71000 Sarajevo, Obala vojvode Stepe 7/11, Post.
Fah 186, Yugoslavia

CHARACTERISTICS OF INSTITUTION:
State-run, nonprofit university

DATE FOUNDED: 1949

TOTAL ENROLLMENT: 24,000 fulltime students
9,000 parttime students

DEGREES AWARDED:
First Degree
   two–three years required
Second Degree
   four–five years required
Third Degree
   Up to two years after Second Degree required
Doctorate

ACADEMIC PROGRAMS:
Faculty of Architecture (including town planning)
Faculty of Arts, Philosophy and Philology
Faculty of Civil Engineering
Faculty of Dentistry
Faculty of Economics
Faculty of Electrical Engineering
Faculty of Forestry
Faculty of Law
Faculty of Mechanical Engineering
Faculty of Mechanical Engineering (in Zenica)
Faculty of Medicine
Faculty of Metallurgy (in Zenica)
Faculty of Pharmacy
Faculty of Physical Culture
Faculty of Political Sciences
Faculty of Science
Faculty of Veterinary Sciences
Faculty of Transportation
Academy of Dramatic Art
Academy of Fine Arts
Academy of Music
School of Economics and Commerce
School of Education
School of Management
School of Nursing
School of Social Work

SPECIAL PROGRAMS:
Institute of Architecture
Institute of Biology
Institute of Computer Science
Institute of Economics
Electroenergetic Institute
Institute of Ergonomics
Institute of Organization and Economics
Institute of Oriental Research
Institute of Thermo- and Nuclear Techniques
Institute of Welding
Institute of Work Production
Cooperative arrangements with 25 other universi-
  ties, including the State University of New York at
  Utica and the University of California

LANGUAGE OF INSTRUCTION: Serbo-Croatian

ADMISSION REQUIREMENTS FOR FOREIGN STUDENTS:
Secondary school certificate, or recognized foreign
equivalent, and entrance examination

TUITION FOR FOREIGN STUDENTS:
None

TOTAL INSTRUCTIONAL FACULTY:
1,225

LIBRARY COLLECTIONS:
Central library
Faculty libraries

UNIVERSITY PUBLICATIONS:
*Bilten Univerziteta u Sarajevu, Doktorske disertacije-Re-
zimei, Univerzitet u Sarajevu-Pregled predavanja*

RECTOR: Prof. Dr. Nenad Kecmanovic

SVEUČILIŠTE U ZAGREBU
(University of Zagreb)
41000 Zagreb, Trg Maršala Tita 14, POB 815, Yugoslavia

CHARACTERISTICS OF INSTITUTION:
State-run, nonprofit university

DATE FOUNDED: 1669

TOTAL ENROLLMENT: 41,200 fulltime students (including 7,300 correspondence students)

DEGREES AWARDED:
First Degree
  two–three years required
Second Degree
  four–five years required
Third Degree
  up to two years after Second Degree required
Doctorate

ACADEMIC PROGRAMS:
Faculty of Agriculture
Faculty of Architecture
Faculty of Civil Engineering
Faculty of Defectology
Faculty of Economic Sciences
Faculty of Electrical Engineering
Faculty of Food Processing and Biotechnology
Faculty of Forestry
Faculty of Geodesy
Faculty of Law
Faculty of Mechanical Engineering and Naval Archi-
  tecture
Faculty of Medicine
Faculty of Metallurgy (in Sisak)
Faculty of Mining Engineering, Geology and Petro-
  leum
Faculty of Natural Sciences and Mathematics
Faculty of Organization and Information Studies
Faculty of Pharmacy and Biochemistry
Faculty of Philosophy
Faculty of Physical Education
Faculty of Political Sciences
Faculty of Stomatology
Faculty of Technology
Faculty of Veterinary Medicine
Academy of Dramatic Art
Academy of Fine Arts
Academy of Music
School of Printing Technology

SPECIAL PROGRAMS:
Institute of Agriculture
Computer Center
Cooperative arrangements with 29 other universities, including Florida State University, State University of New York, Johns Hopkins University, Indiana University, the University of Pittsburgh and the University of California at Los Angeles

LANGUAGE OF INSTRUCTION: Croatian and Serbian

ADMISSION REQUIREMENTS FOR FOREIGN STUDENTS:
Secondary school certificate, or recognized foreign equivalent, and entrance examination

TUITION FOR FOREIGN STUDENTS:
None

TOTAL INSTRUCTIONAL FACULTY:
3,700

LIBRARY COLLECTIONS:
National and university library—1,200,000 volumes
Faculty and institute libraries

MUSEUMS AND GALLERIES:
Museums of Mineralogy and Perography, Geology and Paleontology

UNIVERSITY PUBLICATIONS:
Sveučilišni vjesnik

PRESIDENT: Dr. Duško Sević

BIBLIOGRAPHY

Academic Studies in the Federal Republic of Germany. Bonn: Deutscher Akademischer, n.d.

Commonwealth Universities Yearbook. Vol. 1. London: Association of Commonwealth Universities, 1989.

Etudiants Etrangers les Etudes Superieures en France, 1990. Paris: Ministere de l'Education Nationale, de la Jeunesse et des Sports Direction des Enseignements Superieurs, Bureau de l'Information et de 'Orientation, 1990.

International Handbook of Universities and Other Institutions of Higher Learning. 11th ed. Paris: M. Stockton Press for the International Association of Universities, 1989.

Mohr, Dr. Brigitte, and Ines Liebig, eds. *Higher Education in the European Community.* 5th ed. London: Commission of the European Communities, 1988.

World of Learning. 40th ed. London: Europa Publications Limited, 1990.

INDEX